Christ Church

T006991

KU-518-017

February 1976

WITHDRAWN FROM
CHRIST CHURCH LIBRARY
OXFORD

THE DEVELOPMENT OF
ENGLISH GLASSMAKING 1560–1640

Sir Robert Mansell, Vice-Admiral of England and Glass Manufacturer.

The Development of
English Glassmaking
1560–1640

ELEANOR S. GODFREY

Clarendon Press · Oxford
1975

Oxford University Press, Ely House, London W.1

GLASGOW NEW YORK TORONTO MELBOURNE WELLINGTON
CAPE TOWN IBADAN NAIROBI DAR ES SALAAM LUSAKA ADDIS ABABA
DELHI BOMBAY CALCUTTA MADRAS KARACHI LAHORE DACCA
KUALA LUMPUR SINGAPORE HONG KONG TOKYO

ISBN 0 19 828267 2

© *Oxford University Press 1975*

*All rights reserved. No part of this publication may be reproduced,
stored in a retrieval system, or transmitted, in any form or by any means,
electronic, mechanical, photocopying, recording or otherwise, without
the prior permission of Oxford University Press*

CHRIST CHURCH
LIBRARY
OXFORD

*Printed in Great Britain by
Butler & Tanner Ltd
Frome and London*

PREFACE AND ACKNOWLEDGEMENTS

THIS study of the glass industry in England grew out of an interest in the economic policy of the Crown during the reigns of Elizabeth and the first two Stuarts. Glass making was one of the most important of the industries controlled throughout most of that period by royal grants of monopoly privilege, and along with other such grants has been subjected to severe condemnation, especially in W. H. Price's *English Patents of Monopoly*,[1] long considered the standard work. The limited space and narrow scope of the materials at Price's disposal, however, and his obvious bias in favour of an extreme *laissez-faire* economy made his conclusions sometimes questionable, and suggested the desirability of a more thorough study of one of the industries he discussed. Since the later glass patents were based on the change from wood to coal fuel, a study of the glass patents was also bound to throw light on the thesis of John Nef[2] concerning an early industrial revolution based on the change to coal, either by lending support or suggesting modifications. Both the question of the wisdom of the monopoly patents and the change to coal fuel involved an investigation of an alleged new 'invention' in glassmaking, so the work was necessarily expanded to include technical problems connected with the process and furnaces. Once work was begun, a cursory review of glassmaking in the period soon revealed that the original questions were often less important for an understanding of the industry than such matters as wages, prices, the demand for different kinds of glass, importation, changes in capitalization, management, and marketing. In addition, the question of quality drew attention to such vessel and drinking glasses as remain and also to the extent of the production of glass suitable for use in scientific investigations, primarily lenses. As the ramifications of the subject grew, it became clear that it was desirable to make as inclusive a study as possible, especially since previous accounts were at best brief and fragmentary. Though the emphasis is still on economic and political factors, the aim has been to present a comprehensive picture of English glassmaking at a crucial point in its history when it was being transformed from a medieval craft into something resembling a modern industry.

Since the research has been carried on over a period of more than twenty years, it would be tedious, if not impossible, to give adequate

---

[1] W. H. Price, *The English Patents of Monopoly* (Boston, Houghton Mifflin, 1906).
[2] See especially J. U. Nef, 'The Progress of Technology and the Growth of Large Scale Industry in Great Britain, 1540–1640', *EcHR* v (1934), 3–24.

thanks individually to all the persons who have given me assistance and advice. To all the librarians and archivists of repositories listed in the *Bibliography* I am most grateful for unfailing courtesy, assistance and sometimes valuable suggestions. In particular, however, I should like to express appreciation to Mr. James R. More-Molyneux for permission to use the Loseley Manuscripts at Loseley House and to Major J. C. Mansel for similar privileges in using the Clavell Manuscripts at Smedmore House. To the directors and staff of numerous museums both in England and the United States I am equally indebted for advice, encouragement, and special access to their collections, particularly to those of the Corning Museum of Glass, the Pilkington Museum, and the London Guildhall Museum; and above all to Mr. R. J. Charleston, Curator of Ceramics of the Victoria and Albert Museum. Eric S. Wood of Guildford, D. W. Crossley, G. H. Kenyon, and Mrs. Ruth Vose were helpful in arranging for me to inspect the sites or the results of archaeological excavations. Dr. Cyril Smith of the Massachusetts Institute of Technology made valuable suggestions in regard to the furnaces and Dr. Michael McVaugh of the University of North Carolina helped with the chapter on glass specialities and scientific glass. My greatest debt of all, however, is to my husband, whose patience, encouragement, and support over the years have made the work possible. Needless to say, any errors or shortcomings are my own.

ELEANOR S. GODFREY

Chapel Hill, North Carolina
15 February 1974

CONTENTS

LIST OF PLATES

Frontispiece. Sir Robert Mansell, Vice-Admiral of England and Glass Manufacturer. *Portrait reproduced by permission of Christopher Methuen Campbell, Penrice Castle, Glamorgan*

BETWEEN pp. 228–9

I. An early fifteenth-century glasshouse in the forest-glass tradition. *Reproduced by permission of the British Library Board*

II(a). Unstable urinal. *Guildhall Museum, no. 18399*

II(b). Ale glass (reconstructed) of glossy blue green metal, with folded foot, in-curved rim, and mould-blown pattern. *Guildhall Museum, no. 21309*

II(c). Beaker with chequered spiral-trail decoration. *British Museum, no. 1958, 5–3, 1*

II(d). Green-glass goblet (reconstructed). *Guildhall Museum, no. 15590*

II(e). Green drinking glasses with mould-blown, wrythen, and trailed decorations. *Gloucester City Museum and Art Gallery*

III(a). A Verzelini glass. *Crown Copyright: Victoria and Albert Museum, no. C. 523–1936*

III(b). The Barbara Potters glass. *Crown Copyright: Victoria and Albert Museum, no. C. 575–1925*

III(c). A 'cigar-stem' wine glass. *Guildhall Museum, no. 15535*

III(d). Laddered stem wine glass. *Guildhall Museum, no. 5167*

III(e). Nonsuch wine glass with a simple knopf and baluster stem. London Museum. *Reproduced by permission of the Nonsuch Palace Excavations Committee*

IV(a). Bottle of light apple-green, a modification of the 'steeple-shaped' apothecaries' bottle. *Guildhall Museum, no. 15607*

IV(b). Green-glass bottle with wrythen ribbing. *Crown Copyright: Victoria and Albert Museum, no. C. 1–1910*

IV(c). Hexagonal bottle of green glass. *Gloucester City Museum and Art Gallery*

IV(d). Square bottle of light-green glass. *Waltham Abbey Historical Society Collection*

IV(e). Wine bottle in dark-green bottle glass. *Courtesy of Howard Phillips*

IV(f). Hardwick Hall. *The National Trust. Photograph through the courtesy of Gordon Fraser Gallery, Ltd.*

LIST OF FIGURES

LIST OF TABLES

LIST OF ABBREVIATIONS

Add. MSS.	BM Additional Manuscripts
Ant.	*Antiquary*
A.P.C.	G.B., Privy Council, *Acts of the Privy Council of England*
BM	British Museum
Cal. S.P. Col.	PRO, *Calendar of State Papers, Colonial Series*
Cal. S.P. Ven.	PRO, *Calendar of State Papers and Manuscripts in the Archives and Collections of Venice*
Cal. S.P.D.	PRO, *Calendar of State Papers, Domestic Series*
Chancery	PRO, Records of the Chancery, Chancery Proceedings
Dioc. R.O.	Diocesan Record Office
DNB	*Dictionary of National Biography*
EcHR	*Economic History Review*
Eg. MSS.	BM Egerton Manuscripts
EHR	*English History Review*
Exch. K.R.	PRO, Records of the Exchequer, King's Remembrancer
GLRO	Greater London Record Office
GMR	Guildford Muniment Room
Harl. MSS.	BM Harleian Manuscripts
HMC	Historical Manuscripts Commission
JGS	*Journal of Glass Studies*
J.H.C.	G.B., Parliament, *Journals of the House of Commons*
J.H.L.	G.B., Parliament, *Journals of the House of Lords*
J.R.O.	Joint Record Office
JSGT	*Journal of the Society of Glass Technology*
Lansd. MSS.	BM Lansdowne Manuscripts
LQR	*Law Quarterly Review*
Midd. MSS.	University of Nottingham Library, Middleton Manuscripts
OED	*Oxford English Dictionary*
P.C.C.	Prerogative Court of Canterbury
Port Books	Exch. K.R., Port Books
Post-Med. Arch.	*Post-Medieval Archaeology*
P.R.	Parish Register
PRO	Public Record Office
R.O.	Record Office
R.P.C. Scot.	*Register of the Privy Council of Scotland*
S.P.	PRO, State Papers, Domestic Series
Straff. MSS.	Sheffield Central Library, Strafford Manuscripts
Surr. A. Col.	*Surrey Archaeological Collections*

Suss. A. Col.	*Sussex Archaeological Collections*
Suss. R.S.	Sussex Record Society
VCH	*Victoria County History*

NOTE ON DATES

ALTHOUGH it was customary in the sixteenth and seventeenth centuries for the calendar year to begin on 25 March (the Feast of the Annunciation, also called Lady Day), dates in the text conform to the modern practice and are given as though the year began on 1 January. In the footnotes, however, both years are given for dates from 1 January to 25 March (e.g. in the text, 2 February 1620, in the footnote, 2 Feb. 1619–20).

The quarter sessions of the high courts of England began on the days following Michaelmas (29 September), Hilary (13 January), Easter, and Trinity Sundays (both movable feasts). Business transactions and payments, however, were more frequently marked by the quarter days—Lady Day, Midsummer Day (24 June), Michaelmas, and Christmas.

PART ONE

THE CHRONOLOGICAL HISTORY 1560–1642

I

THE BACKGROUND:
MEDIEVAL GLASSMAKING

WHILE this study is not primarily concerned with problems of
technology, the history of glassmaking even in its political and
economic aspects cannot properly be understood without a few preliminary remarks on the nature of the process involved.[1] Glass in any of
its forms is a composition made by the fusion of silica with one or more
substances of an alkaline nature. Silica is commonly derived from sand,
crushed flint, or white pebbles. Until recently the alkali was usually added
in the form of potash made from the ashes of wood or bracken, or in the
form of soda from the ashes of certain marine plants. Enough lime to give
toughness to the glass was usually present as an impurity in the other
ingredients,[2] so that sand and ashes alone, if fused at the proper temperature and for the correct length of time, produced a workable product. In
practice, however, scraps of broken glass called 'cullet' were added to
hasten the melting process. From Egyptian times colour, translucent or
opaque, had been produced by the addition of the proper amounts of
various metallic oxides. Glass, however, is not naturally the colourless
material we associate with the word, but usually has a decided greenish
cast from the wide prevalence of small quantities of iron oxides in most
sands. If certain melting conditions are present, an amber to brown tinge
replaces the green as a result of the iron present. Other metallic oxides
produce other colours. Although coloured glass deliberately produced
has generally been highly esteemed, the production of an absolutely
colourless and transparent glass has always been one of the chief aims of
the glassmaker and its achievement considered to be the culmination of his
art. Such colourless glass was historically known as 'crystal' from its
similarity to natural quartz crystal, and was so called, whatever its chemical composition, as opposed to the modern use of the word to apply to
high-quality glass with a certain lead content.[3] From time to time when

[1] The following summary is based on such general works as P. Marson, *Glass and Glass
Manufacture* (London, Pitman, 1918), W. B. Honey, *English Glass* (London, Collins, 1946), and
others.
[2] See p. 157.
[3] In the British trade today 'full crystal' is defined as potash glass containing 30% lead, 'half
crystal' as glass containing about half that amount. See Great Britain, Board of Trade, *Working
Party Reports: Hand-blown Domestic Glassware* (London, H.M.S.O., 1947), p. 6. Most American
lead crystal is half-crystal by British standards (ibid., pp. 108, 126).

the perfection of colourless glass was achieved, it was usually through the use of purer ingredient sand the addition of manganese, the 'glass-maker's soap'.

Before the development of chemical analysis it was natural that the recipes for mixing the batch were carefully guarded secrets, sometimes lost and rediscovered.[1] Not only the recipes but the knowledge of the proper making of the melting-pots capable of withstanding very high heat, the controlling of the fire, and the manual dexterity necessary to manipulate the molten glass were mysteries which the trade was unwilling to pass on to any chance apprentice. Even more than other medieval crafts, glassmaking was a family business. Only sons or sons-in-law were generally admitted to full knowledge of the trade and consistent inter-marriage of glassmaking families kept the craft a closed one.

Since several kinds of sand and alkali will suffice for making common glass, the industry was never tied to a particular locality. Moreover, the small furnaces used for melting and working the metal could be quickly and easily built with little outlay of capital. Thus in early medieval times the industry tended to be migratory, often following either the demands of the market, since transportation of such a fragile product was always a problem, or the need for large quantities of fuel, which until the early seventeenth century was invariably wood.[2]

The cheapness of the ingredients, the high value of the product, and a tightly guarded monopoly of skill brought glassmakers prosperity and a high social status.[3] That the *gentilhomme verrier* in France was a member of the lesser nobility has been amply demonstrated. The only dispute is whether the craft of glassmaking automatically conferred nobility upon its practitioners or whether members of the nobility were allowed to practise the art without loss of status.[4] In any event members of the lesser nobility in France, Bohemia, and Italy did practise glass-making. What is harder for the modern mind to grasp was that these *gentilhommes verriers* were not merely the owners of glasshouses, but were also the craftsmen who stood at the furnaces and shaped the molten metal.

---

[1] Even today certain glass firms keep their recipes secret. A pamphlet published by the Viking glass company says: 'No glass company tells the secrets of how its colors are produced. . . . The color room where the chemicals are stored . . . is usually kept locked' (Viking Glass Company, *From American Sands and Artists' Hands* (New Martinsville, W. Va., 1950), p. 36).

[2] For the migrations of the early glassmakers see E. Dillon, *Glass* (London, Methuen, 1907), chaps. v, vi, viii, ix.

[3] W. C. Scoville, *Capitalism and French Glassmaking, 1640–1789* (*University of California Publications in Economics*, vol. xv), (Berkeley, Univ. of Calif. Press, 1950), pp. 83–7.

[4] Ibid.; E. G. Clark, 'Glassmaking in Lorraine', *JSGT* xv (1931), 118. Clark states that in Lorraine glassmakers held noble rank not by virtue of their craft but in spite of it, yet he cites an ordinance of 1604 stipulating that *gentilhommes verriers* must be both practitioners of the art and members of families holding letters patent.

The scale of the enterprises was very small and no more than five or six persons usually worked about the furnace. Yet these owner-craftsmen were men of substance and position, who during the later Middle Ages in Europe held lands and grants exempting them from the usual feudal dues and obligations.[1]

Although early glassmaking was migratory, during the late Middle Ages it had settled down in certain well-defined areas of Europe, each with its own tradition and technique. The Italians produced clear and coloured soda glass for the luxury trade, while glassmakers in northern and central Europe, including England, made a potash glass called forest glass (*verre de fougère, waldglas*) from sand and the ashes of beech-wood or bracken. Forest glass was normally decidedly green in colour, the intensity varying with the purity of the sand and the thickness of the finished product. In the early medieval period it seems likely that both window and vessel glass were made at the same furnace, but as the demand for stained-glass windows came to dominate the market in the great era of ecclesiastical building, this branch of the trade became increasingly specialized.

Window glass of the forest tradition was again sharply subdivided according to the two techniques used in blowing.[2] One method produced circular sheets called *verre en plats* or crown glass. The technique consisted of blowing a bubble of molten glass which was then fixed to an iron rod called a pontil at a point opposite the blowpipe. When the pipe was broken off the resulting aperture was further opened with instruments and the bubble flattened by vigorous whirling motion while the glass was reheated. When the sheet was broken from the rod a characteristic rough thickening, later called the 'bull's eye', remained in the centre. The second method consisted of blowing an elongated cylinder supported by a pontil opposite the blowpipe, then removing both ends of the cylinder, splitting it lengthwise and unrolling it on a flat surface. The resulting roughly rectangular sheets were called *verre en tables* in French, usually 'broad glass' in English.[3] Crown glass was smoother than broad glass and retained a fire polish which broad glass lost in unrolling the cylinders. Crown glass cut to less advantage, however, since the diameter of the

[1] Scoville, p. 84. A fuller account of the exemptions in Lorraine is found in Clark, pp. 102–19.

[2] Nearly all works on glassmaking describe the two processes, but the clearest explanation with accompanying diagrams is found in R. Chambon, 'The Evolution of the Processes used for the Hand-fashioning of Window Glass from the Tenth Century to the Present', *Advances in Glass Technology*, pt. ii (New York, Plenum Press, 1963), pp. 165–78.

[3] During the sixteenth century it is clear from numerous documents that 'broad glass' referred to any kind of window glass, as did the French term '*grand verre*'. See especially the terms of Henry Smyth's patent granted in 1552, which is discussed in Chap.II (see p. 16 and n. 3). By the late seventeenth century 'broad' and, somewhat later, 'muff' were used to mean cylinder glass only and since this usage is common in most books on glassmaking, I have adopted it to avoid confusion.

crowns during the early period was usually under eight inches[1] and for many purposes the bull's eye was not suitable. Perhaps for that reason the cylinder method which had been practised in the Roman Empire[2] became the common one throughout most of Europe and was in fact the only one described by the German monk Theophilus in his treatise written in the eleventh century.[3] Near Eastern glass-blowers, however, preserved the crown technique and possibly as a result of contacts during the Crusades its use spread to parts of Italy and France in about the twelfth century.[4]

The fourteenth century brought improvements in methods and more definite localization. A French tradition ascribes the 'invention' of crown glass to Philippe de Cacqueray at a glasshouse at La Haye near Rouen in Normandy in about 1330.[5] He may have introduced the technique, which had long been known, into France, but it is more likely that his 'invention', if any, consisted in improvements in the founding process which produced a more ductile glass metal capable of being blown into crowns of from fifteen to twenty or even twenty-four inches in diameter.[6] At any rate the de Cacquerays and three other glassmaking families allied to them by marriage—the de Bongards, de Brossards, and le Vaillants—received monopoly privileges for producing crown glass in Normandy, and were granted the noble rank of *écuyer*, and certain feudal exemptions.[7] Their crowns, which were known throughout Europe as 'Normandy glass', achieved great prestige and enjoyed a wide international market. Some later members of these families were to be leaders in the English industry. Meanwhile similar improvements were being made in broad glass. Toward the end of the fourteenth century four other families of glassmakers— the de Hennezells, de Thietrys, de Thysacs, and de Bisvals—migrated from the Bohemian border to the forest of Darney in the Vosges mountains of Lorraine.[8] Like their Norman counterparts, they improved the quality and ductility of their glass metal through careful founding, and in

[1] Chambon, p. 166. Chambon discusses early European crowns of about eight inches (20 cm.) in diameter. Crowns from central Asia of the tenth and eleventh centuries of 17–18 cm. in diameter have been found. See A. A. Abdurazakov, 'Medieval Glass from the Tashkent Oasis', *JGS* xi (1969), 32.

[2] D. B. Harden, 'Domestic Window Glass: Roman, Saxon and Medieval', *Studies in Building History*, ed. E. M. Jope (London, Odhams Press, 1961), pp. 39–63; Chambon, p. 166.

[3] *On Divers Arts: The Treatise of Theophilus*, trans. J. Hawthorne and C. S. Smith (Chicago, Univ. of Chicago Press, 1963).

[4] Harden, pp. 40–1; W. A. Thorpe, *English Glass*, 2nd edn. (London, A. & C. Black, 1949), pp. 79–80.

[5] O. Le Vaillant de la Fieffe, *Les Verreries de la Normandie* (Rouen, 1873), pp. 43–4; 93–9.

[6] The fullest discussion of the improvements and the size of the crowns is in Chambon, pp. 167–9. See also Thorpe, pp. 79–80; Harden, pp. 40–1; J. Lafond, 'Was Crown Glass Discovered in Normandy in 1330?', *JGS* xi (1969), 37–8.

[7] J. Barrelet, *Le Verrerie en France de l'époque gallo-romaine à nos jours* (Paris, Larousse, 1954), p. 55.

[8] Clark, pp. 107–8.

addition altered the technique of manipulation in order to increase the size of the cylinders.[1] The resulting sheets were larger, thinner, and flatter than those made before, so that glass 'in the Lorraine mode', like Normandy glass, achieved a high reputation. The four families, three of whom later became leaders in the English industry, received from the Duke of Lorraine confirmation of their noble rank of *chevalier* and privileges similar to those enjoyed by the Norman families.[2] Never organized in guilds or subject to the authority of corporate towns as were most artisans, and yet never quite accepted by the other lesser nobility as members of the feudal establishment, these men—Norman and Lorrainer alike—became fiercely independent in spirit, proud, clannish, hot-headed, and secretive.[3] Soon after the Reformation most of them became staunch Protestants.

Using their distinct techniques the Norman and Lorrainer families came to specialize exclusively in making window glass, generically called 'great glass' (*grand verre*) to distinguish it from vessel or 'small glass' (*petit verre*). At the same time several families of 'small' glassmakers emerged in Lorraine, including the de Bigaults, the du Houx, the Finances, and the Masseys.[4] There were others scattered about France. Their output and that of German and Bohemian glassmakers varied considerably. Much of it consisted of common flasks, bottles, hour-glasses, and so on, but some of their drinking glasses in rich, watery-green *waldglas*, often decorated with mould-blow ribs and applied threads of glass, achieved considerable artistic merit.[5] Smaller sheets of broad glass were also made by the cylinder method elsewhere than in Lorraine, particularly in the Rhineland area of Burgundy and Hesse and in Bohemia, but since these areas exercised little influence over the English industry, they need not be discussed in detail.

Though the forest-glass tradition, which included both vessel and window glass, produced by far the larger part of the total output in Europe, the glass with the most prestige during the later Middle Ages was undoubtedly of Italian origin. Prompted by a desire for a completely colourless glass, Venetian glassmakers had developed a soda glass called *cristallo* which, though slightly greyish by modern standards, was then the best glass in Europe from the point of view of transparency. Softer and more ductile than forest glass, this soda glass could be blown very thin and

---

[1] Chambon, pp. 170-2.

[2] Clark, pp. 108-9; Barrelet, p. 47; Scoville, p. 84.

[3] Scoville (pp. 85-7) relates many interesting anecdotes about the French glassmakers, replete with quarrels and duels. He states that their reluctance to intermarry with commoners and the resistance of other lesser nobility to alliances with them contributed to the constant intermarriage in glassmaking families.

[4] Barrelet, p. 47.

[5] For styles and shapes see Thorpe, pp. 84-6, and Barrelet, p. 48.

worked into curious and fanciful shapes. Coloured glass, especially blue and red, was often used as decoration and frequently enamel work was applied after the vessel was finished. The fashioning of tableware, especially stemmed glasses of various sorts, salts, cruets, and shallow ornamental dishes valued as *objets d'art*, became a highly lucrative trade. By the early sixteenth century the production of beads, simulated jewels, and rosaries of coloured glass formed another speciality, seldom made elsewhere. The high cost of the ingredients of *cristallo*[1] made it too expensive to be used extensively in window glass, which was never an important part of the Venetian industry, but during the first half of the sixteenth century the making of looking-glasses from *cristallo* plates became a separate and profitable speciality. At Altare near Genoa a rival group of glassmakers achieved a skill similar to that of the Venetian glassmen and made most of the same products with the exception of looking-glasses.

Actually, the 'Venetian' glassmakers lived and worked, not in Venice proper, but on the nearby island of Murano. So jealous was the Venetian Council of Ten under whose jurisdiction they lived, of the skill of these men that while they enjoyed a high standard of living and great prestige they were virtual prisoners on their island. They were not allowed to leave without special permission, and if they attempted to set up works elsewhere or divulge the secrets of their trade, reprisals were made against their families and agents might be sent to assassinate them. The Duke of Altare did allow emigration of the glassmakers from his territory, but required them to send contributions annually to his treasury and forbade them to instruct alien apprentices.[2]

The prestige of the Italian glass industry probably reached its highest point during the early sixteenth century. At the peak of her supremacy, however, Venice saw the emergence of a rival glass industry in the Low Countries. It was natural that Antwerp, the new capital of international trade and finance, should become the seat of one of the chief of the luxury crafts. In spite of the stringent regulations, Muranese glassmen escaped to Antwerp and to such cities as Liège, Namur, and Mézières. Men from Altare, Normandy, and some from Lorraine also settled in these cities. By the mid-sixteenth century these men were producing glass known as *façon de Venise* which was so similar to the original product that even an expert could frequently not detect the genuine Venetian object from the copy.[3] Forest glass, both vessel and window glass in the 'Normandy mode', was also made in the Low Countries, chiefly in the Walloon provinces. 'Flemish' glass soon achieved a high reputation in many different branches of the trade as something approaching an inter-

[1] Ingredients and sources of supply are discussed at length in Chap. VI.
[2] Scoville, p. 21; E. Gerspach, *L'Art de la verrerie* (Paris, A. Quantin, 1887), p. 150.
[3] J. Houdoy, *Verreries à la façon de Venise* (Paris, A. Aubry, 1873), *passim*.

national school developed, drawing inspiration and techniques from different glassmaking traditions. The importance of Antwerp for the development of the English glass industry was considerable, for it was through the initiative of men from Antwerp that craftsmen trained in the traditions of Lorraine, Normandy, Venice, and Altare came to settle in the British Isles.

When these alien glassmakers arrived in England early in the reign of Elizabeth, they came to revive an almost extinct craft. Very little is known of the English industry during the Middle Ages. 'It is curious', writes L. F. Salzman, 'that although there is abundant circumstantial evidence of glassmaking in England during the medieval period, direct records of the manufacture are extremely scarce, and practically confined to a single district.'[1] The district was the Weald of Surrey and Sussex. The records begin[2] about 1226 with a deed to Laurence Vitrearius (glassmaker), a Norman who settled at Dyers Cross, Pickhurst, near the little village of Chiddingfold in Surrey and there made both coloured and 'white' glass for the east windows of the Abbey of Westminster. It seems likely that his son and possibly his grandson continued the trade.[3] In the next century (1351–5) John Alemayne of Chiddingfold sold substantial quantities of white window glass presumably made there for St. George's Chapel, Windsor, and St. Stephen's, Westminster.[4] About 1343 the Shurterre family had appeared in Chiddingfold. By 1367 at the latest John Shurterre, who leased Alemayne's property, was engaged in glassmaking[5] and passed on the craft to several generations of descendants, one of whom sent another consignment of window glass to Westminster in 1400.[6] Three branches of the Shurterre family remained in Chiddingfold throughout the fifteenth and sixteenth centuries, but they seem to have abandoned glassmaking some time during the fifteenth century. In the meantime the Paytowes arrived in Chiddingfold about 1440, intermarried with the Shurterres in 1475, and carried on the glassmaking tradition during the sixteenth century.[7]

[1] L. F. Salzman, *English Industries of the Middle Ages* (Oxford, Clarendon Press, 1923), p. 183. A short anonymous note entitled 'The Earliest Recorded Glassmaker in England' in *Glass Technology* (vol. i, no. 4 (1960), p. 137) refers to a manuscript concerning Henry Daniell, 'vitrearius' at St. Benet's Priory in Norfolk *c.* 1135. I have not seen this MS., but it should be pointed out that 'vitrearius' could mean either 'glassmaker' or 'glazier'. See *Revised Medieval Latin Word List*, ed. R. E. Latham (London for the British Academy, O.U.P., 1965).

[2] GMR, Sadler Deeds 105/1/30, summarized in G. H. Kenyon, *The Glass Industry of the Weald* (Leicester, Univ. of Leicester Press, 1967), p. 26.

[3] Ibid. For some reason Kenyon discounts the evidence he cites, but it seems to me most probable.

[4] J. A. Knowles, 'Medieval Glazing Accounts', *Journal of the British Society of Master Glass Painters*, ii (1927–8), 188.

[5] GMR, Sadler Deeds 105/1/110.

[6] Knowles iii. 25.

[7] Kenyon, pp. 117–18, citing the Sadler deeds.

Except for the Wealden area medieval glasshouses in England seem to have been few and generally short-lived. The abbey of Vale Royal carried on the manufacture of glass from 1284 to about 1309, and Salisbury Cathedral had a 'glashous' in the late fifteenth century.[1] In South Staffordshire there is some evidence of more or less continuous production near Abbots Bromley and Rugeley. In 1380 John Shurterre's widow brought John Glazewryth from Staffordshire to Chiddingfold to make 'brode glass' and vessel glass during the minority of her son,[2] and forty years later John Glasman of Rugeley procured white glass for York Minster presumably made there.[3] A century later (c. 1500) there was a glasshouse in the tenure of the Harvey family on the Bagot estates near Abbots Bromley.[4] Sir Walter Bagot writing in 1616[5] claimed that glass had been made on his family's estates for two hundred years, but since he nowhere asserted that production had been continuous, it may well have been intermittent and seems to have died out by the early 1560s, to be revived by immigrant Lorrainers in 1585.[6]

While these scattered references no doubt do not exhaust the list of medieval glasshouses, it is nevertheless clear that much of the window glass used in England during the Middle Ages and nearly all of the coloured glass came from the continent.[7] Moreover this imported glass

[1] L. F. Salzman, *Building in England down to 1540; A Documentary History* (Oxford, Clarendon Press, 1952), p. 182.

[2] GMR, Sadler Deeds 105/1/117.   [3] Salzman, *Building in England*, p. 183.

[4] D. W. Crossley, 'Glassmaking in Bagot's Park, Staffordshire, in the Sixteenth Century', *Post-Med. Arch.* i (1967), 45–6.

[5] Sir Walter Bagot to Sir Robert Mansell, 1616, quoted in full in W. Horridge, 'Documents Relating to the Lorraine Glassmakers in North Staffordshire, with some Notes Thereon', *Glass Notes*, xv (1955), 26–33.

[6] D. W. Crossley suggests in two articles that glassmaking continued at Bagot's Park from 1544 'up to and beyond 1585' when the Lorrainers arrived. As evidence in the first article (*Post-Med. Arch.* i (1967), 46–7) he notes the death in the Abbots Bromley P.R. of Richard Russell 'glazor' in 1561, George Watkys 'vitrearius' in 1566, and Thomas Rodes 'vitrearius' in 1587. As noted earlier, 'vitrearius' could mean 'glazier 'as well as 'glassmaker' (see p. 9, n. 1), and in the sixteenth century the term 'glazier' normally had its modern meaning, so without further evidence these entries are scarcely conclusive. In the second article, 'The performance of the Glass Industry in Sixteenth Century England' (*EcHR* 2nd ser. xxv (1972), 426–7), though he says again that 'glassmakers and glaziers' continue in the Abbots Bromley records, his evidence rests upon the wills of Richard Russell (20 Sept. 1561), George Watkys (15 Mar. 1567), and Thomas Rodes (15 Mar. 1587) in the Lichfield J.R.O. As I read the wills of Russell and Watkys both were identified as 'glazors' and at the time of his death Russell was clearly a husbandman. The debts owing to Watkys clearly identify him as a glazier in the modern sense, there was another Watkys of St. Ives, Huntingdon, who was a glazier in the 1580s (Lichfield J.R.O., will of John Watkys, 9 May 1588), and the presence of a glazier in a town is no evidence that glassmaking was carried on in the vicinity. A thorough search of the Lichfield J.R.O. failed to turn up the will of Thomas Rodes, 'vitrearius', though there were several Thomas Rodes who died in other years in the area, all yeomen. In any case there is a long interval of twenty years between Crossley's citations. and if Rodes were a glassmaker by 1585 he could have been newly employed in some capacity by the immigrant Lorrainers.

[7] Salzman, *Building in England*, p. 183, said there was no documentary evidence for the making of coloured glass in England; but archaeological evidence now suggests that it was made on

was generally of better quality[1] and enjoyed greater prestige than the homemade product. Rhenish, Burgundian, and Norman glass comprised the bulk of that purchased for York Minster,[2] and the executors of the Earl of Warwick in 1447 expressly commanded that no English glass be used in the windows of the Beauchamp Chapel.[3] Henry VI did indeed bring John Utyman from Flanders in 1449 to make coloured glass for Eton College and King's College, Cambridge, granting him a monopoly for twenty years,[4] but there is no evidence that he or any of his workmen remained after their assigned tasks were completed.

However much glass had been made in England earlier, it is clear that by the middle of the sixteenth century the craft was at a low ebb. Charnock's *Breviary of Philosophy* published in 1557 makes this observation:

> As for glassmakers, they be scant in the land
> But one there is as I do understand
> And in Sussex is now his habitacion
> At Chiddingfold he works of his occupacion.
> To go to him it is necessary and meete
> Or send a servante that is discreete
> And desire him in most humble wise
> To blow thee a glass after thy devise.[5]

Poets are not noted for the accuracy of their information, but in this case there is some substantiation for the gist of Charnock's rhyme. Though glassmakers were indeed scant in 1557, there were at least two furnaces working in the Weald. In that very year Henry Strudwick of Kirdford, Sussex, bequeathed to his sons his glasshouse and all the 'ovyns, irons and other thinges necessaryye' for continuing the craft,[6] and six years later Thomas Peytoe of Chiddingfold whose ancestors had made glass in the parish for a century made a like bequest to his son.[7] That there were no other glassmakers in England at that time is attested by a later petition opposing the glass monopoly.[8] The petition states that the 'two families namely Strodwicks and Petoes' were the only ones at work before the coming of the foreigners in the 1560s.

---

two sites. See Kenyon, pp. 190–1; M. Ridgway and G. Leach, 'Further Notes on the Glasshouse Site at Kingswood, Delamere, Cheshire', *Journal of the Chester Archaeological Society*, n.s. xxvii (1948), pt. i, 133.

[1] Kenyon, who has examined fragments from most of the early glasshouse sites, states (p. 105) that the quality was 'generally poor'.

[2] Salzman, *English Industries*, pp. 187–8.

[3] A. Hartshorne, *Old English Glasses* (London, E. Arnold, 1897), p. 129.

[4] Salzman, *Building in England*, p. 183.

[5] S. E. Winbolt, *Wealden Glass: The Surrey–Sussex Glass Industry, 1261–1615* (Hove, Combridges, 1933), p. 12. Chiddingfold, as noted earlier, is actually in Surrey, near the border with Sussex.

[6] *Transcripts of Sussex Wills*, ed. W. H. Godfrey (Suss. R.S. Publications, xliii (1938), 72).

[7] *VCH, Surrey*, ii. 297.

[8] Smedmore House, Clavell MS. B2/5, 'Answeres to the Pattentees Obiections', undated but from internal evidence *c.* 1621.

Considerable evidence also substantiates Charnock's implication that the output of their glasshouses was limited to vessel glass and apothecaries' wares. In view of the importance of the question of whether window glass was being made in England at that time[1] it is worth recounting. The petition cited above clearly states that both the Peytoes and the Strudwicks practised 'the Art of making drinking glasses' and adds that 'the Art of making window glasse was lost in this kingdom and renewed' only upon the arrival of aliens.[2] As early as 1542 a petition of the Glaziers Company to the Privy Council, wholly concerned with the prices of imported Flemish, Burgundian, and Norman window glass, contains no reference to English-made window glass and clearly implies that none was available.[3] Twenty years later (1562) a contract for glazing the windows of the new Chapel at Trinity College, Cambridge, stipulated that the date for completing the work might be extended without penalty, since it depended upon early 'passedge by sea' from the continent for the necessary glass.[4] In 1567 before the granting of a monopoly patent in window-glass making, the master of a glasshouse near Chiddingfold, presumably a Peytoe, stated that he did not and could not make window glass, but only 'small things like urinals, bottles and other small wares'.[5] Two years later Sir Richard Onslow and William More, prominent members of the Surrey gentry, investigated a quarrel among alien glassmakers recently settled in the area and confirmed the fact that no English glassmaker in the Weald could make window glass.[6] As late as 1590 George Longe claimed to be the only true Englishman skilled in the art.[7] Perhaps most conclusive is the negative evidence. After the granting of the monopoly patent in window glassmaking in 1567 to aliens, there is no record of any protest from an English glassmaker.

Since window glass was certainly made in England during the Middle Ages, the question arises as to why its manufacture died out by the mid-sixteenth century. The answer to this problem is not entirely clear, but

[1] The validity of the first glass patent depends upon this point. Harden (p. 57) states that window glass was still being made in England when the aliens came, without citing any evidence except conversations with Kenyon regarding excavated sites. Kenyon himself (p. 82) tends to agree with Harden but admits the fragments of window glass could easily be cullet. The contemporary documentary evidence cited below, much of which was not known to earlier writers, all points to the opposite conclusion.

[2] Smedmore House, Clavell MS., B2/5.

[3] C. H. Ashdown, *History of the Worshipful Company of Glaziers of the City of London* (London, Black, East and Black, 1919), p. 21.

[4] J. A. Knowles, 'The Source of the Coloured Glass used in Medieval Stained Glass Windows', *Glass*, (Apr. 1926), p. 201. Knowles remarks upon the dependence of the English glass-painter on continental sources for his raw material.

[5] S.P. 12/42, no. 43. I have translated from the original French.

[6] Loseley House, Loseley MSS., Onslow and More to the Council, 17 Aug. 1569, unnumbered letter in a box marked 'Oddments to 5 Nov. 1580'.

[7] Lansd. MS. 59, no. 72.

some light can be thrown on the matter by a consideration of the market for glass. Unquestionably until the time of the Reformation the greatest demand was for stained-glass windows for ecclesiastical buildings, especially the more elaborate structures such as cathedrals, abbey churches, royal and college chapels, and some of the wealthier parish churches. When such large structures were being built and glazed, a nearby glasshouse was not only convenient but economical, since transportation of such a heavy and breakable commodity as glass was expensive. Once the structure was complete, however, only small bits of glass would be needed for replacement and the output of a single furnace might well be unsaleable.

For domestic window glass the market was smaller and much more uncertain. Royal residences and the seats of the nobility and the wealthier gentry often contained considerable glass, as did the town houses of the more prosperous merchants, but were seldom completely glazed.[1] Such work was generally done piecemeal, a few windows at a time, so that small consignments of glass (three to six cases) seems to have sufficed for the orders of most glaziers. The houses of ordinary folk and most parish churches continued to make use of oiled paper or linen for window coverings throughout the later Middle Ages. That the demand was too low to sustain window glassmaking on any scale in England is best illustrated by the fact that as late as 1567 the total amount of all kinds of window glass from Normandy, Lorraine, and Hesse brought into the Port of London did not equal the normal production of one glasshouse.[2] It is understandable that English glasshouses making window glass should have declined. Even continental ones more favourably situated on large navigable rivers and enjoying a wider market were also feeling the effects of over-production by the mid sixteenth century.[3]

In the field of vessels and tableware demand for glass was also low during most of the Middle Ages. The wealthy, perhaps influenced by the papal ban on glass chalices,[4] generally preferred the precious metals for their goblets and bowls, and when a few of the more sophisticated did purchase glass, they imported *cristallo* which the forest glassmen in England had neither the skill nor the materials to make. As for the poor

---

[1] Salzman, *Building in England*, pp. 173–4. For a fuller discussion of the market for window glass see Chap. IX.

[2] A total of 214 cases was imported between Michaelmas 1567 and Michaelmas 1568 by English merchants (Port Books E. 190/4/2). If, as was usual, alien merchants imported less during the same period, the total may have been under 400 cases. More than 400 cases were normally produced in a year in a glasshouse by a single furnace. See below, pp. 185–6.

[3] Clark, *JSGT*, p. 110.

[4] Thorpe (p. 78) thinks that various papal bans robbed glass vessels of their 'snob appeal'. Certainly during the later Roman Empire high-quality glass vessels were valued above those of precious metals, whereas in the Middle Ages the opposite was true, but to blame this trend entirely on the Papacy is an over-simplification.

and those of moderate means, more durable substitutes were available in wood, stoneware, and pewter. For some purposes, however, glass held an undisputed advantage over other materials. Containers for acids and chemicals, and urinals (meaning then a globular flask for urine analysis— one of the most common means of medieval medical diagnosis)[1] enjoyed a small but steady market. One skilled glass-blower with some unskilled help could produce simple flasks and urinals as opposed to the two or three necessary for window glass or fine-stemmed drinking vessels and could even combine such work with farming as a part-time occupation. Transportation presented no problem, for travelling chapmen would hawk the wares. The English glasshouses had long produced vessel as well as window glass, and it is understandable that when orders from the Church and the King's glazier for window glass fell off, glassmakers in England began to rely on supplying the humbler needs of the apothecary, the alchemist, and the physician. Over the years the skill to make window glass was easily lost through disuse and some glassmakers abandoned the craft entirely.[2]

The scanty records of importation early in the sixteenth century confirm the impression that demand for glass of various kinds was low. In 1507 the Book of Rates[3] (a list of the most commonly imported items with valuations for use by the customs officials) lists only Norman and Flemish window glass, spectacles, beads, and 'balme glasses', probably small drinking cups.[4] In the same year each of these items and a few others were actually imported, but the consignments in each shipment were very small, for example, '6 dossen glasbedes, i dosen rennishe glasses', and three or four cases of window glass.[5] By mid-century the size of the consignments had increased noticeably and a number of new items made of glass appeared, particularly hour-glasses and looking-glasses. In 1567 window glass accounted for about half the total value of all glass imported, with looking-glasses second in value.[6] Also notable, however, was the increase of importation of tableware both in green glass and in *cristallo*.[7] Compared with other imported commodities, the glass trade was still relatively small, for in 1565 a list prepared for the Privy Council ranked glass as thirty-fifth at a total valuation of £1,622,[8] less than the valuation

[1] The urinal was a recognized symbol of a physician, used often as a signboard device. See F. H. Harrison, *An Introduction to the History of Medicine*, 2nd edn. rev. (Philadelphia, Saunders, 1917), p. 166.

[2] Kenyon, pp. 117–20; Crossley, *Post-Med. Arch.*, p. 46.

[3] N. S. B. Gras, *The Early English Customs System* (Cambridge, Mass., Harvard Univ. Press, 1918), pp. 695–703.

[4] Thorpe, p. 70.

[5] Gras, pp. 562–80. Gras gives imports only for a short period, so that totals cannot be compared to those of 1567 cited below.

[6] Port Books, E. 190/4/2, London, English merchants, Mich. 1567–Mich. 1568.

[7] Ibid.   [8] Lansd. MS. 8/17, 'Wares brought into London', 1565.

of imported tennis balls or playing-cards in a list drawn up five years earlier.[1] Nevertheless a market existed for several kinds of glass not then being made in England, and a merchant familiar with the import trade might well envisage an opportunity for the establishment of at least a few new glass furnaces in England. Raw materials presented no problem and fuel was then not scarce. What was lacking was the skill, especially in the making of window glass and Venetian *cristallo*. The time was ripe for the arrival of alien glassmakers.

[1] S.P. 12/8/3, 1560. See also A. M. Millard, 'The Import Trade of London, 1600-40' (unpublished Ph.D. thesis, Univ. of London, 1956), p. 67.

II

THE REVIVAL OF GLASSMAKING
IN ENGLAND 1567–1590

T HE opportunity for establishing new glasshouses in England using foreign workmen did not go unnoticed. Before success was achieved there were several abortive attempts about the middle of the century. In 1549 eight glassmakers came from Murano to London to set up a permanent *façon de Venise* drinking glass factory.[1] It would appear that within two years all but one had returned to the continent, presumably frightened by letters from the Council of Ten threatening reprisals against their families.[2] In 1552 a merchant of London named Henry Smyth secured a patent for twenty years giving him exclusive right to make 'brode glass such as is wont to be called Normandy glasse'.[3] He proposed to bring workmen from Normandy, but nothing more was ever heard of his project.[4] Since the Norman glassmakers were Calvinist, it is likely that the accession of the Catholic Mary to the English throne discouraged them from coming. Finally Cornelius de Lannoy, a promoter who was as much alchemist as industrialist, secured privileges early in the reign of Elizabeth for schemes as widely divergent as glassmaking and turning base metals into gold. He made a serious attempt to start a glasshouse in London but apparently failed for lack of sufficient technical knowledge.[5] Success awaited the arrival of a man with more persistence and more experience.

I. JEAN CARRÉ

The credit for re-establishing the making of window glass in England and introducing the manufacture of fine tableware in *cristallo* belongs to

[1] H. J. Powell, *Glassmaking in England* (Cambridge, C.U.P., 1923), pp. 27–9.

[2] Powell (p. 29) says that Iseppo Casseler, who apparently stayed in London, continued to make glass, but he cites no evidence and I have found none. I think it highly doubtful.

[3] G.B., PRO, *Calendar of the Patent Rolls* (London, H.M.S.O., 1926), iv. 323. The quotation in the text and a similar reference to 'broad' glass made by Normans near Alfold (Loseley House, Loseley MSS., More and Onslow to the Council, 18 Aug. 1568) are the clearest indications that the term 'broad' was not restricted to Lorraine-type glass in the mid-sixteenth century.

[4] Eric W. Wood, who excavated a Norman glasshouse site near Alfold, Surrey (described briefly in *Surr. Arch. Col.* lxv (1968), 153–4), found a coin of 1552 and a full crown in the annealing furnace, suggesting the site was abandoned hastily. Since a Henry Smith of Burgate owned land near by, he suggested to me that Smith actually brought Normans who stayed a short time and left after the accession of Mary. This is an interesting possibility, but can hardly be taken as certain.

[5] *Cal. S.P.D.* i. 256. Lannoy blamed his failure on the lack of a sufficiently good clay for the pots.

an alien, Jean Carré. A native of Arras, then a part of the Low Countries, he had lived some years in Antwerp. Largely because of a statement of an Englishman made long after his death, it has frequently been asserted that he was a merchant with no knowledge of glassmaking.[1] In view of his close friendship with glassmakers and his ability to command their loyalty and also his instructions that his son be trained to make 'small glass',[2] it is much more likely that in Antwerp he had been engaged in some aspect of the glass trade, probably as a maker of vessel glass. At any rate early in the spring of 1567 he arrived in London[3] intent upon establishing glassworks and armed with considerable technical knowledge, a sizeable amount of capital, and extensive contacts with glassmakers of several traditions.

Although Carré never mentions his reasons for moving to England, it is noted in the *Returns of Aliens* that he 'came hither for religion'.[4] While this could be a conventional reason, it is likely to be at least in part the true one, for Carré and his family were devout Calvinists.[5] Moreover the date of his arrival in England followed closely upon the religious riots of 1566 in Antwerp which provoked Philip II of Spain to set up the dreaded 'Council of Blood' and to send the Duke of Alva with Spanish troops to stamp out heresy. The rebellion and civil disorder which followed disrupted trade, so that in addition to the fear of religious reprisals Carré may have anticipated economic advantages in the move. There were also personal considerations for choosing sanctuary in England. His favourite daughter Mary who had married Peter Appel, a Flemish cloth merchant, had been living in London with her own family since 1561.[6] As a denizen and householder, Appel was in a position to be of assistance to his father-in-law and it was to his house in St. Swithin's parish that Carré brought his wife and younger children early in 1567.

Upon his arrival Carré lost no time in setting about his project. By July 1567 he had already secured from the Queen a licence to build furnaces for window glass in the Weald and another from the Mayor and Aldermen of London for a Venetian-type furnace for crystal there.[7] By that date he also claimed to have actually built three furnaces, one in London and two in the Weald on leased land in Fernfold Wood, part of the manor of Bury,

[1] Thorpe, p. 86, Kenyon, p. 122, citing Lansd. MS. 59, no. 72, Longe to Cecil, 1590.
[2] P.C.C. Daper 39, will of Jehann Carr, 11 May 1572.
[3] *Returns of Aliens Dwelling in the City and Suburbs of London . . .*, ed. R. E. G. Kirk and E. F. Kirk (Publications of the Huguenot Society of London, vol. x in 4 pts.), (Aberdeen, Univ. of Aberdeen Press, 1900–8), pt. ii, pp. 39–40.
[4] Ibid., p. 39.
[5] P.C.C. Daper 39, will of Jehann Carr, 11 May 1572. Carré established a French-speaking congregation at Fernfold with a resident minister. His brother-in-law was elder.
[6] *Returns of Aliens*, pt. i, pp. 263, 317, 390; pt. ii, pp. 40, 294. Appel was born at Ypres and was 'of the Dutche churche'; Mary was born in Arras and was 'of the Frenche churche'.
[7] S.P. 15/13, no. 89, Carré to Cecil, undated but clearly July 1567.

near the little village of Alfold on the Surrey–Sussex border.[1] He had ordered the soda necessary to make *cristallo* from Spain and part of it had arrived.[2] The letter to William Cecil, Secretary to Queen Elizabeth, in which Carré recites these accomplishments is written in the first person singular and implies that he was working alone. As a later document makes clear,[3] however, by the spring of 1568 at the latest he had formed a 'fellowship' or company in which he held a half interest. Three other members of the company are known with reasonable certainty[4]—Jean Chevalier, Peter Briet, and Peter Appel, his son-in-law, who no doubt assisted him with preliminary arrangements but was not active in the management of the business until after Carré's death. Peter Briet on the other hand was clearly an associate of Carré's from the beginning. Like Carré he was a French-speaking Huguenot from the Low Countries, described in 1568 as 'denizen and broker'.[5] Since he signed a petition to Cecil jointly with Carré early in the summer of 1567,[6] it seems likely that the company had been formed by that time, possibly before Carré left Antwerp.

Although well-financed and equipped with furnaces and supplies, Carré very soon became worried about possible competition. The permissive licences from the Queen and the Aldermen of London were about to be made worthless, he claimed, by a grant of a true monopoly in glassmaking to another person. In a letter to Cecil[7] Carré recalled a previous conversation on the subject, when he had been told that no monopoly in glassmaking was necessary or possible. If one was to be issued, Carré felt that on grounds both of priority in planning and of actual accomplishment he should receive it. This same letter, therefore, requested a monopoly in window-glass making and was followed shortly by a second, signed by both Carré and Briet, asking for another monopoly, in Venetian crystal.[8] Although continental precedents in the way of free housing and exemption from certain taxation were cited, no concessions were asked except freedom from local competition. Apparently the Queen and Council refused to consider the second request and nothing more is heard of a monopoly

---

[1] S.P. 15/13, no. 89; Add. MS. 5701 fol. 150. Although Fernfold Wood is less than two miles from Alfold, Surrey, it is actually in Sussex in the old parish of Wisborough Green.

[2] S.P. 15/13, no. 89.

[3] Lansd. MS. 59, no. 76, enclosure, printed in full in *Tudor Economic Documents*, ed. R. H. Tawney and E. Power (London, Longmans, 1924), i. 32–4.

[4] The company and the financial arrangements are discussed at more length in Chap. VII, p. 162.

[5] *Returns of Aliens*, pt. iii, p. 360.

[6] S.P. 12/43, no. 42, Carré and Briet to Cecil.

[7] S.P. 15/13, no. 89.

[8] S.P. 12/43, no. 42, Briet and Carré to Cecil, undated. *Cal. S.P.D.* (i. 297) dates this petition 9 Aug. 1567 in brackets, but a comparison of this letter with another in Carré's hand (S.P. 12/43, no. 45) dated 9 Aug. makes it necessary to place this one somewhat earlier, probably the end of July.

in crystal until after Carré's death. The production of crystal by virtue of the licence from the City of London could continue, however, and in fact it did. On the other hand the request for a monopoly in window glass eventually resulted in the granting of letters patent.

The other person seeking a monopoly of whom Carré complained was probably Anthony Becku. His signature replaces Briet's in further joint petitions to Cecil and his name precedes Carré's in the final letters patent. Becku seems to have been a merchant born in the Low Countries who had lived in London as a denizen for eighteen years.[1] There is no evidence that he had any previous connection with the glass industry, though he had a son and an English son-in-law who were eager to enter the trade.[2] Becku made it clear several years later that he was never included in Carré's company, although he wished to be, and that the relationship between the two was bad from the beginning of their association.[3] Since Becku and Carré, though ostensible partners in the patent, never relished association with each other, it seems clear that as rival contenders for the monopoly in window glass, they joined forces temporarily in order to secure the patent, either from fear that one might forestall the other or on a direct suggestion from Cecil, such as he made later to another petitioner for a glass patent.[4]

The negotiations which preceded the issuing of the patent need not be related in detail. The chief point to be settled was whether or not window glass was already being made in England. The petitioners stated that they had gone to Chiddingfold and talked with the master of the glasshouse there, who told them that he did not and could not make window glass, but only urinals, vessel glass, and other small wares.[5] There was no mention of glassmakers in Staffordshire. Cecil was apparently satisfied and there is no evidence that anyone objected at the time or later that window glass was already being made in England. Once that point was settled, the specific terms of the grant were quickly agreed upon during the month of August.[6]

The final letters patent, dated 8 September 1567, gave to Becku and Carré the exclusive right to make window glass in either the French

---

[1] *Returns of Aliens*, pt. ii, p. 125; *Letters of Denization and Acts of Naturalization in England 1509–1603*, ed. W. Page (Publications of the Huguenot Society of London, vol. viii), (Lymington, Huguenot Soc., 1893), p. 19. Crossley, *EcHR*, p. 428, states that Becku was a 'Normandy craftsman' who came to England about the same time as Carré, but the *Letters of Denization* prove otherwise.

[2] Lansd. MS. 59, no. 76.   [3] Ibid.   [4] Lansd. MS. 59, no. 72.

[5] S.P. 12/43, no. 43, unsigned and undated petition to Cecil, but clearly in Carré's hand. From internal evidence this petition must date from August 1567, and from the use of plural pronouns must have come from Carré and a partner, presumably Becku by this time.

[6] S.P. 12/32, nos. 43, 44, 45, 46. Dates on these documents range from 9 to 12 Aug. 1567. The last is an outline of the main points of the patent as finally granted and is endorsed in Cecil's hand as approved by the Queen and Council.

(Norman) or the Lorraine manner for the term of twenty-one years.[1] Anyone, native-born or alien, attempting to infringe the patent was liable to confiscation of his works, tools, and supplies and the payment of £100 as fine. The patentees for their part were bound to produce 'enough glass for glassings as shall suffice . . . to be employed within owre saide realme' and to sell the glass as cheap or cheaper than foreign glass had usually been sold. They were also bound to teach Englishmen the art of glass-making, so that after the period of twenty-one years the craft would be largely in the hands of natives. In addition the patentees were to pay the Crown annually such amounts of money which would have been due as customs duty had the glass been imported by native merchants (a shilling in the pound by value), but they were then free to export any surplus not sold in England without further payment of customs. Finally the patent was to become void if by Christmas 1568 Carré and Becku were not producing enough glass to supply the realm.

On the whole the patent seems to be a reasonable one. From the point of view of the patentees the stipulation that they should supply the kingdom with window glass within fifteen months was not unrealistic, for the two furnaces already built could have accomplished this if they were both in full production,[2] and the patentees actually seem to have contemplated erecting more and using the provision for free exportation.[3] From the point of view of the government England would benefit from a new industry. Mercantilist theories then coming into general acceptance held that importation of manufactured wares, especially those deemed 'unnecessary', was detrimental to economic well-being and that the establishment of new industries, particularly if they employed native workmen, was highly desirable. In order to secure the training of Englishmen temporary privileges for a limited time seemed justifiable. In the meantime freedom of importation would hold prices in line with those on the continent and the customs duty on each case of English-made glass would maintain the Crown revenue.

The granting of this first glass patent was not an isolated phenomenon, but rather part of a general policy undertaken by the Council. Although precedents existed in the Middle Ages for the granting of special privileges by royal letters patent, most of these early grants concerned either commercial privileges or the licensing and regulating of certain trades. The idea of industrial monopolies enjoying royal protection seems to have been brought to England from the continent about the middle of the

---

[1] PRO, Chancery Enrolments, Patent Rolls, 9 Elizabeth, pt. 11, mm. 33–4 (8 Sept. 1567).

[2] See Chap. I, p. 13. In addition William More who investigated for the Council two years later assumed in his report that two furnaces for window glass would supply the kingdom. Loseley House, Loseley MSS., More and Onslow to the Council, 18 Aug. 1569, unnumbered letter.

[3] S.P. 12/43, no. 43, Carré to Cecil.

sixteenth century.[1] The policy was at first clearly motivated by the desire to benefit the economic life of the nation through the introduction of new industries by special privileges to foreign workmen. Legally the power to make such grants was conceived to belong naturally to the Prerogative, since the customary law and the rights of native Englishmen were concerned only with industries already established. Monopoly rights for new inventors came to be included among these grants, probably at the suggestion of a Venetian engineer,[2] but in the early years of the patent system the rights of the importer of a new industry were more clearly established than those of the inventor of a new process. Between 1561 and 1570 twenty-two patents of monopoly[3] were issued for industrial production, including both new inventions and importations of industries from abroad. Besides window glass there were letters patent covering the production of salt, soap, alum, saltpetre, and sulphur, as well as others for mechanical inventions, such as machines for dredging. The legal right of the Crown to make such grants was as yet unquestioned. During the first years of the policy the grants were made cautiously; the patent for window glass fitted into the policy of encouraging new industries.

On the other hand it might be argued that the patent was not necessary, since conditions for the development of the industry were so favourable. Two facts seem to bear out this thesis: first, that Carré originally seemed willing to operate without a monopoly, and second, that many other Huguenot glass-workers came to England during the late 1570s when the patent was virtually dead. We must remember, however, that in his letters to Cecil, Carré showed clearly that he was familiar with continental precedents for monopoly grants as well as with the policy of the English Crown to issue such patents. His letters indicate that he was nervous, no doubt justifiably, over the prospect of someone else securing a patent which would shut him out, and therefore he was unwilling to proceed without further protection. In addition, if he was familiar with the limited demand for window glass in England, he probably believed that a rival enterprise begun simultaneously might well spell ruin. As for the later immigration of Huguenots, it should be pointed out that they came largely after the massacre of St. Bartholomew in 1572, an event which could scarcely have been foreseen in 1567.

Once the royal privilege was safely granted, Carré ignored his new partner and carried out the arrangements already made with Chevalier for bringing Lorrainers to England to man one of the furnaces near Alfold. The contract signed in April 1568 with Thomas and Balthazar de

---

[1] E. W. Hulme, 'History of the Patent System under the Prerogative, and at Common Law', *LQR* xvi (1900), 44.

[2] Ibid.

[3] Ibid., xii. 146. Price, p. 8, states that eighteen patents were granted during this period.

Hennezell on the one part and Carré and Chevalier on the other contains no reference to Becku as co-patentee with Carré in the royal privilege.[1] The Hennezells, who were to have a half interest in the glasshouse and share the profits equally with Carré's fellowship, were to come to England as soon as possible, bringing with them four other 'gentlemen glassmakers'. During the summer of 1568 they came and began work at one of the two furnaces at Alfold. At about the same time Peter and John Bungar (Pierre and Jean de Bongard) also arrived and by October were engaged in making crown glass in the other furnace.[2] They were brothers from a prominent Norman family of glassmakers but, unlike the de Hennezells, they were not co-owners of their furnace but were paid a salary. In the arrangements with them, however, Carré did grant Becku a share in the profits of the furnace in recognition of his share in the monopoly privilege,[3] but not any share of the management of either furnace. In fact Carré was wise enough to know that local supervision was not necessary and would be hotly resented by the proud *gentilhommes verriers*. He himself continued to live in London,[4] whence his company handled all marketing from the two furnaces and he gave his attention chiefly to the third of his establishments—the glasshouse for *cristallo* tableware which was not a part of the window-glass monopoly. The crystal furnace was built within the walls of the Crutched Friars, an abandoned monastery near the Tower of London, where his partner in that enterprise, Peter Briet, took up residence.[5] During the first years, Carré's staff there seems to have been Flemish, not Italian, since two Flemish glassmakers, John Levinion and Peter Cant, who was probably his brother-in-law, arrived in London about the same time as he.[6] Carré himself may have acted as the third and chief member of a chair[7] making vessel glass, leaving the marketing of both the window and vessel glass to Briet. Whether or not he carried on the tradition of owner-workman, by October 1568 he had clearly put in operation three furnaces making glass in three different continental traditions, as he had planned.

[1] Lansd. MS. 59, no. 76, enclosure.

[2] Ibid., Becku to Cecil, July 1569; Loseley House, Loseley MSS., More and Onslow to the Council, 18 Aug. 1569, unnumbered letter.

[3] Lansd. MS. 59, no. 76, Becku to Cecil, July 1569; Loseley House, Loseley MSS., More and Onslow to the Council, 18 Aug. 1569, unnumbered letter. Wages are discussed in Chap. VIII.

[4] *Returns of Aliens*, pt. iii, p. 380. This entry of 1568 indicates that he was still living with the Appells, but before 1571 he had become both denizen and householder (ibid., pt. ii, pp. 39–40).

[5] Ibid., pt. iii, p. 360.

[6] Ibid., pt. ii, p. 73; pt. iii, p. 361. Since the returns were taken verbally and names frequently mis-spelled, it is likely that Peter Cant is a mis-spelling for Peter Campe, a name not otherwise found in the *Returns* but mentioned in Carré's will as his wife's brother who was to aid her in supervising his glass furnaces. The *Returns* indicate that both Vinion and 'Cant' were glassmakers.

[7] 'Chair' is a technical term for a team of vessel-glass makers normally composed of three members. See below, p. 184, n. 2.

Carré's success in persuading skilled workmen to come to, and for the most part to remain in, England can be attributed to the same factors that brought him there—the religious troubles and the consequent disruption of economic life in France and the Low Countries. All the glassmakers who emigrated to England (with the exception of a few Italians) were Calvinist, and while they may not have been personally persecuted[1] their lot under Catholic rule, whether of the Guise family, Catherine de Medici, or Philip II of Spain, can scarcely have been secure. The series of religious wars which began in France in 1562, and the efforts of Philip II to subdue the Netherlands, caused a decline in the glass trade by disrupting the normal flow of goods to the export market.[2] Over-production, at least in Lorraine, may also have been a factor.[3] Glassmakers were not the only artisans who faced these difficulties, and in the same period other groups of skilled workmen came from the continent.[4] Flemish clothworkers, for example, brought the 'new draperies' to Colchester and other towns of East Anglia, and Protestant refugees of all trades, from merchant to carpenter, streamed into London.[5] Thus it would seem that while the granting of letters patent in glassmaking may have encouraged Carré in his efforts, the peaceful foreign policy and conciliatory religious policy of the Elizabethan government were at least as important in assuring his success.

As matters developed, the patent itself brought on most of Carré's difficulties. As a result of his forced association with Anthony Becku, friction developed between them over the management of the furnaces in the Weald, and soon resulted in a violent quarrel. The patent contained a provision for the mandatory training of English workmen, a provision which Becku desired, but which the alien workmen whose contracts Carré had arranged were not bound to fulfil. Trouble came first with the Lorrainers. When Becku discovered that Carré had signed the contract with the de Hennezells naming Chevalier instead of himself as co-partner, he attempted to intervene and establish his own rights, including altering the contract to ensure immediate training of Englishmen. Instead of confronting Carré, he sought out his partner Peter Briet and asked him to go to the Weald to be a 'mediator' with the Lorrainers.[6] When Briet arrived and informed the Hennezells that Becku, rather than their kinsman Chevalier, held half interest in the monopoly and was insisting upon the training of Englishmen, they were so incensed that they 'departed owt of the

[1] Clark (*JSGT*, p. 113) states that the de Hennezells were not persecuted in Lorraine, but were 'probably socially ostracized'.

[2] Lansd, MS. 59, no. 72.   [3] Clark, pp. 113–14.

[4] W. Cunningham, *Alien Immigrants in England* (London, Swan, Sonnenshein, 1879), pp. 149–189. Cunningham assumes that most of the aliens came for religious reasons, although he notes that some, especially the Keswick miners, came for business reasons (p. 178).

[5] I. Scouloudi, 'Alien Immigration into and Alien Communities in London, 1558–1680', *Proceedings of the Huguenot Society of London*, xvi (1937–41), 27–49.

[6] Lansd. MS. 59, no. 76, Becku to Cecil, undated but clearly July 1569.

realme and made no further meadle in the sayd works'.[1] Instead of attempting to restrain them, Briet contracted with them to set up a glass furnace at Boulogne in France, saying that they could supply the English market as well from there 'and so . . . kepe the science out of the Realme, for they wolde in no wise have the same to come into England'.[2] Whether or not they actually set up a furnace at Boulogne is doubtful, but leave they certainly did.

The Norman Bungars were still at work, however, and Becku was no less intent upon enforcing his rights upon them. Since Briet had been of no help to him, he sent to Alfold first his son Anthony and then his son-in-law James Arnold as his deputies,[3] with the intent of gaining control of the enterprise and enforcing the training of Englishmen—of Arnold in particular. The fiery Bungars were no more amenable to such a demand than the Hennezells, though their tactics differed. Peter Bungar made a personal assault on young Anthony Becku, driving him away, and later both brothers set upon James Arnold, 'th' one with a great staff, the other with a hot yron hauinge hotte glass metall apon yt',[4] seriously wounding him. Shortly thereafter (July 1569) the elder Becku appealed to the Privy Council.

As a result of Becku's complaint the Council ordered an investigation of the matter to be conducted by William More of Loseley, near Guildford, a former Sheriff and prominent member of the local gentry, and Richard Onslow, Her Majesty's Attorney in the Court of Wards and Liveries. Their instructions made clear that the Council was chiefly concerned that as a result of the quarrel between Becku and the glassmakers 'her Majesties intention to have the science of the making of that kynde of glass (window glass) within her realme is about to be frustrated'.[5] Upon receipt of the letter More and Onslow went promptly to Alfold to interview all those party to the quarrel and fourteen witnesses. Their report to the Council[6] substantiated the tale of violence and recounted the orders they had given to restore peace in the industry. They had required the Bungar brothers to pay Arnold forty shillings for the assault which had nearly cost his life 'besides the contentment of the Surgeon who demaunded no lesse than X li for the cure'. Although the Bungars had promised to demean themselves better in the future, they vehemently declared that they would never instruct Englishmen and were not bound to do so by

[1] Loseley House, Loseley MSS., unnumbered letter, More and Onslow to the Council, 18 Aug. 1569, fol. 3. This document, actually a rough draft of six pages much corrected, agrees to a remarkable extent with Becku's letter cited in the preceding note, but gives much fuller information.

[2] Lansd. MS. 59, no. 76. [3] Ibid.

[4] Loseley House, Loseley MSS., More and Onslow to the Council, 18 Aug. 1569, fol. 1. The report makes clear that Peter and John Bungar were brothers.

[5] Ibid., vol. vii, no. 34, Cecil to Onslow and More, 11 Aug. 1569.

[6] Ibid., More and Onslow to the Council, 18 Aug. 1569. The witnesses are named (fol. 1).

the terms of their contract. Reluctantly, More and Onslow advised the Council that there was, indeed, no hope of Englishmen being trained either by the Normans or by the Lorrainers, whose sudden departure they related. They thought that window-glass making should continue in England, however, in spite of this violation of the terms of the patent, and they tried without much success to get Carré and Becku to resolve their differences. The two agreed that they would indeed continue the operation of the Norman glasshouse under the existing contract with the Bungars, but they declared that they would not 'in any other place dele together'. Carré sent to Lorraine for new glassmakers to work for him and his fellowship alone, while Becku with a new partner sent to Germany for workmen, and in the meantime subsidized an English vessel glass-maker to practise making window glass without instruction from aliens. The Council apparently acquiesced, and took no steps to enforce the terms of the patent, or to assure Becku of a share in its management.

Nothing came of either of Becku's schemes, and he apparently gave up any attempt to engage actively in glassmaking. He did, however, secure the right to collect 6d. a case on all glass made under the patent as com-pensation for his share in the privilege.[1] Nor is there any direct evidence that Carré was able to persuade the original Lorrainers or their kinsmen to resume operation of the second furnace near Alfold.[2] The Bungars, however, continued to make crown glass, while Carré gave most of his attention to the crystal factory in London. There he was not achieving the success he had anticipated with his Flemish compatriots, for in 1570 he brought from Antwerp a Venetian-born glassmaker, Quiobyn Littery, and early the following year another, probably Jacob Verzelini.[3] Sales soon warranted expansion of production, for by June 1571 six men described as 'all his servantes, all glassemakers and all Italians' were living at Carré's house in Broad Street.[4] Carré himself decided to lease the furnace to them on contract and move to the Weald to begin another enterprise for making drinking glasses in the green, forest-glass medium rather than in crystal. With him he took the Flemings,[5] but before the new furnace could be made ready for firing, Carré died at his house in Fernfold Wood in May 1572.[6]

[1] Lansd. MS. 59, no. 72, Longe to Cecil, 1589.

[2] Balthazar de Hennezell, one of the original Lorrainers, returned to Darney in 1570 and eventually died there. See Winbolt, p. 129. It is doubtful if others replaced the first group in Carré's lifetime for there is no mention of Lorrainers in Carré's will. The early parish registers of Alfold are missing.

[3] Returns of Aliens, pt. ii, p. 41. The surname is omitted, but Verzelini soon assumed leader-ship at the Crutched Friars.

[4] Ibid., p. 39.

[5] P.C.C. Daper 39, 11 May 1572; 'Lay Subsidy Assessments for the County of Surrey . . . 1593', Surr. A. Col. xix (1906), 78.

[6] Wisborough Green P.R. Carré was buried in the churchyard at Alfold, the closest church to his house.

Although Carré did not live long enough to see the full fruition of his plans, he left careful instructions for continuing his glassmaking enterprises.[1] If his only son, then 4 years old,[2] should not be capable of directing them all eventually, Carré asked that he should be taught 'the art of making small glasse', as one of the Flemings had promised. In the meantime he directed that his widow, her brother (Peter Campe), and her sons-in-law were to see that the work went forward at the green drinking-glass furnace, his favourite project, and there is every likelihood that his wish was carried out.[3] Campe was also given oversight of the crystal furnace at the Crutched Friars. The half interest in the patent for window glass was bequeathed to his wife with power to appoint a deputy to sit on the board of the company, but he recommended that she rely on the advice of his good friend Peter Bungar, master of the Norman glasshouse. Actually she deputed her son-in-law, Peter Appel.

With Becku's consent[4] Appel, and Peter Briet, Carré's long-standing associate, tried to continue operating the window-glass monopoly, but with notable lack of success. The local people resented the proud, clannish aliens who wore ruffs, carried swords, and styled themselves 'gentlemen' and 'esquire'.[5] They found their ways so offensive that in 1574 a plot was hatched at Petworth 'to robbe the Frenchmen that make glasse and to burne their houses', but the offenders were caught and punished before much damage was done.[6] Such disturbances, though costly, were not as serious as the financial difficulties which soon engulfed the company, which was engaged chiefly in operating the Norman window glass furnace. In 1575 Becku sued the Bungar brothers for debts[7] and the next year the Privy Council was pressing Becku for payment due to the Exchequer in lieu of customs, according to the terms of the patent, an obligation he was not prepared to meet.[8] Briet and Appel were also unwilling to pay the Crown for the window glass already made, since they claimed that sale of their glass was ruined by competition from foreign glass.[9] Instead they applied for a new royal patent to contain a prohibition of importation, and if this were to be granted, they would be willing to enter into a bond to increase their production, which was clearly inadequate to supply the market, and pay the arrears on glass already made as

[1] P.C.C. Daper 39, 11 May 1572.

[2] There is no further trace of the son, who may have died young.

[3] The Vinions, one of whom worked with Carré in London, remained near Alfold making green glass until 1620. See Chaps. III, IV, passim.

[4] Lansd. MS. 22, no. 7.

[5] Kenyon, p. 130; Wisborough Green and Kirdford P.R.

[6] S.P. 12/95, no. 82, Bishop of Chichester to the Privy Council.

[7] Loseley House, Loseley MSS., vol. xii, no. 39, More to the Council, undated but c. 1575. The debt was £30, apparently for arrears in royalties.

[8] Lansd. MS. 22, no. 7, Becku to Cecil, 18 Oct. 1576.

[9] Ibid., no. 6, Briet and Appel to Cecil, 1576.

well as that to be made in the future.[1] Their contention that foreign glass was still supplying most of the English market was probably true. In 1571–2 about as much window glass was coming into the Port of London[2] as had been imported in 1567 and in 1574 the Queen's Glazier bought most of his glass abroad.[3] Briet and Appel said that they could not compete in the open market, as Carré had expected to do, because of high overhead costs which the company had suffered in bringing men from the continent and building new furnaces. They might have mentioned Becku's royalty of 6d. a case for his share of the patent, a levy on the industry they intended to continue in return for his support of their application for a new patent, although Becku seems not to have made a capital investment in the Norman furnace. The high cost of overland transportation from the Weald may also have been a factor, for it was probably greater than sea carriage from Rouen,[4] but in any case the company was failing.

The negotiations for a new patent make it clear that Briet and Appel desired a complete monopoly in window-glass making, with freedom from foreign competition in order to raise prices above that of imported glass. At first Cecil seemed willing, and a note in his hand of the proposed clauses for a new patent included the desired prohibition of importation.[5] The full text of the proposed grant, moreover, contained a schedule of ceiling prices on all types of window glass which Briet and Appel proposed to make in England.[6] Though intended for the protection of the consumer, the ceiling on crown glass was 2s. a case above that of imported Norman glass—this was, however, the lowest price at which Briet and Appel felt that they could profitably carry on. In spite of the advanced state which the negotiations reached, the patent was never granted, no doubt because of the objections of the glaziers to the price increase. While the Bungars continued to make window glass, the company run by Briet and Appel soon failed and nothing more is heard of them. After 1576 the original patent to Carré and Becku, though legally in force, was in effect a dead letter. No attempt was ever made under it to stop the spread of new glasshouses, and no duty was ever paid to the Crown on English window glass during the reign of Elizabeth. That Cecil considered the patent still in force, however, is indicated by the fact that he made another effort to collect the duty in about 1582. He called before him all the glasshouse keepers 'to know who should pay the Queen's custom', but received the answer that 'there was no custom due, but by condition of speciall privilege which no one of them did enjoy'.[7]

---

[1] Lansd. MS. 22, no. 6, Briet and Appel to Cecil, 1576. Both Price and Winbolt give very misleading accounts of this document, for neither noted the request for a prohibition of importation, the essential point.

[2] Port Books, E. 190/5/5.   [3] Lansd. MS. 21, no. 68, 2nd document.

[4] Land-carriage was often twenty times as expensive as sea-carriage. See below, p. 182.

[5] Lansd. MS. 22, no. 8.   [6] Ibid.   [7] Ibid., 59, no. 72.

The patent lapsed, then, through non-observance, and the way was open for other glassmakers to set up factories and move about. The patent itself was probably not an important factor in the establishment of the industry, except that it provided a stimulus and encouragement to Carré and his associates during the first crucial years. On the other hand, since neither he nor his deputies exercised their exclusive privilege to the detriment of competitors, it cannot be said to have hampered the industry, and since free importation was always permitted, it cannot have harmed the consumer. In the final analysis the successful establishment of window-glass making in England was due not to the patent (though this does not mean the policy of the Crown in granting it was unwise) but to the disruption of the continental trade by the religious wars and persecutions, and to the initiative of Jean Carré. To Carré also must be ascribed the honour of establishing the making of Italian *cristallo* on a permanent basis and of infusing new life and better skill into the making of green drinking glasses. Although his achievement has been disparaged, he deserves credit for his persistence and for his personality which could command the loyalty of Italian, Fleming, and Norman glassmakers alike. Nor were his results temporary, for although his company failed, some of the men he brought from the continent and their descendants continued to make glass in the Weald until 1618, and the London glasshouse prospered under new ownership.

II. JACOB VERZELINI

At the time of Carré's death the master of the Crutched Friars glasshouse was Jacob Verzelini, a Muranese glassmaker who had worked in Antwerp for nearly twenty years before coming to London. While in Antwerp he had married Elizabeth Van Buren, who like himself was a member of the minor nobility, and he and his family, like Carré, had become strongly Protestant.[1] Carré seems to have brought him to London to be master of the Crutched Friars in anticipation of his own move to the Weald. There is no indication in Carré's will of the terms of the contract between them or of its duration, but it must have been terminated before December 1574. At that time Verzelini claimed that he 'owned the one ffurneys within the cittie of London'[2] and that the other workmen were his employees, so he had probably accumulated sufficient capital in Antwerp to buy Carré and Briet's interest in the furnace. Legally however he was most

[1] Elizabeth and Jacob Verzelini are buried in the parish church of Downe, Kent, where a handsome commemorative brass displays the arms of Verzelini, Van Buren, and Mace. For his association with the parishes both of Downe and of St. Olave's, Hart Street, London, whose minister was his close personal friend, see Verzelini's will (P.C.C. Prob. 11/109/7, Huddlestone 7, 29 May 1604) and also Thorpe, pp. 97–9; 101. Thorpe gives further biographical details.

[2] Patent Rolls, 17 Eliz. pt. 13, mm. 3–4 (15 Dec. 1574).

insecure. As an alien his right to own property was questionable, and the special licence from the City under which he was operating the glass-works had been granted to the now deceased Carré. There was ample reason for him to seek royal protection.

The sort of monopoly grant which Carré had been denied in the field of Venetian crystal Verzelini received on 15 December 1574.[1] The terms, however, were by no means identical with those of Carré's patent for window glass. In return for the sole right to manufacture drinking glasses in the Venetian style and metal for twenty-one years Verzelini was required only to pay the Queen's customs on such glass as was made and to sell the glasses 'as good cheape or rather better cheape' than those commonly imported. Though the introductory sentences stated that he had under-taken to teach native-born subjects the art, never practised in England before his arrival, such instruction was not made a condition of the grant, as it had been in Carré's patent. Moreover, importation of competing wares from Venice or the continent was strictly forbidden and there was no mechanism included for enforcing the stipulation that prices remain comparable to those of imported wares. This is all the more noteworthy in view of the fact that Carré's patent a few years earlier had permitted free importation of window glass, while the proposed one to Briet and Appel two years later set up an elaborate scheme of ceiling prices for the protection of the consumer. The reasons behind the granting of the patent must therefore receive some consideration.

Since no deliberations of the Council or correspondence with Cecil about the matter are extant, the reasoning which resulted in the grant can only be gleaned from the patent itself and the known thinking of the day. The desirability of establishing new industries was undoubtedly upper-most, and while it was thought preferable to encourage those that might employ significant numbers of Englishmen, this was not the only nor indeed the chief consideration. Instead, current mercantilist thinking laid great stress on the curtailment of 'unnecessary' imports[2] to prevent a drain of bullion from the country, and such luxuries as Venetian goblets were clearly in that category. The patent itself states as the chief reason for the grant that 'heretofore great sommes of money have issued and gone forthe of our said realme for that manner of ware.'[3] The price was of little concern to the Council, for it was assumed that only the very rich, who had been paying prices as high as two pounds a dozen for imported glasses[4], would buy Verzelini's wares. Since many preferred vessels of

[1] Ibid.

[2] A list of imports drawn up for the Council in 1559–60 distinguishes between 'necessary' and 'unnecessary' wares. S.P. 12/8/31.

[3] Patent Rolls, 17 Eliz. pt. 13, mm. 3–4 (15 Dec. 1574).

[4] Port Books, E. 190/5/5, London, imports by aliens, Mich. 1571–Mich. 1572. See also Chap. IX.

plate and could import glasses occasionally on special licence, Verzelini would not be likely to raise his prices above those of imported crystal if he wished to find a ready market, and if he did raise his prices unduly the patent could be cancelled. Another factor relevant to the grant was the quality of Verzelini's products, which samples of his best styles presented to the Queen and her ministers demonstrated was comparable with that of imported crystal.[1] Verzelini no doubt made it clear that if letters patent were not forthcoming, he could return to one of the continental cities, as did later Italians of his distinction,[2] and there secure ample privilege and protection. Since no English glassmaker had the skill to compete with him, and since there was ample room for expansion in the industry outside his preserve (for it must be stressed that his privilege covered only drinking glasses in the Venetian medium, not even such other Venetian specialities as mirrors and beads), the only persons in England who could be hurt by his monopoly were in fact the only ones who protested, the London shopkeepers who dealt in glass.[3] They complained of the new patent, but to no avail, possibly because the Council realized that the sale of fine drinking glasses represented only a small part of their trade.[4]

Within a year of the granting of his monopoly a severe disaster overtook Verzelini, which Holinshed relates as follows:

The fourth of September being Sundaie about seven o'clock in the morning a certain glasshouse which sometime had been in the crossed friars hall neere to the tower of London burst out in a terrible fire: whereunto the lord mayor, aldermen and sheriffes with all expedition repaired and practised their euerie means possible by water buckets, hookes and otherwise to have quenched it. All which notwithstanding, whereas the same house a small time before had consumed great quantitie of wood by making of fine drinking glasses; now itself having within it neere fortie thousand billets of wood was all consumed to the stone walls, which walls greatlie defended the fire from spreading further and dooing anie more harme.[5]

Whether the fire was the result of an accident, or of a plot such as the one at Petworth, the loss of the buildings and supplies was a heavy blow. Nevertheless Verzelini determined to rebuild, but first he applied for naturalization and received his denization papers a year later (26 November 1576).[6] Since he was then entitled to own property, he not only rebuilt

[1] The Queen and the Earl of Leicester both owned fine drinking glasses which could have been made by Verzelini. See Thorpe, pp. 99, 104, n. 1 and 113, n. 2.

[2] Notably Antonia Miotti, whom Mansell brought from Venice in 1619, but who left for Brussels in 1624 to receive special privilege there. See Houdoy, p. 54.

[3] Lansd. MS. 48, no. 78, Petition of glass-sellers, undated but c. 1575.

[4] In 1567–8 English merchants imported only 43 doz. crystal glasses; aliens imported only 50 doz. in 1571–2. Port Books, E. 190/4/2; 5/5.

[5] R. Holinshed, *The Chronicles of England* . . . (London, J. Johnson, etc., 1807), iv. 329.

[6] *Letters of Denization*, p. 246.

the glasshouse but a comfortable dwelling for himself and his numerous family within the walls.[1]

After the fire the new furnace was soon in full production and Verzelini prospered, as the glassmaking colony increased through new recruits from Murano.[2] An engraver of glass also took up residence in London and was naturalized in 1582.[3] Some of the glasses made by Verzelini's men still exist; they are engraved with commemorative legends—an indication of the high regard in which they were held.[4] As he prospered Verzelini made extensive purchases of land in Kent,[5] chiefly woodlands to supply sufficient fuel for his furnace. The manor of Downe he used also as a country residence, and his eldest daughter married a neighbouring gentleman.[6] Yet he never succumbed to the temptation to become a country squire, and even in retirement he kept his headquarters at the house at the Crutched Friars next to the glasshouse.[7] Throughout his long life Verzelini was a well-known figure in the London business community, known familiarly as 'Mr. Jacob'.[8]

Very little information about Verzelini's monopoly is forthcoming from official records, an indication that he had less need than his successors to call upon the aid of the Privy Council in enforcing his rights. In 1579 he did appeal to the Council for protection against a merchant who had sold 'a certaine chest and drifotte of glasses' imported from abroad to someone in Leicestershire, contrary to the terms of the patent.[9] The Lord Mayor was instructed to stop such practices. This is the only mention of official intervention to stop importation of Venetian glasses during Verzelini's control of the monopoly, and the Port Books, as might be expected, record no importation of either Venetian drinking glasses or *façon de Venise*.[10] Though the practice prevailed of allowing noblemen and other persons of importance who travelled abroad to bring back glasses for their own households by special licence, such occasional purchases for

[1] GMR, MS. 20/2/12, Letters testimonial of Richard, Archbishop of Canterbury concerning an undecided case in P.C.C. between Elizabeth, executrix of Jacob Versaline, and their children. Many details of the family affairs not in either Jacob's or Elizabeth's will or in the codicil to Jacob's will are given in the Archbishop's report.

[2] *Returns of Aliens*, pt. ii, pp. 221, 303–4.

[3] *Letters of Denization*, p. 71. Thorpe (p. 113) discusses the work of the engraver, Anthony de Lysle, and several documents about him are cited in full in the *Burlington Magazine*, lxvii. (1935), 155.

[4] See Plate III. Thorpe (pp. 105–13) discusses briefly the best-known Verzelini glasses. There is a fuller bibliography in the *Burlington Magazine*, lvi (1930), 256–7.

[5] Guildford Muniment Room, Miscellaneous MS. 20/2/12.

[6] St. Olave's, London, P.R. Elizabeth Verzelini married Peter Manning, 'gentleman and esquire of the parish of Downe', another daughter a doctor of medicine, and a third a Grocer of London.

[7] GMR, MS. 20/2/12.

[8] Thorpe, pp. 100, 103–4.

[9] *A.P.C.* xi. 155.

[10] Port Books, E. 190/7/8 and 8/1.

private use did not bother Verzelini's trade, for he seems to have found a market for all his wares.

Competition from within England was never a serious problem either, though at least once Verzelini dealt vigorously with an attempted infringement of his monopoly. In the late 1570s a glasshouse was set up at Beckley near Rye, to make beads, bugles,[1] and enamels in the Venetian tradition, by Godfray Delahay, a Frenchman, and Sebastian Orlandini, a Venetian.[2] Since beads and bugles were not included in Verzelini's grant, this was not an infringement and Delahay sold the beads in London for some time without disturbance. Soon, however, Orlandini, the master of the glasshouse, began making drinking glasses in Venetian crystal. At first Verzelini was willing to accept damages as recompense for the violation of his patent rights, but when John Smith, a glazier of London, bought out Delahay's interest and moved the enterprise to Ratcliffe in 1580, the threat of competition near London possibly on a larger scale than at Beckley alarmed Verzelini, and he was unwilling to accept further payments. Instead he appealed to the Privy Council to stop the intended infringement of his rights.[3] In February 1581 the Council obligingly ordered the furnace at Ratcliffe pulled down,[4] although a month later they were investigating what the charge would be for rebuilding it.[5] Apparently they had acted prematurely before any drinking glasses were made at Ratcliffe, and Verzelini was liable for damages to the owners, who were clearly entitled to make beads and bugles. There is no evidence that the furnace was rebuilt, however, and it is likely that there was not a sufficient market to support a factory which produced only beads. Six years later another Italian, named Luthery, a former employee of Verzelini's at the Crutched Friars,[6] set up a furnace in Godalming parish near Guildford to make 'glass and bugells',[7] and surviving fragments would seem to indicate that in addition to beads and buttons he was making green drinking glasses, not *cristallo*.[8] Certainly Verzelini made no com-

---

[1] Bugles were tube-shaped beads made of glass, usually black, used to ornament apparel.

[2] East Sussex R.O., Rye MS. 47/20, nos. 10 and 11, interrogatories and depositions of Sundaye Exante, John Otes, and Stephan Duvall.

[3] Noting a payment to Verzelini, Kenyon misinterprets the incident and states that Verzelini himself owned a third share of the glasshouse (Kenyon, p. 211), but the Rye MS. cited above and the Privy Council Records substantiate the opposing view.

[4] *A.P.C.* xii. 337.

[5] Ibid., xiii. 4–5.

[6] *Returns of Aliens*, pt. ii, p. 41.

[7] GMR, Loseley MS. 1040, Recognizance of Ognybene Luthery. For a fuller discussion of this enterprise see G. M. A. Beck, 'Omniabene Lutheri: A Surrey Glassmaker', *Surrey Arch. Coll.* liii (1952), 90.

[8] Winbolt (p. 30) and Kenyon (pp. 194–9) describe fragments founds on the glasshouse site in Godalming wood which must have been Luthery's. They mention 'puntee knobs, prunts or seals' in addition to green drinking glass fragments, but since sealed bottles were virtually unknown at that time and glass buttons were in steady demand, the 'seals' were probably buttons. There was no evidence of *cristallo*.

plaint of competition. The inhabitants of Guildford and Godalming, however, complained to the Council of the consumption of large quantities of wood.[1] After an investigation by William More the Justices of the Peace forced him to stop making glass.[2] Since Luthery returned shortly to the parish of St. Olave's in London, presumably he went back to work at the Crutched Friars,[3] still on good terms with Verzelini.

There is no other evidence of attempted infringements of Verzelini's patent. His own men seem to have been exceptionally loyal to him and contented with their lot, judging by the frequency with which they named their children 'Jacob' and 'Elizabeth'.[4] Certainly they showed none of the restlessness and dispostion to return to the continent which characterized the later Italian colony under Mansell's employ.[5] Since emigration from Murano was still hazardous, there was little incentive for others to risk retaliation from the Council of Ten unless they had already made arrangements to work at the Crutched Friars. The few that did come to England without such security joined forces with Flemings or Lorrainers, as we shall see, to make not crystal but green drinking glasses.[6] From the granting of the patent in 1574 until the policy of the Crown changed in 1592 Verzelini prospered virtually unchallenged.

III FOREST-GLASS MAKERS

At the same time that Verzelini was prospering, forest-glass makers were increasing in numbers and beginning to spread throughout England. There was nothing to hamper expansion in green glass, for no monopoly restricted production or imposed financial obligations in the way of customs duties or royalties. Since the Port Books record considerable importation of green drinking glasses and other vessels from the continent in the 1570s,[7] it is obvious that a substantial market existed, particularly for glasses of a quality superior to those previously made by native Englishmen. The foreign workmen introduced a higher skill into the making of such wares and as a result they had no difficulty in competing with imported glassware. It is not surprising, then, that whether or not Carré's family continued for long to own the furnace at Alfold for 'small glass', production continued in the area. By the 1590s John Vinion, probably the son of a John Levinion who had worked with Carré in London, had been joined by a newly arrived Flemish alien, Peter Comely,[8]

---

[1] Loseley House, Loseley MSS., vol. xiii, no. 10.
[2] GMR, Loseley MS. 1040.   [3] St. Olave's P.R., 1589.
[4] Thorpe, pp. 103–4, quoting various parish registers.
[5] See Chaps. IV, V, passim.
[6] Price's contention that infringement was a serious problem for Verzelini (p. 69) rests on the unfounded assumption that the makers of green glass also made crystal.
[7] See p. 220.
[8] Returns of Aliens, pt. ii, p. 73; 'Lay Subsidy Assessments . . . 1593', Surr. A. Col. xix (1906), 78.

and their furnace at Alfold was a principal source of 'drinking glasses and other small wares' for travelling chapmen.[1]

In window-glass making the situation was somewhat different. The royal patent lapsed in the late 1570s, as we have seen, and the company managed by Briet and Appel, who were middlemen, failed because they could not undersell imported window glass. Once the profits of the middlemen and the royalties to the patentees were eliminated, however, there was a possibility that the producers themselves could survive. Since the cost of overland transportation from Alfold was high, moving south in order to utilize water transportation to London would help to cut the costs of delivering glass to London. This may have been done before the company failed, for in 1574 window glass which had no doubt come down the Arun from a site near Wisborough Green was being shipped from Littlehampton to London by sea.[2] Whether the glassmakers were newly arrived aliens, or the Bungars who had already moved from Alfold, it is certain that the Bungars had moved before 1579.[3] By that year the glassmaking colony in Wisborough Green was large enough to prompt Peter Bungar to secure a licence from the Bishop of Chichester to 'minister and serve' in French to his compatriots in the local parish church.[4] By that time also Peter owned his own furnace, and thereafter the family continued to make glass in the area, which they sold themselves to dealers in London. They had been forced to reduce their prices, however, considerably below that which Briet and Appel sought to charge.[5]

Even during the 1570s the Bungars faced increasing competition from newly arrived groups of alien glassmakers. Whether or not the original de Hennezells ever returned, other Lorrainers soon appeared in the Weald, their names anglicized to Hensey, Tittery, and Tysack. A few more Normans and Flemish vessel-glass makers came as well. Fear of religious persecution, heightened by the massacre of St. Bartholomew in 1572, and the 'Spanish fury' in Antwerp in 1576, when the troops sacked the city and massacred hundreds of Protestants, sufficiently explains the migration; glassmakers were only a small group among the many Protestants who sought a haven. London, Southampton, and Rye were the chief ports of entry, and so many men of all trades streamed in that in 1575 the town council of Rye forbade the landing of any more 'of the French or Flemish nacion except they be Marchants, gentlemen, common

---

[1] Winchester, Hampshire Dioc. R.O., Consistory Court Book no. 62, 21/M65, fol. 45. The case concerns chapmen who frequented Alfold to buy glasswares.

[2] Port Books, E. 190/740/22, Littlehampton and Arundel, 1574-5. For water transportation and costs, see pp. 182-3.

[3] Previous accounts have assumed that the Bungars worked near Wisborough Green from the beginning, but William More's report to the Council (see above, p. 24) proves that at first they were near Alfold.

[4] Chichester, West Sussex R.O., Consistory Court Book, C. fol. 22v.

[5] A full discussion of prices and costs follows in Chaps. VIII, IX.

postes or messengers'.[1] 'Gentlemen glassmakers' were not thereby barred and a number had already come in. As early as 1574 a glasshouse near Rye began shipping 'English window glass' to London[2] and another 'lately erected' in the neighbouring parish of Northiam also shipped glass to London from 1580 to 1584 in spite of protests from the Rye town council about the glassmakers' destruction of timber.[3] Another short-lived glasshouse was set up within a mile of Hastings in about 1580 by a Hensey (Ansey) to the annoyance of the inhabitants,[4] and between the years 1576 and 1579 there was one glasshouse, and possibly two, at Buckholt in Hampshire, manned by three Lorrainers, four Normans, and a Fleming, all of whom seemed to have come in through the port of Southampton, where they were registered in the Walloon church.[5] At first many of the new arrivals tended to stay in the south of England. Two of the Normans at Buckholt soon appeared on the estates of Knole House in Kent, where they were joined by an Italian and a glassmaker of uncertain origin,[6] while one of the Lorrainers, Jan du Tisac, seems to have moved to Ewhurst, where he appears as John Tysac a few years later.[7]

By the early 1580s some of the glassmakers in the southern counties began to seek new locations in the west and in the Midlands. The documentation of their movements, derived from excavated sites and correlated in some instances by entries in parish registers, need not be related in detail.[8] It is worth noting, however, that this evidence does not bear out the theory of Winbolt, followed by others,[9] that Carré's men, frightened by the Petworth disturbances, took to their carriages in a body and began a clearly defined series of migrations. Instead Carré's men, the Normans and the Flemings at Alfold, stayed in the Weald until 1618; those who migrated were aliens who arrived in the 1570s and later, or their descendants, and they left the Weald at varying times, following no single path of migration. Instead small groups of two or three families fanned out to the west and north, their ranks swelled from time to time by fresh

[1] Lewes, East Sussex R.O., Rye MS. 1/4, fol. 158, Decrees of the Rye Assembly, 15 Feb. 1575.

[2] *The Port Books of Rye*, ed. R. F. Dell. Sussex Record Society, vol. lxiv, pp. 67–82.

[3] Rye MS. 47/24/13; *VCH Sussex*, ii. 255.

[4] *A.P.C.* xxi. 281, 6 Dec. 1581.

[5] *Registre . . . de l'Église Wallone de Southampton* (Publications of the Huguenot Society, vol. iv, (Lymington, The Huguenot Society), p. 12. For the sites, see Kenyon, p. 215.

[6] T. B. Lennard, 'Glassmaking at Knole, Kent', *Ant.* xli (1905), 127–9. Contemporary documents are quoted at length.

[7] Winbolt, p. 20.

[8] See the bibliography, pp. 266f for a listing of articles. One of the fullest is T. Pape, 'Medieval (and later) Glassworkers in North Staffordshire', *Transactions of the North Staffordshire Field Club*, lxviii (1933–4), 74–171. Pape summarized information about sites in other counties.

[9] Winbolt, pp. 17–19. Thorpe, pp. 87–91, accepted the thesis with variation, as did other writers except Kenyon and Crossley, both of whom were familiar with the earlier typescript version of the present work (E. Godfrey, 'The Development of English Glassmaking, 1560–1640', Ph.D. thesis, Univ. of Chicago, 1957).

arrivals from the continent[1] and by younger sons from the established families still in the Weald. They moved about frequently, generally inter-married, though not to the exclusion of an occasional English alliance,[2] and sought to preserve their traditions and their clannish ways. From time to time a few rejoined the glassmaking colonies in the Weald.

Before 1590 most of the glassmakers who left the south settled in Staffordshire. About 1582 one of the earliest groups to leave settled in Bishop's Wood (between Eccleshall and Market Drayton) on land belong-ing to the Bishopric of Lichfield.[3] The then Bishop had been rector of Balcombe in Sussex until 1579,[4] and since he was no doubt familiar with the profitable arrangements which landlords could make with glassmakers in search of fuel, he may have enticed them to come. In any case he owned a share in the new glasshouse.[5] Nearness to the Staffordshire clay used in pot-making[6] (which helps explain the long tradition of glassmaking in the area) provided an additional inducement, and the industry stayed in Bishop's Wood until 1612. At least four furnaces were built, though probably not all of them operated simultaneously. Window-glass makers —the Henseys, Tysacks, and Titterys—arrived first in Eccleshall parish, then as they moved on they were replaced by the Bigos and du Houx, makers of vessel glass, who lived across the border at Cheswardine in Shropshire. As early as 1585 one of the Bishop's employees, Edward Hensey, who had come from the Weald, left Bishop's Wood to settle at Blithefield on the Bagot estates less than twenty miles away.[7] Since glass-making had been practised there earlier in the century, Richard Bagot, like the Bishop, was familiar with glassmaking and eager to profit from the sale of his wood. A month before (15 June 1585) he had already made an agreement with Ambrose Hensey[8] for the sale of supplies and the building of a new glasshouse and furnace.[9] Ambrose soon died[10] and there is no indication of how long Edward stayed at Blithefield, though he certainly had returned to Wisborough Green some time before 1602.[11] After an interval, however, glassmaking continued in Bagot's Park.

[1] Folger Shakespeare Library, Washington, Bagot MS. L. a. 445; PRO Star Chamber Proceedings, 8 Jac. 1, 179/7.
[2] H. S. Grazebrook, *Collections for a Geneaology of the Noble Families of Henzey, Tyttery and Tysack* (Stourbridge, J. T. Ford, 1877), *passim*; various parish registers.
[3] Pape, pp. 101–12.
[4] Horridge, p. 29. The Bishop was William Overton.
[5] Ibid., p. 27, Pflayer, the Bishop's steward, to Richard Bagot.
[6] See p. 88.   [7] Horridge, pp. 27–9.
[8] Horridge, p. 27. Agreement between Richard Bagot and Ambrose Hensey.
[9] There is no indication in any of the documents that glassmaking was then in progress by native Englishmen on the estates, or had been in recent years. See Chap. I, p. 10 and n. 6.
[10] Abbots Bromley P.R., 1586, quoted in Crossley, *Post-Med. Arch.*, p. 47.
[11] Edward Hensey 'of the parish of Greene, Co. Sussex, glassmaker' married Sara Thietry of Eccleshall in 1602; their son was born the following year in Wisborough Green. Eccleshall and Wisborough Green P.R.

Though Staffordshire and the Weald were the chief centres of glass-making in the early Elizabethan period, as they had been in the Middle Ages, there were certainly a number of furnaces elsewhere in the west and in the Midlands.[1] Altogether the growth in the industry was impressive, and by 1590 it was firmly established. Not much of the credit for the revival of glassmaking in England can be attributed to the economic policy of Elizabeth's Government, however, for little initiative was taken directly by Crown or Council, and the aliens who came were motivated less by offers of special privilege, which few received, than by the religious troubles and consequent disruption of markets on the continent. Yet neither can the policy of the Elizabethan Government be said to have been harmful, for the privileges granted in the two patents were not un-reasonable and both were granted to men who had the knowledge and persistence to carry through their plans in spite of considerable difficulties. Neither patent was abused in execution: Verzelini's aroused almost no opposition, and Carré's soon lapsed. Particularly important from the point of view of government policy was the refusal to reissue the window-glass patent on terms which would indeed have hampered the industry, for a prohibition of importation would have allowed the patentees to control the English market, keep the price high and force all new refugees either to cease operations or to pay high royalties for the privilege of making glass. Had this occurred, the rapid influx of new workmen and the expansion of production might not have taken place. At the end of the period, however, no official monopoly hindered the increase in numbers or the movements of the forest-glass men, though to prevent further fall in prices they still attempted to maintain their old monopoly of skill which kept the craft out of the hands of native Englishmen. Verzelini's crystal glass factory, still protected by his official monopoly, was even more firmly established. It seemed as though he could look forward to a peaceful retirement, leaving to his sons a prosperous business and to his sons-in-law the management of the estates which supplied the fuel. The jealousy of native Englishmen, however, and problems of fuel costs soon led to a new phase in the industry.

[1] For the number of furnaces in England in 1590, see p. 211.

III

PROJECTORS, LEGAL BATTLES, AND THE TRANSITION TO COAL

SINCE the English glass industry in 1590 was still divided into two distinct branches—the production of crystal and the production of window and green glass—it is necessary to treat them separately. Different problems presented themselves in the making of crystal, which was located in London, controlled by a single family and protected by a royal monopoly, and in the making of common glass, which was scattered, migratory, and open to any sort of competition. Problems of transportation, fuel costs, and prices all affected the forest-glass makers, but not the crystal-makers to any great degree. Troubles in that branch of the industry came largely from what might have seemed its chief source of strength— its legal status. Monopoly proved to be a not unmixed blessing, for what the Crown gave, the Crown could take away. Moreover the Law Courts and Parliament were beginning to question the right of the Crown to bestow monopoly privileges in industry, and from 1590 to 1615, when the theory of the patent law was developing, the crystal-makers were engaged in almost constant legal battles over a whole series of new patents. By 1614 both branches of the industry were united under the control of a single monopoly based on the change of coal as fuel, a turning-point of far-reaching importance. The battles for domination of the glass industry which preceded and accompanied the change to coal must be considered in some detail in order to understand the most neglected, but perhaps the most important period of this study.

I. WILLIAM ROBSON: ENGLISH ENTREPRENEUR IN CRYSTAL

Although an occasional Englishmen had been admitted to the craft, in the early 1590s aliens and their immediate descendants still controlled both branches of glassmaking. Their monopoly of skill and their successful resistance to the pressure put upon them to instruct native Englishmen might have resulted in their domination of the management of the industry for a much longer period, had it not been for the direct intervention of the Crown. The change in policy, however, resulted not so much from a prejudice on the part of the Crown or Council against foreigners, as it did from a gradual shift in their attitude towards the monopoly patents. It has been pointed out that early in the reign of Elizabeth the letters patent were granted usually from a sincere desire to stimulate the economic life of the nation by the introduction of new industries, whether imported from abroad or 'invented' at home. In theory, and sometimes in practice, the Crown took the initiative in inducing foreign workmen to come[1] and regarded itself as the sole arbiter of the new industry introduced under the protection of its letters patent. But with the multiplication of such patents, the initiative shifted from Crown to patentee, and, as 'projectors' increased in number and persistence, considerations of national good often gave way to those of private profit. The parsimonious Queen soon came to realize the advantage to her Exchequer of granting such privileges to favourites and courtiers in lieu of pensions or annuities. Industrial patents were granted to persons who could not claim to be the inventors or introducers of new industries.[2] Yet to the end of her reign Elizabeth refused to admit a change in the system, and, maintaining the old legal theory and ignoring the rumblings of discontent, she asserted her absolute right of jurisdiction in all cases of disputes arising out of these grants.

In view of the change of policy governing industrial monopolies, it is not surprising that English projectors—courtiers, not glassmakers—should have sought privileges in glassmaking to the detriment of the aliens. The first such attempt proved abortive. About 1590 two of Her Majesty's footmen sought letters patent for the sole making of 'urynalls, bottles, bowles, and cuppis to drink in' such as were not covered by the privileges already granted to 'one Jacob, a straunger'.[3] Such a grant would have invaded the only branch of the industry which indisputably had long been practised in England, and would have put out of business or forced into subjection all the makers of common glass in England. The financial gain of the projectors, that is 'their better maytenance in your Majesties service', was the only reason given for such an outrageous request. The project was turned down summarily, but another as little justified was soon granted.

The successful projector of a new glass patent, a man considerably more important than the footmen, was Sir Jerome Bowes, a soldier and courtier who had earned Elizabeth's admiration as her ambassador to Russia. He knew nothing of glassmaking and never showed the slightest inclination to learn, but his circumstances were such that he felt entitled to some sort of pension for his long service to the Crown.[4] Encouraged by the grants to such courtiers as Sir Walter Raleigh, Thomas Wilkes, and Richard Drake,[5] Bowes sought to control, not the scattered green-glass factories, but the centralized, lucrative crystal factory belonging to

---

[1] Hulme, *LQR*, xii. 151.   [2] Price, p. 8.
[3] Lansd. MS. 59, no. 77, petition of H. Miller and A. Scott.
[4] *DNB*, 'Sir Jerome Bowes'.   [5] Price, p. 17, n. 1.

the prosperous Mr. Jacob. That he was not the first importer or inventor of a new industry did not deter him, for other established industries such as vinegar and starch had already been turned over to courtiers.[1] Nor does the injury to be done to Verzelini and his sons seem to have concerned either Bowes or the Council.

The new glass patent, which was issued to Bowes on 1 February 1592,[2] was strictly speaking a reversion of Verzelini's patent and was to become effective when the latter expired in December 1595. In general the terms of the new grant paralleled those given to Verzelini, except that it was to run only for twelve years and required the payment of a fixed rent of one hundred marks[3] annually instead of the equivalent of customs duty. In addition, while importation of crystal drinking glasses was forbidden, a proviso stipulated that if Bowes failed to produce sufficient glasses for noblemen at reasonable rates, he must 'suffer the said Noblemen and others of Her Majesties Privy Councill to make provisions thereof only to their owne private use' from abroad.[4] Unlike earlier glass patents the preamble contained no justification for its issue except the long service of the patentee to the Queen, and indeed none is possible. The need for protection of the industry had largely passed, and from the point of view of economic policy it would have been far wiser to have allowed Verzelini's patent to expire. From the point of view of legality, however, the exercise of the royal prerogative in making such grants was not yet clearly limited either by statute or by common law. Eager to retain as wide prerogative powers as possible, Elizabeth maintained that the Crown held the right to regulate not only new industries but also the production of 'frivolous' and non-essential commodities. The point was made a decade later in the famous Case of Monopolies, *Darcy* v. *Allen* concerning a monopoly in playing-cards, when Sir Edward Coke upheld the Crown position by arguing that the regulation of 'vanities' such as playing-cards belonged to the prerogative rather than to the common law.[5] Coke lost the case after the death of the Queen, but his argument throws light on the implication in the patent that only noblemen and others of rank bought 'vanities' such as crystal glasses. The provision for private importation, apparently added at Cecil's suggestion,[6] indicates that the Council contemplated that Bowes, the soldier, might not be able to furnish the market as effectively as Verzelini, the glassmaker.

Certainly Bowes's initial difficulties justified their fears. Though in

---

[1] Price., pp. 9, 17. [2] Patent Rolls, 34 Eliz., pt. 15, mm. 62–4 (1 Feb. 1592).
[3] The mark was the equivalent of two-thirds of a pound.
[4] Patent Rolls, 34 Eliz., pt. 15, m. 62.
[5] Price, p. 23, quoting Sir Edward Coke, *Reports* (London, 1777), xl. 84f. Price discusses the case at length (pp. 23–4).
[6] Lansd MS. 67, no. 25. In a draft of the 'materiall poyntes' of the patent the provision for importation was added in Cecil's hand.

March 1596, soon after his grant became effective, he rented part of the former Blackfriars monastery[1] and possibly added a warehouse the following year,[2] it is doubtful if he was producing much if any glass, since it was later stated that he was 'much letted and hindered' by Verzelini's[3] sons, Francis and Jacob, who were managing the Crutched Friars furnace during their father's retirement. The details of this struggle are not clear, but it seems likely that the Verzelinis continued to make glass with their staff of trained Venetians and prevented Bowes from obtaining a new labour supply. In addition they seem to have resorted to a court battle on the legality of the Bowes patent. The Queen had opened the door for such action when, in response to considerable agitation against monopolies of all kinds in the Parliament of 1597, she had stated that although her right to grant patents of privilege was above question, they might all be 'examined to abide the trial and true touchstone of the law'.[4] Some sort of injunction seems to have been issued against Bowes as a result, for he was soon complaining that his 'license and authorities . . . was impugned by the Versalyns' and that he had 'tryed most of his friends for the freeinge of his Patent' to no effect.[5] In desperation he sought the help of two city men, William Turner and William Robson.

There is no reason to think that either Turner or Robson, both members of the Salters Company of London, had then had any experience in glassmaking or had any special access at Court. Both seem to have been ambitious and energetic entrepreneurs with some capital who were eager to profit from the management of monopolies. Turner made a verbal agreement with Bowes to free the patent of the encumbrance under which it stood and secure a new one prolonging the privilege after its expiration in 1607. With Robson he also agreed to take over entire management of the crystal monopoly as Bowes's assignee in return for an annual payment of £500.[6] The pair did indeed succeed in 'freeing' the patent and 'pacifying' the Verzelini brothers. In their own account, the only one extant on the affair, they are discreetly silent as to their methods, except to mention that it required 'exceedinge great costes, chardges, travell and expense'.[7] Whether or not bribery was used, sometime during 1598 Francis Verzelini was committed to prison, where he remained for ten years and was joined by his brother Jacob.[8] The charges are not clear, but violation of

[1] Folger, Loseley MS. 349/63. Sir George More owned the property.

[2] *Notes and Queries*, 1st ser. x, (1854) 348–9.

[3] Exch. K.R., Bills and Answers, E. 112/95/569, *Bowes* v. *Turner, Robson, and Lane.*

[4] Sir S. D'Ewes, *Journal of the . . . House of Commons* (London, 1693), p. 554.

[5] Exch. K.R., Bills and Answers, E. 112/95/569, *Bowes* v. *Turner, etc.* Answer of Turner, Robson, and Lane.

[6] Ibid.   [7] Ibid.

[8] Exch. K.R., Barons' Depositions, E. 133/155/81, *Att. Gen.* v. *Versalyne*, Hilary term, 1606. The case concerns concealed lands in Kent inherited from the estate of Jacob Verzelini the elder, but makes it clear that both sons were already in prison.

Bowes's patent was probably involved. Later the ruin of the unfortunate brothers was completed by a charge of owning 'concealed lands', which prevented them from selling timber from their estates to pay debts.[1] Meanwhile the Council was upholding the legality of the new patent by open warrants issued to assist Bowes and his assignees (Turner and Robson) in suppressing importation and the foundation of glasshouses. The warrants mark a new departure in policy, for though Verzelini had been able to complain to the Council of violations, he had no authority of himself or through his agents to enforce his privileges. Bowes's assignees needed the warrants, however, since they faced considerably more competition at home and from abroad than had Verzelini. In spite of the warrants some merchants were able to import Venetian wine glasses,[2] and at least one glass furnace in Gloucestershire which may have been attempting to produce crystal had to be suppressed by Robson's agents.[3]

With the warrants to protect them, and the Verzelinis safely out of the way, Robson and Turner set about to exploit the Bowes monopoly. The furnace was built at Blackfriars and production was soon under way. Most of Verzelini's former staff seem to have been employed, for Robson mentions 'dead wages' paid to the workmen while the glasshouse was being made ready.[4] Turner supplied most of the working capital, including the rent on the property, while Robson, who lived at Blackfriars, provided actual supervision and management. By 1601 business was flourishing: more space was needed for keeping accounts and for storage of the glass.[5] Bowes, who had no further responsibility for management, should presumably have been drawing 500 pounds per annum from Turner and Robson, from which he was obliged to pay the Crown rent. Apparently he was not being paid, for in September 1605 he was seriously in arrears to the Exchequer.[6] In order to collect from Turner he drew up a new written agreement which called for weekly rather than yearly payments, and one of his men forced Turner to sign it at sword point.[7] About this time (December 1605), however, Turner had become a subcontractor for the alum works in Yorkshire,[8] and thereafter, though he reserved for himself an annuity, he left entire management of the glass monopoly to William Robson.

[1] Exch. K.R., Barons' Depositions, E. 133/155/81; also ibid., Decrees and Orders, E. 124, no. 4, fol. 144v, *Att. Gen.* v. *Versalyne*, 12 Feb. 5 Jac. 1. Concealed lands meant those unlawfully alienated from the Crown. See Price, p. 167.

[2] Port Books, E. 190/11/1, London, aliens, 1599–1600.

[3] *A.P.C.* xxxix. 101–2. It has usually been assumed that this was the Woodchester glasshouse (Thorpe, p. 89 n. 4 and elsewhere), but there is no certain evidence. The Woodchester P.R. has no entries for French or Italian families, only one for an English glassmaker, 'William Mason of the glasshouse', in 1613.

[4] Exch. K.R., Bills and Answers, E. 122/95/569, *Bowes* v. *Turner, etc.*

[5] Folger, Loseley MS. 349/63. Two more rooms were rented at Blackfriars.

[6] S.P. 14/15, no. 53, L. Treas. Dorset to Salisbury.

[7] Exch. K.R., Bills and Answers, E. 122/95/569.   [8] Price, pp. 84–5.

In 1605 securing an extension of the grant was vital, for the original patent to Bowes had only two more years to run. If Robson's story may be believed, a new patent[1] extending the privileges for twenty-one years was actually secured (5 October 1606) more through his own efforts at Court than through any influence of Bowes. Of all the glass patents there is least justification for this one. If the real motive of the earlier grant of 1592 had been to transfer ownership of crystal-making to English hands, that had already been accomplished. Even the tenuous legal justification—that the regulation of frivolous enterprises belonged to the prerogative—had been recently undermined by the Queen's proclamation of 1601 which permitted all patents to be submitted to the test of the common law, and by the adverse decision in the Case of Monopolies, already referred to.[2] Bowes presumably still needed his pension, but he was in his upper sixties at the very least when his patent was regranted for twenty-one years.[3] Since Robson claimed to be instrumental in getting the new grant,[4] and stressed the great amount of money that it cost him, it is very likely that he paved the way by 'gifts' to the proper persons at Court. Moreover, in 1607, in recognition of Bowes's advancing years, Sir Percival Hart and Edward Forcett received a reversion of the monopoly[5] to become effective three years after the death of Bowes. The Bowes patent was set aside before the reversion could take effect, but since Hart was related to Bowes and was probably his heir,[6] one suspects that Robson, after making arrangements to lease its privileges, had as much to do with the issue of the reversion as with the patent of 1606.

With a legal monopoly in the crystal field thus ensured for many years, it would seem as though Robson, the chief lessee, had smooth sailing ahead. Actually his worst difficulties were just beginning. Between 1607 and 1611 in numerous and overlapping suits and counter-suits, as plaintiff in some and defendant in others, Robson was forced to defend his right of confiscation and the suppression of competition, the legality of the patent, and even his right to its privileges as Bowes's assignee. Trouble began in the spring of 1607 over commercial importation. Edward Fawkener, a merchant of London, on his own admission imported ten chests of drinking glasses, forty dozen trencher plates, the twenty 'double bottles', all in crystal, and worth roughly £240 wholesale.[7] Although Robson was

---

[1] Patent Rolls, 4 Jac. I, pt. 21, mm. 24–7 (5 Oct. 1606). [2] See p. 40.

[3] The article on Bowes in the *DNB* gives no date of birth, but states that he went to France with the expedition to avenge the fall of Calais in 1558.

[4] Exch. K.R., Bills and Answers, E. 122/95/569, *Bowes* v. *Turner, etc.*

[5] Patent Rolls, 5 Jac. I, pt. 24, m. 14 (8 Oct. 1607).

[6] When Hart was a minor and a ward of the Queen, Bowes secured custody of Hart's mother, who was *non compos mentis*, and inveigled her into making a will leaving Bowes a considerable legacy (S.P. 12/206, no. 62). For the relationship see *Notes and Queries*, 1st Ser., x, (1854), 348. Bowes had no direct heirs.

[7] Exch. K.R., Bills and Answers, E. 122/96/628, *Fawkener* v. *Robson, Robson and Beane*.

making large amounts of crystal drinking glasses,[1] his prices, inflated by the high rent to Bowes, were enough above Venetian crystal to tempt Fawkener to run the risk. But Robson's men were vigilant. Afraid to unload the glass from the ship, Fawkener persuaded Viscount Fenton, who as a nobleman was entitled to import for his own use, to secure a licence from the King for importation of the glass in his own name. Though Fenton was willing to oblige, by the time he had secured a signet bill from the King it was too late, for Robson's men had already seized the glass.[2] Under the penal terms of the patent, half of the value of all confiscated goods went to the King, and after some obscure negotiations Fawkener used Fenton's signet bill to 'compound for the King's half' for £40, which in effect was an admission that Robson was entitled to keep all the glass, as indeed he did. The confiscation had occurred in May 1607, but by the autumn Fawkener, smarting from his losses, had begun a suit in the Court of King's Bench[3] to recover the confiscated glass, and in addition to test the validity of the patent itself. The case was heard three times during Michaelmas term 1607 by the Lord Chief Justice, but was continued without a judgement until the Easter term following. In the meantime, the patent under which Robson had been operating was due to expire (15 December 1607), and therefore when the case was resumed he would be obliged to defend his rights under the extension of the monopoly which had been granted the year before. Bowes then saw his chance to get a higher share of the profits of the flourishing crystal trade. The new patent was still in his possession and he refused to turn it over to Robson for use in the Fawkener case, apparently hoping either to force Robson to sign a new agreement at a higher rent or to get rid of him and hire new management. Robson retaliated by stopping payment of the weekly rent due to Bowes on 15 December, the date when the old patent expired. Bowes then began a suit in February against Robson and the other assignees[4] in the Court of Exchequer, charging them with infringing his rights by producing glass contrary to the terms of the new patent of 1607, as though no agreement existed between them. The defendants, however, were in a strong position, for Turner produced the written indenture of 1605 giving them full authority to exercise all privileges of both the old and new patents, his subsidiary contract with Robson, and the acquittances proving that the weekly rent had been paid in full to Bowes until the previous December. The Court ruled[5] that although Robson had to

[1] Exch. K.R., Bills and Answers, E. 112/95/569, *Bowes* v. *Turner, etc.*

[2] Ibid., Bills and Answers, E. 112/96/628, *Fawkener* v. *Robson, etc.*; ibid., Barons' Despositions, E. 133/52/46.

[3] I have not found this suit, but details of it are related in the suit cited in the preceding note.

[4] Exch. K.R., Bills and Answers, E. 112/95/569, *Bowes* v. *Turner, Robson, and Lane.* This case reviews the relationship of Bowes and his assignees from the beginning.

[5] Ibid., Decrees and Orders, E. 124, vol. 5, fol. 176, *Bowes* v. *Turner, etc.*, interim decree, 12 Feb. 5 Jac. I. No final order could be found and this decree apparently stood.

deposit arrearage since December pending a final decision, he could continue making glass, and that Bowes was to hand over the new patent immediately so that Robson could prove his right to seize drinking glasses illegally imported.

Though he was now better prepared for his defence against Fawkener, Robson, knowing the fate of the playing-card monopoly at the hands of the common law, next sought to get the Fawkener suit transferred to a prerogative court. Therefore in the Easter term he himself began a suit in the Court of Exchequer for illegal importation, not against Fawkener but against a 'merchant unknown'. Simultaneously he secured an injunction from the Exchequer staying the suit already pending in King's Bench.[1] No direct records are available for the new suit, but on Fawkener's own testimony Robson won the case and the confiscation of Fawkener's glass was validated. In June 1608 the Privy Council issued new warrants to Robson assisting him in continuing confiscation at all ports.[2] Finally in 1610 Fawkener, still protesting that he should have been allowed to proceed at common law so that the validity of the patent itself could have been ruled upon, was ordered to sue 'by English Byll in the Exchequer Chamber' on the matter of validity. This last suit was clearly the most significant,[3] but unfortunately Robson's defence of the monopoly is missing, as is the final decree. Nevertheless it is clear that Robson again triumphed, for the Privy Council still considered Bowes's patent valid in 1613.[4]

While Robson was defending his rights against Fawkener, a new threat to his monopoly arose. Another glasshouse for crystal began production during 1608, operated by Edward Salter who had taken the precaution of securing a royal grant giving him exclusive right 'for making of all manner of drinking glasses, and other glasse and glasse workes not prohibited by former letters patent'.[5] At first glance this would seem to include all glass not covered by the Bowes patent, including window and green glass, but apparently this was not Salter's intent. Instead he aimed at the production of crystal fashioned into types of tableware which were not specifically mentioned in the Bowes patent. With five partners[6] he erected a new furnace at Winchester House in Southwark, brought in a new group of Muranese workmen, and began making cruets, trencher plates, salts, and stills in *cristallo*, and also crystal beakers and straight-sided

[1] Ibid., Bills and Answers. E 132/96/628, *Fawkener* v. *Robson*.
[2] *A.P.C.*, xxxii. 142, where in similar, later orders, warrants of June 1608 are cited as a precedent. The Privy Council records for 1601–13 are missing.
[3] The suit (E. 122/96/628) reviewed the entire case.
[4] *A.P.C.* xxxiii. 142, 497–8.
[5] Patent Rolls, 6 Jac. I, pt. 1, m. 9 (15 Feb. 1608).
[6] Peter Sentell, Thomas Sparkes, Peter Adby, Jesper Tyson, and Humphrey Westwood. Exch. K.R., Barons' Depositions, E. 13/25/21 *Bowes* v. *Salter*.

beer glasses.[1] It is possible that both Verzelini and Robson had made similar tableware,[2] but it is equally clear that neither of their grants had specifically covered anything but drinking glasses 'in the Venetian manner'. Robson, however, had successfully confiscated Fawkener's cargo of tableware and bottles as well as his wine glasses. Assuming therefore that all crystal was covered in his grant, he brought suit in the name of Bowes against Salter for infringing Bowes's patent.[3] The case turned upon two technical points: first, whether or not the metal in Salter's tableware was true *façon de Venise* and second, whether his styles were truly Venetian and therefore included in the privileges reserved for Bowes. Salter's own workmen testified that the metal was indeed as true a *cristallo* as could be produced in England, but that the straight-sided drinking glasses and beer glasses were not customarily produced in Murano, except when they were bespoken. Robson asserted in rebuttal that since they were occasionally made in Venice they were covered by the terms of the Bowes monopoly. Though the final decree is missing, it is likely that one was handed down during 1609, shortly after the testimony was taken.[4] It would seem that Salter won some sort of victory, for his patent was certainly not cancelled. But Robson was a man of resource, and there remained the alternative of buying out his competitor. Several years later Robson informed the Privy Council that he had leased Salter's privileges for a yearly rent of £166 13s. 4d.[5] Thereafter Salter made no more glass,[6] but there is no indication that Robson leased his furnace at Winchester House. It is possible that the decree, while not invalidating Salter's patent, did restrict his right to make cylindrical glasses and ale glasses in crystal, and that the trade in other tableware, though a profitable side-line at Blackfriars, was not large enough to sustain operations in a separate establishment.

In any case, by 1610 at the latest William Robson was in complete control of the English market in *cristallo*. Production and profits at the Blackfriars furnace must have increased, for Robson was prosperous enough to pay high rents to both Bowes and Salter regularly. Judging from a specimen which remains,[7] the quality of the glass made by his Italian workmen was evidently as good as Verzelini's; some Englishmen

---

[1] Exch. K.R., Barons' Depositions, E. 13/25/21, especially the deposition of Symon Favaro.

[2] See Thorpe, pp. 104, n. 1, and 132, n. 5 for possible examples.

[3] Exch. K.R., Barons' Depositions, E. 13/25/21, *Bowes* v. *Salter*.

[4] Ibid., Decrees and Orders, E. 124/7, fol. 158; E. 124/6, fol. 270. *Bowes* v. *Salter*. These are interim decrees.

[5] *A.P.C.* xxxiii. 162–3.

[6] *Commons Debates, 1621*, ed. W. Notestein, *et al.* (New Haven, Yale Univ. Press, 1935), iii. 257.

[7] See Plate III(b), the Barbara Potters glass inscribed with the date 1602 and displayed in the Victoria and Albert Museum. Earlier authorities often ascribe it to Verzelini or refer to it as English, 'of uncertain attribution'. See Thorpe, p. 105.

also were being trained.[1] Though wary of the common law he had successfully vindicated his rights before the equity side of the legal system,
and he received frequent help from the Privy Council. He is even said to
have harassed the green-glass makers with his open warrants,[2] and there
is no doubt that he was an aggressive, ruthless, blustering entrepreneur
who well deserved the name 'Roaring Robson' by which he was later
known.[3] Clearly it was Robson and not Bowes, the nominal holder of the
patent, who became the first English-born glass monopolist, and in 1612
he seemed to be in an even stronger position than had Verzelini in 1590.
In the last resort, however, his success depended upon the support of the
Crown, and when that was withdrawn to bolster the change-over to coal
as fuel, his domination of the crystal market collapsed.

II. THE FUEL PROBLEM

Since Nef proposed the theory of a critical wood shortage resulting in an
early English industrial revolution which was based on a change to the
use of coal as fuel,[4] there has been considerable interest in the true
extent of the shortage and its effect upon industrial growth in the early
Stuart period. Glassmaking was one of the industries which successfully
made the change in fuel, so serious consideration must be given to the
problem. During the reign of Elizabeth there were frequent contemporary
complaints of a shortage of wood, and figures on rising prices leave no
doubt but that there was some justification for growing concern,[5] but it
has since been shown that the shortages were not evenly distributed
throughout England and were more critical for certain kinds of wood than
for others.[6] For domestic uses small faggots and billets of wood gathered
on the wastes and commons or purchased in towns were used, but for
construction purposes, especially for ship-building,[7] only timber (very
large trees), preferably of oak would serve, and the expense of land-
carriage made a supply of timber near coastal towns essential for ship-
yards. Wood was also burned by a variety of industries, notably iron-
making, which consumed large amounts of charcoal.[8] Pollarding[9] was

[1] Notably John Worrall. See S.P. 14/124, no. 110.
[2] Exch. K.R., Barons' Depositions, E. 133/25/21, Bowes v. Salter.
[3] Clavell MS. B2/3, Baggeley to Clavell, 12 Apr. 1621.
[4] Nef, EcHR, pp. 3–24.
[5] See J. U. Nef, Rise of the British Coal Industry (London, Routledge, 1932), i, 158; J. E. T.
Rogers, A History of Agriculture and Prices in England, vol. iv (Oxford, Clarendon Press, 1882),
p. 388; S. T. Bindoff, Tudor England (Pelican, 1950), p. 11.
[6] G. Hammersley, 'The Crown Woods and their Exploitation in the Sixteenth and Seventeenth Centuries', Bulletin of the Institute of Historical Research, xxv (1972), 136–59.
[7] R. G. Albion, Forests and Sea-Power (Cambridge, Mass., Harvard Univ. Press, 1926),
pp. 7–11.
[8] T. S. Ashton, Iron and Steel in the Industrial Revolution (Manchester, Univ. of Manchester
Press, 1924), p. 9; notes kindly supplied by G. Hammersley.
[9] Pollarding means lopping off branches to produce a tall trunk with a bushy head.

sometimes practised, but it was more usual to cut over an entire woodland.

Before the alien glassmakers arrived, there was already concern for the
supply of timber for the navy, occasioned partly by the effect of the
enclosure movement and partly by the growth in iron-making.[1] As
early as the reign of Henry VIII Parliament had enacted a statute requiring
that at least twelve 'standills' or tall trees be left standing on each acre of
woodland cut over,[2] and in the first year of Elizabeth's reign another
statute forbade the cutting of timber more than one foot square at the
base for iron-making, within fourteen miles of the sea or any navigable
river, although the Weald was expressly exempt.[3] Much of the English
iron industry was concentrated in the Weald at the time, yet it is clear that
when the alien glassmakers arrived in the Weald during the 1560s and
1570s wood suitable for fuel, as opposed to timber, was still relatively
plentiful, especially the beech which they preferred.[4] They began to consume large quantities of fuel,[5] and although they claimed later in their own
defence that they used only the 'lop and top', unsuitable for anything but
fire-wood,[6] it is clear that often wood of any size was used, though if
large logs were cut, they had to be 'cleft small' before being fed into the
furnace openings. Eager for quick profits, many landlords began to denude
their properties to feed the new glass furnaces as well as the iron-mills
already present. Henry Percy, ninth Earl of Northumberland, for example,
has left a graphic account of how the 'axe was put to the trees' on his
estates at Petworth, where there was a glasshouse,[7] in order to pay his
personal debts occasioned by 'hawks, hounds, horses, dice, cards, apparel
and mistresses'.[8] Although he admitted later that the total destruction of
his woodlands came about because of his ignorance and the careless
husbandry of his stewards, nevertheless he was forced to write to his son
that 'the memory of good trees in rotten roots doth appear above ground
at this day; being forced now for the fuel relief of your house at Petworth
to sow acorns, whereas I might have had plenty if either they had had
care or I knowledge.' If the Earl was so bereft of fuel, it was not surprising
that the inhabitants of Petworth plotted against the 'Frenchmen' who
wasted the woods for fuel for their glass furnaces. Entrepreneurs who
leased estates showed the same lack of concern for conservation as the
Earl. The steward employed at Knole House, where there was also a
glasshouse, wrote to his master of the systematic denudation of the park at
Knole. 'Adams and George doe work at the Painted Gate', he wrote, 'and

[1] Ashton, pp. 4–10.

[2] G.B., Parliament, *Statutes of the Realm* (London, Eyre, 1811–28), iii. 977–80, 35 Henry VIII,
c. 17.

[3] Ibid., iv. 377, 1 Eliz., c. 15.   [4] See p. 161.

[5] See pp. 191–2.   [6] S.P. 14/162, no. 64, 1624.   [7] Kenyon, pp. 206–7.

[8] Henry Percy, *Advice to his Son, 1609*, ed. G. B. Harrison (London, Benn, 1930), pp. 81–2.

they do not sett up the cords halfe so fast as they are caryed away, therefore yf you will have the glassmen to contynew at worke you must either graunte that more cutters may be sett at worke or else suffer them to carry out of some other place in the parke, for all the clefte woods that were in Hookwood area are caryed to the glasshowse already.'[1] The steward did indeed 'view the trees' periodically, perhaps to comply with the statute regarding standills, but as the systematic felling continued day after day and month after month, the 'rotten roots' at Knole must soon have resembled those at Petworth, and it is understandable why the glasshouse at Knole operated for only about three years.

By the 1580s the increase in the number of both iron works and glasshouses in the south of England was causing concern not just about the destruction of timber suitable for the navy but about the supply of wood for fuel for all purposes. In 1581 Parliament enacted a statute forbidding the erection of new iron works or the cutting of any wood whatsoever for iron-making within twenty-two miles of the Thames, four miles of the downs of Sussex, or three of the coast.[2] A single exception was granted to an ironmaster whose 'woods have been preserved and coppysed for the use of his iron works', which seems to imply that the practice of re-afforestation was then not general. Four years later another statute forbade the erection of new iron mills in any part of the Weald unless the owner had enough wood on his own proper land to supply his fuel needs.[3] In this same Parliament there was for the first time an attempt to restrict the new glass industry. A Mr. Newkener, Member from Sussex, brought in a bill (8 December 1584) authorizing the suppression of all glasshouses operated by 'dyvers and sundry frenchmen and other straungers' or their children, and providing further that native Englishmen could not pursue the craft within thirty miles of London.[4] The 'preservacion of tymber and woodes spoyled by glasshouses' was given as sufficient justification, and, if passed, the bill would have driven most of the glassmakers from England. The bill was sent to committee, however, and in February Newkener reported that it had been amended on more lenient terms. The new bill allowed a foreigner to keep a glasshouse, provided that he employ and instruct one native Englishman for every two aliens and that no glasshouse be located within twenty-two miles of London, seven miles of Guildford, four of the coastal towns, or anywhere in the downs of Sussex.[5] The only exception was Verzelini's crystal factory, which was expressly exempt. In its revised form the bill received the assent of both Houses, but the Queen refused her signature.[6]

---

[1] Lennard, p. 127.   [2] *Statutes of the Realm*, iv. 667, 23 Eliz., c. 5.
[3] Ibid., iv. 726–7, 27 Eliz., c. 19.
[4] House of Lords Library, Victoria Tower, House of Lords MSS., 'An acte against the making of glasse by straungers . . . and for the preservation of tymber and woodes', 9 Dec. 1584.
[5] Ibid., draft of a bill with the same title, 16 Feb. 1585.   [6] HMC *Third Report*, p. 5.

That the bills against iron works and glasshouses were passed by a Parliament composed largely of landowners indicates genuine concern for the conservation of woods in the Weald. In addition, the bill against glassmakers demonstrates the extent to which aliens still controlled the craft and with rare exceptions, refused to train Englishmen. It was probably the requirement for making such training compulsory that kept the bill in its original form from becoming law, for if Cecil and the Council remembered the violence at Alfold, prompted by Becku's attempt to force English apprentices on the recalcitrant Bungars,[1] they may well have advised Elizabeth that enforcement of the bill was not practical. Furthermore, since the glassmakers were largely aliens, the Council could suppress any furnaces which caused a local outcry, as indeed they did while the bill against glasshouses was being debated.[2] There were far fewer glasshouses than iron works,[3] so the Council no doubt felt that such occasional action was sufficient to protect the fuel supply in critical areas.

Though the establishment of new glass furnaces was never restricted by law, the glassmakers themselves, whose numbers increased significantly during the 1580s, were nevertheless affected by shortages of fuel which they had helped create. There was still wood to be had, but there is every indication that the price was beginning to rise,[4] and what was even more ominous, the price of glass on the London market was falling rapidly.[5] Caught between rising costs and falling profits brought on chiefly by overproduction in one area, glassmakers faced three possible solutions to their predicament. They could move to more heavily wooded areas, provided that they could find sufficient markets or cheap transportation; they could remain in the Weald facing their economic difficulties as best they could; or they could find another fuel. Different groups tried each of these three solutions. Their efforts will be discussed in the following three sections.

III. THE DISPERSAL OF THE GLASSMAKERS

Late in the reign of Elizabeth cheap wood for fuel was still to be had in certain districts. Transportation of such fuel was prohibitively expensive, however, and since glass furnaces were easily and cheaply constructed, it was profitable to move as often as necessary. 'As the woods about here decay,' wrote a resident of Worcestershire in the 1590s, 'so the glasshouses remove and follow the woods with small charge.'[6] The reception accorded to the glassmakers varied, for though in Staffordshire, as we have seen, they found friendly landlords as well as plentiful woods in the 1580s, in

---

[1] See above p. 24.   [2] Luthery's glasshouse near Godalming, Surrey. See p. 33.
[3] For the number of glasshouses, about fifteen, see Chap. IX, p. 211; for iron works, see C. Wilson, *England's Apprenticeship, 1603–1763* (New York, St. Martin's Press, 1965), p. 86.
[4] See below, p. 191.   [5] See below, pp. 204–12.   [6] *VCH Worcester*, ii. 248–9.

other places 'the people rose in tumults and expelled the foreigners by force.'[1] Local shortages of fuel brought on by their furnaces might indeed be temporary, but the local inhabitants were seldom in a mood to be patient while the woods grew again. Moreover, the supply within easy carriage of the glasshouse might well be exhausted within a few years, and since transportation of wood for as little as three miles often doubled its price,[2] few glassmakers were willing to enter into contracts for fuel for more than three years duration, even when they were welcomed.[3] Migration became for most of them a way of life.

There were other considerations than the supply of wood, however, to be taken into account when choosing locations. Nearness to the Stourbridge clay was one—though clay was often transported for long distances[4]—and another was the availability of suitable sand; but neither of these was as important as favourable marketing conditions. In this respect the makers of drinking glasses and vessel glass had a decided advantage, for travelling chapmen often came to the furnace door for supplies, relieving them of marketing problems.[5] As a result they were free to spread over a wide area. (Numerous sites have been found from Herefordshire to the North Riding of Yorkshire,[6] dated mostly after 1590.) Few stayed long in one place, and a catalogue of locations or an attempt to trace the movements of particular individuals is hardly justified. Window-glass makers were more restricted in choosing their locations, for their product was not only expensive to transport but exceedingly breakable. Before the turn of the century, when the market for window glass in the Midlands was brisk, glaziers, like chapmen, often came to buy at the furnace door. Occasionally a glasshouse was set up for the customary three years on estates where extensive building was taking place. One notable example of this was the glasshouse on the Shrewsbury estates at the time when the Dowager Countess, better known as Bess of Hardwick, was building Hardwick Hall.[7] For many glassmakers, however, local markets could not absorb all of their output, and in order to transport the glass cheaply to other parts of England, they settled as near as possible to navigable rivers. A notable concentration of glasshouses developed in

[1] *VCH Warwick*, ii. 244.

[2] Hammersley, *Bull. Inst. Hist. Research*, p. 156.

[3] See especially Folger, Bagot MS. L. a. 445. The glassmakers signed a three-year contract and insisted upon paying for their furnace so that they could 'leave it when we goe'. See also Chap. VI, p. 143.

[4] See Chap. IV, p. 88.

[5] See p. 165.

[6] N. P. Bridgewater, 'Glasshouse Farm, St. Weonards', *Transactions of the Woolhope Naturalists' Field Club*, xxxvii (1963), 300–15; F. A. Aberg and D. W. Crossley, 'Sixteenth-Century Glass-Making in Yorkshire', *Post-Med. Arch.* vi (1972), 107–28. For other articles see the Bibliography.

[7] Longleat House, Marquess of Bath MS. 114A, vol. E, pp. 68–70; Chatsworth House, Hardwick MS. 10, fol. 25v.

Gloucestershire near the Severn. By 1590 a merchant of Bristol, where there were no known glasshouses until the mid-seventeenth century,[1] was exporting window glass to Bayonne in southern France.[2] After the turn of the century substantial shipments of window glass from Gloucester to Bristol by merchants from Shrewsbury and Birmingham[3] suggest that the glass had come down the Severn and its tributaries. Shipments were directed chiefly to other coastal towns in the west and almost none reached London until 1614.[4]

By the 1590s the dispersion of glassmaking throughout England and the concentration near rivers had again brought attention to the fuel shortage in areas outside the Weald. There were more bills in Parliament, repeating the pattern of the 1580s, but with even less success. A bill introduced in the Parliament of 1589–90 was even more drastic than Newkener's first bill of 1585. Its proponent, a man named George Longe who claimed to be the only true Englishman skilled in glassmaking, had conceived an ambitious scheme for monopolizing the industry by moving it to Ireland where wood was cheap. In 1589 he had already produced some glass there, but found he could not induce 'the glassmakers to remain and work in Ireland so longe as they had liberty here in England'.[5] As a result he sought to persuade Parliament to suppress all the glasshouses in England without exception in order to conserve fuel, and at the same time secure from the Queen a monopoly for making glass in Ireland intended to supply the English market. Though the shipwrights supported his bill and Longe claimed that 'the House well liked of it', it was not read and committed until towards the end of Parliament and then, according to him, 'the committyes chosen being such as sould woodes to the frenchemen for that purpose, kept the bill and neuer sate thereon, and so it rested undetermined.'[6] The bill was indeed referred to a committee composed among others of Sir William More, chairman, and Mr. George More.[7] Whether or not the Mores of Loseley sold wood to glassmakers,[8] they represented the view of the gentry who did. It is probable, however, that the monopoly aspects of the bill, to which Parliament was increasingly opposed, influenced the committee at least as much. In spite of a generous bribe offered to Cecil,[9] Longe's projected patent failed to get any more consideration than his bill, and his Irish project fell through. His experience demonstrated again the seemingly unbreakable monopoly of skill

[1] F. Buckley, 'Early Glasshouses in Bristol,' *JSGT* ix (1925), 36–60.
[2] Port Books, E. 190/1130/17, Bristol, exports, 1590.
[3] Ibid., E. 190/1146/12, Gloucester, coastal, 1612.
[4] Ibid., E. 190/1134/5, Bristol, coastal, 1613–14.
[5] Lansd. MS. 59, no. 75, Longe to Cecil.
[6] Ibid.   [7] D'Ewes, *Journal*, p. 475.
[8] The Loseley MSS. give no direct evidence, but there were glasshouses nearby.
[9] Lansd. MS. 59, no. 72, Longe to Cecil.

guarded by alien families, and the difficulty of making changes in the industry without their co-operation. A later English entrepreneur who tried to make glass in County Cork seems to have suffered a failure similar to Longe's;[1] and although in 1606 Sir Roger Aston received a monopoly patent for glassmaking in Ireland,[2] he made no attempt to exploit its privileges until the successful change to the use of coal as fuel had been made in England.

The fuel shortage in the 1590s was most noticeable near navigable rivers, and it had been brought about by the consumption of wood in iron and steel works as well as glasshouses. In the Parliament of 1593 a more reasonable bill than Longe's was introduced, which sought to prevent the erection of new iron, steel, or glass works within eight miles of a navigable river and also the cutting of wood of any size, not just timber, in these areas for use in the industries named.[3] The bill failed, however, through the influence of landlords who found wood a profitable crop. In at least some areas convenient for glassmaking wood for fuel was still to be had, though it is also true that where glassmaking had been carried on for any length of time, the price of wood went up rapidly. The rise in the selling price of the glass in the country, however, was not at all commensurate with the increased costs of production; in fact, largely because of the prevailing marketing conditions, it rose hardly at all.[4]

As a result of the squeeze between rising costs and stable prices, some of the glassmakers suffered economically. The clearest example of this comes from the glasshouse in Bagot's Park. Glassmaking was resumed therein about 1607 after an interval of at least ten years,[5] and the glassmakers paid substantially more for wood than had their predecessors in 1585.[6] They moved on after a short time, but were replaced by Jacob Hensey and his associates, who continued making window glass until 1615, paying Walter Bagot even higher prices for wood at the end of that time.[7] By 1615 Jacob was seriously in debt to Bagot for wood and also to a merchant of Leicester for other supplies. As a result he eagerly accepted an offer to work on a salary for Sir Robert Mansell,[8] who at that time had recently secured control of a new patent for the coal process in glassmaking. There is no evidence, however, that Hensey had made an

---

[1] M. S. D. Westropp, *Irish Glass* (London, Herbert Jenkins, 1921), pp. 23–4.

[2] Patent Rolls, 4 Jac. I, pt. 21, mm. 15–9, 28 Oct. 1606.

[3] HMC *Third Report*, pp. 88–9, House of Lords MSS.

[4] See pp. 202–3.

[5] Richard Bagot died in 1597. His son Walter wrote to Mansell in 1616 (Horridge, p. 32, Bagot to Mansell) that glassmaking on his land had been carried on continuously for only eight years previous to 1615, though it had been practised there earlier, in the lifetime of his father.

[6] Folger, Bagot MS. L. a. 445. See also pp. 191f.

[7] See p. 192.

[8] Mansell's career is dealt with in more detail in later chapters. For this incident see p. 84.

attempt to experiment with coal as fuel, and it seems likely that if he had exhausted his wood and supplies he would have made some small profit, though an amount greatly reduced from that of earlier glassmakers. As we will see later, he was not alone in his willingness to work for Mansell, so it seems likely that others were in much the same situation. Some glassmakers, however, who were working in more favourable locations seem to have been in better circumstances than Jacob Hensey. The few window-glass makers who fought Mansell's patent in 1621 were probably in this category. One came from Newent in Gloucestershire[1] and another had worked in both Lancashire and Cheshire.[2] Wood was probably still plentiful in these counties. It would seem that the rising cost of wood had had an effect on the glass industry in stimulating migrations and in reducing profits, but before 1612 it had not hampered production in the west and north to any great degree. The glassmakers in these areas, however, were not supplying the important London markets.

IV. ISAAC BUNGAR AND THE LONDON MARKET FOR WINDOW
       GLASS

It was in the Weald and along the south coast that the shortage of wood for fuel is said to have been most critical, yet many glassmakers chose to remain there and a few of those who left to work elsewhere eventually returned.[3] Even though their numbers were thinned by departures, representatives of all the original immigrant families stayed in Surrey and Sussex, where they constituted the largest single concentration of glassmakers in England. Among them were vessel-glass makers, mostly of Flemish descent, and second generation Normans and Lorrainers—the Bungars, Henseys, Titterys, and Tysacks—who continued to supply nearly all the window glass for the London market. The way in which they met the problem of fuel can best be understood by considering the career of one of their number.

Isaac Bungar, 'the truculent Bungar' who inherited the arrogance and the fiery disposition of his forebears, was the English-born son of Peter Bungar[4] whom Carré had brought from Normandy to Alfold. After Peter's death his widow with the help of Isaac and of Ferrand, who was probably a younger son, carried on the production of crown glass at a furnace near Wisborough Green. Their early lead in supplying the London

---

[1] Abraham Liscourt, who is discussed below, p. 62.
[2] Francis Bristow. See [E. Nicholas], *Proceedings and Debates of the House of Commons in 1620 and 1621* . . ., ed. T. Tyhwhitt (Oxford, 1766), ii. 71.
[3] Notably Edward Hensey. See Chap. II, p. 36.
[4] S.P. 14/162, no 231 A; statement of Isaac Bungar; Le Vaillant de la Fieffe, p. 14.; Guild-hall Library, London, Guildhall MS. 5758, no. 5. From these three sources it is easily deduced that Pierre de Bongar married Madelin de Cacqueray in Normandy and that Isaac was their son born in England.

market seems to have brought at least modest prosperity, but by the 1590s the price of window glass on the London market had fallen sharply, as indicated by a contract dated September 1596 between the Bungars and a London goldsmith named Lawrence who was acting as a wholesaler in glass. Lawrence contracted for the glass at the lowest price recorded for the entire period,[1] less than half that paid thirty years earlier,[2] and also stipulated that the Bungars should not sell any glass other than the 500 cases he had ordered until he had disposed of his stock. The implication of an over-supply in London and a voluntary limitation of shipments from Sussex in order to prevent a further fall in price is quite evident.

The lesson in economics which Bungar learned in his dealings with Lawrence was not lost upon him and soon he aspired to control the market himself. As one of the chief producers, bound by close ties of kinship and pride of craft with the Henzeys and other Wealden men, he could count on co-operation. Needing a London ally with established connections to help in the marketing, he enlisted the aid of a man named Lionel Bennett, a dealer in glass who was probably a member of the Glaziers Company by the early 1600s.[3] Bungar himself, while not relinquishing his factories, acted as a dealer as well, and by 1605 the pair had managed to get an effective corner on the market. Their helpless customers, the glaziers, have described so graphically the means whereby they maintained their control that their words deserve quotation:

First about the year 1605 beganne Bungar and Bennett the sole engrossings of all the glasse made in Sussex. . . . Through theire cunninge practizes and devices, wee weare constrained to pay them xxiis. vid. per case, which was of soe small a size that by proporcon of that glasse which wee now have from New Castle . . . was not worth above xviis. att most, and if at any tyme wee paid lesse, yt was when another man sett upp a ffurnace, And then they woulde advaunce theire size and fall theire price to the vallue of a noble in a case differnce, though yt weare by their owne protestacon to theire losse 200 £; of purpose to over-throwe the party, which in a short time they effected; By which theire policie they brought the market to theire owne desires, and so shrincke their size and raise their price as before they had done.[4]

Without benefit of letters patent or litigation Bungar and Bennett had secured a monopoly of the London window-glass market no less effective than Robson's legal monopoly in crystal.

There is other evidence that Bungar's control of the market was based

---

[1] Guildhall MS. 5758, no. 5.

[2] For a full discussion of prices see pp. 201–14.

[3] Guildhall MS. 5758, no. 9, Indenture dated 2 Dec. 1612. Bennett was then a member of the Court of Assistants and to have achieved that position he must have been a member of the company for some time. When Bungar himself became a member of the Glaziers is not clear, but it was certainly before 1624 (ibid., no. 13).

[4] S.P. 14/120, no. 89, Glaziers' Petition, 15 Apr. 1621.

on effective control of the production in the Weald. In 1611 would-be rivals in glassmaking complained that 'all the glasshouses are for the most parte ingrossed by such marchantes who use their glassmakers as servantes and instrumentes . . . for their own private gaine for the en-hauncinge of the prices of glasse and do often forbid the bringing of yt into the Cittie . . . untill such tyme as they fynde great scarctie.'[1] Without such control and without sufficient capital to undersell competition tem-porarily, Isaac and his associates could hardly have maintained their posi-tion for nearly ten years. He himself was the largest single producer since he owned at least two furnaces, perhaps more, and had a substantial interest in others.[2] Edward Hensey of North Chapel, Sussex, was the second largest,[3] but instead of competing, the two co-operated closely. By 1614 (probably by 1605 as the Glaziers said), all the other known masters of window-glass furnaces in the Weald, seven in number, were described as 'servants' of one or the other.[4] There is no certain evidence of the tactics used in acquiring domination of the Wealden glass industry, but apart from Bungar's aggressive nature, control of the fuel supply was an important factor.

The early prosperity of the Bungar family in the late 1570s, before the influx of large numbers of glassmakers, provided the capital. Isaac, as a native born Englishman, could hold land and he began leasing and buying woodlands, at first for use in his own furnace. Though the exact extent of his land is not known, in 1615 when the use of wood was forbidden he sold Lionel Bennett the manors of Sydney and Sedgehurst near Alfold for the large sum of £500 on which there were extensive woods and two glasshouses, neither of which Isaac himself worked.[5] He also owned land at Chiltington,[6] Sussex, and possibly elsewhere. Owning his own wood-lands meant that he could avoid local resentment and the threat of govern-ment suppression, for the statutes against iron-makers in the Weald[7] make it clear that persons who owned their own fuel supply were accorded special consideration. It also meant he could practise coppicing, pollard-ing, and reafforestation in order to avoid the increase in price which local shortages produced. As he was able to buy land on which other glass-

---

[1] Bodleian Library, Oxford University, North MS. a.2, fol. 145, Feb. 1610/11.

[2] *A.P.C.* xx. 290; Star Chamber Proc., 5 Jac. I, 179/7. See also the discussion of his con-tinued operations in 1616–17, pp. 85f.

[3] *A.P.C.* xxxiii. 658, 670.

[4] Ibid.; see also pp. 72f. below.

[5] PRO Records of the Chancery, Enrolments, Close Rolls, C. 54/2277, no. 17, indenture between Bungar and Bennett, June 1615. Bungar was then living at Billingshurst. One of the furnaces of Sydney Wood was undoubtedly worked by Vinion and Comely making vessel glass (see p. 94) and the other by Tobias Hensey of Alfold (*A.P.C.* xxxiii, 648), who had mar-ried Susan Bungar, apparently Isaac's niece rather than his daughter. *Cal. of Sussex Marriage Licenses*, ed. E. H. W. Dunkin, pt. iii. Suss. R.S. Publications, ix (1909), 43.

[6] Kenyon, p. 136, citing Bungar's will.

[7] See above, p. 49.

houses stood, he could supply the masters with fuel in return for a share of the glass and acquire the same sort of control that landowners and merchants in the Midlands exercised over the glasshouses they financed. But as his operations expanded he was forced to buy more and more woodlands, often in partnership with others,[1] a process too expensive to be pursued endlessly, for the glasshouses consumed wood faster than it could grow. It was sometimes necessary for both Bungar and the glass-makers he financed to buy wood, but in doing so there was the risk of local troubles. About 1607, for example, Albert Hensey who worked 'by procurement of Isaac Bungar' on a small parcel of land leased from a yeoman bought his wood locally, but claimed that within the first year two of his employees at the glasshouse were starved and beaten and all the wood seized by a band of local inhabitants.[2] Bungar even had difficulty in controlling the supply from his own woodlands, for one of the minor partners in his numerous purchases, who acted as agent, sold wood which Bungar had intended for his own glass furnaces to other industrialists, probably iron masters, at higher prices than those agreed upon for the glasshouses.[3] Thus it would appear that though Bungar sought an answer to the fuel problem in the ownership of woodlands, as time went on this proved to be less and less satisfactory.

The scarcity of window glass in London, which Bungar and Hensey contrived in order to hold up prices, was certainly related to the high price of fuel in the Weald. Bungar could have sold more glass at his usual price than he did, for the glaziers complained that frequently glass was so scarce in London that they were obliged to cast lots for the available supply and many could not obtain enough to make a living.[4] It seems clear that he was forced to curtail production to an amount which his own woods would support for the most part, supplemented by occasional small purchases. In view of this artificial scarcity, it is surprising that foreign window glass was not imported,[5] for there was no prohibition, or that more glass did not reach London from outlying areas.[6] Bungar's price must have been below that of imported glass and apparently the glaziers were unwilling or unable to pay more. As for the glass produced in the

[1] Chancery, C. 5/593/19, *Bungar* v. *Martin*, 18 Mar. 1619/20. The case reveals that Bungar and several partners, including Martin, bought woodlands worth £174 in 1612 and another tract worth £105 in 1614. Neither of these was the Sydney Wood property, and Bungar put up most of the capital.

[2] Star Chamber Proc., 5 Jac. I/179/7.

[3] Chancery, C. 5/593/19, *Bungar* v. *Martin*, 18 Mar. 1619/20 Bungar claimed that Martin had invested only £20 out of £279 in the woodlands, and had no right to determine the price or sale.

[4] S.P. 14/120, no. 89. Glaziers' Petition.

[5] See Table 4, p. 210.

[6] Although the coastal port books are sketchier than those for London, the only record found of shipments to London from the outports was of 100 cases in 1614. Port Books, E. 190/1134/5, Bristol, 1613–14.

west of England, transportation costs, including those of reshipment to London, and profits of middlemen no doubt made it more expensive than Bungar's, and he could always resort to temporary price-cutting in order to discourage its sale.

At a time when the scarcity of window glass in London was most acute, there was a daring attempt to supply the market from a new source. London merchants in the newly formed Virginia Company decided to establish a glasshouse in the struggling settlement at Jamestown, Virginia, which was barely a year old.[1] There was much to be said for the project, for wood for fuel and other supplies, were abundantly available at nominal cost, and transportation could be provided by ships returning from provisioning the colony. The chief problem was skilled labour; but warned by Longe's experience in Ireland, the merchants induced eight Poles and Germans, some of them skilled glassmakers,[2] to join the new group of settlers who arrived in 1608. Work was so soon under way that when Captain Newport returned to London, later the same year, he took with him samples from the new glasshouse for the inspection of the London merchants who were financing the project. Both window glass and vessel glass were made for a time,[3] but the 'starving winter' of 1609–10 brought an end to the venture. Had the colony been better managed and provisioned, the project might well have succeeded; but the fact that it was begun at all demonstrates the seriousness of the scarcity of glass in London, and the high price that window glass had reached as a result of the heavy cost of fuel.

Lest it might be thought that the deliberate and voluntary curtailment of production in the Weald might seem an unwarranted assumption, it would be well to point out that Scoville has shown that in the next century when wood became scarce and dear in France, glassmakers had to shorten their 'season' because of the fuel problem.[4] In 1746, for example, the Provençal producers, fearful lest the King might refuse to renew their charters because of the high cost of wood in Marseilles, offered to work only seven months a year, whereas previously they had worked ten and then nine months; while in Languedoc in 1725 the glassmakers promised to work only half the year for the same reason. Scoville concludes that except for the Lorraine furnaces and the dark-bottle furnaces then burning coal, the common-glass industry in France, which included the glasshouses

[1] The two best accounts of the Jamestown glasshouse are the article by C. E. Hatch, 'Glass-making in Virginia, 1607–25' (*William and Mary College Quarterly Magazine*, 2nd ser. xxi (1941), 119–38; 227–38, and the pamphlet by J. C. Harrington, *Glassmaking at Jamestown* (Richmond, Dietz Press, 1953).

[2] Harrington, pp. 6–8.

[3] Ibid., p. 30. It is frequently stated that beads for the Indian trade were made at Jamestown, but this was true only in regard to the second glasshouse there.

[4] Scoville, p. 20.

operated by Bungar's Norman relatives, suffered severe depression during the early eighteenth century, largely because of the fuel shortage.

The successful change to the use of coal as fuel was responsible for the relief of the similar state of affairs found at an earlier date in England. By 1610 the attempts to move the industry to Ireland or to America had failed. The 'Frenchmen' in the west and north led a precarious and migratory existence, while the London market was firmly under the control of Bungar's regime. But by 1612, possibly by 1611, the technical changes permitting the use of coal solved the fuel problem and placed the British glass industry far in advance of the French. Bungar's economic empire and that of Robson were alike threatened. But the 'truculent Bungar' was not prepared to give up the traditional ways of his noble forebears without a long and bitter battle.

V. THE INVENTION OF THE COAL PROCESS

The change from the use of wood as fuel to that of coal was a most significant occurrence in the English glass industry. The adoption of coal was not simply a matter of overcoming prejudice against a more obnoxious fuel: serious technical difficulties had barred the way. Although a discussion of the technical changes belong more properly to a later chapter,[1] it must be stated here that the solution of the technical problems was sufficiently complicated to demand a new invention, and that the crux of the invention consisted in changes in the glass furnace itself.

In spite of the difficulties, more than one glassmaker experimented with coal as fuel, but success was a different matter. Since it is natural for an inventor to protect himself by a patent, the question of the true inventor of the coal furnace for glassmaking is bound up with the issue of new letters patent. The first such patent, issued on 28 July 1610 to Sir William Slingsby and others,[2] reflects the fact that inventors were seeking to profit by using coal for all kinds of industrial purposes. The terms of the grant included exclusive right to 'erect ovens, furnaces, and engines for brewing, dyeing, baking brick, tile and pot-making, refining and melting glass, ordnance, bell-metal, latten, copper and other metals with sea-coal and pit coal' for twenty-one years. Slingsby, who had leased coal mines at Seaton Delaval, Northumberland, at about the same time (1610),[3] apparently thought that the same furnace could be used for either glassmaking or metallurgy, but he had not yet perfected one. The next year he admitted that 'our busynes hathe as yett butt slow progression'.[4]

The next patent, issued within a year[5] in spite of Slingsby's protests, turned out to be based on more definite accomplishments. It was not concerned with metallurgy but only with the making of glass with coal.

---

[1] See Chap. VI. [2] Patent Rolls, 8 Jac. I, pt. 12, m. 20. [3] Wilson, p. 82.
[4] S.P. 14/61, no. 113. [5] Patent Rolls, 9 Jac. I, pt. 29, m. 19 (25 Mar. 1611).

The patentees included not only, as usual, courtiers—Sir Edward Zouch and Bevis Thelwell—but also others familiar with the trade—Thomas Mefflyn, the King's Glazier, and Thomas Percival to whom the invention was attributed. The grant gave them the exclusive right to make glass with sea- or pit-coal for twenty-one years upon payment of a nominal rent of twenty pounds to the King and ten pounds to the Prince of Wales. The type of glass was not specifically stated, but it is clear from later debates in the Council[1] and also from notes drawn up before the granting of the patent[2] that window glass was all that was intended. There was nothing in the patent to hinder the wood-users from continuing with their old methods, or to restrict importation.

In view of the importance of this patent and of its successors granted for the coal process, it is worth noting the lengthy arguments for and against it as presented to the Council.[3] The petitioners outlined eight reasons in favour of their project. The first and most important concerned the preservation of the woods; it was followed by others relating to lowering the price, improving the glass, and providing more Englishmen with work. It was argued that the projectors would be reimbursed for the heavy expenditure incurred in perfecting their experiments, and, finally, 'other men encouraged to exercise theire wittes for new inventions by the benefit that cometh from this'. On the opposing side three objections were brought against the proposal: first, that former patentees would be injured; second, that 'gentlemen well wooded would be hindered in the sale of theire woodes'; and third, that many families of independent glass-makers would be ruined.

The first objection Zouch disposed of summarily by stating that Slingsby was the only patentee whom his patent could possibly injure, that his own invention consisted of a very different type of furnace from Slingsby's, and that if Slingsby could prove otherwise he would pay him whatever he asked.

The lengthy answer to the second objection indicated the extent to which the gentry and the great lords benefited from the sale of wood to glassmakers. Zouch attacked the objection from several angles. First of all, he said, the scarcity of wood was so great that Parliament in its wisdom had written 'many penall and stronge lawes' for its preservation. Furthermore, where wood was still plentiful there were already many iron forges and glasshouses 'which doe faster consume yt than it can growe', and these could continue to operate. Because of the competition, however, he conceded that 'some few gentleman might receive some small hurt.' His most interesting argument was expressed in the following terms:

---

[1] *A.P.C.* xxxiii, 192–3, dating from 1613–14.
[2] Bodleian Library, North MS. a.2, fol. 145.
[3] Ibid. The following discussion is all taken from this lengthy paper.

Besides our graunt (as we conceive) wil be rather beneficiall than hurtfull unto them [the wood-producing gentry] by restrayninge all others from making yt as we intend to doe, for the excessive price of woodes woulde in tyme make all glasse makers learne our invencon and use our fuell by reason that it is cheaper than the other, and so leave the use of wood in the making thereof altogether, but being prohibited by our graunt must keep on making it of wood as now they do.[1]

Zouch was obviously concerned lest the interest of landowners who had been selling wood to glassmakers would prevent the issue of his patent, and he was at pains to show that in fact his patent would protect their sales for a time, since he was asking not for a monopoly but simply for a patent in the modern sense—protection for his process, for a limited period, from use by others. He clearly expected to compete successfully with the wood-burners in the open market.

Zouch's answer to the third objection, that glassmaking families already established would be injured, shows the extent to which the descendants of the Huguenot glassmakers were still considered alien and undesirable. These men's feelings should not be considered unduly, Zouch said, for their forebears received a patent from Elizabeth which they forfeited by not keeping its terms in regard to payment of customs or instruction of Englishmen. Furthermore, the commonwealth would benefit by an increase in the number of glassmakers, who would force these men to increase the size of their window glass and to sell it more cheaply. While he did not mention Bungar by name, Zouch repeated the Glaziers' story that the market in window glass was controlled by a few men who deliberately created scarcities. If competition from his furnaces forced them out of business, Zouch said that he stood ready to hire them or their workmen. In any case he asserted that it would be better to have a few foreign families hurt than to deprive the commonwealth of a better and cheaper supply of glass. Zouch realized that he was threatening the domination of the London market by the Wealden glassmakers, and being familiar with Bungar's tactics, he had ample reason to desire royal protection.

Zouch presented his case to the Council[2] so well that there is little to add by way of commentary. If his assertion that one of his partners was the first inventor of the new coal process was true, then his patent was legal by modern standards and was certainly the most legitimate of all the glass patents granted. He claimed that Thomas Percival had already achieved success before the patent was applied for in 1611. If this is true, there is no doubt about priority, for others who claimed credit for the

---

[1] Ibid.
[2] The petition was referred first to the Lord Treasurer and the Lord Privy Seal, with instructions to discuss it with others of the Council. Lansd. MS. 266, fol. 110.

invention seem to have been experimenting with coal no earlier than 1612. No rival claims were publicly stated until the debates in the Parliament of 1621, when Mansell's glass patent of 1615, along with other monopolies, was under attack. At that time Isaac Bungar, who was fighting the patent by every means, made a claim to prior invention[1] which was clearly false. All his furnaces were in the Weald, and while there are indications at three sites there that some of his men experimented with coal,[2] there is no evidence that any of them achieved success. Furthermore Bungar purchased additional woodlands expressly for fuel for his furnaces, after coal was used successfully in London; and there is ample evidence in the Council records that he continued to burn wood until forced to abandon glassmaking in 1618.[3] The only other claims during the Parliamentary investigation were made by another glassmaker, Abraham Liscourt, representing the scattered glasshouses in the west. He asserted that Claude and Ambrose Hensey made glass with 'sea coal and pit coal' in Staffordshire and that he himself and Paul Tysack did the same.[4] His claim on behalf of the Henseys is clearly as false as Bungar's. The only known Ambrose Hensey, who was making glass on the Bagot estates in 1585 and died soon afterwards, certainly used wood,[5] as did Claude Hensey, who erected a new furnace on the same estates about 1607.[6] Walter Bagot, who supplied the fuel, later protested about his losses from wood which had been cut ready for use in the glasshouse when it was abandoned in 1615; he never mentioned any use of coal, even on an experimental basis.[7] As for Liscourt himself, it has usually been assumed from the fragmentary account of his testimony in the *Commons Debates* that he was an associate of Tysack on the Dudley estates.[8] This was not the case, for there is no record of him in the Stourbridge area. Instead in 1607 he was tenant-at-will for land and a glasshouse on the manor of Yartleton, near Newent, Gloucestershire, owned by Sir John Wintour, where he remained until at least 1617.[9] Wood was fairly plentiful there,[10] and though he may have experimented with coal, Mansell's counsel maintained that he used the

---

[1] *Commons Debates, 1621*, iii. 196.

[2] The sites were Sidney Wood at Alfold, Somesbury near Ewhurst, and Petworth Park. See Kenyon, pp. 202, 205, 207.

[3] For Bungar's purchases see above, p. 57; for the Council orders see below, pp. 73, 86–8.

[4] *Commons Debates, 1621*, iii. 195.

[5] Horridge, p. 27, quoting in full the agreement between Richard Bagot and Ambrose Hensey, 5 June 1585.

[6] Horridge, p. 32; Folger, Bagot MSS. L. a. 144, 445, 446.

[7] Ibid., nos. 144, 508, 147.

[8] *Commons Debates, 1621*, iii. 196. The notes say 'as did he and Paul Tissick for the Lord Dudley in Staffordshire'.

[9] Glos. R.O., D4 21/13, Rental of the Wintour estates, 1607; Newent P.R. (Bishops' transcripts), burial of the wife of Abraham Liscourt, 1617.

[10] See G. Hammersley, 'A History of the Iron Industry in the Forest of Dean Region, 1562–1660', unpublished Ph.D. thesis, Univ. of London 1972.

old style of furnace meant for wood and, like Bungar, had no success with coal.[1] Liscourt himself under cross-examination admitted that he 'gave over, being sent for by the patentees', this was probably in about 1618, when he seems to have moved to Newcastle-on-Tyne and Mansell's employ.[2] In any case he pressed his claims to priority no further.

There is more to be said for Paul Tysack.[3] Lord Dudley was present at the investigation of 1621 and asserted that Tysack made glass with coal on his estates 'two years before the patent'.[4] In addition a petition of Bungar and his friends who opposed Mansell's patent stated that a 'sisters sone of Isaack Bungard, glassmaker, betrayed by faire promises brought the art of makinge glass with Coale to the patentees, who were never the Inventors of the same'.[5] They were probably referring to Paul Tysack, for Isaac's sister Mary had married John Tysack of Ewhurst, Surrey, in 1585,[6] and Paul could have been their son. If so, he was trained in the Weald, and with his father may well have participated in experiments in burning coal there.[7] In the year 1612 Paul arrived in the parish of Kingswinford near Stourbridge and began making glass, presumably on the Dudley estates.[8] There is no firm evidence of his whereabouts before coming to Stourbridge. It has often been assumed that he was working in Bishop's Wood before moving to the Stourbridge area,[9] and indeed there was a family of Tysacks there as early as 1585,[10] but there were also other Tysacks working near North Chapel, Sussex.[11] Paul could not have invented the coal process in either location, however, since there is no evidence that coal was ever burned successfully in the Weald, or even tried on an experimental basis in Bishop's Wood. Mansell's counsel claimed that Tysack was a 'servant of the patentees' at the time of his success[12] and if he first used coal near Stourbridge, this was undoubtedly true, for his arrival there followed the issue of the first patent. Lord Dudley's vague claim to the contrary can hardly be relied upon, since neither he nor Tysack made any attempt to secure a patent for the coal process in glass-making, in spite of the fact that Dudley was instrumental in securing one

[1] Commons Debates, 1621, iii. 197, 255.
[2] All Saints, Newcastle P.R., 1 Jan. 1619/20, marriage of Ann Liskoe (Liscourt), probably Abraham's daughter.
[3] The spelling varies. 'Tissick' is also found, but Kingswinford P.R. spells the name 'Tysack'.
[4] Proc. and Debates, ii. 38–9; Commons Debates, 1621, v. 153.
[5] Harl. MS. 6806, fol. 234.
[6] Wisborough Green P.R.
[7] John Tysack lived first in Ewhurst, then in Kirdford. On glasshouse sites near both places coal cinders have been found near wood-burning furnaces which would not have proved workable with coal. See Kenyon, pp. 202, 207.
[8] Kingswinford P.R., Apr. 1612.
[9] Pape, p. 115; D. B. Guttery, From Broad Glass to Cut Crystal (London, Hill, 1956), p. 8.
[10] Eccleshall P.R., burial of Catherine Tysack, 26 Jan. 1584/5.
[11] A.P.C. xxxiii. 658.
[12] Commons Debates, 1621, iii. 255.

a few years later[1] on behalf of his natural son, Dud, who claimed to have invented a coal process for iron-smelting. Most notable is the fact that Paul Tysack himself, a man of substance, did not attend the Parliamentary investigation, or contradict Mansell's statement, or in any way make a claim for himself as the true inventor of the coal process. There seems to be no justification for awarding him that honour.

Another reference to an early use of coal does not make clear the ownership of the establishment involved. Simon Sturtevant's *Metallica* published in May 1612, says apropos of using coal in metallurgy that 'very lately, by a wind furnace, green glass for windows is made as well by pit coal at Winchester House in Southwark as is done in other places with much waste and consuming of . . . wood fuel.'[2] It will be remembered that a glass furnace at Winchester House had been erected by Salter for making crystal glass into salts, cruets, and the like; and that Robson, representing Bowes, had sued Salter in 1608. We also know that Salter stopped glassmaking in about 1609 and sold his patent rights to Robson. Buying the patent rights, however, would not necessarily imply leasing Salter's furnace. While it is theoretically possible that Robson was in command at Winchester House when coal was being used in 1612, it does not seem at all likely, for in his bitter fight with Zouch and Company during the year 1613 Robson never mentioned the use of coal, nor did Salter. No one, in fact, ever disputed the claims of Zouch and Percival to priority in the use of the coal process except Bungar and Liscourt.

By a process of elimination, then, we are led to assume that Zouch and his partners themselves leased the Winchester House factory from Salter after he sold his patent rights to Robson, and that this occurred long enough before 1612 for the necessary changes to have been perfected and noted by Sturtevant: most probably in 1609 or 1610.[3] Another reason for assuming that the Winchester House furnace was Zouch's is that if, on the contrary, it had belonged to a competitor who used coal so openly that it was known to Sturtevant, surely Zouch would have tried to prosecute on the basis of the 1611 patent, but no record of such prosecution can be found. By 1613 Zouch and Thelwell owned another coal factory for window glass at Lambeth, but since this is described as 'lately-erected' in that year,[4] they must have been operating earlier elsewhere. Much time has been devoted to this problem because of the imputation[5] that Zouch

---

[1] Dudley's patent was granted in 1621. Price, pp. 193–6.

[2] S. Sturtevant, *Metallica* (London, George Eld, 1612), partially reprinted in Price, pp. 176–192.

[3] Since the decree is missing, we do not know when the decision was handed down in the case of *Bowes* v. *Salter*, but 1609 is likely.

[4] Loseley House, Loseley MSS. vol. v, no. 182, 13 July 1613.

[5] Price, pp. 71–2, 80; L. Stone, *The Crisis of the Aristocracy, 1558–1641* (Oxford, Clarendon Press, 1965), p. 353.

and his partners were not first in the field. The best evidence, however, seems to indicate that they were successful at Winchester House early in 1612, possibly by 1611 as they claimed. There is no evidence that the men in Staffordshire were successful at such an early date—or, indeed, that they were successful at all before they had come to an arrangement with the patentees. In this connection it is particularly significant that there is no record of prosecutions under the patent until 1614, when the use of wood was forbidden.

Little is known about Thomas Percival, later known as 'Doctor Percival',[1] or his previous connection, if any, with glassmaking. The change which he made in the furnace at Winchester House shows that he was familiar with experiments using coal for other industrial purposes,[2] and his association with the King's Glazier, who knew of the scarcity and high price of window glass in London, may well have suggested concentration on glassmaking alone. He surely needed the help of trained glassmakers, and it is possible that he hired either Paul Tysack himself, or others of Isaac Bungar's numerous relatives. No French names are recorded in Southwark before 1615, however; and the known presence of one Italian and one English glassmaker[3] suggests that these men may have been employed to help with early experiments. In any case the initiative was English, as was the capital which financed the experiments. The fuel problem provided a motive for experimentation, for there was hope of large profits if it could be solved; but if Percival was indeed the true inventor of the process—and there seems to be no reason to deny this—it cannot be justly said that the established green-glass makers were forced by the fuel problem—however serious—to change to coal: it was a newcomer to the industry who was responsible for the change.

VI. THE TRIUMPH OF ZOUCH AND COMPANY

The successful use of coal threatened the livelihood of the wood-users, and they were not slow to perceive the danger. For nearly fifteen years after the granting of the patent of 1611 a battle for ascendancy was waged on many fronts, involving not only competition in the market but the varied uses of sabotage, litigation, orders in Privy Council, the prerogative, and agitation in Parliament. Of the two established leaders in the industry Bungar was to be the more persistent opponent of the coal patentees; but in the years before 1615, which concern us now, Robson was the more strenuous antagonist.

[1] A.P.C. xxxiii. 464.   [2] See p. 151, below.
[3] GLRO, P92/SAV/262, Token Book of the Liberty of the Clink, 1614. Vincent Serino, Robert Goddard, 'workman at the glasshouse', and John Leech, clerk, were all employed in 1614. Benjamin Hensey arrived in 1615 (ibid., P92/SAV/264). James Bristow was in Southwark also (St. Saviour P.R.); his trade is unknown, but Francis Bristow is known as a glassmaker by 1621. See below, p. 90.

Robson was in complete control of the crystal trade, and his rights under Bowes's patent were protected by being specifically exempt from the terms of Zouch's grant, but he had made no effort until 1611 to produce window glass. It speaks for Robson's alertness and the success of the early experiments with coal that he saw immediately possibilities for further profit for himself from the new situation. In the same month that Zouch received his first patent, March 1611, Robson bought for 100 marks per annum the dormant patent rights secured by Sir Roger Aston in 1606 for making green and window glass in Ireland, and he set about forming a company to exploit Aston's patent.[1] Always an opportunist, he was foresighted enough to see that while the use of coal fuel might break Bungar's domination of the London market and drive him out of business, the way would then be open for successful competition from Ireland, where wood was still sufficiently cheap. Nothing much happened during the early part of 1612, perhaps because Robson was waiting to judge the full effectiveness of Zouch's process, but in September he was roused to further action when Zouch began producing crystal as well as window glass.[2] During 1613 Robson was engaged in a two-pronged offensive designed to protect and enlarge his economic empire.

Before Robson could proceed with his plans, he found it necessary to arm himself with suitable weapons. The Privy Council obligingly provided him with a series of open warrants, dated from May to July 1613,[3] for the enforcement of his three patents (Bowes's, Salter's, and Aston's). These he could use to protect his rights in the making of crystal against the encroachments of Zouch, and also to clear the way in Ireland for a new enterprise. A letter from the Council to the Lord Deputy for Ireland called attention to the fact that the combined rights of Bowes[4] and Aston covered the entire field of glassmaking in Ireland, and that all furnaces not owned by the assignee of these patentees (namely Robson) should be promptly pulled down and importation to England of wares which had already been made forbidden. In the meantime Robson had formed a company to finance his venture, and in July he dispatched to Ireland[5] a relative, whom he had trained at the Blackfriars furnace, and other workmen. Window glass was soon being produced in considerable quantity, and in 1614 frequent consignments of 100 cases were shipped to

[1] Exch. K.R. Bills and Answers, E. 112/100/1122, *Holloway and Holloway* v. *Robson*. This case rehearses the history of Robson's Irish glasshouse.

[2] *A.P.C.* xxxiv. 196–7, 9 June 1615, Order in Council for damages to Bowes and Robson by Zouch.

[3] Ibid., xxxiii. 29–30, 61–2, 142.

[4] Bowes's patent for Venetian crystal covered Ireland as well as England. See Patent Rolls, 4 Jac. I, pt. 15, mm. 24–7 (5 Oct. 1606).

[5] Exch. K.R., Bills and Answers, E. 122/100/1122. *Holloway and Holloway* v. *Robson*. It is curious that all the details of this venture are noted except the exact location: 'Ireland' is all that is indicated.

London. The glasshouse continued to operate until 1618, and there is no record that Bungar attempted to drive this enterprise out of business by underselling, for he was threatened more seriously by Zouch, as Robson had no doubt foreseen.

While Robson was successful for a time in Ireland, in London he was waging what turned out to be a losing battle against Zouch. At first he seemed to have the advantage. When his open warrants failed to be effective against Zouch, he appealed directly to the Privy Council, on the grounds that Zouch's patent for the coal process was limited to the production of window glass.[1] The Council ordered Zouch and Thelwell to appear with their counsel and in the meantime to stop making drinking glasses in crystal. Zouch ignored the command and received a second to the same effect.[2] The case was then referred to a committee which included Sir Francis Bacon, then Attorney-General, and Henry Yelverton, Solicitor-General. Eventually Thelwell appeared before the full Council,[3] and both parties to the dispute gave testimony to the committee. Finally in October the Council issued an order[4] based on the committee's report, that Bowes's patent held by Robson should stand in law, that Zouch must stop making glasses either in the metal or the fashion prejudicial to Robson, but that the two parties should settle the dispute over Salter's rights (for crystal other than drinking glasses) by direct discussion without further troubling the Council, since the committee did not have time to investigate the technicalities.

It would seem as though Robson had won a substantial victory, but in fact the dispute was far from ended. Zouch and Thelwell gained a hearing from the King, who 'was pleased to take note of the controversy'.[5] He informed the Privy Council that in his opinion Zouch's patent benefited the kingdom more than the previous ones and he wished the matter to be reopened. Consequently the Council ordered that Sir Edward Coke (at that time Chief Justice of the Court of King's Bench) together with the King's learned counsel should call in the parties once more and certify their opinion of the case. At a Council meeting three days later Coke expressed the committee's opinion as strongly in favour of Zouch; this was largely because they were convinced that other glass works were 'injurious to the publique by the expending of wood'.[6] The question before the Council then became that of outright cancellation of the patents to Bowes and Salter, but the difficulty lay in the tenacity of William Robson and the strong support that he received from certain Lords of the Council. Zouch expedited matters somewhat by offering to

[1] *A.P.C.* xxxiii. 162–3, 29 July 1613.   [2] Ibid., p. 173, 6 Aug. 1613.
[3] Ibid., pp. 192–3, 31 Aug. 1613.   [4] Ibid., p. 250, 31 Oct. 1613.
[5] Ibid., p. 269, 14 Nov. 1613.
[6] S.P. 14/75, no. 9, Suffolk to Sir Thomas Lake, 17 Nov. 1613.

pay £1,000 a year to the previous patentees if their privileges were terminated.[1] The Earl of Suffolk writes that after the meeting Coke volunteered to handle the matter personally. He recounts it thus:

Sir Edward Coke . . . came and desired me to send his Majestie word, what his opinion was, for a fitting course, which is this; that seeinge they [Bowes and Robson] will not yeald to reasonable condicons that his Majestie will be pleased to send a Commandement for a new Pattent to be drawne, to Sir Edward Zouch and his Company, which my L. Coke will oversee, which being graunted by the King with assurance taken from them for performance of that thousand poundes a year to be paid to the King for the use of thother pattentees. . . . By this course my L. Chief Justice saith he will enforce them to yeald to that reasonable composicon which hath bene offered by setting this just patent affote which overthrowes thother that is so offensive to the common good of the Kingdom.[2]

Since we know that the King took Coke's advice, we may assume also that Coke actually supervised the drafting of a new patent to Zouch, and undertook to deal with Robson, whose prosecution of Zouch had backfired.

The new patent to Zouch, which was granted on 4 March 1614, contained provisions[3] strikingly different from those of the earlier one. The patentees remained the same (except that Robert Kellaway replaced Mefflyn, by then deceased); but the patent rights were extended to cover every conceivable type of glass. For this privilege the patentees were to pay the King £1,000 annually, and though the patent did not specify the use to which this was to be put, the Council understood that it was to be used in paying off the previous patentees. All other glass patents were revoked and their holders forbidden to make any further glass with wood. The makers of green and window glass were not specifically mentioned, but the implication was clear that they also were not to use wood. All importation of foreign glass was at the same time prohibited, and the retail glass-sellers were expressly enjoined not to enter into contracts with foreign workmen. The monopoly was to continue for twenty-one years. Thus for the first time a patent was granted which covered the entire field of glassmaking and, in addition, protected its holders from foreign competition.

The terms of this patent were virtually identical with those of a somewhat more strongly worded patent, granted the following year, which Sir Robert Mansell came to control. Since the policy embodied in the two patents is a controversial one, attacked alike by contemporaries and later

---

[1] S.P. 14/75, no. 9, Suffolk to Sir Thomas Lake, 17 Nov. 1613.
[2] Ibid. For the drastic change in Coke's attitude towards this patent, see below, pp. 113–14.
[3] Patent Rolls, 11 Jac. I, pt. 16, no. 4.

writers, the considerations behind the granting of the patent of 1614 merit attention. There seems to be no valid reason to doubt that conservation of the woodlands was the chief motive which prompted the King and his advisers, including Sir Edward Coke, to approve the patent. Whether or not the shortage of timber, and of the smaller wood used for fuel, was sufficiently acute to warrant such a complete monopoly is debatable; but clearly the King and the majority of his advisers were of that opinion. They were influenced by the fact that glassmaking, unlike iron-making, was still considered an unnecessary luxury. The King's proclamation of the following year forbidding the use of wood stated that 'it were the lesse evil to reduce the times unto the ancient manner of drinking in Stone, and of Lattice-windows, then to suffer the losse of such a treasure.'[1] The Court of James I was notoriously corrupt, but there is no evidence of any bribery in connection with this patent; and it is particularly notable that no such charges were made in the attack on the glass patent in the Parliament of 1621, although bribery was the chief charge in that Parliament against Francis Bacon, then Lord Chancellor, in connection with his judicial duties. Nor can Crown revenue have been a motive for granting the patent, for the high annual Crown rent was intended as compensation for the previous patentees, and was actually paid to them.

Once the benefit to the kingdom from the suppression of wood-burning glasshouses had been agreed upon, the only concern of the King and Council was to make certain that Zouch had achieved sufficient technical success. In July 1613, before the issuing of the patent, they sent Sir George More (who had long been familiar with the glass trade), Sir Edmund Boyer, and certain members of the Glaziers Company of London to view the works and inspect the glass. Their report indicated that they found the glass 'for the metal to be clear and good, but in some places uneven and full of spots, by reason of the negligence of the workmen'. Though this might seem to be faint praise, the glaziers went on to affirm that they had 'at sundry times bought glass as good and as cheap there as any other of the same size' and to express a strong opinion that the coal works should not be 'overthrown'. In addition they suggested that the unevenness, which resulted from poor workmanship in blowing, not from the founding process, was the result of sabotage by workmen who had been both threatened and bribed, probably by Isaac Bungar,[2] and that they had often bought glass of poor quality from wood-burning furnaces as well. The same or even greater success must have been achieved in the

[1] S.P. 14/187, no. 42, 23 May 1615; printed also in Hartshorne, p. 413.

[2] Loseley House, Loseley MSS., vol. v, no. 182, 13 July 1613. Price (pp. 71–2) quotes only the first part of this report, out of context, in an effort to prove that the coal process was not successful. In connection with the sabotage the report said 'Isaac Bungar is vehemently to be suspected'.

use of coal for the production of crystal, for if Zouch's men had not been making crystal good enough to provide real competition, Robson would hardly have carried his case to the Privy Council.

Thus the reasons for the grant of the monopoly seem to be established; but the question arises whether it would not have been wiser to have issued a new patent to Zouch which would cover all types of glass made by the coal process, but to have allowed other glassmakers to continue until competition in the market drove them out of business. There were several reasons why this was not done. In the first place Zouch claimed that he faced financial failure in spite of his technical success, chiefly because of his great investments and losses in perfecting the process,[1] but freedom from competition would enable him to recoup his losses and expand sufficiently to supply the kingdom. Secondly, the glaziers who accompanied Sir George More to the glasshouse had supported Zouch's contention that 'unlawful practices have been used to overthrow the work, against which it were good some speedy course were taken, that the same may better proceed'.[2] Finally, a new patent to Zouch covering crystal-making with coal would invalidate Bowes's patent and ruin Robson's trade, but if Zouch were to be obliged to pay them off, as agreed, he could hardly be expected to compete with wood-users while paying such high overheads.

In spite of such arguments, not all the great officers of state were convinced of the wisdom of the policy. Baron Ellesmere, the Lord Chancellor, delayed the patent at the Great Seal for over a month. 'I knowe his Majesties great care for preserving of the woodes,' he wrote to Lake, 'and thinke all the good meanes that can be devised in that behalf to bee too little. But upon hearing of this Bylle read . . . I doe fynde some partes of yt, as yt is contrived and penned, very considerable in my poor opinion.'[3] He asked 'a little staye in the case' in order to hear a resumé of the debates in the Privy Council, which his illness had forced him to miss, especially since he wished 'for his Majesties affayres in Parliament . . . a fare and quiett passage, and happy successe, and I am afrayd that some partes of his Booke might give more occasion of speeche and question, in this hopefull Parlement than is yet foreseen.'

In spite of his doubts Ellesmere put the seal to the patent on 4 March 1614,[4] but his fears for trouble in the 'hopefull Parlement' were soon justified. On 20 April a petition was exhibited in the House of Commons against the glass monopoly. In the debate that followed the monopoly

[1] The preamble to the patent cites such losses, along with the saving of wood, as the chief reason for granting it. The amount of capitalization and the extent of the losses is discussed in Chap. VII.

[2] Loseley House, Loseley MSS., vol. v, no 182.

[3] S.P. 14/76, Ellesmere to Lake, 23 Feb. 1614.

[4] Patent Rolls, 11 Jac. I, pt. 16, no. 4 (4 Mar. 1614).

was declared to be a dangerous precedent, for what applied to glass might soon be applied to iron and then to all other commodities. Nothing was said in defence, and the House ordered the patentees to produce the patent for consideration by a committee. On 4 May Sir Edwin Sandys reported for the committee; but the record of his statement is unclear, except for the fact that the committee had resolved that the cancellation of the patents previously granted to Bowes and Salter in crystal-making was a just measure.[1] In the debate that followed, this same view was expressed by several merchants, who argued that all patents for glass should be cancelled, since they could supply the country with cheaper glass from abroad. Little window glass had been imported in the preceding years when its importation was freely permitted,[2] so it is evident that they were speaking of the crystal trade from abroad, which had been cut off by the patents. Another speaker then denounced all monopolies, stating that patents should not be granted for new processes, but only for the invention of new things, a view never adopted by the common law.[3] Nevertheless the views of the merchants prevailed, the Zouch patent was denounced as a monopoly, and the patentees were again ordered to deliver it into the keeping of the House. Two days later Kellaway, protesting vigorously, was forced to surrender it.[4]

Whether or not the House of Commons thought that their action in taking custody of the patent amounted to formal cancellation, Zouch and his partners did not so interpret it, and they proceeded to enforce their rights. They had already protested to Bacon and Yelverton against Robson's importation of glass contrary to the terms of their patent.[5] The next step was to force him to cease production in England, which he refused to do. In order to placate Robson the Council appointed a committee[6] to apportion among the former patentees the £1,000 payable by Zouch. The committee reported in July that Bowes should have a pension of £600, Robson and Turner should divide £240 between them, and Salter should receive the balance of £160 per annum. A further order in December changed the allocation slightly. Bowes was to receive the same amount as before, Salter £150, Turner and his sister £150, and Robson a mere £100; the pensions were to be paid only during the lifetime of Bowes and for three years afterwards.[7]

Under this arrangement Bowes was better off than when the patent was in force, and had no reason for complaint. Salter and Turner had ceased to have an active interest in the business, although they had probably invested money on which they expected a return. They, too, seem to

---

[1] *J.H.C.* i. 469, 472.   [2] Port Books, E. 190/18/3.   [3] See Hulme, *LQR*, xii. 148.
[4] *J.H.C.* i. 475.   [5] *A.P.C.* xxxiii. 476–7.
[6] Ibid., pp. 497–8. The committee was composed of Lord Zouche, Lord Knollys, Lord Wotton, and the Chancellor of the Exchequer.
[7] Ibid., pp. 659–60, 11 Dec. 1614.

have been satisfied with the new arrangements. Robson alone was outraged. We do not know the exact amount of his profits from the business, but it must have greatly exceeded £100 per annum. Moreover, Bowes was already in his seventies, and the payments were to cease three years after his death.[1] Consequently, after the first announcement of the pensions in July Robson, in defiance of the Council, continued to make glass at Blackfriars.[2] Their Lordships committed him to the Marshalsea for contempt, but in September allowed him to leave long enough to consult with the Chief Justice, Coke, about the legality of the various patents.[3] Robson was soon back in prison;[4] indeed Coke's attitude might have been anticipated had Robson known the part played by the Justice in the grant of the new patent to Zouch. The Blackfriars glasshouse continued in operation during Robson's absence; but in October he reluctantly commanded that the fire should be extinguished, a few days before a Sheriff came with orders from the Council to put it out forcibly.[5] Then Robson was released[6] and troubled Zouch no more.

Having finally subdued his powerful London competitor, Zouch next turned his attention to the provincial makers of green and broad glass. On 18 November 1614, Paul Tysack received a summons from the Council for setting up furnaces in Staffordshire and Worcestershire in defiance of Zouch's patent.[7] One would very much like to know whether he was using coal successfully at this time. The summons made no mention of the fuel used, nor can this be inferred, for a like summons was soon served on the owners of furnaces known to have been wood-burning. No further order concerning Tysack appears in the Council register until 1621,[8] when he was Mansell's leasee, paying for the privilege of using the coal process.[9] It seems unlikely that he had discovered the entire coal process independently before 1614—though he may have been making experiments—for if so, he would have protested about his arrest more vigorously. It seems much more likely that, as a result of the summons, he became, as Mansell's counsel asserted, a 'servant of the patentees' in return for further instruction.[10]

Some of Tysack's Wealden relatives and friends (six Henseys and two Tysacks) were summoned next by the Council[11] for infringing Zouch's patent; they were all wood-users. Although not named in the warrant, Isaac Bungar turned up as one of their chief spokesmen. With Edward

---

[1] Bowes actually died in 1616 (*DNB*, 'Sir Jerome Bowes').
[2] *A.P.C.* xxxiii. 498, 11 July 1614.   [3] Ibid., pp. 545–6, 6 Sept. 1614.
[4] Ibid., pp. 574–5.   [5] Ibid.   [6] Ibid., p. 585.
[7] Ibid., pp. 634–5.   [8] *A.P.C.* xxxviii. 8.
[9] Ibid.; cf. Guttery, p. 8.
[10] Guttery (pp. 3–4) assumes, without citing sources, that Zouch licensed all the Tysacks and Henseys in 1613 or earlier. The Council register disproves this.
[11] *A.P.C.* xxxiii. 643, 30 Nov. 1614.

Hensey of North Chapel[1] he maintained that if the new patent to Zouch were to be strictly enforced, he and Hensey ought to be allowed to use up their materials, including wood already cut, before shutting down their furnaces, or else the new patentees should be forced to buy their supplies.[2] The Council chose the latter alternative, and agreed to secure 'certain gentlemen of quality' living nearby to estimate the value of the materials. As in nearly every dispute in the glass industry, Sir George More was named chairman.[3] Hensey and Bungar promised for their part that their workmen would accept employment with the patentees, who in turn agreed to pay reasonable wages. The patentees were not bound to buy the materials, however, unless the workmen behaved themselves and worked properly, since 'for divers causes they have reason to feare some indirect and underhand practices of the sayd Hensey and Bungard, thereby to seduce and corrupt those servants whome sometymes they imployed in their glassworkes'.[4] Such fears for the future were well justi-fied, for the matter was far from settled. Bungar was not so easily per-suaded to cease production or to abstain from sabotage, and nothing was accomplished under the agreement for several years.

The known opposition of Bungar and the Wealden men seems to have prompted further strengthening of the monopoly, for within two months of these men's indictment a new patent was issued to Zouch's company, expanded to include five new members of the company. One of the five, Sir Robert Mansell, came to control the enlarged company and his regime begins a new chapter in the history of the glass industry. Before he took over, however, the monopoly was already formed in all its essential characteristics, prosecution of the wood-users had begun, and the pen-sions of former patentees had been decided upon. All that was lacking was a stronger hand than Zouch's to steer the monopoly through the troubled waters that lay ahead.

Although former accounts of glassmaking have passed over the years covered in this chapter with the briefest of mention, surely it was one of the most crucial periods of the time studied in this book. The technical problems involved in the use of coal as fuel had been solved, even though much remained to be done before the change-over could be effected throughout the industry. The domination of the alien glassmakers had also been at least partially broken through the patent system, and management of the industry transferred to English hands; and although this resulted in undoubted injustice to men such as Verzelini's sons, the industry eventually profited from the elasticity of mind of men not bound by

[1] Two men named Edward Hensey were summoned; the other one from Wisborough Green was the same man who had worked at Bishop's Wood and Bagot's Park (see above, p. 36), and was probably in Bungar's employ in 1614.

[2] A.P.C. xxxiii. 668–9. The wood was the chief source of contention later.

[3] Ibid., p. 690.   [4] Ibid., pp. 668–9.

ancient traditions. Nevertheless in other ways the policy of issuing letters patent was harmful. Certainly the two patents to Bowes merit the term 'parasitic',[1] nor were any real contributions made to the legal theory of the patent law by Robson's lengthy law suits in defence of them. He discovered that the royal prerogative was a precarious foundation for an industry; while the opponents of the patent system learned that an attack in the courts of law was not sufficient, and that the prerogative must be limited by statute if similar patents were to be prevented in the future. Although Zouch's patent of 1611 was clearly as justifiable as any modern patent for a new process, the reluctance to abandon earlier, less sensible policies soon hampered its operation. The decision in the summer of 1613 to suppress the old patents and outlaw the use of wood not only created a true monopoly, but since the Council could not bring itself to do away with the Bowes patent without compensation, burdened the new coal-burning company with the payment of heavy pensions as the price of entrance into the crystal field. Such payments were at least part of the reason for the company's inability to drive the wood-users out of business through competition, and brought on drastic measures to suppress the wood-burners which prolonged the strife in the industry.

[1] Price said (p. 80) that every glass patent after 1582 was 'parasitic, being in no instance granted in reward of invention'. His remark has been frequently quoted.

IV

MANSELL'S ADMINISTRATION: THE TROUBLED YEARS 1615–1620

T HE third patent to Zouch's expanded company was issued on 19 January 1615. From that date until the attack on monopolies in the Parliament of 1621 the new company was principally engaged in trying to increase production from their coal furnaces sufficiently to supply the entire kingdom with all types of glass. In spite of their monopoly rights, the patentees faced a variety of problems. The company itself had to be reorganized on a sound financial basis; suitable locations chosen near coalfields for new furnaces; adequate management and labour secured; and solutions sought for some technical problems which were still imperfectly understood. The most troublesome problem, however, was the suppression of all competition from abroad and at home. Robson had already capitulated through pressure from the Council before the granting of the new patent in 1615, but Bungar's role as chief antagonist was just beginning and he was to find many allies. Finally, the patentees, whose privileges were based on the prerogative, faced the problem (brought home by Robson's career) that every investigation by the Council of their monopoly was not just a possible source of support, but a possible threat. The strong personality of Sir Robert Mansell provided leadership for the monopoly during its most difficult period; and since he continued to dominate glassmaking until 1642, it is of interest to see what manner of man it was who was able to hold the position of glass magnate for the better part of thirty years.

I. MANSELL AND COMPANY

Sir Robert Mansell has been described as a Welshman with the manners of an Admiral and the brains of a financier.[1] His career illustrates the methods adopted by younger sons of county families in seeking a fortune. Robert was the eighth son of Sir Edward Mansell of Margam in Glamorganshire.[2] Though the family was an ancient one that stood well in the

[1] Thorpe, p. 115.
[2] Harl. MS. 2218, fol. 65, genealogy of the Mansell family. There is some disagreement on the number of Sir Edward's children and on Robert's place in the family: for this and other biographical details see E. P. Statham, *History of the Family of Maunsell (Mansell, Mansel)* (London, privately printed, 1917–20), i, 249f.; *DNB*, 'Sir Robert Mansell'; G. T. Clark, *Some Account of Sir Robert Mansell, Kt.* (Dowlais, privately printed, 1883).

county, his best chances for advancement lay through Baron Howard of
Effingham, a distant relative on his mother's side,[1] who commanded naval
forces preparing to resist attack from Spain. At the age of fifteen young
Robert saw service under Lord Howard against the Spanish Armada, and
in the expedition against Cadiz he earned a knighthood. The next step was
to arrange an advantageous marriage. At some time before 1600 he married Elizabeth, daughter of the Lord Keeper, Sir Nicholas Bacon. She
was already a widow[2] and some years his senior. With her he took up
residence at Petney in Norfolk, where he cemented friendships with her
relatives, the Gawdys, and entered Parliament for King's Lynn in 1601.[3]
Though he served later for other constituencies, Sir Robert seems not to
have made much of a mark in Parliament; but his personal bravado[4] and
fiery temperament served him well in the Navy, and by 1603 he was Vice-
Admiral of the Narrow Seas. At sea his bold tactics won him praise, but
also exposed him to the risk of official censure when he came near to
stirring up further trouble with the Dutch.[5]

    In 1604, through the influence of Howard (at that time Earl of Notting-
ham and Lord High Admiral), Sir Robert secured the reversion of the
office of Treasurer of the Navy upon surrender of that office by Sir Fulke
Greville.[6] There is some disagreement as to his ability and integrity in
the execution of that office.[7] Perhaps the judgement expressed in the
Dictionary of National Biography is fairest: 'The administration of the Navy
was notoriously corrupt during the reign of James I, but there seems no
ground for charging Mansell while Treasurer with any gross dishonesty.
He made no large fortune in office.'[8] Moreover he sold the office of
Treasurer of the Navy in 1618 in order to devote his full time to the glass
business, at a time when the monopoly was far from producing a profit.
Certainly there were some irregularities in Mansell's administration; and
these, together with the rivalry of a faction opposing the domination of
the Howards, led to the appointment in 1613 of a commission to investi-

---

[1] His father was Chamberlain of Chester and Sheriff of Glamorgan; his mother was Lady
Jane Somerset, daughter of the Earl of Worcester. See Statham, ii. 339f. for further details.

[2] Accounts of Mansell's marriages are extremely confusing, but the identity of his first
wife is clearly established by her extant letters to Sir Bassingborne Gawdy, and to her brother,
Sir Nathaniel Bacon of Stiffkey. See BM Egerton MS. 2714, fols. 199, 200; ibid., Additional
MS. 41140, fol. 114.

[3] J. E. Neale, *The Elizabethan House of Commons* (New Haven, Yale Univ. Press, 1950),
pp. 57–60.

[4] Mansell fought a bloody duel with Sir John Haydon in 1600. See Neale, p. 57; S.P. 12/265,
no. 89.

[5] HMC, *Lord de l'Isle and Dudley MSS.*, iii. 93.

[6] *DNB*, 'Sir Robert Mansell'.

[7] Price, p. 75; M. Oppenheim, 'The Royal Navy under James I', *EHR* vii, pt. ii (1892),
471–96; Clark, p. 34; Statham, i. 85; Thorpe, p. 115.

[8] *DNB*, 'Sir Robert Mansell'. The possibilities for graft were great, since in 1604 alone at
least £10,000 passed through his hands for repair of the Navy. Harl. MS. 1645 (Mansell's
account book).

gate the administration of the Navy. Mansell, showing his customary rashness, opposed the appointment of the commission on constitutional grounds and soon found himself in gaol for attacking the prerogative[1]— though rumour had it that he was imprisoned for 'some irreverent speech used to the Lady Elizabeth'.[2] Eventually he was released after an apology, and the commission never issued a report.[3] In 1621 he again risked royal displeasure by engaging in a violent quarrel with the Duke of Buckingham, then Lord High Admiral and the King's favourite, in spite of the fact that his glass patent was in jeopardy of cancellation. Mansell had sold his office of Treasurer of the Navy,[4] but he had been given the title of Vice-Admiral of England, and when the quarrel occurred he had recently returned from command of an expedition against the pirates.[5] Though the cause of the quarrel has been lost, it probably concerned Mansell's command. Buckingham prevented him from receiving any further commissions for sea duty and Mansell retaliated with tart and uncomplimentary remarks about the Duke in the Parliament of 1624–5.[6]

In the meantime, following the death of his first wife Sir Robert had married again. In 1617 he was married to Elizabeth Roper, lady-in-waiting to the Queen.[7] The Queen herself gave the wedding banquet at Denmark House, and, it was rumoured, also gave the pair £10,000 as a wedding present.[8] Although this was obviously an advantageous marriage, Sir Robert seems to have been influenced largely by sentiment, since the lady was referred to as his 'old mistress' to whom he had long been attached.[9] The choice was a fortunate one, for she was well educated, resourceful, and thoroughly capable of administering her husband's business interests in his absence.

There is no indication of exactly how or when Mansell became interested in the production of glass. Even James I 'wondered [that] Robin Mansell being a seaman, whereby he had got so much honour, should fall from water to tamper with fire, which are two contrary elements'.[10] For a number of years before investing in the glass monopoly, however, he had been active in speculative companies, especially those engaged in overseas trade and colonization. He had 'adventured' in the East India Company,[11] and in 1612 he was an incorporator of the North-West

---

[1] A.P.C. xxxiii. 211, 217.   [2] HMC Marquess of Downshire MSS., iv. 133.
[3] Oppenheim, p. 479.   [4] DNB, 'Sir Robert Mansell'.
[5] See below, pp. 102, 117.
[6] D. H. Willson, Privy Councillors in the House of Commons, 1604–1629 (Minneapolis, Univ. of Minnesota Press, 1940), 184 and n. 37.
[7] Most biographical accounts say that his second wife was Anne Roper but an extant letter dated 1621 is signed 'Elizabeth Mansell' in her own hand. S.P. 14/124, no. 112. She was probably the daughter of Sir John Roper who purchased the Barony of Teynham in 1616.
[8] S.P. 14/89, nos. 33, 122.
[9] Ibid.   [10] J. Howell, Epistolae Ho-Elianae . . . (London, 1737), p.103.
[11] Cal. S.P. Col., vol. ii, East Indies, pp. 194, 240, 304, 334, 442.

Passage Company.[1] He seems to have been most interested of all in the Virginia Company; for in addition to investing money, he solicited other investors, and was a member of the council.[2] It was probably in meetings of the council of the Virginia Company that he first became interested in glassmaking, for the members surely discussed the scarcity of window glass in London and costs of production before authorizing the glassmaking venture that was made in the new settlement. When the glasshouse in Virginia failed, Mansell no doubt turned his attention to Zouch's experiments with the use of coal; and when the opportunity to become a member of the company controlling the coal process presented itself early in 1615, he was willing not only to invest, but almost from the first to undertake direction of the expanded company.

It is clear that the new patent granted to Zouch's company in 1615 was issued only so that the names of the five new patentees, including Mansell, might be included; for except for somewhat stronger wording to forbid importation and the use of wood as fuel, the terms of the new patent[3] were virtually identical with those of the Zouch patent of 1614—a complete monopoly in all types of glassmaking for twenty-one years. Apart from Mansell, the new patentees were Philip, Earl of Montgomery, and Sir Thomas Howard[4] (both well-connected courtiers, high in the favour of James I); Sir Thomas Tracy (a country squire from Gloucestershire[5]); and Thomas Hayes (a young merchant, son of a former Lord Mayor of London[6]). The five new members were already well acquainted. They had had numerous business dealings with each other previously in the East India Company and in the Virginia Company,[7] and they were clearly men willing to risk capital in highly speculative enterprises. From Zouch's point of view, their inclusion in the monopoly was desirable both for the additional capital which they could contribute and for their influence at Court, in the Privy Council, and in the City of London. Except for Mansell, however, they were all comparatively young[8] and uninterested in providing the remaining factor needed for success—vigorous management. That factor the energetic Sir Robert was more than willing to provide.

[1] Cal. S.P. Col., ii. 238–9. Later Mansell sat on the Council of the New England Company. C. M. Andrews, The Colonial Period of American History (New Haven, Yale Univ. Press, 1934–8), i. 356.

[2] Records of the Virginia Company, ed. S. M. Kingsbury (Washington, Govt. Printing Office, 1906–35), i. 595; iii. 29, 32, 40, 85, 329.

[3] Patent Rolls, 12 Jac. I, pt. 3, no. 9.

[4] There were several Thomas Howards, but this one is identified in a later patent as Viscount Andover (later Earl of Berkshire) who was second son of the Earl of Suffolk, Lord High Treasurer in 1615.

[5] Tracy was related to Montgomery by marriage. For the connection and other family details see A.P.C. xxxviii. 464, and DNB, 'Sir Horace Vere' and 'Richard Tracy'.

[6] Cal. S.P. Col., ii, 375.

[7] Ibid., pp. 194, 240, 304, 334, 335, 442; Records of the Virginia Company, iii. 32, 84, 85, 89.

[8] All seem to have been under 30. Mansell was 42.

Immediate financial problems faced the new patentees, for Zouch's old company was virtually bankrupt. The rent of £1,000 per annum owed to Bowes and his assignees according to the patent of 1614 was overdue, and Bowes was clamouring for the arrears.[1] The question of responsibility for payment was complicated, however, since Zouch claimed damages because of Robson's production of crystal for six months after the patent of 1614 forbidding it, while Robson claimed damages from Zouch for making crystal for eighteen months (September 1612 to March 1614) contrary to the terms of Bowes's patent. The Privy Council appointed a committee to arbitrate the claims, which reported in March, and again in June,[2] when a final order was given that Robson should pay about a third of the arrears and the new patentees should provide the remainder. Still no money was forthcoming from either party. Robson was soon imprisoned for contempt of the Council[3] and after about a month Mansell appeared before the Council to speak for the new patentees. He told the Council that he was prepared to pay Bowes immediately 'for himself and the others' but asked the assistance of the Council 'if the patentees should refuse to make an allowance thereof unto him on accompt'.[4] In the six months since he had joined the board of Zouch and Company, Mansell had assumed direction of the Company's financial affairs, but he was having difficulty in getting all the members of the board to agree to necessary expenditure.

Perhaps because of such difficulty in getting the full board to agree, Mansell bought out his eight partners at some time during the summer of 1615,[5] guaranteeing each of them an annuity of £200. At the same time he assumed all the debts of the Zouch company, which he seems to have paid eventually,[6] as well as other current obligations. At once he began to set the financial affairs of the company in order. By November he had paid the arrears to Bowes, and also the first half-year's rent under the new patent.[7] At Bowes's request he arranged to pay him directly in the future, instead of through the Exchequer. Thereafter little is heard of the other patentees in connection with the monopoly, with the exception of Bevis Thelwell, who was owner and manager of the Minories glasshouse in

[1] A.P.C. xxxiv, 15-6, 13 Jan. 1615; Chancery, C. 108/226/2.

[2] Ibid., 95-6, 196-7. The committee was composed of Sir George More, Sir Thomas Vavasor, and Sir William Waade.

[3] Ibid., p. 340.   [4] Ibid., pp. 250-1, July 1615.

[5] S.P. 14/104, no. 21, July 1618; Chancery, C. 108/226/1; Midd. MS. 5/165/131. Mansell's, petition of 1618 gives details of the agreement, discussed at length in Chap. VII, but no date, and it has previously been assumed that the agreement took place in that year. The petition in the Chancery Proceedings, however, indicates that the purchase took place during 13 James I, and the Middleton MS. places it before November 1615.

[6] Chancery, C. 108/226/1. In addition the Privy Council records refer to a debt owed by Zouch's company to a widow of Lambeth, for rental of property, which Mansell eventually paid. A.P.C. xxxiv. 155; xxxvii. 246.

[7] Ibid., xxxiv. 329, 18 Nov. 1615.

London several decades later.[1] It is probable that Thelwell had been the active manager under Zouch, and continued as overseer of one of the plants. Although Mansell was in complete control of the monopoly, the prospects of the company making a profit were still remote. At most the company owned only two furnaces, one at Winchester House and one at Lambeth. Apart from the heavy debt, Mansell was obliged to pay out a total of £2,800 annually. Of this sum, all the Crown rent and some of the annuities to the other patentees did not represent actual investment. Such high unproductive overheads put him at a disadvantage in trying to under-sell wood-burning competitors who were still operating in spite of the prohibition. Moreover it was necessary that new furnaces should begin operation immediately if the market was to be supplied; and to do this the co-operation, or at least the acquiescence of skilled workmen was essential. Mansell was totally without experience or established connections in a highly technical and secretive craft. It took a bold man indeed to assume entire responsibility in this situation.

II. THE LONDON FACTORIES FOR CRYSTAL GLASS

When Mansell took control of the glass monopoly, he was faced with far fewer problems in the making of crystal than in any other sector of the industry. As we have seen from Robson's strenuous opposition, the technical problems stemming from the use of coal in crystal-making had been successfully solved by 1612,[2] though probably very little crystal was made during the first few years. After the new furnace for window glass was built at Lambeth in 1613 more of the production at Winchester House could be devoted to crystal. Vincent Serino, a skilled Venetian, moved to the parish of St. Saviour's, Southwark, from the parish of St. Olave's across the river, and worked with a staff that seems to have been largely English.[3] After Mansell took control he introduced the making of plates for looking-glasses[4] at Winchester House. Nicholas Closson, a looking-glass maker of Amsterdam, appeared in the Liberty of the Clink in 1615, as did three window-glass makers from the Weald,[5] whose technique in blowing cylinders from forest-glass could be utilized in blowing plates from *cristallo*. Since Closson and a number of glassmakers (several with

---

[1] PRO Records of the Chancery, Decree Rolls 28/1212, no. 8, *Batson* v. *Lewin*.

[2] French glassmakers had much greater difficulty in making crystal with coal than in making other kinds of glass. See Scoville, pp. 43–4, and pp. 149–50 below, for the technical problems.

[3] Serino had lived in the parish of St. Olave's, Hart Street, since 1604, and he could have crossed the Thames to work at Winchester House much earlier than 1614. For the others see GLRO, p92/SAV/262, Token Book of the Liberty of the Clink, 1614.

[4] 'The True State of the Businesse of Glasse of all Kindes' (n.p., n.d.), anon. pamphlet, but clearly written by Mansell *c*. 1635. See below, p. 236.

[5] GLRO, P92/SAV/263; St. Saviour P.R. The glassmakers were Hector Cawkery, Benjamin Hensey, and John Bennett, probably the same John Bennett who was employed by Albert Hensey in 1607. See Star Chamber Proc., James I, 179/7.

English names) stayed in the parish of St. Saviour's until at least 1624,[1] it is likely that the making of crystal plates was carried on at Winchester House until that date, and possibly throughout the Mansell regime.[2] By 1617, however, Mansell had converted part of the extensive structure of Winchester House into store-rooms for window glass shipped from his outlying furnaces,[3] and he had built a new furnace for crystal drinking glasses in Broad Street[4] within the City. As manager for his new plant he hired William Robson, the most experienced Englishman in the production of crystal. Although Robson's own furnace at Blackfriars had been shut down, he now held no grudge against Mansell for supplanting him and instead became his strong supporter[5] and life-long employee. Italians were employed at Broad Street, probably many of them Robson's former employees.

Once the Broad Street factory was running smoothly, Mansell found that there was a greater need for Robson's initiative in managing the sale of window glass brought from Newcastle-upon-Tyne.[6] In about 1618 his place at Broad Street was taken by James Howell, a young Welshman who is better known for his literary career. Howell knew little of glass and found the work uncongenial. 'Had I still continued Steward of the Glasshouse at Broad Street,' he wrote, 'I should in a short time have melted away to nothing amongst those hot Venetians, finding myself too green for such a charge'.[7] Fortunately the hot Venetians were so highly skilled that they needed no direction—in fact they resented it. High wages (promptly paid), good materials, and freedom from interference were their chief demands[8]. When Howell became dissatisfied at Broad Street, Mansell sent him on an expedition to the continent to contract for supplies of the best materials for crystal glass, and to recruit more skilled workmen. In all respects the mission succeeded, and though Howell at his father's insistence soon left Mansell's employ,[9] the Broad Street works prospered.

Captain Francis Bacon, who had commanded Mansell's flag-ship when

[1] St. Saviour P.R.; *List of Foreign Protestants and Aliens, Resident in England, 1618–1688*, ed. W. D. Cooper Publications of the Camden Society, O.S. vol. lxxxii (1862), 97, 99. Closson kept four servants, all Englishmen, and the glassmakers were Richard Bailye, John Foster, and William Wellar.

[2] Mansell did not mention the Winchester House furnace after 1624, and it may have been closed down.

[3] S.P. 14/112, no. 67, Dines to the Privy Council, c. 1617–18. For a description of Winchester House and the wharf see Winchester, Dioc. R.O. MSS. 155/646/1–2, Survey of 1649.

[4] The furnace was probably in the property known as Austin Friars, Broad Street. See Powell, p. 29, who ascribed this location to Verzelini.

[5] S.P. 14/112, no. 66.

[6] Ibid., nos. 66, 67.

[7] Howell, p. 20.

[8] S.P. 14/112, no 28, statement of an Italian glass-blower.

[9] Howell, p. 103. Howell's father felt that the glass business was 'too brittle' for the building of a successful career. For the mission abroad, see Howell, pp. 60, 65.

Mansell was Vice-Admiral of the Narrow Seas and was no doubt a relative of his first wife's, took over the supervision of the Broad Street works.[1] He seems to have been a harder task-master than young Howell and to have understood the Venetians less well than the experienced Robson. Under his supervision and that of Lady Mansell, who came to take an active part in the management of the business, there were often labour troubles at Broad Street, and defections as the workmen broke their contracts and went elsewhere. It is clear from the testimony of some of the workmen, however, that whenever possible Mansell himself kept a firm hand on the management of the factory, and he was more successful in securing co-operation than his subordinates.[2]

The Broad Street furnace became a mainstay of the monopoly from a financial point of view, and Mansell maintained a residence nearby.[3] The styles of the drinking glasses he produced seem to have been limited, but the quality of the metal on the whole was good[4] though it varied with the quality of the materials used and the skill of the workmen employed at any one time. Drinking glasses of various kinds were the best-selling items, but other tableware in crystal was occasionally made, and in addition Mansell introduced a cheaper line of drinking glasses made from a native, instead of the imported, soda.[5] His greatest interest, however, lay in improving and expanding the production of crystal plates for mirrors and spectacles.[6] That his efforts were successful is attested by the Venetian Ambassador, who reported to the Doge in 1620 as follows:

Various subjects of your Serenity, some outlaws who have taken refuge in this kingdom, where many natives of Murano may now be met, work at making looking glasses or flint glass or teach how to make them. One of them, so I am informed has given instructions how to make curved flint glass, Murano fashion, another how to make it better, so that there are many English who work admirably, and the crystal attains a beauty not sensibly inferior, but of quite equal quality to that of Murano, which used once to have the pre-eminence and was the pride of all the world.[7]

In order to achieve such notable success Mansell had spent considerable sums on recruitment of Italian workmen and on bonuses given to them for training Englishmen.[8] As a result, more specialists in the finishing processes for looking-glasses came to settle in England from the Low

[1] Howell, p. 20.

[2] S.P. 14/112, no. 28.

[3] Straff. MS. 15/96, Mansell to Wentworth, dated from 'Marqueshowse Broad Street', 1635. Earlier letters are also dated from Broad Street.

[4] From fragments excavated in London it is difficult to differentiate between English and continental-made glass.

[5] See Chap. IX, p. 215.

[6] S.P. 14/162/231 B, Mansell's Statement, 1624; and 'The True State of the Businesse of Glasse'.

[7] *Cal. S.P. Ven.*, xvi. 212.   [8] S.P. 14/162/231 B.

Countries,[1] and spectacle-making began to flourish.[2] The making of crystal with coal fuel was well established, and though Mansell had introduced improvements, few basic changes had been made.

III. RELOCATING THE WINDOW-GLASS FURNACES

Early in 1615 the only furnace in the Zouch company's possession that was making window glass with coal was in Lambeth, and it operated at a loss.[3] More furnaces of this type needed to be put into production as soon as possible in order to supply the market, and costs had to be cut, especially the cost of fuel. While coal is usually assumed to be a cheaper fuel than wood, in fact it varied widely in price[4] according to the kind and grade of the coal and the distance it was transported from the pits, and it varied as well in its properties of burning. When the coal process was being developed in the years before 1615, only hard Scottish coal was burned in both of Zouch's furnaces in London, in spite of its high price, about 14s. a ton.[5] The price presented no problem in crystal-making, for the high value of the finished product had always permitted high fuel costs, even during the time when wood was burned. In window-glass making, however, it was not possible to use Scottish coal at the current London rate unless prices of the finished glass were raised considerably above that for glass coming from the wood-burning furnaces. The differential between reasonable fuel costs in the two branches of the industry had encouraged Zouch's early entrance into the crystal field, but he had continued to use Scottish coal in the window-glass furnace in spite of heavy losses, since it was then assumed that it was the only sort suitable for glassmaking. Five or six tons of coal were required to make a ton of window glass,[6] so it was clearly desirable that, if it was found that coal other than that from Scotland could be used in the industry, the furnaces should be moved to the coal-fields. When he took control of the monopoly Mansell realized this and determined to make immediate changes; he attempted to use other kinds of coal, but he was forced to resort to a process of trial and error over several frustrating years before success was finally achieved.

During the year 1615 he made three attempts to find a suitable location for the window-glass furnaces, two of the sites he tried being near the sea. The Lambeth works were shut down and the workmen were moved first to Kimmeridge in Dorset on the Isle of Purbeck.[7] There the landowner, Sir William Clavell, had been mining soft coal from shallow veins for the

---

[1] Returns of Aliens, pt. iii, pp. 140, 217; S.P. 16/521, no. 148.
[2] See below, p. 241.
[3] S.P. 14/162/231 B.
[4] See p. 194.
[5] S.P. 14/162/231 B; Nef, British Coal Industry, i. 118.
[6] See below, p. 194.
[7] S.P. 16/282, no. 99.

manufacture of alum,[1] and had built a 'huge peere of stone one hundred foote long' in Kimmeridge bay to provide shipping facilities.[2] After heavy losses Clavell had been forced to abandon the manufacture of alum[3] and he welcomed the glassmakers. They stayed only briefly, however, complaining that the coal, which contained a high sulphur content, was 'unusefull'.[4] Since vessel glass was made there successfully with the same coal within a few years, the chief problem was probably the objections of the glassmakers to the coal fumes, which according to a contemporary 'yeelded such an offensive savour that the people labouring about those fires were more like Furies than men'.[5] A Welshman naturally thought next of his native area and Mansell tried again at Milford Haven in Pembrokeshire, but there, he said, 'the Cole proved neither serviceable nor transportation of glass possible to be had'.[6] He was probably right. There was little shipping from Milford Haven at that time, and the hard anthracite coal, emitting little gas or smoke, did not burn with the long, hot flame necessary in a reverberatory furnace.[7] It is not known how long experimentation continued in Wales, but meanwhile the market in London was in such short supply that Mansell felt obliged to bring the workmen back to London for a time, even though the glass was again made at a loss.

About the same time that the Purbeck venture was begun Mansell also set up an experimental glasshouse near the Trent River, close to Nottingham, on the manor of Wollaton belonging to Sir Percival Willoughby. For it he recruited new workmen by instigating first the publication of a proclamation forbidding the use of wood in glassmaking, and then immediately the arrest of three prominent offenders.[8] One of the three, the Jacob Hensey who had become indebted while working on the Bagot estates, agreed to enter Mansell's employ at once and set off for Wollaton without even returning to Staffordshire to collect his tools and belongings.[9] Upon arrival he found that John Squire, a drinking-glass maker

---

[1] For Clavell's background and the alum venture see J. C. Mansel, *Kimmeridge and Smedmore* (Dorchester, Friary Press, n.d.) Mansel quotes from the Clavell MSS. still at Smedmore House, Kimmeridge.

[2] J. Coker, *Survey of Dorsetshire* (London, J. Wilcox, 1732), pp. 46–7. The survey was made n the reign of James I.

[3] Clavell MS. B1/1B. See also A. F. Upton, *Sir Arthur Ingram, c. 1565–1642* (Oxford, O.U.P., 1961), *passim*, and Price, pp. 82–101.

[4] S.P. 14/162, no. 231 B.

[5] Coker, p. 46.

[6] S.P. 14/162, no. 231 B.

[7] See Nef, *British Coal Industry*, i. 109–22, for a discussion of the qualities of this and other coal. See Chap. VI, for the furnaces and their requirements.

[8] *A.P.C.* xxxiv. 198, 15 June 1615. The three were Jacob Hensey of Blithefield, Staffs., Jacob Hensey of Winnansuch, Glos., and —— Sparkes of Wednesbury, Staffs.

[9] Folger, Bagot MS. L. a. 144, Bagot to Willoughby, 5 Aug. 1615; Horridge, p. 32, Bagot to Mansell, 1617.

who had worked in Bishop's Wood until 1612, had preceded him and was already supervising the construction of two new coal-burning furnaces, one for vessel and one for window glass.[1] It is possible that Squire had previously had some instruction from Zouch's men in London, for at Wollaton there were no technical problems with the furnace or with the coal. In fact, after work was well under way the men declared that 'they had never made glass so good'.[2] By December success seemed certain and Mansell signed a contract[3] with Willoughby for seven years, leasing the land and necessary buildings, and agreeing on the price of the coal to be supplied from Willoughby's coal-mines nearby.

Though glass was made in both furnaces until some time during 1617, Wollaton was not a satisfactory location, for financial rather than technical reasons. Mansell was chiefly concerned with supplying the London market, and as he himself said, 'coles and transportation arose to a greater charge than the business could beare'.[4] His agent's detailed cost accounting leaves no doubt as to the truth of this assertion.[5] The long journey down the Trent and the Ouse to Hull and thence by sea involved considerable cost and expensive delays, while the coal, though excellent for glassmaking purposes, was too expensive to make the usual selling price at the furnace door a profitable one. Willoughby himself could see this, and though Mansell's agent tried to persuade him to undertake financing the works,[6] paying Mansell a fee for the privilege, he wisely refused. Reluctantly, the works were closed down and the final and successful trial at Newcastle upon Tyne was determined upon.

During the time the Wollaton glass works were still operating, window glass was extremely scarce as a result of Mansell's vigorous suppression of the wood-burning glass furnaces by means of warrants sent out by the Privy Council.[7] Most of the glass for the London area had previously come from the Weald; and it will be remembered that the Council had ordered Bungar and Hensey to cease production in November 1614, with the understanding that they would be compensated for their wood and other materials.[8] They appear to have complied, but their workmen were still in the Weald, and the committee appointed by the Privy Council to

---

[1] Midd. MSS. 5/156/138 and 131, Squire to Willoughby, and the contract between Mansell and Willoughby.

[2] Ibid., 5/165/133, Fosbrooke to Willoughby, 1616.

[3] Ibid., 5/165/141, no. 1, contract 8 Dec. 1615. Many of the Midd. MSS. pertaining to the Wollaton glasshouse are summarized or transcribed in R. S. Smith, 'Glass-making at Wollaton in the Early Seventeenth Century', *Transactions of the Thoroton Society of Nottingham*, lxvi (1962), 24–32.

[4] S.P. 14/162, no. 231 B.

[5] Midd. MS. 5/165/139, no. 4. See Chap. VIII for an analysis of costs at this glasshouse.

[6] Ibid., 5/165/141, nos. 1, 2.

[7] A.P.C. xxxiv. 344, 371. The warrants called for the arrest of glassmakers in Worcestershire, Devon, Staffordshire, and North Wales.

[8] See Chap. III, pp. 72–3.

appraise the materials had never made a report. In order to satisfy the London glaziers while he 'settled' his furnaces, Mansell agreed in April 1616 that instead of receiving compensation the Wealden men might work out their wood and materials, for a term of sixty weeks at Bungar's furnaces, for thirty weeks at Hensey's.[1] With the glass supply for London assured, Mansell could again stop the financial drain from the unprofitable London glasshouse by closing it down.[2]

The patent of 1615 had prohibited importation of all kinds of glass, but at first Mansell paid little attention to enforcing this provision, since only small amounts of glass were being imported.[3] During the spring of 1616, however, he secured a royal proclamation calling attention to the prohibition of importation and strictly forbidding merchants to buy foreign glass.[4] In spite of this, during the summer of 1616 a merchant named Leeche imported a fairly large shipment of window glass from Ireland made in the furnace owned by the company formed by Mansell's own employee, William Robson.[5] Glass had been made in Ireland by Robson's firm since 1613, but its shipment to England had not caused Mansell any special concern during his first year as manager of the monopoly. In September 1616, however, he confiscated a shipment and Leeche sued in the Court of King's Bench to recover his glass.[6] Before a decision could be reached, Mansell countered with a suit in the Court of Exchequer,[7] and what began as a simple enforcement of his patent rights turned into the first test of the extent of his privileges. Leeche based the defence of his right to import Irish glass on the validity of Aston's patent (whose rights Robson had purchased), which he claimed included the right to sell in any of the King's dominions. Mansell, citing the prohibition of importation in his own patent, maintained that Aston's patent nowhere contained the right to import glass into England, and this was what the Court, too, decided.[8] The decision, concerned only with the importation of glass, contained nothing to hinder Robson from continuing to make glass in Ireland; but he was anxious not to antagonize his new master further, and he decided to abandon the enterprise—whose chances of success were, in any case, limited without the possibility of selling in London. He closed down the furnace, leaving his partners to

[1] *A.P.C.* xxxiv. 469–70.

[2] S.P. 14/120, no. 89, statement of the Glaziers Company, who claimed that Bungar persuaded Sir Robert to 'put out his fires' in London so that he could again control the market.

[3] See Table 4, p. 210.

[4] *A.P.C.* xxxiv. 472–3, 7 Apr. 1616.

[5] See Chap. III, p. 66.

[6] Exch. K.R., Bills and Answers, E. 112/99/1053, *Mansell and Dowle* v. *Leeche*, Leeche's answer to the Bill of Complaint.

[7] Ibid., Bill of Complaint.

[8] The decree is missing, but the case of *Holloway and Holloway* v. *Robson* (Exch. K.R., Bills and Answers, E. 122/100/1122) indicates that Mansell won the case.

sustain the losses.[1] It is clear that the Irish glass sold more cheaply in London than did Mansell's, so that Mansell profited most from the episode, both by cutting off potentially disastrous competition and by vindicating his extensive privileges in the courts.

For the time being the victory was a hollow one. Mansell's coal-burning furnaces were still producing little window glass. Bungar, who had been licensed to supply the London market, took advantage of his monopoly situation to raise the price and sell inferior and undersized glass. The Glaziers Company complained to the Privy Council in April 1617.[2] Bungar and Bennett, they said, though 'promisinge that they would furnish the market with store, . . . kept yt so bare and scant that whereas one man would have had tenne cases (to avoid a mutany) they weare faine to caste lottes for one case. . . . And notwithstanding that which they did bringe to the markett, much of yt was so ville and badd that yt was not fitt for any use, in respect that they cullt out the best and reserved great quantities thereof for the ende of theire termes permytted them to worke, of which they would not sell under xxvs. or xxvis. per case, as Bennett himself has affirmed.'[3] Mansell was forced to admit to the Council that he could do nothing to relieve the shortage, since his factories were still not 'settled', and the Council saw no alternative to giving Bungar an extension of time under close supervision. A new agreement sanctioned by the Council on 6 July 1617[4] permitted Bungar to work two furnaces until August 1617 and one furnace until April 1618. Sales were to be supervised by two members of the Glaziers Company, one appointed by Mansell and the other by Bungar, who were to check the price, the quality, and the fairness of the division of the glass amongst the glaziers.

Mansell could not hope to maintain his monopoly long by such expedients, and it was imperative to achieve success quickly. Though the date when he first determined to experiment at Newcastle and built his first furnace there is uncertain,[5] it was most probably during 1617 after the glaziers had complained to the Council. The advantages of Newcastle-upon-Tyne now seem obvious—coal at less than half the price of that at Wollaton,[6] and reliable water transportation at moderate rates in the colliers that sailed frequently. However the soft coal from Newcastle, much of which was sulphurous and full of saltpetre, was then thought to be entirely unsuitable for glass-making and it was, as he said, 'his last refuge, contrary to all mens opinions to make triall at Newcastle'.[7]

[1] Exch. K.R., Bills and Answers, E. 122/100/1122.
[2] A.P.C. xxxiv. 232–3, 23 Apr. 1617.
[3] S.P. 14/120, no. 89.   [4] A.P.C. xxxiv. 290–1, 6 July 1617.
[5] There is no certain evidence for the date, but late 1617, after the closing of the Wollaton works, seems most likely. The familiar names appear in the parish registers in 1619, but that is clearly too late. Nef claims (i. 180, n. 3) that glass was probably made at Newcastle in Elizabeth's reign, but I find no evidence even in his reference.
[6] See Chap. VIII, p. 194.   [7] S.P. 16/282, no. 99.

To his surprise the coal proved satisfactory, but during the first two years of operation there were other troubles, most of which he blamed on the 'truculent Bungar'. Procuring clay for the pots was a serious problem: for though the workmen at first imported Stourbridge clay, according to Mansell jealous glassmakers remaining in Staffordshire corrupted it so that it was useless, and he was forced to import from Rouen, and from Spawe in Germany.[1] Finally, after a long search, a suitable vein of clay was discovered in Northumberland. The workmen who were brought from the Weald and from Staffordshire were members of the families of French descent (the Henseys, Titterys, and Tysacks)[2] who were friends and relatives of Bungar. Some came willingly, but others soon defected or engaged in sabotage, such as deliberately breaking the pots. Mansell claimed that Bungar bribed the workmen '(being his nephews and neere kinsmen) to ruin the workes, showing them a bagge of money and promising them that they should never want whilst that lasted'.[3] There was probably some truth in the allegation, for Sir George More, who had investigated the industry for the Privy Council many times, later agreed that there were indeed illegal 'devises to spoile the glasse'.[4]

In the face of all difficulties Mansell persisted, and by April 1618 when the agreement with Bungar expired, the Newcastle furnaces were producing substantial amounts of glass for the London market. Sir Robert no longer felt any necessity for prolonging the licence and he insisted that all wood-burning furnaces be shut down. Nonetheless he sought to retain Bungar as he had retained Robson, and offered him £200 a year to manage one of his coal factories.[5] Bungar refused and according to Mansell told a gentlemen of his acquaintance that 'he had £1,000 left to counfound him and his patent'.[6] Since Bungar continued to make glass, Mansell prosecuted him in the Court of Exchequer,[7] and as a result the fires in Bungar's furnace were finally extinguished sometime during 1618. It soon became evident that his opposition to Mansell was greatly increased as a result of the suppression of his furnaces; although the Henseys with whom he had been associated seemingly co-operated with the monopolist.

The establishment of the Newcastle glasshouses did not end the complaints of the London glaziers or Sir Robert's troubles. Late in 1618 or early in 1619 members of the Glaziers Company again petitioned the

[1] S.P. 14/162, no. 231 B.
[2] All Saints P.R., and St. Nicholas P.R., Newcastle-upon-Tyne.
[3] S.P. 14/162, no. 231 B.
[4] *Commons Debates, 1621*, iii. 256.
[5] S.P. 14/216, no. 231 B.
[6] Ibid.
[7] I have found no record of the case, but many records have been lost. Mansell stated (S.P. 16/282, no. 99) that he did prosecute him successfully; and Bungar sold his extensive woods in about 1618 (Chancery, C. 5/593/19, *Bungar* v. *Martin*).

King,[1] complaining not of a scarcity of glass but of poor quality, high prices, and an 'artificial darth' due to unfair distribution. The blame was laid partly on Mansell, and partly on his agents or 'undertakers', Launce-lot Hobson and John Dines, who were selling the glass that came from Newcastle. Hobson and Dines were both glaziers themselves and accord-ing to the others they 'culled out for themselves and such as they ffavored' the best glass, leaving for the rest the 'refuse', which was foul, so brittle that it broke under their tools, and too small in size for the price charged. The glaziers added that they had heard that there was a new glass factory under way in Scotland, and they wished that the King might permit it to go forward in order that the kingdom might be better supplied.

Mansell answered the petition in great detail.[2] He admitted a temporary shortage of glass from Newcastle because of a visitation of the plague, which had taken twenty employees—masters and workmen. He had since replaced them, however, and had erected new works first at St. Catherine's, London, and then at Woolwich,[3] which operated at a loss, in order that when difficulties prevented shipments from Newcastle, the kingdom might be better supplied. The poor quality of the glass he blamed upon the difficulty of securing wood ashes and cullet. Wood ashes (one of the chief ingredients of window glass) his predecessors had secured as a by-product from their wood-burning furnaces; and knowing their value, they had kept the ashes in a pure state. But Mansell was forced to buy wood ashes, and in spite of paying more than he had formerly, he could not find a supply that was not corrupted with turf and peat. Cullet was also indispensable, but the glaziers refused to sell him their cuttings except at very exorbitant rates, and sometimes they would not sell them to him at all, preferring to export them to France. In an effort to improve the quality of the glass, Mansell claimed that he had been using zaffer, 'a thing not formerly used in this kingdom'.[4] As for the price, Mansell quoted figures to show that both coal and ashes cost him more than formerly, and yet he sold glass cheaper than had Bungar, who did not have to buy ashes at all. Finally, as to the charge of unfair distribution, he stated that 'the whole company [of glaziers] have been offered to make choice of any 3 or 4 men whom they might trust for the sole disposition thereof, which hitherto they have refused or neglected to doe.'[5]

---

[1] S.P. 14/113, no. 48, undated, 'The humble petition of a great number of London', signed by a majority of the Glaziers Company. The *Calendar* (*Cal. S.P.D.*, x, 134) dates this petition 1620, but that cannot be correct since the petition mentions Dines as Mansell's agent and he had been discharged before November 1619 (S.P. 14/112, nos. 66, 67; *A.P.C.* xxvii. 85, 156). A Council letter of December 1618 (*A.P.C.* xxvii. 329) mentions complaints of bad glass from Mansell's furnaces, and that seems the most likely date for this petition.

[2] S.P. 14/113, no. 49, 'The humble answere of Sir Robert Mansell'.

[3] Mansell implied that these furnaces operated successively, not simultaneously.

[4] For the use of zaffer (cobalt), see p. 160.

[5] S.P. 14/113, no. 49.

The glaziers found little to say in reply.[1] They would sell Mansell their cullet for 11s. per barrel, but 'under that price we sell for France'. Mansell could afford a rise in the cost in this and other materials, they insisted; and they said that they would be satisfied if he restored the price of glass to that which they had paid formerly. Their answer is torn at the bottom, leaving the last sentence to read 'that Hobson may . . .'. It probably read 'that Hobson may continue as undertaker but that Dines be replaced', for that is certainly what happened. Hobson remained as Mansell's agent until 1637,[2] but by 1620 Dines was no longer in Mansell's employ and had in fact become his bitter enemy.[3] Dines never explained the cause of the bad feeling between them, but since the glaziers called Dines 'an unnatural brother' during the time when he was Mansell's broker, it is likely that Mansell fired him to please the glaziers and that Dines retaliated by joining Bungar in implacable opposition to the monopoly. In addition to replacing Dines as undertaker, Mansell lowered the price to its previous level, as the glaziers requested.[4] No order in Council required this, but it was to Mansell's advantage to please his chief customers, lest their complaints should influence the Council to cancel his privileges. As for the quality of his glass, it is clear that there was a wide variation in different meltings; but it is equally clear that by 1619 Mansell was technically well-informed about the glassmaking process and energetic in his efforts at improvement. The Admiral had turned glassmaker in earnest.

The Newcastle works, owned outright by Mansell's company, were intended to supply the London market and some areas of the east coast. The rest of the country he intended to supply not through his own factories, but through a system of sub-leasing the privilege of working with coal to independent glassmakers. Of these Paul Tysack of Stourbridge was one of the most prominent, and possibly the first.[5] Another was Francis Bristow of Coventry.[6] The number and location of such licensed subsidiaries is difficult to determine, but there were certainly several, for Mansell said in 1624 that there were nine broad-glass furnaces in England.[7] Two other lessees whose names are known were John Moose, and Edward Percival,[8] no doubt a relative of Thomas Percival who was credited with the invention of the coal furnace. Opponents of the monopoly in the Parliament of 1621 said that these firms were not sufficient in number or properly located to serve the country markets satisfactorily, and also that

---

[1] S.P. 14/113, no. 50, 'Glaisyers exceptions to Sir Robert Mansell's allegations'.
[2] S.P. 16/378, no. 58.
[3] S.P. 14/112, no. 67, statement of John Dines.
[4] S.P. 14/162, no. 231 B; see also Chap. IX.
[5] See above, p. 72.
[6] *Commons Debates, 1621*, iii. 257.
[7] S.P. 14/162, no. 231 B.
[8] Moose and Percival had contracts with Mansell in 1621 (*A.P.C.* xxxviii. 8), as did others who were probably drinking-glass makers, but their locations are uncertain.

the price was higher than before the patent.[1] The justification for first charge is doubtful. There was considerable movement of glass on the Severn estuary,[2] and there was nothing to prevent additional glassmakers who were willing to use coal from becoming Mansell's lessees. Moreover, some wood-burners continued to make glass in remote parts of England in an effort to escape the Council warrants.[3] Admittedly there may well have been local shortages during the period when the furnaces were being relocated, and the price at the furnace door was probably higher.[4] On the whole, however, by 1620 Mansell had overcome the chief problems in resettling the window-glass industry.

IV. GREEN DRINKING GLASSES AND OTHER VESSEL GLASS

By 1615, and very probably throughout the reign of Elizabeth, the making of green drinking glasses and other vessels such as bottles, urinals, and vials was carried on in separate furnaces from those producing window glass.[5] The demand for such glass was substantial[6] and profits were at least as high and sometimes greater than for window glass.[7] It is remarkable, therefore, that Mansell expended so little of his capital and time in the production of vessel glass. The explanation would seem to be that though the London market was considerable, it was not yet controlled by an organized company[8] which could pressure the monopolist through appeals to the Privy Council. As we have seen, the Glaziers did pressure him for an adequate supply, and since he was forced to invest such large proportions of his relatively limited capital into abortive attempts to relocate the window-glass furnaces during the first troubled years, he had little money or energy left for the vessel-glass trade. With a few exceptions he resorted instead to the system of subleasing, which he also used as well for the scattered broad-glass furnaces in the west and the Midlands.

When he first assumed control of the company during the summer of 1615, Mansell intended to enter both branches of the trade equally, for he dispatched Squire, a green-glass maker, to Wollaton in July to work in a furnace which the company owned.[9] Though Squire stayed only a year before moving to a new location on his own as Mansell's lessee,[10] his place was taken by a glassmaker named Coxe who remained at Wollaton until the glasshouse was shut down in 1617.[11] There was then a proposal to erect a new green-glass furnace on the nearby manor of Awsworth

---

[1] See below, pp. 106–10.　　　[2] Port Books, E. 190/1134/9, Bristol, coastal trade, 1616–17.
[3] A.P.C. xxxviii. 8, 47, 324.　　　　　　　　　　　　　[4] For prices see Chap. IX.
[5] Midd. MSS. 5/165/131 and 140. Two furnaces, each for a single team, were built at Wollaton and the accounts kept separately. See below, pp. 194–8.
[6] See below, pp. 220–3.　　　[7] See below, p. 198.　　　[8] See below, p. 130.
[9] Midd. MSS. 5/165/138 and 140.　　　　　　　　　　[10] A.P.C. xxxviii. 8.
[11] Midd. MS. 5/165/133, Fosbrooke to Willoughby, 29 Nov. 1616.

belonging to Francis Willoughby,[1] but, if it ever materialized, it was a subsidiary enterprise operating on a lease. The records of Mansell's 'undertaker' (or agent) for the Wollaton glasshouse indicate that profits at the furnace door from green drinking glasses were slightly higher than those from window glass,[2] but Mansell's insistence upon shipment of the glass to London made the venture uneconomic. Had the glasses been sold locally to chapmen, it might have prospered, as the agent pointed out.

Within a year of the establishment of the Wollaton furnaces a scarcity of vessel glass developed in London. Shipments from the one furnace there could not supply the demand, and importation had been forbidden by the proclamation of 1615, except on licence from Mansell. In spite of the proclamation, several London merchants began importing substantial quantities of drinking glasses during the winter and spring of 1615–16. At Mansell's behest the Privy Council intervened in April 1616 to stop such illegal importation,[3] but Mansell was then obliged to make other provision to supply the shopkeepers. The cost and breakage involved in transporting the vessel glass from distant areas indicated the desirability of a local site, so a furnace was built at Ratcliffe and sub-let immediately to a group of four London merchants headed by Thomas Robinson,[4] all of whom owned shops which sold glassware.[5] Mansell charged them the high yearly rent of £300, in return for which he granted them a monopoly of the London market in drinking glasses with the express stipulation in their contract that no glass made in any other furnace owned or licensed by him could be brought into the London area and sold there. Several other lessees were licensed at about the same time, or somewhat earlier, but it is likely that their contracts restricted them to selling in their own area. Such a clause was certainly included in the proposal to build a green-glass furnace at Awsworth.[6] During 1615 vessel-glassmaking with coal was begun in Haughton Green, Denton, near Manchester.[7] Isaac De Houx

[1] Midd. MS. 5/165/137.
[2] Ibid., no. 140, Pauncefoote's accounts; analysed at length below, pp. 187–99.
[3] A.P.C. xxxiv. 472–3, 7 April 1616. The offenders were described as 'retailers of drinking and other glasses'.
[4] Exch. K.R., Barons' Depositions, E. 133/84/64, Mansell v. Clavell, depositions of Richard Robson and Thomas Robinson.
[5] Ibid., deposition of William Brierly of Gray's Inn. Apart from Robinson the partners were Thomas Harwood, John Kirby, and Thomas Phillips.
[6] Midd. MS. 5/165/137, agreement between Pauncefoote and Nicholson concerning the erecting of a glasshouse at Awsworth, 23 July 1617.
[7] It has sometimes been maintained that glassmaking began in Haughton Green in 1605. The only evidence is an entry in the P.R. of Hyde, Cheshire, near Haughton Green, of the burial on 31 July 1605 of an infant of 'one Dionise, a Glaseman'. At that time 'glassman' normally meant a chapman trading in glass. See p. 165, below. By itself, this entry is hardly conclusive. There are no other entries until January, 1615/16 when Isaac, the son of Robert Hartley, glassmaker, was baptized. Isaac de Houx's daughter was baptized 8 Sept. 1616, and he could well have arrived in the area the preceding year. I can discover no firm evidence that glass was made at Haughton Green, or elsewhere in the area, before 1615.

(De Hooe), the chief glassmaker there, was working on a leasing arrangement with Mansell in 1621,[1] and probably from the time of his arrival in Denton. Though the terms are not known, his sales also may have been restricted. Even if they were not, transportation problems were such that little of De Houx's glass could have reached London, so the merchants who operated the Ratcliffe furnace were assured control of the market in the city.

As Mansell continued to license vessel-glass makers, he was careful to protect the London market restricted for the Ratcliffe glasshouse by precise stipulations in their contracts. The one about whom most is known and who proved to be the most troublesome for him was Abraham Bigo, descendant of the Lorraine de Bigaults, who had worked for many years with John Squire in north Staffordshire.[2] Possibly he may have also worked with Squire at Wollaton, for in 1617 he was familiar with the coal process[3] and eager to go into business independently. He needed to find financial backing in a coal-bearing region, however. This he gained from Sir William Clavell, on whose estates at Kimmeridge in Purbeck Mansell's first attempt to move window-glass making to the coal-fields had been made. If Bigo had heard of the 'onusefullness' of the Purbeck coal or of its obnoxious odour from Mansell's men, this did not deter him, and Clavell was equally eager for profit from his otherwise almost unsaleable coal. First Bigo signed the necessary contract (17 November 1617) with Mansell.[4] By its terms Bigo received the right to make green drinking glasses in Purbeck for nine years at a yearly rent of £100, on the express condition that sale of the glass should be restricted to the counties of Dorset, Wiltshire, Hampshire, Devonshire, and Cornwall. He then went to Kimmeridge and for a time used the furnace that Mansell had built, until success in making glass with the Purbeck coal was assured. Then in February 1618 he and Clavell entered into partnership. They signed a formal contract, detailing the financial arrangements between them and the disposition of the glass. Although ostensibly they were equal partners and shared the responsibility for payment to Mansell, Clavell supplied most of the capital and was chiefly responsible for the sale of the drinking glasses. Bigo built a new and bigger furnace with the intention of employing a sizeable staff of glassmakers,[5] which he apparently was able to do, and for the first eighteen months of its existence Clavell and Bigo kept the agreement with Mansell and their glasshouse prospered to the satisfaction of all parties.

---

[1] *A.P.C.* xxxviii. 8. [2] Pape, pp. 101-2.

[3] Bigo had the technical knowledge to supervise the building of a new furnace at Kimmeridge.

[4] Clavell MS. B2/1, contract between Bigo and Clavell, 16 Feb. 1617/18, which mentions the date and terms of the Mansell-Bigo contract.

[5] The contract cited in the preceding note stipulates four pots in operation, whereas one was usual.

In order to protect the drinking-glass market for his lessees and to force additional glassmakers into similar contracts, Mansell, in the spring of 1618, turned his attention to suppressing all drinking-glass furnaces which still persisted in burning wood. The principal one was worked by Paul Vinion and Peter Comely at a site in Sydney Wood near Alfold, Surrey, on land belonging to Isaac Bungar.[1] In April 1618 Mansell complained to the Privy Council that Vinion and Comely were burning wood for glass-making. They were soon arrested and imprisoned,[2] but in May Sir Robert asked for their release on condition that they give bond not to repeat the offence.[3] If he wished to secure their services as employees or lessees, however, he was soon disappointed, for Vinion, like Bungar, was adamant in his opposition to Mansell. He began a series of petitions, the first of which[4] asked that he be permitted to work out his wood and materials, which he estimated would take fourteen months; he was willing to pay Mansell 20s. a week for the privilege. If he was not to be allowed to continue making glass, he asked for compensation for his wood. To both requests Mansell's answer was a firm 'no'.[5] Bungar had been licensed to continue burning wood, Mansell pointed out, only to relieve a temporary shortage of window glass, and he could hardly afford to compensate all the wood-burning glassmakers for fuel cut when their furnaces were suppressed. Similar pleas from Walter Bagot in Staffordshire had already been turned down.[6] Mansell did say, however, that he would be glad to hire Vinion at 40s. a week, the going rate for green-glass blowers.[7] Vinion refused the offer of employment unless he was first permitted to work out his wood.[8] Several years later he was still negotiating for the privilege of working, and was offering several alternative deals.[9] He would pay Mansell £60 for the privilege of being allowed to work for sixty weeks and to sell all the glass to Mansell or his agents; he would pay £100 and sell the glass himself; or he would try to negotiate directly with the 'shop-keepers of glasse' (the Ratcliffe firm) whom he understood held the exclusive privilege of making drinking glasses for the London market. Needless to say all these suggestions were refused, for Mansell would not countenance wood-burning furnaces or invasion of the London market contrary to his agreements.

[1] S.P. 14/105, no. 19, Petition of Paul Vinion and Peter Comely; GLRO DW/PA/7/11, fol. 403, will of Peter Levinion, brother of Paul Vinion. For Bungar's ownership of Sydney Wood, see p. 56, above. For the site and fragments of the drinking glasses, seen Kenyon, pp. 203–6 and Plates XIV, XVI.

[2] *A.P.C.* xxxvi. 115.   [3] S.P. 14/97, no. 54, 4 May 1618.

[4] S.P. 14/105, no. 16, 10 Jan. 1619.   [5] Ibid., no. 17.

[6] Folger, Bagot MS. L. a. 295, Brown to Bagot, 12 June 1617. Brown told Bagot that Mansell would not pay him for the wood.

[7] S.P. 14/105, no. 18, undated but probably 1619, although the *Calendar* gives the date as 1620 with a question mark.

[8] Ibid., no. 19.   [9] Ibid., no. 20, undated but apparently *c.* 1620 or 1621.

Vinion described himself in his petitions as a 'poor man', and since Bungar owned the land on which he was working, it is likely that though theoretically he was independent, in fact he was working on shares, as was customary[1] (receiving fuel from Bungar in return for a share of the glass made), and that Bungar had been selling his glass in London. Few other glassmakers put up such lengthy resistance after their first arrest, and few except Bungar and Vinion refused Mansell's offer of employment after their furnaces were suppressed. It is very probable, then, that Vinion's persistence in attempting to continue the use of wood as fuel was prompted and supported by Bungar. Certainly Vinion, even though he was unwilling to become a salaried employee, could have moved to a coal-producing region and become Mansell's lessee on terms similar to Bigo's, which required only slightly more rent than Vinion offered in order to continue burning wood. Later another Vinion, perhaps his son, came to terms with Mansell and became a bottle-maker.[2] In any case Paul Vinion eventually gave up in resisting the change in fuel.

V. COMPETITION FROM BUNGAR AND HIS ALLIES

Although by the spring of 1619 Mansell had, from his own point of view, accomplished much in establishing coal-burning glasshouses and in suppressing wood-burning ones, serious trouble still lay ahead. He continued to be in debt, and, in order to meet his high unproductive overhead,[3] his prices were high: an open invitation to illegal competition. His system of sub-leasing with variation in the rents and the marketing restrictions was bound to produce jealousy among his lessees. Bungar had become the arch-enemy of the monopoly, with every incentive to destroy it, for once his wood-burning furnaces were forcibly closed, he stood to lose the profits not only from manufacturing but also from his retail trade (both in window and vessel glass) from the Wealden furnaces. In order to break the monopoly he sought allies among those already hostile to Mansell, especially Dines, or those who might profit by defying him, such as Sir William Clavell. Together these men were the instigators of three separate disputes concerning the sale of glass in London which were laid before the Privy Council during 1619. The Council found itself embroiled in a lengthy controversy which resulted in a second royal proclamation concerning the glass monopoly which embodied a somewhat different policy.

The first dispute concerned Mansell's right to enforce his restriction of the sale of green drinking glasses in London to the four merchants headed by Thomas Robinson. It would seem that their furnace had never produced enough glass to meet the London demand and they had tolerated the sale of drinking glasses made by Vinion and Comely without

---

[1] See Chap. VII for an analysis of usual working contracts.
[2] See below, p. 228.   [3] See below, pp. 170f.

protest. When Vinion's wood-burning furnace was shut down in 1618, Robinson secured from Mansell a licence to import from France a specified number of drinking glasses,[1] a privilege restricted to the patentees by the terms of the grant. Bungar, who could not hope to secure such a licence, decided instead to bring glass from Mansell's other factories to London. Clavell's furnace was the nearest, and although Clavell and Bigo had previously kept to the terms of their agreement with Mansell,[2] they began consigning glass to London during the early summer of 1619 at Bungar's persuasion.[3] There it was sold 'some by Clavells servantes and some by Isaac Bungar'[4] at prices lower than the London merchants could afford to charge—or so they claimed—since they paid Mansell three times as much rent as did Bigo and Clavell. As a result they broke their contract with Mansell for management of the Ratcliffe works and refused to pay any further rent.[5] In July Mansell determined to enforce his contracts, and through the Privy Council secured the arrests of Bungar, Clavell, and Bigo.[6] The Council heard the case; but since it emerged that Robinson could not supply the London market and was importing glasses on licence from Mansell, they referred the matter to the Chief Justice of King's Bench and the Chief Baron of the Exchequer for further investigation.[7]

Before a report could be brought in, a second dispute came before the Council concerning the importation of window glass. John Dines, it will be remembered, had been discharged by Mansell early in 1619[8] and thereafter he worked with the King's glazier, a man named Baggeley. Both parties nursed hard feelings over the discharge, however, and Robson deliberately sold Dines 'eight or nyne cases of glasse of the worst sort' because 'both the kinges glasier and Mr. Dynes . . . spoke against his master Sir Robert Mansell'.[9] Later, after more angry words, Mansell himself drew his sword on Dines and refused to sell him any glass at all for the King's buildings unless he brought a purveyor with him.[10] Dines then prompted two merchants (Howgill and Greene) to secure a licence directly from the King to import sufficient glass for glazing the King's house at York. During the summer and early autumn of 1619, they imported considerably more glass than was necessary for the royal buildings and sold it to other persons. Mansell objected to the Council, and Howgill and Greene, who would not promise to stop importing window glass, languished in the Marshalsea prison for some sixteen weeks.[11]

---

[1] A.P.C. xxxvii. 155.

[2] Exch. K.R., Depositions by Commission, E. 134/22, Jac. I/Eas. 24, Mansell v. Clavell, depositions of Short and Culliford.

[3] Exch. K. R., Barons' Depositions, E. 133/84/64, Mansell v. Clavell, deposition of Norman.

[4] Ibid., deposition of John Kirby.

[5] Ibid., deposition of Thomas Robinson.

[6] A.P.C. xxxvii. 14.

[7] Ibid., p. 68.

[8] See above, p. 90.

[9] S.P. 14/112, no. 66.   [10] Ibid., No. 67.   [11] A.P.C. xxxvii. 85.

The third case, which came before the Council while the other two were still unresolved, proved to be by far the most difficult. It concerned importation from Scotland, and became a question, as in Robson's Irish enterprise, of whether glass could be imported from 'other the King's dominions' in competition to Mansell's glass. The Scottish glasshouse was operating under a patent granted in December 1610 to Sir George Hay[1] (who later became a member of the Privy Council for Scotland), with terms similar to Sir Roger Aston's patent for Ireland, which Robson had leased. Like Aston, Hay had no particular plans for exploiting his patent, and it remained dormant until 1617. In that year two separate attempts were made to establish glassworks in Scotland without permission from Hay, one by a Scot named Crawford, the other by two London merchants (members of the Goldsmiths Company).[2] The Goldsmiths persuaded John Maria del Aqua, one of Mansell's Venetians at Broad Street, to become their foreman at a high wage.[3] He worked for them for eight or nine weeks; but since the Scottish Privy Council, following a complaint from Hay, had ordered the factories shut down,[4] Maria worked instead for Crawford, who seems to have leased Hay's patent rights as a result of the complaint. After a year with Crawford, Maria left in June 1618, 'for want of materialls and wages', in order to sign a new contract with James Ord, who replaced Crawford as Hay's lessee. Ord had as little capital as Crawford,[5] and Maria himself paid not only for the new coal-burning furnace but also for the operating expenses for five months.[6] During the summer of 1619 he broke his contract with Ord in disgust and remained unemployed for a time. After his departure Ord determined upon a new policy. He procured a considerable amount of new capital from the group who were opposing Mansell's monopoly ('Sir William Clavell, Worrell a broker, Dines a glasier and Bungar the sonne of an alien glassmaker'),[7] and turned from crystal, which Maria had been making, to the production of window glass for the London market. Since Mansell had already vindicated his right to exclude glass from 'other the King's dominions', however, Ord prompted Hay, who held the Scottish rights, to appeal for support from the Scottish Privy Council. In July the Scottish Council obliged with a petition to James I asking that the importation of the

---

[1] I have not found the full text but its date and terms are referred to frequently in other documents. See especially R.P.C. Scot. xi. 138-9.

[2] The men were Agmondesham Pickayes and William Ward. S.P. 14/112, no. 28, statement of Pickayes.

[3] S.P. 14/112, no. 28, statements of Pickayes, Ward, and John Maria del Aqua, all of which agree substantially.

[4] R.P.C. Scot. xi. 138-9, 21 May 1617.

[5] Crawford later secured a patent for transporting glasshouse clay to England in recompense for his losses at the glasshouse. Ibid., xi. 484-5, 1 June 1619.

[6] S.P. 14/112, no. 28, statement of John Maria del Aqua.

[7] S.P. 16/521, no. 147, statement of the Glaziers Company.

Scottish glass to London should be allowed on the basis of the benefits that would accrue to his realm of Scotland from glass manufacture, and alleging that Ord must be allowed to export if he were to succeed, since the sale of glass in Scotland would 'not uphold the glasse workes the space of ane month'.[1] If importation of window glass to England was not to be allowed, then they asked that an old statute forbidding the export of Scottish coal should be enforced—an obvious attempt to pressure Mansell into compliance, for Scottish coal was then thought necessary for his crystal furnaces. When the petition went unanswered, Ord went to London in person with a second to the same effect.[2] But Mansell would make no concessions, and Ord could get no answer from the King that was satisfactory to the Scottish patentees. Without permission Crawford's factory at Wemyss began shipping to London window glass which Mansell's agents promptly confiscated. The matter was then laid before the English Privy Council in November.[3]

Notes prepared for the deliberation of the Council indicate the arguments which were presented on either side.[4] Ord, representing the Scottish firm, claimed that Hay's patent was granted before Zouch's, which was indeed true, and that he and his associates were 'anterieur in their making of glasse', which was clearly false, as Maria and several other witnesses testified.[5] The real question, however, was not priority of manufacture, but whether a glass factory operating legally in Scotland could export glass to England in spite of the prohibition in Mansell's patent. The Council came to the same decision as had the courts of law in the Irish case: that it could not. At the same time the Council was still considering the case of Clavell and Bungar (who were selling drinking glasses from Purbeck in London) and that of the merchants, Howgill and Greene (who were importing window glass from abroad at Dines's instigation). It was desirable that a policy should be laid down which was broad enough to cover all these cases and any other troublesome situations which might arise.

The new policy was embodied in a proclamation (25 January 1620)[6] which stated that the provision in the glass patent of 1615 for importation under licence from the patentees was intended only as a temporary measure until the glass works were 'brought to perfection', and that henceforth neither the patentees nor others could import any kind of glass except on the express permission of a new committee called the 'Lords Commissioners for the Glasse-workes'. The ruling was made explicit in regard to Scotland, with the proviso that in time of great scarcity of glass

---

[1] National Library of Scotland, Denmilne MS. ix, no. 13, 22 July 1619.

[2] Ibid., no. 23, 19 Oct. 1619.

[3] Lansd. MS. 162, no 97 fol. 67.   [4] Ibid.   [5] S.P. 14/112, no. 28.

[6] A.P.C. xxxvii. 108, 19 Jan. 1619/20; S.P. 14/187, no. 76, proclamation dated 25 Jan. 17 Jac. I.

in England, the Glass Commissioners might permit importation from Scotland alone. The Commission, already appointed two weeks before,[1] consisted of two Scottish lords, the Duke of Lennox and the Marquess of Hamilton, and two English lords, the Earls of Arundel and of Pembroke. They were given full authority to enforce the proclamation and settle all future disputes, provided that their orders were signed by at least two Commissioners, one of whom must be Scottish and the other English.

Ord and his English backers were not prepared to give up glassmaking, if the loophole permitting importation in time of scarcity could be exploited. No sooner was the ink dry on the proclamation than Ord was petitioning the Commissioners to that effect.[2] Dines, whose financial interest in the Scottish firm was probably not generally known at that time, sent in another petition, also complaining of a 'want of glass' in London.[3] As a result the Glass Commissioners undertook a thorough investigation of the price, quality, and supply of window glass from Mansell's furnaces. At their request the Glaziers Company appointed a committee to inspect and report on the glass in the warehouses. One statement, apparently a minority report written by only one person, said briefly that Mansell's glass was 'for the most part . . . unserviceable and for no use'.[4] It was probably written either by Bungar or Dines, both of whom were then members of the Company. A more lengthy report, signed by the Warden of the Company, one of the assistants, and two other members who were retailers of window glass one of whom was Bennett, Bungar's former partner, reported as follows:

. . . in the ffirst parcell wee found some badd glasse, and for the most part reasonable good, and in the second parcell wee found as abovesaid some badd, but the greater parte good, and in the third parcell, which came last in, so farre as we could see, to our judgment it is good and merchantable glasse, and the ffourth parcell which we viewed, it was indifferent good glasse.[5]

In addition Inigo Jones, Surveyor of Works for the King and Thomas Baldwin, Comptroller, accompanied the glaziers on their inspection trip at the request of the Glass Commissioners, and later made a second visit alone before producing a separate statement.[6] Like the glaziers, they found a mingling of 'the best and worst sortes togeather', and added that many of the tables were blown too thin. They added, however, that this was a

[1] Clavell MS. B2/2, Commission of James I to the Glass Commissioners. 10 Jan. 17 Jac. I. It is significant that Clavell was sent a copy.

[2] S.P. 14/113, no. 47, petition of James Ord, 25 Feb. 1619/20.

[3] S.P. 14/120, no 89.

[4] S.P. 14/113, no. 52. The report, written in the singular, is unsigned and the writer indicates that he disagreed with the others.

[5] Ibid., no. 51. Report signed by Habbacuck Kerby, Warden, John Inman, Lionel Bennett, and Richard Spearman.

[6] Ibid., no. 53, statement of Jones and Baldwin.

defect which 'the glasiers that were sent, seemed not desirious to have reformed, beinge a thinge that will redowne to their benefitt as we conceave' by making more repairs necessary. Jones and Baldwin recommended that thicker sheets be blown and the glass graded for quality and 'severally pryst'. None of the reports commented on either the price or the quantity of glass available, but the amount on hand in the storehouses disproved actual shortage. That there was indeed plenty of glass is also indicated by another letter of the glaziers to the Commissioners a year later, reminding them of Dines's unjust complaint in 1620. As a result of the investigation then conducted at the Commissioners' order, they said, 'the Citty of London was founde soe plentifully stored and with soe good, as none of us could truly say that ever wee knewe the Citty better provided than att that very tyme'.[1] Lest such a statement might seem unwarranted in view of the reports of both good and bad glass in Mansell's storehouses, it should be pointed out that the glaziers had complained of the bad quality of Bungar's glass which they had previously used, and even more strongly of that from Scotland.[2]

After the investigation, the order stood that no more glass could come into England from the Scottish factory. Instead Ord turned to supplying the market in Scotland, for, contrary to the statement of the Scottish Privy Council when the quarrel began, there was indeed an ample market there which was being supplied by imported window glass, chiefly from Poland. In the autumn of 1620 the Privy Council of Scotland conducted their own investigation into glassmaking with a view to cutting off such foreign importation. The detailed report of a committee which they appointed leaves no doubt but that the glass then made in Scotland was not up to the English standards.[3] The window glass, like Mansell's worst, was too thin and brittle; and they recommended sending to London for samples of drinking glass to be used as a standard 'for trying the sufficiencie' of the Scottish glass. Nevertheless they decided that it was feasible to cut off importation from abroad, subject to review if the quantity made in Scotland proved to be insufficient.[4] The Scottish patentee, then, like his English counterpart, had a monopoly of the internal market in his own country; but neither could compete with the other except in times when it was accepted by the Glass Commissioners that there was a scarcity of glass.

Once the troublesome Scottish case was disposed of, the other cases still pending before the Council could be quickly dealt with on the basis of the proclamation. After four months in gaol Howgill and Greene surrendered their licence and promised not to attempt further importation.[5]

---

[1] S.P. 14/120, no. 71, petition of the Glaziers Company, 1621.   [2] Ibid.

[3] R.P.C. Scot. xii. 428, 439–41. The committee consisted of Sir George Hay, Lord Carnegy, Sir Andro Hamilton, Sir Archibald Naper, and James Murray, Master of Workes, together with such merchants and glaziers as they wished to assist them.

[4] R.P.C. Scot. xii. 451–2.   [5] A.P.C. xxxvii. 155–6.

Robinson's licence from Mansell was also revoked, and the drinking glasses he had ordered (which had not yet arrived), were to be sequestered and bond given for their re-exportation.[1] The Commissioners then ordered the re-exportation of all glass expected from abroad, with a few exceptions. One exception was made for the Earl of Arundel, one of their number, who was expecting six chests of Venetian glasses for his private use;[2] and another for a merchant who had just received hour-glasses, tin spectacles and vials of small value.[3] In general, however, the agents whom the Commissioners appointed to inspect shipments[4] took seriously the strict enforcement of the proclamation forbidding all importation of glass, whether by Mansell or by independent merchants. The surest indication of their vigilance is the fact that by September the Merchant Adventurers were complaining of the restraint of their trade, occasioned by the pro-hibition of importing 'all thinges made of glass'.[5]

One last dispute remained to be settled—the case of Bigo and Clavell, who had sold in London drinking glasses made in Purbeck, contrary to Mansell's restrictions. The proclamation did not cover such internal arrangements; but in March 1620 the Glass Commissioners nevertheless reviewed the case, and at the same time considered the petition of an hour-glass maker who had been buying vials at the Ratcliffe furnace.[6] Like Clavell he objected to Mansell's marketing restrictions and wanted to be allowed to purchase glass at any of Mansell's furnaces instead of only in London, where he said the price was high and glass suitable for working was scarce. Mansell said that his contract with the agent for the Ratcliffe works only continued until the following Midsummer Day (15 July 1620),[7] so the Commissioners ordered that after that date hour-glass makers should be at liberty to buy glass at whichever of Mansell's works they wished; and in the meantime they should be served at reasonable prices. They assumed that Mansell would not renew the Ratcliffe contract on the same terms, and that thereafter glass from any of his furnaces could be freely sold in London. Mansell however disregarded their intention, and in July he re-let the Ratcliffe works on similar restrictive terms.

On the whole the lengthy investigation had resulted in a victory for Mansell. He had lost his right to import glass, and he had to expand his own production in order to supply the kingdom himself, but this he was eager to do. In April he prevented the issue of letters patent for the finishing processes in looking-glass making, on the grounds that it would

---

[1] Ibid., p. 155.   [2] Ibid., p. 201.   [3] Ibid., p. 195.
[4] Ibid., p. 165. The agents were Sir John Suckling and Sir John Woolstenholme.
[5] Ibid., p. 282.
[6] S.P. 14/113, no. 20, March 1619/20, petition of Ralph Coulbourne, hour-glass maker.
[7] A.P.C. xxxvii. 342–3, Order in Council of 7 Feb. 1620/1, which refers to a hearing and an order by the Glass Commissioners on 12 Mar. 1619/20. See also a note on the bottom of Coublourne's petition, to the same effect (S.P. 14/113, no. 20).

interfere with the freedom of workmen he had brought from the continent for that purpose, and also that not being bound to buy plates from him, the proposed patentees might attempt illegal importation.[1] At the same time he was anxious to put all his affairs in order, since in January 1620, just before the Glass Commissioners reached their decision, the Privy Council had appointed him Commander-in-Chief of an expedition against the pirates infesting the Algerian coast.[2] Before he left, it was essential for him to settle his differences with his chief enemies, Bungar and Clavell. Some years later Clavell said that after the proclamation was issued, Mansell 'did then hold himself satisfied for all complaintes formerly made' and was on friendly terms with him and with Bungar.[3] In addition he said that Mansell made a contract with Bungar 'for a glasseworke in or neer London'. It is possible that Bungar took over the Ratcliffe works since the contract for them expired in July 1620; but it is more likely that Mansell intended to set up a new glasshouse under Bungar's management, to relieve the shortage of glass in London. One final matter remained: the state of Mansell's account with the Crown. In August Mansell drew up a statement[4] which showed that in discharge of the Crown rent of £1,000 he had, during the previous year, paid £600 directly to the former patentees: £350 to Bowes's heirs (instead of the £600 that Bowes himself had received), £150 to Salter (as agreed), £100 to Turner (instead of the £150 originally awarded to him), and nothing at all to William Robson, who had been Mansell's employee for some time. The balance of £400 had not been paid in cash, but had been 'delivered in glasses to the Kings Majestie': apparently Mansell's tableware pleased the royal taste. At the same time that the account was drawn up, he handed over the administration of the glass monopoly to his wife and Captain Francis Bacon. In October Mansell's fleet set sail, to be gone for nearly a year. Though his affairs seemed to be in order, during his absence Lady Mansell faced the most severe threat that the monopoly had yet encountered.

[1] S.P. 14/113, nos. 20, 80, petition of Sir Ralph and Anne Bingley, March 1620, and Mansell's answer, April 1620.
[2] A.P.C. xxxvii. 105, 12 Jan. 1619/20.
[3] Exch. K.R., Barons' Depositions, E. 113/84/64, *Mansell* v. *Clavell*.
[4] S.P. 14/116, no. 86.

V

MONOPOLY TRIUMPHANT

THE period from the late autumn of 1620, when Mansell left for sea, until the disappearance of the monopoly in 1642 saw the climax of the struggle between the Mansell monopoly and its adversaries. In spite of an unfavourable Parliamentary investigation the monopoly not only survived but was reissued to Mansell, to him alone this time, and then later extended by indenture, thus ensuring his domination of the glass industry until the outbreak of the Civil War. During the latter part of this period—the eleven years when Charles I ruled without Parliament—the few troubles which the monopoly encountered came more from internal problems than from outside pressure. Before 1624, however, the storm which broke upon the monopoly nearly swept it away.

I. LADY MANSELL AS ADMINISTRATOR

Although Lady Mansell, perhaps attempting to make capital of male gallantry, referred to herself as a 'poor, weak woman',[1] she proved herself anything but a weak administrator in her husband's absence. Captain Francis Bacon shared her responsibility in regard to the Broad Street factory, but she herself handled administrative problems. She had been prepared for this task by considerable experience in receiving accounts, giving acquittances and dealing with sub contractors.[2] Although Mansell had temporarily composed his differences with Bungar and Clavell before going to sea, he was scarcely gone when Bungar broke his contract and engaged in a violent quarrel with Lady Mansell. The cause of the quarrel is not clear, though it probably concerned either certain restrictions in the contract or the hiring by Bungar of Mansell's workmen. At any rate before February 1621 Bungar had uttered such 'disgraceful speeches' against Sir Robert that he was imprisoned in the Marshalsea.[3] In addition Clavell and Bigo were continuing to send drinking glasses from Purbeck to the London market, an action which the Order in Council of the preceding March appeared to have authorized. Lady Mansell objected to such shipment as 'prejudiciall to an agreement between Sir Robert Mansell and his farmers', and took the matter to the Glass Commissioners for review.[4]

---

[1] S.P. 16/521/147, petition of Dame Elizabeth Mansell, undated but *c.* 1621.
[2] Exch. K.R., Barons' Depositions, E. 133/34/64, *Mansell v. Clavell*.
[3] *A.P.C.* xxxvii. 342–3.   [4] Ibid.

She complained as well that Clavell was enticing her workmen to leave London and work in the Scottish glasshouse in which he had an interest.

So persuasive was Lady Mansell that the Glass Commissioners supported her claims and reversed their previous order. On the technicality that their commission did not extend to supervision of Mansell's internal arrangements, they recalled their order permitting buyers to purchase glass at any of Mansell's factories, adding the proviso that aggrieved persons could find a remedy in the courts of law.[1] Moreover, in the specific dispute with Clavell, they tried to help her to enforce the contract signed between Mansell and Bigo. Noting that Bigo was too poor a man to enter bond for the performance of his contract, and that he had made over part of the works to Clavell, who had never signed a contract with Mansell and claimed not to be bound by the marketing restrictions, they ordered that Clavell should enter into the same contract with Mansell as had Bigo.[2] Clavell was unwilling to do this, and circumvented the order by making over the entire ownership of the business to Bigo, who was then forced to pay all of Mansell's rent and in addition supply Clavell with large quantities of glass in payment for coal, supplies, and rent of the buildings.[3] As for the workmen who had allegedly been enticed away from London, the commissioners declared that they were not satisfied with Clavell's evasive answers, that such tactics were unjust, and that if another incident occurred he would be duly punished.[4]

When these orders were issued (7 February 1621) Bungar was still in gaol. Lady Mansell wrote an adroitly worded letter to the Council concerning his case.[5] She did not really desire his imprisonment, she said, but only asked that he sign a statement before the Glass Commissioners, promising that he would not be a 'malitius disturber of Sir Robert Mansells workes or contracts from hensforth'. Bungar's answer is a measure of his respect for her as an adversary. 'For that which is required by the Lady Mansell,' he wrote, '. . . not knowing how far my Lady may straine any such promise to draw me into further trouble . . . I do humbly desire to be excused from setting my hand to anything that may engage me to my future inconvenience.'[6] It is not clear whether or not he changed his mind and signed the paper, but since he was soon free,[7] he probably made at least verbal promises to stop troubling Lady Mansell. He did not sign another contract for managing one of Mansell's London glasshouses, however, and the works he had managed were apparently re-let to another.

Shortly after his imprisonment Bungar tried to cause further trouble for

---

[1] *A.P.C.* xxxvii. 342–3.   [2] Ibid.
[3] Exch. K.R., Depositions by Commission, E. 134/22, Jac I/Eas. 24, *Mansell* v. *Clavell*, depositions of John Jenkins, clerk, and Richard Robson.
[4] *A.P.C.* xxxvii. 342–3.
[5] S.P. 14/124, no. 122, 'Lady Mansell concerning Bungarde with Bungards Answeare'.
[6] Ibid.   [7] *A.P.C.* xxxvii. 343, 9 Feb. 1621.

Lady Mansell by interfering with the supply of fuel for the London glasshouses making crystal, which had continued to burn nothing but Scottish coal. Since the earlier attempt to do this through the petition of Ord and the Scottish Privy Council had failed, he went instead to the masters of shipping in Scotland, who had supplied Mansell's coal, and persuaded them to raise the price from 14s. a ton to 24s. a ton, and then to cut off supplies entirely for a time.[1] For three weeks the furnaces were without fuel, until, as Mansell admiringly related, his wife, determined not to be thwarted, 'adventured upon the working with Newcastle cole (a thing never before attempted or thought possible)'. The change worked so satisfactorily that thereafter Newcastle coal was always used at the crystal furnaces, and Bungar had unwittingly brought about a reduction in his adversary's cost of production. In all these dealings Lady Mansell showed herself to be a person of decision who was not easily intimidated by rivals or recalcitrant contractors. These qualities she needed, for in a few weeks she was to face an even greater threat to her husband's monopoly.

II. INVESTIGATION IN THE PARLIAMENT OF 1621

When Parliament assembled early in January 1621 matters of foreign policy and supply were uppermost in the minds of the King and his counsellors. It soon became evident, however, that the Commons were intent upon redress of grievances, particularly the monopoly patents of all kinds. When Noy, a Cornish lawyer, moved on 19 February that an inquiry should be held into the monopoly patents, he did not specifically mention that for glass:[2] but as one of the chief patents, it was inevitably included in the investigation. The various accounts of the debates of the Commons and the committee meetings show, however, that the glass patent did not arouse the storm of opposition which greeted more flagrantly abused grants. The attack on the so-called 'Buckingham ring' patents for inns, ale-houses, and gold and silver thread brought forth violent speeches and led to the revival of the impeachment process against Sir Giles Mompesson and Sir Francis Mitchell, two of the chief offenders.[3] Buckingham himself felt it necessary to repudiate those of his relatives and dependants who were involved, while Bacon's responsibility for approving the granting of some of the objectionable patents led to the bringing of charges of corruption against him. All this is well known: but the emotional tension in the House and the high feeling against all

[1] S.P. 14/162, no. 231 B, Mansell's statement, 1624. Nef's figures on the prices of Scottish coal in London seem to corroborate the charge. See Nef, *British Coal Industry*, ii, app. E, 391–3.

[2] *Commons debates, 1621*, iv. 78.

[3] S. R. Gardiner, *History of England . . . 1603–1642* (London, Longmans, Green, 1894–96), vol. iv, chaps. 23–5, gives one of the fullest accounts of the attack on monopolies in 1621. He discusses the glass patent briefly, but his statements are not entirely accurate.

monopoly patents must be kept in mind as a contributing factor in the investigation of the glass patent.

The records of early debates of the House of Commons on monopolies contain no mention of the glass patent. It was included in Alford's list of monopolies,[1] however, as a result of two petitions handed in to the House, one from the 'familie of Bungard' and other glassmakers, the second in the name of Isaac Bungar, John Worrall, Paul and Peter Vinion, Abraham Liscourt, and 'diverse others'.[2] All patents on the list were referred to the Committee of Grievances. During March and early April both Houses were concerned with the most objectionable grants, especially the 'Buckingham ring' patents. In the midst of the hearings the King came before the Lords (26 March) to state his intention of 'striking dead' by proclamation the patents which were causing so much trouble.[3] Encouraged by this pronouncement and by the punishment meted out to Mompesson and Mitchell, the Commons revised the list of other objectionable patents and ordered systematic hearings on them. Glass came up in its turn.

In advance of the hearings, all those who stood to gain or lose from a possible cancellation of the glass patent made a strenuous effort to strengthen their positions. Petitions and counter-petitions appeared and were circulated widely.[4] Lady Mansell got wind of a rumour that Baggeley, the King's glazier who worked with Dines, was using his influence at Court to overthrow the patent, and was planning to testify before the Parliamentary committee in favour of the Scottish firm.[5] She countered by threatening him with losing his position with the King if her husband's patent were cancelled, and she sent Robson to under-bid him for a contract in regard to glazing the remaining windows in the royal buildings then under construction. Baggeley appealed to Clavell for help, and Clavell showed his letter to the King[6] in an effort to thwart Lady Mansell's threats. It seems that Baggeley did not lose his job—but neither did he testify in Parliament.

On 30 April the Committee on Grievances spent the afternoon in examining the charges made against the glass patent,[7] and ordered further hearings. Lady Mansell, being ill, sent in a petition on 7 May, asking that the House withhold its judgement on the patent until her husband's return; but she added that 'according to the uttmost of her poore

---

[1] Alford Papers, Harl. MS. 6806, fol. 234, printed in *Commons Debates, 1621*, vii. 539–40.

[2] Harl. MS. 6847, fols. 269ᵛ–70, in *Commons Debates, 1621*, vii. 540–1.

[3] *J.H.L.* iii. 69.

[4] Apart from the petitions already cited, there is another, slightly different, among the Clavell papers at Smedmore (Clavell MS. B2/5).

[5] Ibid., B2/3, Baggeley to Clavell, 12 Apr. 1621.

[6] Ibid. The letter is endorsed in Clavell's hand 'The Kinges glasiers letter which I shewed to his Majestie'.

[7] *Commons Debates, 1621*, iv. 282, 353.

hability' she had instructed her counsel as requested.[1] In spite of her petition the committee proceeded the same day to hear counsel both for and against the patent, to consider petitions and affidavits, and to hear oral testimony. The hearings were continued on 14 May.

It is worthwhile to examine the character of the evidence which was presented on both sides during the several hearings.[2] In his diary Pym drew on the brief prepared by counsel against the patent; this counsel was apparently hired by Bungar and the others who signed one of the petitions.[3] The brief outlined eight charges made against the patent: (1) that making glass with coal was not a new invention; (2) that there had been an unwarranted increase in price, especially in the provinces; (3) that the glass was worse than that formerly available, and contained less feet to the case; (4) that all window glass on the London market was already cut into quarrels; (5) that all types of glass were included and restricted from importation, although the patentees did not make all types; (6) that crystal and amber beads that had been imported were seized by the patentees; (7) that numerous people had been imprisoned unjustly; (8) that twelve loads of wood were used in every firing in the Venetian-type glasshouse.[4] The Barrington diary adds that much was also made of the condemnation of the Zouch patent by the Parliament of 1614.[5] Together these cover the main points in a list of twenty 'Articles of obieccions' against the patent found in the Alford papers.[6]

Counsel for the defence, ably instructed by Lady Mansell, answered the charges in detail. That twelve loads of wood were used to start each fire at Broad Street was readily admitted to be true, but it was pointed out that this was the case only in that one factory and that firing occurred only four times a year, so that the use of wood was negligible compared with the former consumption.[7] Abuses in the management of the patent, such as unwarranted seizure of glass and imprisonment, were not conceded as proved; but even if they did exist, it was argued that they did not touch the validity of the patent iself, but were administrative matters which could be corrected.[8] As for the charge that the patentees restricted importation of all glass, though they did not make all kinds, this, too, could be

---

[1] Ibid., iii. 195.

[2] Ibid., pp. 195–7; *Proc. and Debates*, ii. 38–9. These two are the fullest accounts, though Pym's summary of the three committee hearings (*Commons Debates, 1621*, iv. 353–4) is better organized. The Barrington diary and the Holland diary (ibid., iii. 203–4; vi. 144–5) add an interesting anecdote about Sir Charles Morrison, Clement Coke, and some ribald verses about 'asses and glasses'. Neither were paying much attention to the hearings.

[3] Alford Papers Harl. MS. 6847, fols. 269v–70. Bungar, Worrall, Liscourt and the Vinions are named, but not Clavell who claimed not to be a glassmaker at this time. He may however, have helped hire the counsel.

[4] *Commons Debates, 1621*, iv. 353.

[5] Ibid., iii. 196.

[6] Ibid., vii. 541–5, printing full text of Harl. MS. 6847, fols. 271v–4.

[7] Ibid., iii. 255; iv. 354; ii. 366.   [8] Ibid., iii. 255.

corrected, and they were indeed making more specialities than had pre-viously been made in England.[1]

The greater part of the defence rightly focused on the first three charges —the genuineness of the invention, the price of glass made under the patent, and its quality. The counsel admitted that various other people had tried to make glass with coal, but insisted that they used 'the old furnace proper for Wood' with no success,[2] and that Paul Tysack in particular was already 'a servant of the patentees' when he succeeded.[3] The brief then dealt in some detail with prices of window glass at that time as compared with those during the reign of Elizabeth in order to prove that they had been lowered.[4] It was admitted that relocation of the industry near coal-fields at Newcastle had caused some rise in prices in certain inland communities, for while London could be cheaply supplied by water, other areas, which had formerly had wood-burning furnaces nearby, faced transportation charges from the new factories. Even so, counsel for the patent maintained that prices were not excessive, and that attempts were being made to establish the industry over a wider area. As for the quality of the glass and the number of feet to the case, written affidavits from the glaziers were presented which indicated satisfaction and support for the patentees.[5]

Besides the briefs, both parties submitted considerable testimony, both written and oral. On the question of the invention the chief witnesses against the patentees were Bungar and Liscourt themselves, along with Lord Dudley (for, as has been pointed out in an earlier chapter,[6] none of the other men on whose behalf claims of prior invention were made came forward to testify). Since their testimony and its reliability has already been discussed, it need not be repeated, except to point out that Sir George More, who had often acted as chairman of committees investigat-ing the glass business, including disputes between Bungar and Mansell, was sitting in the House and testified in favour of the patentees.[7] It seems that Thomas Percival did not appear to defend his claim as inventor, yet there is little doubt that Mansell's counsel succeeded in establishing the fact that the design of the coal furnace was first perfected by him and that the new furnace was essential for success in burning coal for glassmaking. Bungar's counsel admitted as much in the final summing up on 14 May when he argued that 'if the fornace were the only helpe to the Manufac-

---

[1] The truth of this point is implied by points nos. 16 and 17 in the 'articles of objieccion' (Harl. MS. 6847, fols. 271v–4) which asserted that the price of chemical glass, then made in England, was higher than it had been on such glass formerly imported.

[2] *Commons Debates, 1621*, iv. 353.

[3] Ibid., iii. 255.

[4] Ibid., iii. 256; iv. 354.   [5] See below, p. 110.

[6] See above, pp. 62–4.

[7] *Commons Debates, 1621*, iii. 256. Exactly what he said is not recorded.

ture, then the patentees showld have reward for the fornaces and not for the glasse'.[1]

The witnesses who gave evidence about the price and quality of the glass contradicted each other vehemently. Bungar and other witnesses supporting him asserted that Bungar himself had previously sold glass at the furnace door cheaper than the current price.[2] Assertions of excessive prices came chiefly from the country, especially Coventry, where it was said that the price had risen by as much as 7s. a case.[3] The names and occupations of the witnesses are not always given in the records, but from the statements made it would seem that most of the unfavourable testimony came from the small group of glassmakers who opposed the patent and wished to continue using wood. Unfavourable testimony did indeed come from Inigo Jones, Surveyor of Works for the King; but this was not so much about the price as the quality of Mansell's glass.[4] He asserted that the King had lost as much as £150 to £200 annually through bad glass supplied for use in royal buildings. Jones's statement is not surprising, however, in light of the quarrel already recounted[5] between Mansell and his agents on the one hand and Dines and the King's Glazier on the other, resulting in deliberate selling of bad glass. About an equal number of witnesses testified for Mansell. One 'old man, *pro* Sir Robert, saith that Sir Robert hath since the work was perfected made better glass then before was and as good, and as good a penniworth as Burgundy or Normand glass', while another said 'for drinking glasses [they are] as cheape and good as this 40 years have ben, and as large'.[6] When an unfavourable witness intervened to say that glass was 'worse, deerer now than before', a third and still a fourth stated that it was 'as good, large, cheape'. It was to be expected that each side could muster a certain number of people who were willing to testify in its behalf and it is difficult to evaluate the validity of the oral testimony. Enough has been said, however, to indicate that it was far from one-sided, as has sometimes been assumed.[7]

The written affidavits and petitions from groups who were not Mansell's rivals but rather purchasers and consumers of glass seem more reliable. One of these, the apothecaries of London, favoured Bungar's side. Their petition has been lost, but the nature of their complaint is summarized in Alford's list of objections to the patent which mentions the high price of 'chimicall glasses, as Retorte heades and bodies, boulte heades and other like used for extractions distallacion and other Chimicall uses'.[8]

---

[1] Ibid., p. 258.   [2] Ibid., pp. 256–7; *Proc. and Debates*, ii. 71.

[3] *Commons Debates, 1621*, iii. 256–7; *Proc. and Debates*, ii. 71.

[4] *Commons Debates, 1621*, iv. 354; *Proc. and Debates*, ii. 73.

[5] See above, Chap. IV, p. 96.   [6] *Commons Debates, 1621*, iii. 256–7.

[7] Price, pp. 74–5. Price wrote before the publication of the *Commons Debates, 1621*.

[8] *Commons Debates, 1621*, vii. 544.

Formerly, they said, such complicated retorts had been imported from Germany, but recently Mansell had been making them and charging excessive rates. No doubt the accusation of high prices was true; one may compare the complaint of the hour-glass makers during the previous year that glass vials suitable for their purposes were both scarce and dear. The complaint of the apothecaries, however, was aimed at removing the restrictions on importation rather than allowing the use of wood, since they clearly implied that such complicated chemical glass had never been made in England before Mansell's time.

Two other consumer groups supported the Mansell monopoly. The petition of the spectacle-makers, noted in the record as 'for Sir Robert Mansell',[1] has also been lost, but it is clear that they were satisfied with the price, quality, and supply of the crystal plates from his furnaces which they ground into lenses. So also were the largest single group who bought glass wholesale—the Glaziers Company of London. Two of their petitions are extant. The first, dated 4 April 1621 and signed by sixteen glaziers, deserves quotation regarding Mansell's window glass:

1. First, for the price it is as cheape sold as it hath ben usually sold to us for the space of twenty yeares before the grant of the Pattent, and by reason of the increase of the Size wee do afforde to the Commonwealth Glasse wrought cheaper than heretofore by Tenn poundes in the hundred.
2. Secondly, For the Goodnes the Glasse is as good and as well Condicioned as anie hath benn since our memories and use of the Trade.
3. Thirdly, For Store, wee have had, and have sufficient quantitie to exercise our Trade and to furnishe all buyers, and such as have use of the Comoditie by recourse to this Cittie. And whereas his Majestie hath been Informed by Bungar and Dynes that Glasse hath been before the Pattent sold for Fourteen Shillings per case, wee averre that we thinke that by privat Contractes betweene Bungar and Bennet it might be soe sold; but wee the Glassers for many yeares before the Pattent payd to Bungar and Benett Twenty two shillings six pence per Case, they being the Sole Ingrossers whoe keept great Store of Glasse in their handes of purpose to make a scarcitie whereby they might uphold their price. Soe that wee finding greater benefitt and ease by haveing ready and Constaunt Markett by the Pattent—are fearfull to fale to our former Subiection to persons of our owne fraternity who have Terinized over us.[2]

The final paragraph of the petition deals with glass recently brought from Scotland, which the glaziers found 'soe thin and unserviceable' that they much preferred to pay 22s. 6d. for Mansell's glass than 20s. for the Scottish glass. A further petition of 15 April, signed by forty-six persons who apparently comprised the entire company, except for the few like

---

[1] *Commons Debates, 1621*, ii. 366; iii. 256.   [2] S.P. 14/120, no. 71.

Bungar and Dines who opposed Mansell, made the same points in stronger terms and greater detail.[1]

It is hard to find any adequate ground for discounting the statements of these men whose livelihood was at stake.[2] Had Mansell's glass actually been more expensive and of poorer quality than that made by Bungar or the Scottish company, it is difficult to see why the glaziers supported Mansell when an opportunity arose to overthrow the patent. Bungar himself was hard put to explain what he admitted to be the support of almost the entire company for Mansell's patent. Since he could hardly continue to deny the truth of their assertions that Mansell's glass was good, cheap, and plentiful, he said that their reason for supporting Mansell was that as a body they controlled the distribution of all Mansell's glass from the Newcastle furnaces and that they 'kept themselves in worke by cutting out great quantities of glasse into quarryes [quarrels] with which they serve the kingdome to the utter undoinge of the glasiers of the countrie and enriching of themselves'.[3] Taking all the testimony into consideration, it seems clear that most of the country, including London, was being supplied with glass from Mansell's furnaces of a reasonable quality and price, at least equal to that which had been made in the wood-burning furnaces, but that prices were indeed higher in some country areas and in provincial towns. It is equally clear that Mansell has introduced the production of several types of glass not previously made in England, but that he had been more successful in making plates for the manufacture of looking-glasses and spectacles than in supplying the needs of apothecaries and hour-glass makers.

The debate in committe which followed the hearing of testimony confirms this impression. Little was said about the issues argued by opposing counsels—the validity of the invention, the quality and price of the glass. Instead the striking thing about the debate as recounted by Pym[4] is that the testimony in favour of Mansell was ignored, and further arguments were presented against the patent, based not on harm to the commonwealth from the monopoly, but on loss to the King. Various members said that the King was losing the customs on looking-glasses and hour-glasses to the amount of £170 yearly, that he suffered through bad glass supplied to his own works, and that the rent of £1,000 due to the Crown

---

[1] S.P. 14/120, no. 89. The originals of both this petition and the one cited in the preceding note have long lists of signatures appended, though the transcripts in the appendix of the *Commons Debates, 1621* (vii. 545–9) omit the signatures. A comparison of the signatures with other documents of the Glaziers Company (Guildhall MS. 5758, nos 9, 11 ,14) indicates that the Warden, several former Wardens and assistants, as well as nearly all the company signed the second petition, except for Bungar, Bennett, and Dines.

[2] Price (p. 74, n. 1) calls the second petition a 'single and somewhat suspicious testimonial'.

[3] Clavell MS. B2/5 'Answeres to the Pattenttee obiections', undated. This petition is not referred to in the *Commons Debates, 1621*.

[4] *Commons Debates, 1621*, iv. 354.

went instead to previous glass patentees. All of these statements were true, though the last was hardly Mansell's fault, or to his liking. The first point, the loss of customs duty, could be construed as redounding to the benefit of the kingdom through an increase in manufacturing in spite of a relatively small loss to the Exchequer—less than Mansell was then paying to the King following the reduction in the pensions paid to previous patentees.[1] Remembering the protest of the Merchant Adventurers during the preceding autumn,[2] it seems likely that their loss of profits from importing products now made by Mansell was a more important factor in the condemnation of the patent than concern over the King's revenue. Only one speech touched on the essential point of the patent's validity. Mr. Mallett was against it 'in creation and execution' since extending monopoly powers over the entire industry on the basis of an invention of one process in glassmaking was an unwarranted as 'a man for the invention of goloshoes showld have the sole making of shooes'.[3] This statement indeed conceded the genuineness of the new process.

Such was the temper of the committee that the condemnation of the grant was almost a foregone conclusion and few spoke out in its defence. Salter felt constrained to apologize for his pension from the proceeds of the monopoly, and hastened to explain that he held his pension by letters patent and would receive it in any case, so that it was a matter of indifference to him whether the glass patent stood or fell.[4] Sir William Herbert likewise explained that he came by his shares as a result of a bad debt.[5] Even Sir George More, who was in the best position to speak as an independent authority, failed to take a strong stand. He apologetically explained that his certificates given earlier in the hearings in favour of Mansell were based on his knowledge of 'devises to spoil the glass, and that made him . . . to certify as he did'.[6] Only three members of the House spoke in favour of the patent. Sir Cary Reynolds seems to have said that the King by his prerogative could prohibit importation.[7] Sir Edward Sackville, who was one of the few supporting the Crown policy in general in the Parliament,[8] pointed out that, if the patent were suppressed, England would be deprived of the manufacture and Scotland enriched.[9] Lastly Sir Robert Heath, the very able Solicitor-General, who was nevertheless unpopular with the Commons,[10] pointed out that the use of coal in

---

[1] See Chap. IV, p. 102.   [2] See Chap. IV, p. 101.
[3] *Commons Debates, 1621*, iv. 354.   [4] Ibid.
[5] *Commons Debates, 1621*, iv. 354. One wonders if the debt was owed to him by Philip Herbert, Earl of Montgomery, one of the original nine shareholders. The relationship of Sir William to the Earl is not clear, but he is said to have held his seat in this Parliament through Pembroke's influence (Willson, p. 183), and the Earl of Pembroke was Montgomery's elder brother.
[6] *Common Debates, 1621*, iii, 256.
[7] Ibid., p. 259. It is difficult to make much of the report of this speech.
[8] Willson, p. 156.   [9] *Commons Debates, 1621*, iii, 25.
[10] Willson, pp. 213–5. Willson calls Heath a man of outstanding ability.

glassmaking was in the best interests of the nation and that the patent
was 'a very considerable thing to helpe manufactures into the Kingdome'.[1]
'Notwithstanding,' remarked Pym, 'it was adjudged by the Committee
to be a Greevance.'[2]

On 16 May, Coke reported on the glass patent for the Committee of
Grievances, and upon his recommendation without further debate the
House proceeded to condemn the patent. There is no doubt that Coke's
influence was such that his opinions helped to sway both the committee
and the full House. His speech to the House when making his report is
therefore particularly important. The patent, he said, was a grievance both
in creation and in execution.[3] His reasons were as follows: (1) that the
patent was 'for no new invention' as was proved by certificates and by
three witnesses; (2) that the new invention was only for a new type of
furnace, and should neither have been the basis for rights over the entire
industry nor have excluded the making of glass with wood; (3) that the
restraint on importation hindered trade; and (4) that the time of twenty-
one years was too long. As for the execution of the patent, he said that it
was 'doubtful' whether the glass was as good as it had been formerly, and
that it was likewise 'doubtful' whether the price was not higher than it
had been before the patent. Coke thereby admitted that the charge of poor
quality and higher prices had not been proved; as for the seeming contra-
diction in his first two assertions, another diarist records that Coke
reported that 'the fornace [was] the chiefe thing of their invention'.[4] In
spite of conceding this point Coke urged condemnation of the patent, not
for its abuses but for its illegality. Such a stand was to be expected from
the general tenor of the investigations of other monopolies, and from the
obvious desire of Coke and the Commons to limit the prerogative in the
granting of such patents; nevertheless, it is remarkable in view of the fact
that Coke himself had been primarily responsible for the terms of the glass
patent of 1614,[5] which was almost identical with that of 1615 which he
called illegal. As was pointed out earlier, in 1614 he had acted not only
as a Privy Councillor but as the chief 'referee', charged with determining
the genuineness of the invention and also the general policy to be adopted.
Moreover the point which Coke stressed the most in 1621[6]—that the
patentees should not have given a complete monopoly on the basis of the
new invention of the coal furnace, nor should the wood-users have been
hindered from continuing to make glass—was in fact the very matter on
which he had taken the most vigorous stand in 1614 on the opposite side.
Then he had urged that it was in the national interest to suppress the use

[1] *Commons Debates, 1621*, ii. 258.   [2] Ibid., iv. 355.
[3] Ibid.; *J.H.C.*, i. 222.   [4] *Commons Debates, 1621*, iii. 272.
[5] See Chap. III, pp. 67f. above.
[6] Several of the *Commons Debates, 1621* diaries mention this as Coke's only argument.

of wood entirely in glassmaking, and he had volunteered to draw up the terms of the new patent and to force Robson, then the chief opponent, to cease production. The explanation for such a change in attitude was that Coke, though still a Privy Councillor,[1] had thrown in his lot with the Commons and was attacking the prerogative by any means possible. In the process he had made more than one volte-face. For instance, in connection with the cloth trade, it is related by Miss Friis that although Coke had been one of the promoters of Alderman Cockayne's project, he later turned to attack the new company 'with the greatest eagerness' and that 'it did not improve his mood that he was often reminded that he had been one of the agents in the formation of the new company'.[2]

The glass patent was one of the last to be voted a grievance by the Commons, and on the same day (16 May) a committee was appointed to draw up a list of all such condemned patents.[3] The Commons realized that their action in formally labelling the patents as grievances did not cancel them in law, and they intended to petition the King, who on 26 March had declared his intention of abolishing the most abused grants, to proceed with the promised action. Before a petition based on the list could be formally drawn up, however, Parliament was suddenly prorogued until the autumn. The Commons then ordered that none of the condemned patents should be in effect during the summer vacation.[4] It is doubtful if they had the legal right to do this without the concurrence of the Lords and the King but, as earlier in the same session, their zeal outran law and precedent.[5]

The King kept his word in regard to the most objectionable patents. A royal proclamation of 10 July 1621 abolished eighteen, including most of those on the list drawn up by the Commons, and ordered that sixteen other patents, if abused, might be proceeded against in the ordinary courts of law.[6] The glass patent, however, was not in either category, for by then it had already received special attention.

Though Bungar, Clavell, Dines, and Worrall, all of whom had shares in the Scottish glass company, had hoped to overthrow Mansell's monopoly entirely, they apparently sought to compromise for the time being by securing the right to import Scottish glass into England. They may have been aided by the Scottish Privy Council in securing the King's attention. In any case Sir George Hay, a member of the Scottish Privy

---

[1] Willson, p. 99.

[2] A. Friis, *Alderman Cockayne's Project and the Cloth Trade; The Commercial Policy of England in its Main Aspects, 1603–1625* (London, O.U.P., 1927), p. 292.

[3] *Commons Debates, 1621*, iii. 270. Glass was included in the final list (Add. MS. 14031, fols. 43–43ᵛ) as number nineteen out of twenty.

[4] *Commons Debates, 1621*, ii. 423.

[5] The Commons had already been forced to retreat over the impeachment of Sir Francis Mitchell, one of the patentees for inns, and of Sir Robert Floyd.

[6] Price, pp. 166–8. The full text of the proclamation is printed.

Council, under whose patent they were operating, secured from the King (14 June 1621) a licence to import glass from Scotland in any amount without the prior consent of the Glass Commissioners.[1] This was followed in a few days by a Council order[2] to the effect that Mansell's patent should remain in force until his return from sea, and that in the meantime all other glass furnaces should be suppressed. Noting that importation from Scotland would deprive Mansell of some profit, however, since the Scottish patentees paid no high rent to the Crown and could undersell Mansell, the order said that by the King's pleasure payments to the Crown and to the other shareholders in the patent should be suspended until the matter was finally decided.[3]

III. THE MONOPOLY UPHELD AND REISSUED

The Council's order that Mansell's patent should remain in force until his return from sea was designed to counteract the impression that the action of the Commons in ordering its suspension was valid. Word had quickly spread that the patent was no longer in force. Acting upon that assumption, a number of glassmakers (some of whom had been present at the hearings in the Commons)—the Vinions, Liscourt, Bristow, William Beare, and Edward Hensey[4]—immediately set up new glasshouses. Mansell's own sub-contractors stopped paying their rents, and merchants began to import glass from abroad. Lady Mansell appealed to the Privy Council for enforcement of their order that the patent should stand, and on 10 July warrants went out for the arrest of the owners of new glasshouses and for their appearance before the Council.[5] After this, most of these glassmakers seem to have complied with the order, either by accepting contracts with Mansell or by ceasing to operate, although Paul Vinion spent a few days in the Marshalsea first,[6] and Francis Bristow eluded the Council messenger. On the same day (10 July), letters were sent to Mansell's lessees, seven in all,[7] instructing them to make regular payments to Lady Mansell or to come before the Council to explain their refusal. Again most of them complied without further protests, although Bigo and Clavell ignored the order. In November the Council sent again

---

[1] Patent Rolls 19 Jac. I, pt. 8, 14 June 1621.   [2] *A.P.C.* xxxvii. 400–1.

[3] Ibid. The order says that Mansell should be remitted '£2,800 in his payment to the King', but this must have been a misunderstanding. Mansell paid only £1,000 to the King, the balance to his partners. See below, p. 171.

[4] Liscourt and Bristow had both testified. One Edward Hensey was already Mansell's employee in Newcastle; this one had moved from Wisborough Green to Oldswinford (Stourbridge) where he died in July 1621, leaving a son of the same name. P.C.C., Prob. 11/95/20, will of Edward Hensey.

[5] *A.P.C.* xxxviii. 8.   [6] Ibid., pp. 17, 23.

[7] Ibid. The lessees were Abraham Bigo, Paul Tysack, John Squire, John Moose, Edward Percival, John and Isaac De Houx, apparently working separate furnaces. Sir William Clavell, though not formally Mansell's lessee received a similar letter from the Council. Clavell MS., B2/4.

for Clavell, Bigo, and Bristow and in addition summoned Bungar, Dines, and a glassmaker named John Nymm.[1] Dines, who was probably importing glass, soon obeyed the Council's instructions. Nymm had to be imprisoned in the Marshalsea for a few days before he would comply.[2] The fires in Bristow's furnace near Wigan in Lancashire were finally extinguished forcibly,[3] but the resistance of Clavell and Bigo was to continue for a long time.

In the meantime Bungar tried another scheme for thwarting Mansell. During the summer of 1621 he and John Worrall (a drinking-glass maker trained at Blackfriars under Robson and a member of the Scottish glass firm), petitioned the Council with new proposals. Bungar's petition asked that Mansell's patent should be declared void on the grounds that the Commons had judged it a grievance, and that Bungar and 'other English natives' should be permitted to make green glass in return for an annual rent to the Crown of £500.[4] Worrall's petition 'on behalfe of himselfe and other glassmakers' unnamed, increased the offer to £1,000 and asked for the privilege of making Venice glass, as well as green glass of all types.[5] Though the two appeared to be separate offers—as Mansell assumed when recounting the incident[6]—Bungar himself said that Worrall's petition was a joint offer which incorporated his own and that the rent offered was higher in order to cover the privilege of making every kind of glass.[7] He also said several years later that he and Worrall were not asking for a monopoly but only for the 'free use of their trade for themselves and other natives'.[8] Such a claim can hardly be substantiated by the wording of the petitions, which asked for assurances that they would not be 'disturbed by foriners and others not brought up in that mistery unles it be from Scotland onely', a clear reference to Mansell, his English managers who had not been trained as glassmakers, and his Italian workmen. Moreover it is difficult to see how they expected to realize enough profit to pay the high Crown rent without some sort of monopoly, legal or contrived, which would enable them to force competing glassmakers into subjection or into leasing arrangements. The exact nature of their scheme remains obscure, since it was never put into operation. Both petitions were refused: as Mansell said, the Council saw no reason for issuing a new monopoly to the men who had been attacking the current one, especially since Bungar clearly wanted to return to the use of wood as fuel.

A last effort to secure cancellation of the patent was made when Parliament re-convened in November 1621. Since matters of political impor-

---

[1] A.P.C. xxxviii. 91.   [2] Ibid., p. 16.
[3] Ibid., pp. 47, 113.   [4] S.P. 14/124, no. 111.
[5] Ibid., no 110. Both petitions are undated, but a later statement by Bungar (S.P. 14/162, no. 231 A) indicates that both were sent in during the summer of 1621, and that his preceded Worrall's.
[6] S.P. 14/124, no. 231 B.   [7] Ibid., no. 231 A.   [8] Ibid.

tance were uppermost in the minds of the members, and the royal proclamation of July had abolished the most unpopular patents, much less
was heard in this short session about monopolies. On 18 December, however, it was reported that certain grievances had been considered in
committee, including the glass patent.[1] As a result of a resolution passed
that day, the Commons sent a request to the Lord Treasurer asking that he
should influence the King to suppress the patent for glass.[2] The King,
angry with the Commons over the matter of privilege, was hardly in a
mood to take the request seriously and the patent stood, as had been
ordered in June.

In the meantime Sir Robert, who had been commanded to return to
England in July, more for naval and diplomatic reasons than to defend
his monopoly, arrived during the late summer. His privileges were still
intact, offenders were being prosecuted, and glass that was illegally imported in June had been ordered to be sequestered and delivered to his
own agents.[3] But the clique which opposed him—Bungar, Dines, Worrall,
and Clavell—had scored one triumph, for glass could be freely imported
from their Scottish firm. By July large amounts of common green drinking
glasses and window glass were arriving from Scotland, consigned to either
Dines or Clavell.[4] Upon his return Mansell also began to import, though
the Council had not given him permission: he brought in from France
an even larger number of coarse drinking glasses than had come from
Scotland, and also some glass bottles and bowls. Several merchants,
including Thomas Robinson, the shopkeeper who had owned a share in
the Ratcliffe glasshouse for a time and who was still retailing Mansell's
glass, imported substantial quantities of fine crystal drinking glasses from
Venice and some looking-glass plates. Since Mansell's firm was at the
same time importing large amounts of barilla,[5] a soda used only in the
making of crystal, production at his furnaces can hardly have ceased or
even lessened to any extent, yet neither he nor the Council made any
move to stop importation. The explanation for the importation by
Mansell, his friends, and his enemies, once the Council began ignoring
the ban on importation, clearly lies in the price. Mansell's glass could not
be sold at prices comparable to that coming from either Scotland or the
continent so long as he was obliged to carry high overheads in the form
of the Crown rent and dividends due to his partners on their holdings of
watered stock.[6] These dues had been temporarily suspended in June
1621[7] at the same time as the proclamation allowing importation for that
very reason, but it was understood that the respite would stand only until

[1] *J.H.C.* i. 668, 18 Dec. 1621.　　　　　　[2] S.P. 14/124, no. 58, 19 Dec. 1621.
[3] *A.P.C.* xxxviii. 17, 16 July 1621.
[4] Port Books, E. 190/24/4, London, English merchants, 1620-1.
[5] Ibid.　　　　　　　　　　　　[6] *A.P.C.* xxxviii. 329.
[7] Ibid., xxxvii. 400-1.

DEG—E

Mansell's return, when the entire patent was to be reconsidered. For over a year nothing was done, but in October 1622 Mansell sent in a petition asking that the matter should be settled without delay.

The Privy Council considered his petition at a full meeting on 12 October, and 'in regard of the great importance of this business' referred it to a committee, composed of the four Glass Commissioners (Lennox, Hamilton, Arundel, and Pembroke) and in addition Lionel Cranfield (recently made Lord Treasurer and Earl of Middlesex), the Earl of Carlisle, Viscount Grandison, and Sir Richard Weston (the Chancellor of the Exchequer).[1] Cranfield had taken an active part in the impeachment of Bacon in the recent Parliament and had also attacked the monopoly policy as a restraint on free trade. The committee made several proposals to Mansell[2] in an attempt to meet the objections of the House of Commons, and heard his replies. In February 1623 they made their report.[3] They were not in favour of upholding the old patent 'because it hath been complained of in Parliament as a grievance', yet they found Mansell a 'deserving servant' who had been abused by his opponents and was still in debt. They proposed, therefore, that a new patent should be granted to him alone, forbidding the making of glass with wood and freeing him from payment of any rent to the King, but permitting free importation of all sorts of glass subject to an imposition out of which the King could make up the loss of the rent. The Council agreed to the report and ordered that the King should be informed and urged to act accordingly.

The provision for importation in the proposed patent met the principal objection of the merchant class to the old patent. Bungar and his friends could be expected to continue their opposition; but the Commissioners stated that numerous petitions and certificates from the glass-sellers, looking-glass makers, glaziers, and spectacle-makers presented in and since the last Parliament had convinced them that the glass made by Mansell was as good as or better than that made with wood and that there was 'sufficient store made not only to serve England but also to serve other countries if need were'.[4] As a result of their report, the Council continued the suppression of sporadic new glasshouses, some of which may have been wood-burning,[5] and ordered John Worrall and others to stop troubling the Council with petitions against Sir Robert Mansell.[6]

Since the new patent was to apply to Sir Robert alone, it was to be

[1] *A.P.C.* xxxviii. 329–30; S.P. 14/162, no. 231 B, Mansell's account, which states that Prince Charles was present at this meeting.

[2] *A.P.C.* xxxviii. 329–30.

[3] Ibid., pp. 406–7, 5 Feb. 1622/3.

[4] Price, p. 219, from the preamble to the patent of 1623; he prints the patent in full, pp. 214–215. The preamble reviews the report of the committee and the petitions which they examined.

[5] *A.P.C.* xxxvii. 423. The warrant mentions the proclamation forbidding the use of wood in glassmaking.

[6] Ibid., p. 465, 8 Apr. 1623.

expected that some of the holders of the nine shares in the old patent would protest. Lady Vere, wife of Sir Horace Vere, wrote to her brother-in-law, Viscount Conway, who was one of the principal secretaries of State, that she had inherited a share in the patent from her brother, Sir Thomas Tracy, and that since it seemed likely that annual payments to her would stop, she wanted the matter heard before the Council.[1] Conway recommended her petition to the Earl Marshal,[2] and after some delay a hearing was held.[3] Besides Lady Vere, Percival (the inventor of the coal process), Sir Edward Leech, and Sir Richard Smith[4] were heard; but the Council found no cause to change their course. They ordered the new patent to proceed, and 'as for the interest and losse pretended by the said patentees, if they have suffered any (which did not appeare unto the Boarde) the Lordships leave them to such course of lawe or equitie as they shall think fit to take'.[5] Actually Mansell did not stop all payments to his shareholders, for three years later he gave as a reason for the continuance of his patent the fact that its overthrow would cause loss to the 'old patentees', who, so long as he managed the business, were 'sufficiently secured'.[6] This statement, together with the statement of the Council that they could see no justice in the complaints, leads one to suppose that after he was granted the patent of 1623 Mansell paid only those shareholders whose shares represented actual investments and paid them in proportion to the investment made. Percival had probably not contributed any capital.

The sealing of the new patent occurred on 22 May 1623. The policy which it embodied was clearly an improvement over that in the patent of 1615. At last Mansell was free of unproductive overheads, and could hope to recoup some of the losses which he still claimed to be incurring. Unrestricted importation from Scotland and elsewhere would operate as a check on prices and satisfy the merchants. But Mansell still faced troubles, in spite of the fact that his monopoly was intact so far as rival glassmakers in England were concerned. Bungar remained adamant in opposition, and began again his endless petitions;[7] several glassmakers persisted in setting up wood-burning furnaces, and were called before the Council;[8] and Sir William Clavell persisted in circumventing Mansell's restrictions on the sale of drinking glasses in London, and in enticing Mansell's workmen to move to the Scottish glasshouses.

[1] S.P. 14/138, no. 32, Mary, Lady Vere, to Conway, 13 Feb. 1622/3.
[2] S.P. 12/214 (Conway's letter book), p. 7.
[3] A.P.C. xxxviii. 443–4, 450, 464.
[4] For the transfer of shares, see below, p. 172.
[5] A.P.C. xxxviii. 464.   [6] S.P. 16/521, no. 148.
[7] HMC Fourth Report, p. 283, Earl de la Ware MSS., 'Petition of Isaac Bungard for himself and other glassmakers . . .', 'Another petition from the same', dated 1623.
[8] A.P.C. xxxviii. 423. The places mentioned were Bradfield in Staffordshire, Hawkeley in Lancashire, and Raulborne in Denbigh.

The case concerning Clavell which Mansell brought before the Privy Council in the summer of 1623 was complicated. Mansell complained[1] that Clavell had not obeyed the Council order of February 1621, which had instructed him to enter into the same contract with Mansell for the glass-works in Purbeck as had Bigo; and that although Clavell and Bigo were in fact partners, Clavell had continued to ship large quantities of drinking glasses to London to the detriment of Mansell's other glassworks. More-over the rent due to Mansell had not been paid for two and a half years, since the time of the order. Clavell answered that instead of entering into the contract he had renounced his interest in the glasshouse on his estates; and though he readily admitted to selling glass since that time in London, he said that he came by it not as part-owner of the furnace but 'by some other title'. Technically Clavell was correct, for as noted earlier, he had indeed dissolved his original partnership with Bigo and entered into new arrangements by which he received finished glass in payment for rent, coal, and other supplies.[2] The arrangement had been made so that he could circumvent the Council order, and it left Bigo far worse off financially than he had been under the first arrangement. As a result Bigo was forced to give Clavell larger and larger amounts of the glass, and he could not afford to pay Mansell's rent, for which he was solely responsible. Most of these facts must have come out in the hearing, for after long debate the Council found Clavell's defence 'illusory' and ordered the furnace to be destroyed and the glass seized by Mansell's agents.[3]

The second charge, made against Clavell and John Worrall jointly, that they had 'seduced' workmen from Mansell's factories to work in Scotland at higher wages, had also been made in February 1621. Clavell had then been ordered to stop such practices. In this second hearing he denied that he had violated the order, and claimed instead that Mansell had enticed his own workmen from Wemyss to work in England.[4] The Council referred these allegations to Sir William Beecher, Clerk of the Council, for further investigation and examination of witnesses. Two weeks later Beecher reported entirely in favour of the truth of Mansell's assertions.[5] Clavell and Worrall were present in person; but after hearing what they had to say for themselves, the Council found them guilty of disregarding the Council's previous directive, and ordered them both to be committed to the Marshalsea, where Clavell remained for the better part of the summer.[6] The Council then issued to Mansell a letter of assistance, stating that although by the declaration of the old patent to be void and the issue of the new patent to Mansell, all former contracts were

---

[1] *A.P.C.* xxxix. 11–12.

[2] Exch. K.R., Depositions by Commission, E. 134/22/Jac. I/Eas. 24, *Mansell* v. *Clavell*, depositions of John Jenkins (Clavell's clerk), and others.

[3] *A.P.C.* xxxix. 11–12.   [4] Ibid.

[5] Ibid., pp. 34–5, 27 June 1623.   [6] Ibid., pp. 34, 82.

cancelled, no one was to presume to make glass without entering into a new contract with Mansell. In order to make certain that cases like Clavell's were covered, the letter further stated that no one was to rent buildings or grounds to glassmakers or to sell them coal unless they were satisfied that such persons were lawfully licensed by Mansell and were keeping their agreements.[1] Nevertheless, Bigo's back rent was still not paid and he continued to make glass.

Since the non-payment of the rent was a legal matter enforceable by the courts, the Council referred Mansell to the Court of Exchequer, where he secured a writ against Bigo for the arrears. Clavell's brother bribed the Under-sheriff of Dorset to ignore the writ for some six or seven weeks,[2] until finally Mansell's lawyer went down from London, and after some harsh words, saw to it that the writ was executed and Bigo's furnace was actually pulled down. Bigo then left for Ireland, where he signed a lease for a new glasshouse and happily seems to have prospered.[3] Mansell was still unsatisfied in respect of Bigo's rent arrears, which the glass seized at the Purbeck works would not cover, and he also claimed damages for the sale of Bigo's drinking glasses in London, contrary to his contracts. Consequently he pressed his suit against Clavell in the Court of Exchequer[4] for both the arrears and the damages. When the case had dragged on for two full years without a decision, in 1625 he began yet another suit against Clavell in the Court of King's Bench. Clavell then petitioned the Council,[5] asking that both suits should be dismissed, since he had been ruined financially and punished enough for his defiance of Mansell. Perhaps his petition was granted—but in any case Mansell had effectively enforced his right to enter into restrictive contracts with his lessees, and glassmaking on Clavell's estates had ceased.

The overthrow of the Bigo–Clavell glasshouse was a test case and a warning to other glassmakers. For a time Mansell's business proceeded peaceably. When Parliament convened again in 1624, however, there was another attempt to destroy the glass monopoly by action of Parliament, though the threat was never as great as in 1621. Since Buckingham and the Prince had returned from Spain and wished to call off the unpopular

[1] Ibid., pp. 57–8.

[2] Exch. K.R., Barons' Depositions, E. 133/84/64, *Mansell* v. *Clavell*, deposition of Richard Robson; Exch. K.R., Depositions by Commission, E. 135/22 Jac. I/Eas. 24. *Mansell* v. *Clavell*, deposition of John Harbin, Under-sheriff of Dorset.

[3] Westropp, p. 11. Bigo leased land from the overlord of Birr Castle on 9 Oct. 1623, and arranged to buy wood for his glasshouse. Philip Bigo, no doubt a descendant, owned glasshouses and land near Birr Castle in the 1660s (ibid., p. 32), although another named Anthony Bigo returned to the Stourbridge area about the same time (Guttery, p. 9).

[4] This was the case to which both the Barons' Depositions (E. 133/84/64) and the Depositions by Commission (E. 135/22 Jac. I/Eas. 24) frequently cited in this work pertain.

[5] Clavell MS. B2/6, 'Petition of Sir William Clavell to the Council; undated but clearly *c*. 1625. In the petition Clavell mentions both suits: the records of that in King's Bench have not been found, but the complexity of legal records is such that they may still exist.

negotiations for the Prince's marriage to the Spanish Infanta, the Commons were in a somewhat better mood. Moreover, the worst of the monopolies had been abolished by royal decree. Also, Sir Robert was present in person as a member for his native Glamorganshire, and he was popular with some of the other members, since he was known as an opponent of Buckingham even though his open opposition to the military policy of the favourite was not to begin until 1626.[1] In the Parliament of 1621 the Commons had passed a bill against monopolies, but the House of Lords had thrown it out during the autumn session.[2] Substantially the same measure in somewhat altered form was re-introduced in 1624, and without much difficulty passed both Houses and received the royal assent.[3] In the substance this law, known as the Statute of Monopolies, declared that all monopolies consisting of commissions, licences, and patents for the sole buying, making, working, or using of any commodity were against the law.[4] It did, however, exempt chartered companies, and patents for new manufactures and new inventions, so that the beginning of the modern patent law was laid down. All such patents, however, were to be subject to the test of the common law. Nine grants already made were specifically exempt from the provisions of the statute, including the one to Sir Robert Mansell.

As in 1621, Sir Edward Coke took the lead in drawing up the provisions of the bill. On 19 April he reported from a conference with the Lords about the bill and mentioned that certain exceptions should be made to the general provisions.[5] Mansell's patent was among those ordered to be brought in so that its provisions might be studied. Three days later the House considered all patents to be exempted, as well as the provisions of the bill itself,[6] and on 1 May Coke reported on the completed bill and urged its approval. The meagre report of his speech gives no indication of his reasons for granting immunity to patents which three years earlier he had condemned, except that he wanted them included as exceptions 'not in Love to these Patents, but to the Passage of the Bill'.[7] He must have judged that the House would not pass the bill without the exceptions, most of which were for industrial enterprises such as saltpetre and gunpowder, and the making of ordnance and shot. Several were associated with the increased use of coal: that to the Hostmen of Newcastle-upon-Tyne, the patent for alum (like glass a relatively new industry in England), Lord Dudley's patent for iron-making with coal, and Man-

---

[1] *DNB*, 'Sir Robert Mansell'; Willson, p. 184. Mansell attacked Buckingham 'with sume violence and more heate then judgment' in 1626.

[2] *J.H.L.* iii. 177, 1 Dec. 1621.

[3] *J.H.C.* i. 691, 696, 703, 704, 710, 711; *J.H.L.*, iii. 362, 393–4, 397, 400, 402, 412.

[4] *Statutes of the Realm*, 21 Jac. I, cap. 3. The full text is printed in Price, pp. 135–41.

[5] *J.H.C.* ii. 771.

[6] Ibid., pp. 772, 773.   [7] Ibid., pp. 696, 781.

sell's glass patent.[1] Though this does not show that there was a general policy of exempting industries which had received monopoly privileges of some sort on the basis of the use of coal, the assumption that the change from the use of wood to coal in the glass industry was in the best interests of the nation was certainly an important factor in preserving Mansell's monopoly. There is no record of the debates on the matter, but Mansell defended his interest in a lengthy brochure[2] printed for the benefit of the members of Parliament. In addition to reviewing the case presented on his behalf in 1621 (which proved the genuineness of the invention of coal-burning glass furnaces, and the reasonable price and quality of the glass made in them), he claimed that since then he had built more furnaces to provide a better supply, and with the exception of window glass he had lowered all his prices as a result of being relieved of the Crown payments. The schedule of prices which he appended indicated the extent of the price reductions. He then related the counter-offer from Bungar and Worral for a monopoly of their own at a higher rent, as evidence that they were attacking him for reasons of private gain rather than concern for the public welfare, which was best served by his patent. The point which he stressed most was the saving of that valuable national resource, wood—both timber, and small wood used for fuel—effected by his patent.

Bungar answered Mansell in another printed pamphlet[3] which also circulated widely among members of both Houses, and John Worrall sent in a petition supporting Bungar.[4] Bungar made little attempt to dispute Mansell's price reductions, except to claim that window glass could be sold cheaper if there were no patent. Instead he denied the monopolistic nature of the counter-offer he and Worrall had made, and pleaded for the use of wood in glassmaking on the grounds that it was not really injurious to the country. Only light branches were used, he said; besides, if Parliament wished the use of wood outlawed they should pass a law to that effect, instead of which he pointed out that 'by several Actes of Parliament Iron Works, which are greater consumers of wood than glasshouses, are allowed'. Finally he pleaded for sympathy for the poverty-stricken glassmakers, who being kept from 'their lawful trade, have starved and perished, and their children doe begge their bread'. However, the House of Commons was not sympathetic to Bungar's case—though he

---

[1] The other patents exempted were those for licensing taverns, for transporting calf skins, and for making smalt, a deep-blue glass substance containing cobalt which was pulverized and used in decorating pottery. Mansell never made smalt and Abraham Baker had received the patent, 20 Feb. 16 Jac. I.

[2] S.P. 14/162, no. 231 B.

[3] Ibid., no. 231 A. In spite of the numbering it is clear from internal evidence that Mansell's was printed first.

[4] Ibid., no. 64, petition of John Worrall.

was justified in his claim that the use of wood was still permitted in iron-making.[1] The Lords were even more inclined than the Commons to favour Mansell, who had strong support from Pembroke[2] and the other Glass Commissioners, and the bill passed easily.

In spite of his failure to overturn the monopoly through blocking its exemption from the Statute of Monopolies, Bungar's opposition did not cease. From the wording of the statute it was not entirely clear whether exemption meant that the excluded patents merely escaped being automatically made void by the act, or whether they were exempt from the clause providing for testing of the validity of all patents and grants at the common law. Bungar decided upon the former interpretation, and at some time during early 1626 he began proceedings by *quo warranto* against Mansell in the common-law courts.[3] At first the Privy Council allowed Bungar to proceed with his suit, although they were of the opinion that Mansell's patent was 'agreeable to the late statute of monopolies', and warned Bungar against any encroachments on its provisions during the course of the trial.[4] But Mansell, fearful of the outcome of the trial and weary of the continuing expense of defending his rights, petitioned the King to stay the suit.[5] He stressed the damage to the King's prerogative and to the prestige of the Council which would result if a patent so often reviewed and approved by the Privy Council and specifically upheld in the recent Parliament were to be overthrown by the law courts. After due deliberation the Council concurred in his opinion and intervened to stop the proceedings.[6] The patent was ordered to stand as valid in law and the Attorney-General was notified to stay all suits or prosecutions pending against it. Bungar was also warned to stop troubling the Council with petitions, and not to make any further attempt to overthrow the patent by any means whatsoever.

The legal triumphs over Bungar, a representative of those who wanted to re-establish wood-burning glasshouses, and over Clavell, the most obstinate of the rebellious coal-burning lessees, ended Mansell's difficulties in enforcing his monopoly. Until the Long Parliament assembled there were no more prosecutions, and since Mansell was willing to hire trained men at the going rate or to finance them in semi-independent concerns, most glassmakers accepted his employment. Liscourt, who had testified

[1] Dudley had never demonstrated the effectiveness of his coal process. See Ashton, pp 11–12.

[2] Mansell was of Pembroke's 'party' and had been elected to Parliament through his influence. See Willson, pp. 183–4.

[3] I could not find the records of this case, but knowledge of it was derived from the Council order and Mansell's petition, cited in the following notes.

[4] Order in Council, 19 June 1626, quoted in Price, p. 77.

[5] S.P. 16/521, no. 148, *c.* 1626. Mansell gave other reasons than damage to the prerogative, but they are all familiar.

[6] S.P. 16/41, no. 37, 6 Dec. 1626.

against him in 1621, seems to have been employed at Newcastle,[1] and Bristow is found in 1631 on the estates of Thomas Wentworth, later first Earl of Strafford, as Mansell's lessee.[2] For at least ten years there were no further complaints of a scarcity of window glass or of its high price.

Though Mansell controlled the production of glass in England, importation of all kinds of glass was freely permitted by the terms of his patent of 1623 and by orders of the Council. The possibility of competition from Scotland, where glasshouses were still operating, or from the continent was no problem for Mansell in window glass, for none at all came from Scotland in 1626 and very little from the continent.[3] Clavell was importing very large quantities of drinking glasses from Scotland in that year, however, and other merchants were also importing large numbers from France, Flanders, and Venice.[4] Mansell's own production was low, and he blamed his troubles not on price competition, but on the regularity with which Clavell attracted to Scotland workmen from Mansell's furnaces,[5] in spite of the Council orders intended to suppress this practice. He finally determined to solve the problem by buying out the one enterprise which he could not otherwise control, and in 1627 he purchased from Sir George Hay the patent rights for Scotland for £250 per annum, using Thomas Robinson as his agent. He shut down the drinking-glass furnace in Scotland immediately in order to secure the return of the workmen— although, according to Mansell's story, they were so disaffected that they deliberately made bad glass and he was forced to send to Mantua for a new group.

Drinking glasses could still be imported from the continent, but for several years the numbers were not large enough to bother Mansell's sales. About 1630, however, a man named Vecon who was Mansell's 'principall clarke' absconded to France with all the accounts and much of the firm's money.[6] With the stolen money as capital, and using the technical knowledge he had learned in Mansell's employ, Vecon set up a drinking-glass factory across the Channel intended to supply the English market. For labour he hired most of Mansell's staff from Broad Street. Mansell immediately complained to the Privy Council that fourteen glass-blowers, all Italians, had 'on the suddaine runne away', and he asked for a diligent search both on land and in all ships leaving England.[7] The fugitives were never apprehended, however, and soon such large amounts of drinking glasses in *façon de Venise* crystal were being imported and sold

---

[1] All Saints, Newcastle-upon-Tyne, P.R. The names of several Liscourts, often with the designation 'glassmaker', appear well into the Restoration period.

[2] Straff. MS. 20/30, Marris to Wentworth, 12 Apr. 1631.

[3] Port Books, E. 190/131/3, London, English merchants, 1626.

[4] Ibid.   [5] S.P. 16/282, no. 99.   [6] Ibid.

[7] *A.P.C.* xlv. 336. The Italians included John Maria del Aqua, who had once before left Mansell's employ for Scotland.

in London that once again his sales were damaged. Mansell's petitions to
the Council resulted in a new order, given on 25 June 1630,[1] which
altered the previous order of February 1623 regarding importation. When
the previous order was made, their Lordships said, there was little importation from France and Flanders in drinking glasses; but because of
the competition from Vecon's establishment, no further importation of
drinking glasses or looking-glasses was to be permitted, except from
Venice itself. Nothing was said about window glass, common green glass,
or bottles, since Mansell could meet competition in these areas, and after
the order the Broad Street factory resumed production, presumably with
new workmen.

IV. EXTENSION OF THE MONOPOLY AND THE FINAL YEARS

After 1630 a decade of moderate prosperity for the monopoly began.
Mansell's numerous glasshouses were supplying the English market
adequately in window glass, common green drinking glasses, spectacles,
and bottles, and by about 1633 there was even a surplus for exportation
in small quantities.[2] Such glass as was imported, though small in quantity
was sizeable in value, for it consisted of articles in the luxury category—
beads, delicate Venetian stemmed ware, and some fine looking-glasses
and plates.[3] Obviously Mansell was still having some difficulty in the
production of crystal, in the form of both fine drinking glasses and plates
for looking-glasses. It is doubtful whether he ever regained a staff of
Italian workmen who could fashion wares intricate enough to compete
with those of Murano. A good many Englishmen had been trained, however, and Broad Street certainly turned out large numbers of simpler
drinking glasses, which sold at cheaper rates than those from Venice.[4]
Mansell invested heavily in improving the quality of his crystal plates for
looking-glasses during the 1630s (the quality of these had apparently
fallen off since the favourable comments of the Venetian Ambassador in
1620[5]), and in this he had notable success, as the increase in the numbers
of craftsmen engaged in the finishing processes, and the exportation of
some of their wares attest.[6]

Although the Privy Council, when they issued the new patent to
Mansell in 1623, had agreed that the glass monopoly should not be
renewed when it expired in 1638, the financial straits of the Crown during
the years when Charles I ruled without Parliament prompted negotiations
for an extension. Other monopolies operating under royal grants, the
alum and soap monopolies in particular, were yielding substantial revenue

---

[1] *A.P.C.* xlvi. 27–8, no. 91.

[2] Port Books, E. 190/38/7, London, exports, 1633–4. The market and the amounts of glass
imported and exported are discussed at length in Chaps. IX, X.

[3] Port Books, E. 190/38/5, London, Imports, English, 1633–4.

[4] S.P. 16/282, no. 99.   [5] See above, p. 82.   [6] See Chap. X.

during the 1630s,[1] and the King's advisers, Wentworth in particular,[2] saw no reason why the glass monopoly should not make its contribution. Mansell was agreeable, provided the terms were satisfactory, and at some time during 1632 Charles I promised Mansell an indenture prolonging his monopoly in return for an annual rent of £1,000, with a proviso that the importation of all kinds of glassware was to be prohibited except from Venice and Scotland. Importation from Venice was to be solely in the hands of Mansell's agents, and since Mansell still controlled the patent for glassmaking in Scotland,[3] he would be once again in complete control of the English market.

Before the arrangements were complete, however, Mansell became alarmed about the possible grant of a rival glass monopoly. Sir Percival Hart, who had held the reversion of Bowes's patent for crystal-making in both England and Ireland,[4] had petitioned the King for a new monopoly of glassmaking in Ireland,[5] with the intention of selling in the English market, as Robson had done twenty years earlier. Mansell wrote to Wentworth, asking for his help in stopping Hart's project, for he claimed that 'importation from thence will ruyne the work here'. In order to supply Ireland adequately with glass, he offered to set up as many glasshouses as necessary himself in whatever locations Wentworth thought desirable. Wentworth was willing to stop Hart's project;[6] but with an eye to increasing the King's revenues still further, he suggested incorporating Ireland in the terms of the new indenture, and raising the total Crown rent to £1,500, of which £250 was to be expressly paid 'for the Irish privilege'. However, this did not end Mansell's difficulties: next he heard that 'some of great power' opposed him, and were offering to pay even more rent for a glass monopoly with the same privileges as those proposed for his own.[7] For the benefit of the Council he drew up a lengthy defence of his own claims, which stressed that he, if anyone, deserved the monopoly on the basis of the great costs, losses and difficulties he had encountered in establishing the coal-burning furnaces on a profitable basis.[8] Twice the Council debated the matter at length when the King was present, and finally Charles himself ordered the passing of the grant.

[1] Price, p. 42.

[2] Straff. MS. 18/65, 21 June 1638. Mansell to Wentworth. This letter implies that the suggestion for the extension with new terms had come from Wentworth.

[3] S.P. 16/467, no. 66, Mansell's statement, 10 Sept. 1640. Mansell said that he was then paying £300 to 'my Lord of Kenool (formerly Sir George Hay) at his Majesties order' for the Scottish patent. The original patent to Hay should have expired in 1631, but apparently it had been reissued, and Mansell forced to pay £50 more per annum than the original purchase price.   [4] See above, p. 43.

[5] Straff. MS. 13/165, Mansell to Wentworth, 4 Jan. 1632/3.

[6] Straff. MS. 18/65, Mansell to Wentworth, 21 June 1638.

[7] Ibid.   [8] S.P. 16/282, no. 99, Mansell's statement, 28 Jan. 1634/5.

The indenture, dated 1 March 1635,[1] incorporated the provisions that Mansell had requested (including glassmaking in Ireland) at the agreed rent of £1,500. It was followed shortly by a proclamation prohibiting the importation of all sorts of glass made in foreign parts, except from Scotland.[2] Mansell kept his part of the bargain, and until the Scots invaded Newcastle in 1640 the rent seems to have been paid.[3] The officers of the Exchequer, hoping to enrich the royal treasury further, soon lodged a suit against Mansell in Chancery, attempting to prove arrears in the Crown rent dating back to the first Zouch patent for the coal process in 1611; but Mansell was able to establish the fact that it had all been paid[4] except when it had been specifically remitted by the Council, or when none was due, as was the case under the terms of the patent of 1624. It is evident from this case that the King's interest in the glass industry was purely financial. Indeed, apart from the Crown's need for revenue, there was no possible justification for the extension of the monopoly in 1635 to Mansell or anyone else. By 1635 the coal process was well established and Mansell's company was solvent; but, thanks to the King, free competition in the industry was not yet in sight.

Mansell was growing old and had lost much of his energy. Soon after 1635 an extended illness delayed his attempt to set up new glassworks in Ireland in fulfilment of his pledge to Wentworth. Moreover, there was considerable opposition in Ireland itself. Burning coal there was clearly uneconomic and the furnaces would have to be fired by wood; but in view of the extent of the woodlands in Ireland, it is surprising that the objections were based on the supposition that new glass furnaces would consume valuable timber.[5] Mansell asserted that he intended to burn not timber, but brushwood, which had been offered him free in return for clearing it. (This was the justification that Bungar had presented in 1621, in very different circumstances.) In a querulous letter to Wentworth, Mansell came close to rebuking him for permitting costly delays in his attempt to fulfil an obligation which Wentworth himself had fastened upon him. Even for Wentworth's help in forestalling Hart and the others Mansell said that he could not return more thanks 'than can . . . [be] expected from me beyonde ye merit of a glassemaker, though I enjoye ye title and fee of Vice-Admerall of England'.[6] Mansell also complained that he was

---

[1] The full text dated 1 Mar. 1634/5 is printed in Price, pp. 226–41, but Price misinterprets the date as 1634 not 1635. [2] *Cal. S.P.D.* ccxciv (1635), 429, 14 Oct. 1635.

[3] F. C. Dietz, 'The Recipts and Issues of the Exchequer during the Reigns of James I and Charles I', *Smith College Studies in History*, xiii, no. 4 (July 1928), 150. Payments are not shown for every year, but the records are incomplete. Mansell said in 1640 that he had paid regularly (S.P. 16/467, no. 66).

[4] Chancery, C. 180/226, no. 2, 'The case touchinge the arreares due upon the severall patentes for the glasse business'.

[5] Straff. MS. 17/296, 23 Feb. 1637, Mansell to Wentworth.

[6] Ibid., 18/65, 21 June 1638, Mansell to Wentworth.

having great difficulty in realizing enough profit from his English glass-houses to offset the Crown rent which he had already paid, and which he 'labored to recover' so that he might 'dye with a conscience unburthened with debt'. Clearly he found the new privilege burdensome, and had sought it only to protect himself from a monopoly granted to others.

Mansell's method for recovering the capital paid out in revenue to the Crown was already apparent—he had raised the price of window glass by 2s. in the case, the first increase in twenty years. The Glaziers Company promptly complained to the Council of the higher prices and also of the 'badnesse and scarcity of glasse'.[1] In addition they said that they wanted the glass to be shipped to London in large sheets, instead of being cut into quarrels in Newcastle, as had been the practice for some time. Their Lordships immediately called in Mansell to justify himself. The scarcity was brought on, he said, by the latest visitation of the plague at Newcastle; but he had replaced the workmen who had died, and there was plenty of glass in his storehouse there waiting for shipping, which he was unable to obtain.[2] The price rise he blamed on the increased cost of coal—though surely the necessity of paying the Crown rent was at least as important a factor.

Their Lordships thought Mansell's answers were satisfactory concerning the price and the scarcity. They were not satisfied about the quality, however, and stated that 'by experience in their owne buildings and others in the ordinary use of glass [they] found that the same was not so faire, soe cleare nor soe strong in wearing as the same was wont to be'. Mansell was accordingly warned to attend to the quality of his glass and to bring it back to reasonable standards. Concerning the cutting of glass, they sided with the glaziers, and ordered that the glass should be shipped to London uncut, and the master cutters should be recalled to London. The distribution in London was to be removed from the jurisdiction of Launcelot Hobson, Mansell's agent, and entrusted to representatives selected by the Master and Wardens of the Glaziers Company until they had satisfied their needs, when Hobson could dispose of the remainder. Mansell's objection that, in that case, he could not recover the cuttings for cullet was met by an order to the glaziers to deliver all their cuttings to Sir Robert 'at reasonable and indifferent rates', and in no circumstances to export any. The moving of the cutting operation to London would seem to be a most uneconomic measure, for the cut glass weighed less, packed better, and was less liable to breakage, beside making unnecessary the re-shipping of the cullet back to Newcastle. The Master and Wardens of the London company, however, and the more prosperous glaziers who dealt in wholesale window glass, profited from control of the cutting

[1] S.P. 16/378, no. 58, 12 Jan. 1638, account of proceedings in the Privy Council.
[2] Ibid.

operation; and Bungar and Dines, who were still members of the company,[1] had special reason to welcome the new arrangement, for no doubt they had felt that Hobson had discriminated against them in the distribution of glass, as a result of the old enmities.

At about the same time as the Glaziers Company produced their petition, the newly formed Company of Glass-sellers of London sent in another, which was extremely favourable to the Mansell monopoly. Far from criticizing Mansell's glass in any way, they were at great pains to point out the benefits of his patent, and the large quantities of glass which, under its terms, were not only sold in England but 'much thereof transported by them into foreign parts'.[2] Their grievance was rather against the Court of Alderman of the City of London, who had refused to enrol the charter of incorporation which the glass-sellers had recently secured from the King for a substantial price.[3] Their new charter gave them a monopoly of the retail trade in drinking glasses of all kinds, glass tableware, looking-glasses, hour-glasses, and all types of glass objects except spectacles and window glass, which were already controlled by separate companies. In addition they were to control the finishing processes in the making of looking-glasses and hour-glasses, and all artisans who practised such trades were to be forced to become members.[4] The new company was dominated by shop-keepers who dealt in glass, among them Thomas Robinson, all of whom had previously belonged to other London companies, and who wished to eliminate the army of petty chapmen who roamed the London streets as well as the countryside. They could not enforce their newly bought privileges, however, and compel independent retailers to be translated from other companies without enrolment of the charter. Their petition was addressed to the King: but although he had been willing enough to sell them a charter, its enforcement against the wishes of the City was almost impossible at that time. There is no record of any answer from Charles or the Council, and the glass-sellers had to wait until 1665 before their charter became effective.[5]

Five members of the company who were hour-glass makers tried a different approach. They petitioned the Council in December 1637,[6] complaining of the poor quality and high price of the vials which they used in making hour-glasses, and also that Mansell's agents sold not only to

---

[1] Ashdown, p. 114, naming the Assistants and Warden of 1638.

[2] S.P. 16/475, no. 57, 'Petition of the Master, Warden and Commonalty of the Glasse-Sellers of London'.

[3] A. L. Howard, *The Worshipful Company of Glass-Sellers of London* (London, for the Company, 1940), pp. 20–1.

[4] Guildhall MS. 5559, Ordinances of the Company of Glass-Sellers.

[5] S. Young, *History of the Worshipful Company of Glass-Sellers of London* (London, Barker, 1913), p. 21.

[6] S.P. 16/373, no. 82, 15 Dec. 1637, petition of five men describing themselves as hour-glass makers.

them, who were 'of the Company of Glass-Sellers of London', but also to others who had never served a proper apprenticeship. Since they dwelt on this last point at length, it was obvious that desire to enforce apprenticeship in the company was their chief goal. Mansell was ordered to reply to the charges and the investigation which followed vindicated his position. Their Lordships decided that the glass vials were neither bad nor dear, and the complaints on every score were 'merely clamorous'.[1] The following month Mansell's agent and the five petitioners signed an agreement for the delivery of vials at a specified price, but there was no guarantee that Mansell's glass would not be sold to others.

From the investigations of these two petitions it is clear that the price of window glass had risen, largely as a result of the new patent with its high rent to the Crown, and that the quality had deteriorated. The supply was still adequate provided shipping was available, however, for window glass was exported in 1640. That so little rise in price had occurred under monopoly conditions is worthy of note. In all other kinds of glass the price was, if anything, lower. Supplies were sufficient for export as well as for the domestic market, and—except for the finest Venetian styles which Mansell still imported to some extent—were satisfactory in quality as well. In glassware England had passed from an importing to an exporting country in less than twenty years.

The outbreak of war dealt the Mansell monopoly a blow from which it never recovered. When the Scots invaded Newcastle in the summer of 1640, work at the Newcastle glass factories abruptly ceased. In September 1640, Mansell wrote to the Privy Council that upon the approach of the Scottish army his workmen fled with their wives and children, leaving the fires in the furnaces and the pots full of metal.[2] He was obliged to pay them 'dead wages' to prevent them from leaving the country. Glass already made could not be shipped to London because of the presence of the Scottish army. In addition, a stoppage of work in the London glasshouses resulted from the interruption in the supply of coal from Newcastle. Because of these difficulties Mansell asked to be relieved of payment of the half-yearly rent due at Michaelmas; he also wanted ships to be made available to help solve his troubles. However, in the autumn of 1640 the Council had more serious matters to discuss than the state of the glass industry. Whether or not they remitted Mansell's rent, no ships were forthcoming to fetch his glass and coals from Newcastle. The stoppage of work in London naturally resulted in shortages, which several merchants attempted to relieve by once again importing in defiance of the monopoly.

[1] Ibid., Orders in Council, 12 Jan. and 3 Feb. 1637/8, attached to the petition.
[2] S.P. 16/467, no. 66, 'The state of my workes for windowe glasse seated neare Newcastle . . .' 10 Sep. 1640.

When the Long Parliament assembled in November, all sorts of grievances abounded, but the issues of religion and arbitrary government so overshadowed all others that the House of Commons had little time for considering those stemming from individual monopolies. In January 1641, however, the House of Commons received three petitions against Mansell's monopoly,[1] which were referred to the Grand Committee for Grievances on 10 February.[2] No hearing was held on the petitions for over a year. Knowing that his best hope of support lay with the Lords, Mansell petitioned the upper House in May,[3] complaining that several 'inconsiderable persons' were acting as though Parliament had already overthrown the monopoly, though in fact there had not been so much as a hearing. The Lords referred the matter to their own Committee for Petitions and ordered the offenders against the patent to appear and testify. In the meantime they issued an order (13 May 1641) that Mansell's patent should stand 'in full power and force . . . until the Parliament order the contrary'.[4] The Lords' committee was as busy as that of the Commons, however, and the promised hearings were never held.

Relying on the Lords' order that his patent should be enforced until Parliament had reviewed it and taken further action, Mansell secured the arrest and imprisonment of Richard Batson, a cutler who had been importing large quantities of glass.[5] The Lords upheld Mansell's action[6] in spite of Baton's plea that his case be transferred to the jurisdiction of the Commons' committee for a hearing.[7] In January 1642, at Mansell's request, bonds for good behaviour were taken of three more men accused of violating the terms of his patent.[8] Two of them, Francis Bristow and Jeremy Bagg, were making glass without paying rent; the third was Isaac Bungar. Whether or not Bungar had resumed glassmaking or was merely the object of Mansell's unfounded suspicions, nothing more was heard of his case.[9] Bagg and Bristow, however, refused either to put out their fires or to pay Mansell, and at his insistence the Lords heard their case in March. The result was their imprisonment for contempt of the Lords' order of the preceding May;[10] and in spite of several pet-

[1] Longleat House, Whitelock Collections, vii, fols. 254–7. There is no mention of the petitions in the *J.H.C.*

[2] Ibid.; HMC *Fourth Report*, House of Lords MSS., p. 92.

[3] House of Lords Library, House of Lords MSS., Mansell's petition, 13 May 1641.

[4] *J.H.L.* iv. 248.

[5] Ibid., p. 322; Chancery, Decree Rolls, C. 78/1212, no. 8, *Batson* v. *Lewin*. Lewin was also named in the order of 13 May 1641.   [6] *J.H.L.* iv. 335.

[7] House of Lords MSS., Batson's petition, 30 July 1641.

[8] Ibid., Affidavit of William Chapnell, 16 Jan. 1641; Longleat, Whitelock Coll. vii, fols. 254–7.

[9] Bungar died the following year at Pulborough, Sussex. Since his daughter Anne had married John Bristow 'clerk' (see Kenyon, pp. 135–6) it is possible that he was related to Francis Bristow by marriage and had been associated with him.

[10] *J.H.L.* iv. 669.

itions, asking that their case should be heard by the committee of the House of Commons, they remained in gaol for some time.[1]

In April the Commons finally took up the matter of Mansell's patent, not because the case was referred from the Lords, but because of the complaint of another merchant whose imported glass had been seized by Mansell's agents. The House ordered that his glass should be returned, subject to payment of the customs, and that the same ruling should be applied in all other cases.[2] Mansell was also ordered to bring in his patent and give his reasons for the seizure. Though Mansell sent in a petition of protest, it was ordered that he should attend the Grand Committee of Grievances the following week. There is no record of a debate on the patent in the committee, although it is likely that some discussion was held. The result was almost a foregone conclusion, given the general attitude of the Commons toward Crown monopolies: it was decided that the patent should be cancelled. On 30 May 1642 Sir Robert was ordered to surrender his patent to the Clerk of the House,[3] with the clear implication that surrender implied its demise. The Lords did not concur in the action, nor did they give further consideration to the case. At the time, the struggle over the Militia Bill was occupying the attention of both Houses and of the King, so it is not surprising that the glass patent received so little discussion. In August the King raised the royal standard at Nottingham: civil war had begun. There was now no possibility that Mansell could revive his claims. In fact the Commons suggested that he should be placed in charge of the forces in Glamorganshire, under Sir Thomas Fairfax;[4] while one of the King's advisers suggested him as a possible commander for the royal fleet.[5] Because of his age, neither suggestion was acted upon.

The cancellation of Mansell's patent did not prevent him from restoring the works at Newcastle and continuing to operate them. He faced new competition there in 1645, however, when a merchant of London and a Mr. Harris of Newcastle signed an agreement with the Common Council of Newcastle for 'two glasshouses new buylt' and part of a dock.[6] Some difficulties between Mansell and his competitors were referred to the House of Lords in the same year,[7] but it would seem that both the new and the old glasshouses flourished. Mansell, a glassmaker to the end, petitioned the Common Council for an extension of his own leases in 1652,[8] even though they had six years still to run; but he died soon

---

[1] House of Lords MSS., petitions of Bagg and Bristow, 23 Apr. 1642; 16 May 1642.
[2] *J.H.C.* ii. 523, 12 Apr. 1642.   [3] Ibid., p. 569, 30 May 1642.
[4] Ibid., p. 160; *J.H.L.* iv. 342.   [5] *DNB.* 'Sir Robert Mansell'.
[6] Newcastle-upon-Tyne, *Extracts from the Newcastle-upon-Tyne Council Minute Books, 1639–1656* (Newcastle-upon-Tyne, Northumberland Press, 1920), p. 55.
[7] *J.H.L.* iv. 328.
[8] J. Brand, *History . . . of Newcastle-upon-Tyne* (London, B. White, 1789) ii. 45.

afterwards,[1] and his furnaces eventually came into the possession of the Henseys and Tysacks,[2] who had worked them from the beginning.

After the cancellation of Mansell's patent, Bristow and Bagg seem to have been discharged from their bonds and allowed to resume glassmaking as independent men,[3] and probably the same applies to Mansell's other lessees. There is no indication of the fate of the Broad Street works, but certainly glassmaking continued in London, though hampered somewhat by uncertain transportation of coal and finished glass throughout the period of the war. Freed from the restraints of the monopoly, glass production seems to have increased during the Commonwealth, and bottle works in particular multiplied. A much larger increase in production, however, occurred during the period of the Restoration. Output of both window glass and bottles took on a new dimension, and in the field of fine glassware Ravenscroft discovered a formula for making lead crystal, which was far superior to glass made elsewhere in Europe either for tableware or for scientific instruments. The crystal was produced with coal, and it has been argued that its invention resulted from experimentation with new formulae as a result of the adoption of coal as fuel. This has never been clearly demonstrated: but certainly the breaking of old traditions and the experimentation in the industry as a result of the change to coal provided a congenial climate and a stimulus for the inventor. After the patent lapsed there was never a return in England to the use of wood as fuel in any branch of the glass industry, so the monopoly had accomplished its stated purpose. The great expansion in the number of English glass-houses and in total production during the last years of the century is in decided contrast to the French glass industry, which remained stagnant so far as the making of common glass was concerned, and the Venetian industry, which went into a long decline. The use of the cheaper fuel in England was certainly one important factor in the expansion.

It is not possible to issue any final judgement on the glass patents before other considerations have been taken into account. It could be argued, for example, that the change to coal would have occurred in England without the patents, as a result of economic pressure alone; but this can hardly be discussed before the comparative costs of using the two fuels, and the resultant prices have been investigated. What can be said here, however, is that there was some justification for the policy followed by the Crown of upholding the glass monopoly in 1621, and reissuing it in 1623 with provisions for free importation of glassware and remittance of the Crown rent. There is no reason to doubt that James I and his

---

[1] Mansell died in 1656 (*DNB*, 'Sir Robert Mansell').

[2] 'Jacob Henzey', 'William Tizacke', and 'Daniel Tittery' took a lease of the western glasshouses in Newcastle on 21 Sept. 1678. Brand, ii. 45.

[3] Longleat, Whitelock Coll. viii. 256.

advisers thought that they were acting in the best interests of the national economy by allowing special privileges which bolstered the change to coal, since Mansell's debts and Bungar's persistent opposition might otherwise at that time have forced the company into bankruptcy and delayed the changeover. The indenture of 1635, however, was certainly unwise from every point of view except that of Crown revenue—but fortunately it was swept away before much harm could result.

PART TWO

ECONOMIC ASPECTS OF GLASSMAKING

VI

TECHNICAL PROBLEMS
IN PRODUCTION

MOST of the problems that English glassmakers faced in the period under study were those that were common to all industries, such as costs, marketing, and prices. There were other, special problems in glassmaking of a technical nature, however: they must be considered first, since they have a bearing on other economic aspects of the industry. As the narrative history has made clear, the chief technical problem which was successfully solved during the period was that of the changes in the process associated with the use of coal as fuel, which, as all parties to the dispute concerning the patents for the use of coal in glassmaking agreed, involved the invention of a furnace of a new design. This controversial invention deserves careful attention; but there were also other technical problems which plagued glassmakers, some of which concerned the furnaces and the pots, regardless of the fuel burned, while others were associated with the kind and quality of the materials used, and the total proportions of the ingredients used in a batch.

I. FURNACE CONSTRUCTION AND POTS

Glassmaking as practised in this period required the application of heat in three distinct stages.[1] In the first, or 'fritting' process, sand and alkaline substances (usually potash or soda) were heated and stirred together on the floor of a furnace until they were partially fused into large lumps. In the second, or actual melting operation, the frit was broken up, mixed with cullet and sometimes with decolourizers, placed in clay pots or crucibles and subjected to a very much higher heat for a longer period during which a scum called 'sandever' was removed with a ladle. When samples showed that fusion was complete, the glass-blowers worked out the molten metal into sheets or vessels, which were then ready for the third operation, known as annealing, which consisted of subjecting the finished glass to a heat somewhat below its melting point and then cooling it very gradually in order to remove the stresses which resulted from

[1] This discussion and much else concerning the technical process is taken from A. Neri, *The Art of Glass . . .*, trans. C. Merret (London, 1662), *passim*. Merret's long commentary which follows Neri's text is based on knowledge of English glassmaking: it is cited hereafter as 'Merret'. Neri's own work, first published in Italian in 1612 and based on Italian methods is cited as 'Neri'.

manipulation of the glass and sudden cooling. This last process, which is still necessary in glassmaking, must be done carefully or glass of any composition and thickness will shatter at the least tap. It was accomplished in an oven known as a 'lehr', either by moving the glass slowly

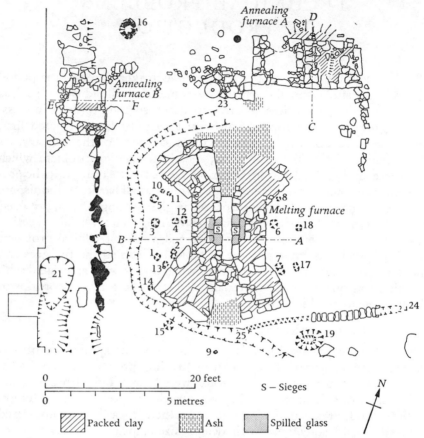

Fig. 1. Plan of an excavated glasshouse near Rosedale, Yorkshire, *c.* 1595. From D. W. Crossley and F. A. Aberg, 'Sixteenth Century Glass-making in Yorkshire' *Post-Med. Arch.* vi (1972), 119, reproduced by permission of the Society for Post-Medieval Archaeology.

down a long tunnel away from the source of heat, or by gradually reducing the heat with the glass stationary in the lehr.[1] In addition heat was necessary for firing the pots and then pre-heating them before they were filled with frit.

Since the three processes and the firing of the pots required different

[1] Both methods are still used, either by placing the glasses on a moving belt or by a thermostatically controlled lehr.

degrees of heat for different periods of time, separate furnaces were often built. From medieval times there is a clear example of this at Blunden's Wood, Surrey, where excavations revealed a working furnace and two smaller ovens, one with two compartments, intended for fritting, annealing, and pot-curing.[1] There was a similar arrangement in the glasshouse built at Jamestown in Virginia by the Polish and German glassmakers who went there in 1609.[2] When making vessel glass, forest-glass makers sometimes carried on the annealing and other heating operations in a tunnel-like extension of the main furnace, while the Venetians often combined the working and annealing processes in one furnace by the use of a tower built above the melting chamber.[3] At a few sites in England immigrant forest-glass makers built furnaces with four 'wings' or extensions at ground level,[4] whose purpose, though this is somewhat speculative, was probably pot-curing, as would be suggested by the way they are labelled in an illustration of an eighteenth-century 'English' glasshouse remarkably similar in plan to a glasshouse site in Yorkshire.[5] Heat could be drawn from the main furnace through openings in the wings, thus effecting some small savings in fuel. If the wings were also used for annealing vessels,[6] however, separate fires were usually built there and allowed to die down, since a gradual reduction in temperature is essential in annealing. For window-glass making it is certain that the Normans built separate furnaces for annealing, with horizontal slits to accommodate the finished crowns,[7] and the Lorrainers (at least when making window glass) also seem to have used separate auxiliary furnaces.[8] During the wood-burning period there was no particular incentive for window-glass makers to reduce their fuel consumption, since they needed large quantities of wood ashes, a by-product of their fires, to make their glass.[9] Vessel-glass makers,

[1] E. S. Wood, 'A Medieval Glasshouse at Blunden's Wood', *Surrey Arch. Col.* lxii (1965), 56.

[2] Harrington, pp. 25–7.   [3] See below, p. 147, and Fig. 3.

[4] Four English sites with winged furnaces are Buckholt in Hampshire, Luthery's furnace at Vann, near Godalming, Surrey, and Hutton and Rosedale in Yorkshire. See Kenyon, pp. 195–8, 215–17, figs. 17 and 20; Crossley and Aberg, *Post-Med. Arch.* vi (1972), 11–19 and plan facing p. 112.

[5] See Fig. 1 (site plan at Rosedale, Yorks.) and compare with Fig. 6, p. 152.

[6] Although he found separate annealing furnaces at Hutton and Rosedale, Crossley suggests that the wings were also used for annealing. Crossley and Aberg, *Post-Med. Arch.* vi (1972), 126.

[7] E. S. Wood, *Surrey Arch. Col.* lxv (1968),153–4.

[8] Three of the winged furnaces in England made vessel glass (Vann, Hutton, and Rosedale). The fourth (Buckholt) probably did so too: there were window-glass makers working in the vicinity, but also vessel-glass makers (the du Houx, Perne); and since there are two sites, only one of which has been excavated, the winged furnace probably belonged to vessel-glass makers. The furnace at Bishop's Wood, usually associated with Lorraine window-glass makers (see above, p. 36) and that at Jamestown, Va., which made broad glass, had separate auxiliary furnaces and no wings.

[9] The rate of consumption of wood ashes and the question of lowered costs, which Crossley attributes in part to the winged furnaces (Crossley, *EcHR*, p. 431), is discussed at length in Chap. VIII.

who seem to have used proportionately fewer ashes,[1] had more reason to combine as many heating operations in one furnace as possible, as did coal-burning glassmakers of all kinds, though they, too, built additional fires in the wings when wings were used for annealing.[2]

Whatever the annealing arrangements, the most important part of the working furnace was the central chamber. As opposed to furnaces used for smelting iron ore, glass furnaces were reverberatory in nature: in fact, glassmakers seem to have discovered the principle of the reverberatory furnace. A furnace of this type was clearly described by Theophilus as the

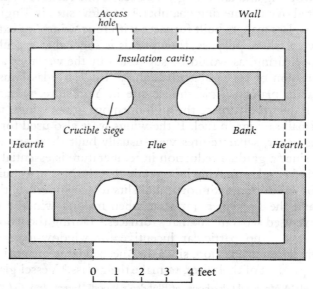

Fig. 2. Floor plan of the working furnace at Blunden's Wood, Surrey, *c.* 1350. From E. S. Wood, 'A Medieval Glasshouse at Blunden's Wood, Hambledon, Surrey', *Surr. A. Col.* lxii (1965), 54–79 and fig. 5. (Mr. Wood has since suggested a possible alternative placing of the access holes. See D. Ashurst and E. S. Wood, 'Glasshouse at Gawber and Blunden's Wood: 'A Further Note', *Post-Med. Arch.*, vii (1973), 92–4.)

usual form of glass furnace in the eleventh century,[3] and as Rhys Jenkins remarks, 'Glass technology seems to have been a thing apart and we have a long interval before we learn of the use of the reverberatory furnace in other industries.'[4] It was only during the early sixteenth century that German gun founders used such a furnace for melting bronze,[5] and none were used in the English brass and copper industry before the late seven-

---

[1] See below, p. 197.   [2] Merret, p. 244.   [3] Theophilus, Bk. II.
[4] R. Jenkins, 'The Reverberatory Furnace with Coal Fuel; 1612–1712', *Transactions of the Newcomen Society*, xiv (1933–4), 67.
[5] Ibid., p. 68.

teenth century.[1] Long before then glassmakers working in different traditions had developed distinct types of the reverberatory furnace which they introduced into England. Both in medieval times and in the late sixteenth century forest-glass makers built furnaces which were rectangular at the base, though the rounded corners and arches sometimes gave them an oval appearance.[2] Along either side of the interior there were sieges or ledges to hold the pots. The fire was built directly on the floor between the sieges, or occasionally in an elongated tunnel opening into the main furnace. The crown of the furnace was a low arch which ensured that the flames and gases continually beat down upon the metal lying in the open pots. There was no chimney; but in some furnaces, there was an opening at one end for the placement and removal of pots during the working process, in others the openings were along the sides next to the places where the pots were to stand. In either case the openings were stopped up during the melting process. When they were located on the sides there were removable coverings containing small working-holes for gathering the molten metal on blowpipes.

Frequent replacement of the pots and repair of the furnace itself were necessary, in spite of the fact that the pots were made of the best fire-clay available and the interior of the furnace itself was built of very hard stone cemented with fire-clay instead of mortar.[3] The heat was intense, especially in green-glass making,[4] and even the best clay softened under heat very little above that to which the interior of the furnace was subjected.[5] Any imperfections in fashioning the crown of the furnace increased the likelihood of cracks which quickly widened into fissures. There is an instance of a French glass furnace which collapsed twice during the first year of firing;[6] and Merret stated that the crown of a green-glass furnace often 'rends in a quarter of a year, or else furrows be made in it'.[7] Moreover, molten glass dissolves clay just as surely as water dissolves sugar,[8] though not so rapidly. The pots were constantly eaten away, and if they cracked, leakage of the glass attacked the sieges, gradually destroying them in turn. Even though broken pots were removed as quickly as possible, at best there was such frequent damage to the interior of the furnace that extensive repairs were necessary several times a year, and the life of a furnace was seldom longer than two to three years.[9]

[1] G. Hammersley, 'Technique or Economy? The Rise and Decline of the Early English Copper Industry', *Business History*, xv (1973), 20.

[2] See Fig. 2 for the plan of the furnace. Plate I indicates the external appearance.

[3] Marson, p. 45.

[4] Merret, p. 242.

[5] C. J. Phillips, *Glass: The Miracle Maker* (New York, Pitman, 1941), p. 142. The author, who was connected with the Corning Glass Company, describes modern techniques and difficulties.

[6] Scoville, p. 38.

[7] Merret, p. 245.

[8] Phillips, p. 142.

[9] Scoville, p. 37.

(A) Lower chamber of the other second furnace   (D) Its opening

(B) Middle one   (E) Round opening

(C) Upper one   (F) Rectangular opening

Fig. 3. A Venetian glasshouse of the mid-sixteenth century with one furnace cut away to show the horizontal divisions. From Georgius Agricola, *De Re Metallica*, trans. and ed. H. C. and L. H. Hoover (New York, Dover Publications, 1950), p. 589.

Furnaces were sometimes rebuilt on the same site,[1] but their short life contributed to the tendency of the glassmakers to make frequent migrations.

The working furnaces used by Italian glassmakers shared some of the characteristics of the French design, but they were larger and somewhat

(A) Arches of the second furnace

(B) Mouth of the lower chamber

(C) Windows of the upper chamber

(D) Big-bellied pots

(E) Mouth of the third furnace

(F) Recesses for the receptacles

(G) Openings in the upper chamber

(H) Oblong receptacles

Fig. 4. A similar Venetian glasshouse, showing a working furnace with an attached annealing furnace. From Agricola, p. 588.

more permanent structures. Round at the base rather than rectangular, and shaped like a large beehive, the Italian furnace was strengthened by ribs or arches which helped prevent collapse; and since the temperature required to melt *cristallo* was lower than that for green glass,[2] expensive

[1] E. S. Wood, pp. 153–4.   [2] Merret, p. 245.

(A) Blow-pipe   (B) Little window   (C) Marble   (D) Forceps
(E) Moulds by means of which the shapes are produced

Fig. 5. A Venetian glasshouse in operation, showing the tools, and clearly indicating by the smoke that there was no opening in the top. From Agricola, p. 591.

accidents from cracked pots were less frequent. Several variations of Italian furnaces, differing chiefly in the lehr and annealing arrangements, were clearly described and illustrated by Georgius Agricola, a sixteenth-century physician and mining expert who lived in Venice for two years.[1] The working furnace differed from the French forest-glass furnaces by being horizontally divided into three separate chambers.[2] The fire was built on the floor of the lower chamber, and the flames and gases entered the middle chamber through a round hole in the partition and were deflected down onto the pots by the low arched crown of the second chamber, thus making the furnace more truly reverberatory. The arched openings with their covers and working-holes resembled those in the French furnace. The third chamber was heated like the second by an opening in the centre; although there was no chimney in the top, there was sometimes a small opening in the back which opened into a separate annealing furnace, which was heated in addition by its own fire.[3] Another arrangement omitted the separate annealing furnace and made use of the top chamber itself for the lehr, with openings to make it possible to place and move about the clay receptacles containing the finished glass. The total height of the furnace was twelve feet—more than twice that of the low French furnace—and the workmen found it necessary to stand on a bench to reach the lehr.[4] Later refinements in annealing resulted in the use of a lehr in the form of a tunnel-like structure some five or six yards long, opening at one end into the tower or top chamber of the working furnace and at the other end into a separate and cooler room of the glass-house, called the 'sarosel'.[5] After the glasses had been reheated in the tower they were pulled along the lehr by hand in the receptacles. The furnace used in England by Verzelini may have been similar to those seen by Agricola; but Salter's Winchester House furnace for crystal glass, which was described by his Italian workmen,[6] had the tunnel-like lehr leading from a high tower to the sarosel room which Merret described as usual in London crystal-making glasshouses of the 1660s.[7] As we have already seen, it was in the Winchester House furnace built by Salter that coal was first used successfully,[8] after Percival had made certain modifications.

Before discussing the probable nature of the changes made in the Winchester House furnace to permit the use of coal, it would be well to

[1] G. Agricola, *De Re Metallica*, trans. H. C. and L. H. Hoover (New York, Dover Publications, 1950), pp. 584–92.

[2] See Fig. 3. 　　　　　　　　　　　[3] Agricola, p. 588. See Fig. 4.

[4] Ibid., p. 590. 　　　　　　　　　　[5] Merret, pp. 243–4.

[6] Exch. K.R., Barons' Depositions, *Bowes* v. *Salter*, E. 133/25/21, depositions of Symon Favaro and Francisco Butso. The meaning of the terms used by the Italians is explained by Merret's descriptions of the same lehr arrangements.

[7] Merrett, pp. 243–4.

[8] See above, pp. 64–5.

review the problems involved. From the experience of French glass-makers, Scoville pointed out three difficulties: the coal smoke coloured the molten glass lying in open pots; the obnoxious fumes escaping from the working-holes hampered the workmen; and the furnaces built for wood did not have a strong enough draught when used with coal to melt the batch.[1] The objections of the workmen were probably not an important factor in delaying the use of coal, though it is worth noting that it was in England, where the prejudice against coal for domestic fuel had been largely overcome, that successful experiments were first carried out. The discolouration made the glass unsaleable, however, especially in the case of fine crystal and clear window glass. The problem could be solved by covering the pots during the melting process, but if this was done a higher furnace heat was necessary. This might seem improbable from the analogy of cooking in a covered pot on a stove; but the analogy does not hold, for with cooking the steam contained in the pot raises the temperature inside. In glassmaking this was not the case, for a small opening had to be left in one side of the cover of the pot for access to the glass.[2] Much more important was the fact that the cover over the surface of the metal prevented the long flames and hot combustible gases generated in a reverberatory furnace from playing over the surface of the melting batch. This reduced the temperature inside the pots and made it necessary to redesign the furnace in order to raise the total furnace heat: hence it was not the covered pots nor a new formula but the furnace that constituted 'the chiefe thing of the invention'.

There are few contemporary references to closing the pots in the early seventeenth century, and though it has usually been assumed that this was done, there is enough dissent to warrant discussion of the evidence.[3] The problem of discolouration of the glass was not new, for wood as well as coal contains carbon, though each material varies considerably in chemical composition. Some wood, if burned when green, gives off sufficient carbonaceous material in the flame and gases to act as a reducing agent and cause discolouration.[4] If the wood was thoroughly dry, however, this seldom happened, and glassmakers normally had their wood cut long in advance of its use[5] and sometimes stored it in the rafters of the glasshouse above the furnace to dry further.[6] Neri showed understanding of this

[1] Scoville. p. 41.

[2] See the illustration of covered glass pots, Marson, p. 44.

[3] The late W. E. S. Turner, a notable authority, assumes the pots were not closed as part of the coal process, though much of his evidence seems to me to suggest the opposite. See W. E. S. Turner, 'Tercentenary of Neri–Merret's *Art of Glass*', *Glass Technology* iii (1962) 194.

[4] W. E. S. Turner, 'Studies in Ancient Glasses and Glassmaking Processes', *JSGT* xl 1956), 294t.

[5] When ordered to stop burning wood Bungar, Edward and Jacob Hensey, and the Vinion brothers all had large quantities of wood already cut.

[6] See Plate 1.

when he wrote in 1612 that the fire in a glass furnace must always be made of 'hard and dry wood, taking heed of its smoak, which always hurteth . . . *especially in furnaces where the vessels and pots stand open* and the glass will then receive imperfections and notable foulness'.[1] His stress on special care when the pots were left open clearly implies that sometimes they were closed in Venice. The Venetians did indeed use covered pots: but only when they used lead oxide in the batch to make simulated jewels,[2] for the presence of lead materially increases the susceptibility to contamination from carbon. Since the batch for simulated jewels contained a lower silica content and hence melted at a lower temperature than potash glass, the Italians could occasionally close the pots without needing to redesign the furnace to achieve greater heat. For forest-glass making, and even for crystal (which contained no lead before Ravenscroft's invention of the 1670s)[3] there was no reason to close the pots when dry wood was burned.

When coal was substituted for wood as fuel, the danger of contamination from carbon in the smoke was greatly increased. Therefore hard coal which gives off little smoke was used in the early English experiments for all kinds of glass and until 1620 for making crystal.[4] Even with hard coal, however, some discolouration was inevitable (given the technology of the time) unless the pots were covered.[5] The experience of French glassmakers confirms this, as the following quotation for *L'Encyclopédie méthodique* indicates:

Coal-burning furnaces have been experimented with, but no matter what care, skill or intelligence is given to the experiment, the color of the glass is never as bright and clear as that melted in log-burning furnaces . . . One cannot hope to attain the same perfection in glassmaking with a coal fire that one does with a wood fire *unless one succeeds in using covered crucibles in the melting process.*[6]

Since some of Mansell's men used a very soft, sulphurous coal which burned with a sooty smoke[7] they must surely have protected the glass metal from contamination. The use of some sort of cover was probably a part of the invention of the coal process, perhaps on the suggestion of the Italian employed at Winchester House,[8] who like Neri, would have known of the occasional use of closed pots in Murano. Though they are not mentioned in written documents, there is also no contemporary

---

[1] Neri, p. A 4. My italics.   [2] Ibid., pp. 33–4.
[3] Merret, p. 315.   [4] See above, p. 105.
[5] By the nineteenth century, however, the use of more efficient furnaces had so improved combustion that clear soda-glass could be melted in open pots. See Marson p. 31.
[6] Scoville, pp. 42–3, quoting *L'Encyclopédie méthodique*: *Arts et métiers*, viii (Paris, 1791), 486–7. The translation and italics are Scoville's.
[7] Especially Abraham Bigo, the smoke from whose furnace 'blackened those who are about it considerably'. J. Hutchins, *History and Antiquity of the County of Dorset* (4 vols., Westminster, Nicholas & Sons, 1861–70), i. 555–6.
[8] See above, p. 65.

description of the furnace changes, the second and, as the French glass-makers discovered, more difficult part of the invention.

That covered pots were used in the making of lead crystal after its discovery by Ravenscroft in the 1670s has long been taken for granted, but there is evidence of their use earlier than that in Merret's commentary on Neri's work, written in 1662. Merret describes large pots 'twenty inches broad at the top but much narrower at the bottom' and then a 'second sort of pot which they call piling pots because [they were] *set upon the greater* into which they put their finest or coloured metall'.[1] In another passage he describes the openings in the furnace into which 'eight or more pots are set and *on these* the piling pots'.[2] If small pots were set upon larger ones which were wider at the top than the bottom, there must have been some sort of cover to prevent the smaller pots from falling in. Though Merret wrote the commentary in 1662, his knowledge of glass-making methods went back at least to the 1640s when he was associated with experimentation at Gresham College; in fact it was for this reason that he was commissioned to translate Neri's work by the Royal Society.[3] Merret, an accurate observer, does not suggest that the piling pots were a recent innovation.

Finally, evidence that the use of open pots in Mansell's coal-burning furnaces produced a dark, almost black glass comes from the bottle indus-try. A dark, strong bottle came to be made in the Mansell period, different in appearance from the light-coloured bottles made earlier.[4] The pots were left open deliberately, so that the heat to which the melting batch was subjected (already higher in coal-burning furnaces than in those burning wood) could be further increased. The formula for the batch could then be altered to melt a stronger glass with a higher silica content. The dark colour resulting from contamination from the coal fumes was not con-sidered to be a disadvantage in this case; in fact the dark bottles were copied by the French long before they understood English furnaces suffi-ciently to burn coal fuel for other kinds of glass.[5] Apart from bottle-mak-ing, open pots may also occasionally have been used in England in green-glass furnaces. Fragments of black glass have been found at the site of Bigo's coal-burning furnace in Purbeck,[6] and an attractive black glass vessel was unearthed in excavating the Du Houx furnace at Haughton

[1] Merret, p. 246. Italics are mine. Turner (*Glass Technology* iii. 198) argues that the piling pot 'stood above and on one side of the large pot' but this is not what Merret says. Turner does not discuss the problem of contamination from coal smoke.

[2] Merret, p. 241.

[3] Ibid., Dedication to Robert Boyle, unnumbered pages.

[4] For a full discussion of the bottle industry, see below, pp. 225–32.

[5] Scoville, pp. 11–12. See also Diderot's *Encyclopédie* (17 vols., Geneva, 1751–65), xvii. 102f.

[6] Fragments found by the author when examining the probable site of the glasshouse at Kimmeridge Bay, Purbeck, through the courtesy of the owner, Major J. C. Mansel. For Bigo, see pp. 93, 120–1, above.

Green.[1] The dark colour may have been deliberate, or it may have been accidental, the result of attempting to make green glass (the usual product at both furnaces) in open pots with coal as fuel.

It remains to discuss the changes which were made in the furnace to increase the internal heat sufficiently for covered pots to be used successfully. The changes were probably suggested by experimentation currently in progress in London concerning the use of coal in metallurgy. The problems were thought to be similar, as the efforts of Slingsby[2] and other early seventeenth-century inventors indicate, since iron, like glass, was contaminated by coal fumes, and if separation of the metal from the flame was effected, a higher working temperature was necessary. A number of people experimented with 'wind furnaces' and 'wind tunnels' in order to produce a stronger draught and increase the rate of combustion. In general a 'wind furnace' meant one with a grate for the fire, unlike the wood-burning glass furnace in which the fire was made directly on the floor of the furnace. When Sturtevant reported in his prospectus that he had seen glass successfully made with coal at Winchester House in 1612, he said it was done in a 'wind furnace'.[3] He failed to describe the furnace in detail, but the next year John Rolvenson described several furnaces with which he was experimenting for metallurgy, both 'with bellows, or without bellows, as wind furnaces, which are best and least chargeable'.[4] In a wind furnace, he says, 'the fewell is alwayes lying on grates without the cisterns or hearth, through which grates the aire or wind gathered and so maketh the fire to burne, the ashes falling through the grates'. He also mentions tunnels underneath the furnace to bring in air from outside to increase the draught and aid combustion. Whether or not he had seen the furnace at Winchester House after the conversion to coal, his description of the grates almost exactly parallels Merret's description of coal-burning glass furnaces in 1662.[5] In addition the excavation of a coal-burning glass furnace at Haughton Green probably erected soon after Mansell took control of the glass monopoly confirms the use of a wind tunnel in the early furnaces, for it revealed a large, long archway or tunnel of brick running below the sieges and parallel to them.[6] The plan and cross-section of an 'English' glasshouse in Diderot's L'Encyclopédie[7] also indicate grates and a wind tunnel. There is little doubt but that Percival built a similar tunnel under the furnace at Winchester House in order to convert it into a 'wind furnace'.

[1] The glass is in the Pilkington Glass Museum; the excavation was carried out under the supervision of the Assistant Curator, Ruth Hurst Vose. See a note in *JGS* xii (1971), 149. For the Du Houx see above, pp. 92–3.   [2] See above, p. 59.

[3] Price, p. 179, from the text of Sturtevant's prospectus.

[4] John Rolvenson, *Treatise of Metallica* (London, T. Thorpe, 1613), p. C.3.

[5] Merret, pp. 239–41.

[6] Film of the excavation, shown to the author by Mrs. Vose.

[7] See Figs. 6 and 7.

Since the effect of grates and a wind tunnel in increasing the draught, and hence the furnace heat, was common knowledge among inventors and even among other glassmakers, such as the French who tried unsuccessfully for many years to copy the English furnace,[1] it is likely that

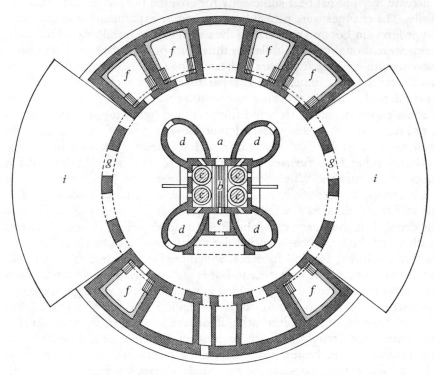

(a) The furnace
(b) Grates for coal
(c) The pots
(d) Ovens for curing the pots before putting them in the furnace

(e) Calcinor for preparing the frit
(f) Small furnaces for receiving the glasses after they are made
(g) Door

Fig. 6. Plan of an eighteenth-century English glasshouse. From Diderot and D'Alembert, *Receuil des Planches sur les Sciences, les Arts Liberaux et les Arts Mechaniques avec leur Explications*, vol. x (Paris, Briasson, 1771), 'Verrerie Angloise', Plate II. The translation of the key is mine.

Percival made another seemingly slight but extremely important change in the operation of the furnace at Winchester House, by employing the use of a chimney. It is generally conceded that the effect of a chimney in

---

[1] Scoville, pp. 42–3. Figs. 6 and 7, taken from a French source, may not be entirely accurate, for the accompanying article notes the French difficulty in copying English methods. The wind tunnels should no doubt extend outside the building. See below, p. 154.

producing a strong draught was not understood in the early seventeenth century. The German alchemist Johann Glauber is usually credited with discovering the principle of the chimney, but his work was not published on the continent until 1646 or translated into English until 1651.[1] The

Verrerie Angloise.

(a) Chimney to draw off the smoke   (e) Tunnel

(b) Interior and conical form of the hall   (f) Pot in the furnace

(c) Entrance   (g) Pot drying out on the furnace

(d) Interior of the furnace   (h) Exterior of the potarches

Fig. 7. Vertical cross-section of the English glasshouse. From *Receuil des Planches . . .*, x, 'Verrerie Angloise', Plate III, fig. 2.

chimney was certainly very little used industrially until the late seventeenth century,[2] and though domestic chimneys began to come into general use somewhat earlier, they were thought of as a means of drawing off the coal smoke and not as an instrument for increasing the draught and the

[1] J. Glauber, *Furni Novi Philosophici* (Amsterdam, J. Fabel, 1646); English trans. *A Description of New Philosophical Furnaces . . .*, set forth in English by J. F., D. M. (London, T. Williams, 1651).

[2] Jenkins, pp. 75–7; J. N. Goldsmith and E. W. Hulme, 'History of the Grated Hearth, the Chimney and the Air Furnace', *Transactions of the Newcomen Society*, xxiii (1942–3), 1–12.

intensity of the fire. In this connection Rolvenson's description of the wind furnaces he knew is most interesting. 'The furnaces may be made either close at the top, with some vent-holes', he said, 'and so merely reverbaratory . . . or else the furnace may be made with one or more funnels, as it were chimneys on the top or in the sides'.[1] He would hardly have regarded the chimneys as optional had he been aware of any relationship to the draught, but it is possible that he had seen such 'funnels' on the top of the wind furnace at Winchester House without understanding their function.

Some small pieces of evidence lend support to the suggestion that there was either a chimney of sorts on the Winchester House furnace, or modifications in the furnace or in the glasshouse itself which created the effect of a chimney. It has already been shown that the furnace at Winchester House was not the low rectangular furnace common in forest-glass making but the tall beehive shape used by the Italians, which was constructed by Salter for making crystal glassware.[2] Moreover Simon Favaro, one of Salter's workmen who had recently arrived from Murano, testified in a lawsuit that it was built even taller than usual. 'The fogaro or place where ye put the fire in this of Winchester House is larger than those of Murano,' he said, 'and the lare or topp of the furnace in Winchester House is much higher than those in Morano.'[3] Francisco Butso, his co-worker, also testified to the unusual height.[4] The furnace was wood-burning when the testimony was given, and there is no indication of the reason for the unusual height; however, when Salter's firm was forced out of business and Zouch's company took over Winchester House for experimental glassmaking,[5] the height of the furnace there may have given Percival an accidental advantage. After the wind tunnels and grates were installed, if an opening was made in the top of the furnace and a 'funnel' such as Rolvenson mentioned installed, the draught and the furnace heat would have been materially increased. Even without the funnel a small opening near the top would have had the same effect, since the furnace was already probably sixteen feet high.[6] If in addition the glasshouse was tall and narrow, with an opening in the roof directly above the furnace, and if the air tunnels extended outside the building itself, by closing all the doors and windows during the melting process a very strong upward draught would have been created. Even if the modifications were simply

---

[1] Rolvenson, p. C. 3.

[2] See above, pp. 45–6.

[3] Exch. K.R., Barons' Depositions, E. 133/25/21, *Bowes* v. *Salter*, deposition of Simon Favaro.

[4] Ibid., deposition of Francisco Butso.

[5] See Chap. III, pp. 46, 64.

[6] As stated earlier, the Italian furnaces were twelve feet high. A difference of less than three or four feet would hardly have attracted such explicit comment.

intended to draw off the obnoxious coal smoke,[1] the same effect would have resulted.

Merrett's descriptions of the glasshouses of 1662 support this theory of the development of the furnace. He describes both the Italian-style circular furnace for crystal, and the furnaces for green glass which were square at the base; in both cases, he notes, the furnaces were tall and the annealing was done in chambers above the working furnace.[2] The workmen had to mount steps to reach the annealing tunnel. He mentions that from the mouth of the small oven used for preparing the frit 'the smoke flieth very black';[3] but he does not mention smoke coming from the big working furnace. Instead he says that it was to 'defend their eyes from excedency of heat and light' that the workmen wore 'straw broad brim'd hats'.[4] The heat was so intense, he says, that three days after the fire was extinguished a straw put into the chamber immediately ignited.[5] In the old low-crowned wood-burning furnaces, smoke poured out of the working-holes just as it did from the mouth of the fritting furnace; but the inference from Merret's remarks is that, in the coal-burning furnaces, it must have been drawn off near the top.

The most convincing argument that the glasshouse itself acted as a large chimney is supplied by the well-known glasshouse cones, which were built during the second half of the seventeenth century.[6] These tall, conical brick structures, open at the top, were the glasshouse buildings; their shape had nothing to do with the shape of the furnace, which could be either square or circular at the base. They operated on the principle just described—that is, the few openings in the cone were closed during the melting process; the wind tunnels, extended beyond the building itself, brought in cool air from outside; and the entire building acted as a giant chimney which created a strong draught by drawing off the furnace heat through the open top. A modern authority has asserted that, in the absence of such modern techniques as gas regenerators, some such arrangement is necessary in order to reach the melting temperature of glass when using coal as fuel.[7] In cementation furnaces for blistered steel the same principle was used, though there is no evidence of specific borrowing of the idea in either case. The coal-burning glass furnace seems to have been developed first.[8] The fact that French glassmakers tried to house English-style coal-burning furnaces in low rectangular glasshouses

[1] Note that in Fig. 7, p. 153, the French author describes the purpose of the chimney as 'to draw off the smoke'.

[2] Merret, pp. 243–4.   [3] Ibid., p. 239.

[4] Ibid., p. 248.   [5] Ibid., p. 245.

[6] At Catliffe, Yorkshire, one of these cones is still standing. Its shape is similar to that of the glasshouse illustrated in Fig. 7.

[7] R. Gunther, 'Rausgaskegel auf alten Glashuten', *Glastechnische Berichte*, xxiv (1961), pp. 559–62; reprint in English entitled 'Old Glasswork Cones' kindly lent by R. J. Charleston.

[8] Goldsmith and Hulme, pp. 8–10.

without chimneys and with the doors and window open[1] explains their failure to melt glass successfully in covered crucibles.

It would be helpful to know the size and shape of the particular building in the complex known as Winchester House which housed the glass furnace; but for later glasshouses high buildings do seem to have been used. Mansell's Broad Street furnace was probably housed in the abandoned monastic church of the Austin Friars which was no doubt vaulted, and at Wollaton Mansell's two new coal-burning furnaces were housed in a 'great barn' which was built for the purpose[2]—though it was probably constructed of wood and not of brick. In Ireland a glasshouse forty feet square and thirty-six feet tall was built in 1621.[3] The glassmaker who operated it burned wood, but he probably came from England and reproduced the style of tall glasshouse with which he was familiar there, for such a high structure was hardly necessary to house a wood-burning furnace.

Admittedly, the addition of the principle of the chimney is conjecture; but it can reasonably be said that in total the changes made by Percival constituted a new invention. Using covered crucibles (with which a Venetian employee would have been familiar), and starting with a Venetian furnace taller than usual, he added grates and a wind tunnel extending outside the building itself; and in addition he very probably opened up the top of the furnace or the top of the building, or both, which created a strong enough draught and a hot enough fire to melt the glass. Since the effect of the chimney was so little understood at the time by other glassmakers and by most other industrialists, the true significance of what seemed to be merely a convenient means of drawing off unwanted smoke may not have been realized. That it was not copied immediately is not surprising, for Percival himself may not have understood fully why his furnace operated as it did; and if he did know, he kept his secrets well.

II. SUPPLIES AND INGREDIENT OF THE BATCH

In 1620 James Howell, who had recently been employed by Mansell at the London crystal works, wrote to his brother that it was 'a rare kind of Knowledge and Chymistry to transmute Dust and Sand (for they are the only main Ingredients) to such a diaphanous pellucid dainty Body as you see a Crystal-Glass is'.[4] He had good reason to be somewhat in awe of the glassmaker's skill, for though sand and ashes were indeed the chief ingredients, their combination to produce good quality glass was not an easy thing. Before the age of chemical analysis glassmakers had to depend upon tradition, experience, and frequently on trial and error in selecting the ingredients. Although formulae for the approximate proportions were

---

[1] Scoville, p. 42.   [2] Midd. MS. 5/165/131.
[3] Westropp, p. 30.   [4] Howell, p. 67.

handed down, they could never be relied upon entirely, for the materials varied in their chemical composition. Much depended upon the judgement of the founder in varying the proportions as the melting progressed; and in a new location, a batch mixed in the usual proportions sometimes failed entirely.

Sand (silica) was always the largest ingredient by volume, but as Merret knew 'there is great variety in this material, for some soon melts and mixeth with the ashes and becomes glass'[1] whereas some does not. Of the impurities in sand lime was one of the most important, for in order to make the types of glass usual in this period the presence of sufficient lime together with either soda or potash was necessary to assist in the melting process and produce a stable glass.[2] Most glassmakers seem to have been unaware of the necessity for lime, and it was never added deliberately to the glass batch in England,[3] although Venetians added it when they made *cristallo* from crushed white pebbles instead of sand.[4] Enough lime is often present in sand—sometimes far more than is necessary[5]—and it occurs also, in some wood ashes.[6] The percentage in sand does, however, vary widely, and it was no doubt insufficient lime that caused experienced glassmakers such as the Henseys to label some sand 'unuseful'.[7]

Iron oxide, an even more common impurity in sand, affects the colour rather than the stability or the melting point of glass. An amount as small as one-tenth of one per cent renders the glass decidedly green, though the effect can be counteracted by decolourizers. If iron is present in slightly larger amounts, decolourizers are less satisfactory, for the glass becomes cloudy; and amounts up to three or four per cent, which are not uncommon, produce a dark green glass which cannot be disguised except by rendering the glass dark brown or black.[8] Under certain melting conditions the green tinge is replaced by an amber one. Glassmakers had long known that sands from different locations produced varying degrees of colour, and they chose their supplies accordingly. In London, for example, the crystal-producing glasshouses used a 'fine white sand from Maidstone in Kent', while the green-glass furnaces used a harder sand from Woolwich.[9]

As for the alkali that was melted with the sand, different forms were used for the making of *cristallo* essentially a soda glass, and forest glass,

[1] Merret, p. 261.

[2] F. W. Hodkin and A. Cousen, *A Textbook of Glass Technology* (London, Constable, 1929), p. 65.

[3] There is no record of purchases of lime in any of the accounts. See also Merret, p. 31.

[4] Neri, p. 16.

[5] Hodkin and Cousen, p. 66.

[6] Turner, *JSGT* pp. 282f. Turner gives detailed chemical analyses of all ingredients used in this period.

[7] Westropp, p. 34.   [8] Hodkin and Cousen, p. 66.   [9] Merret, p. 261

essentially a potash glass. Both forms of alkali were derived from ashes, and it has usually been assumed that the ash of marine plants yielded only soda (Na_2O), and that of woody land plants only potash (K_2O). Turner has shown, however, that there is some potash in the ash of marine plants and some soda in that of land plants; while both contain many other constituents, including compounds of magnesium, in varying proportions.[1] Nevertheless there is in general enough difference between the two kinds of ash to produce glass with different characteristics.

So long as they used wood as fuel, glassmakers had a ready source of free potash in the ashes from their furnaces. (Only in a new location, before work was begun, was it necessary to buy ashes, usually from the land-lord;[2] once production was under way, the purchase of ashes disappears from the records.) The ashes were of high quality, especially when beech wood was burned, and the glassmakers, knowing their value, kept them free from impurities which might contaminate the glass.

When coal was substituted for wood as fuel, necessitating the purchase of ashes, discrimination in the choice of ash was practised whenever possible. The agent on the Willoughby estates, after careful investigation, said that 'wiche asse [witch elm ash?], beanestraw asse and green ferne asse are all good', 'pease-straw asse and gorse asse are not so good', and 'dry fern asse is not good'.[3] Neri also recommended the ashes of fern 'cut when green', which made glass that 'bended much better' than that made with any other vegetable ash.[4] For his large furnaces in urban areas Mansell could not be so particular, since the ashes available there were expensive, scarce, and frequently of poor quality from intermixture with dirt and other extraneous materials.[5] As Merret said, 'for green-glass in England they buy all sorts of ashes confused one with another, of persons who go up and down the country to most parts of England to buy them.'[6] As a result the quality of the glass made both in London and in Newcastle deteriorated, for though sieves were used to remove some of the foreign matter,[7] the process of leaching the ashes to extract a purer form of potash was not practised in Mansell's time. The problem of securing an adequate supply was made worse by competition from other industrialists who also needed potash, which frequently had to be imported.[8] The Soapboilers bought ashes in great quantity, but it was the saltpetremen who gave Mansell the greatest difficulty, claiming that he was getting more than his fair share of the very limited supply. After a lengthy dispute Mansell signed an agreement with the Company of Salpetremen, which stipulated that all ashes entering London were to be landed at his warehouses, but that a commissioner appointed by the gunpowder and saltpetremen

---

[1] Turner, *JSGT*, p. 285*t*. [2] Lennard, p. 128; Westropp, p. 27.
[3] Midd. MS. 5/165/139, no. 1, 'Observacions for glasse', 1615.
[4] Neri, p. 13. [5] S.P. 14/113, no. 49, Mansell to the Council.
[6] Merret, pp. 264–5. [7] Westropp, p. 26. [8] Port Books, *passim*.

should see, that while two-thirds was retained by Mansell, they received the remaining one-third at a reasonable price.[1]

Whereas raw ashes were used in their natural state for making both green and window glass, the makers of crystal required a fairly pure form of soda extracted from the ashes of various marine plants. Most of that used in England for true *cristallo* was imported from the Mediterranean under a variety of names—soda, barilla, polverine, rochetta, and natron.[2] Carré, Verzelini, Mansell, and Ord (for the Scottish firm) all imported barilla from Spain,[3] though when the Spanish trade was interrupted in 1589 Verzelini ordered 'Sevonus ashes' from Antwerp as a substitute.[4] The Venetian glassmakers, however, thought that natron from the Near East was superior to barilla, producing crystal that was 'less inclined to a blewness'.[5] Late in his career Mansell imported natron from Alexandria,[6] perhaps in an attempt to improve the quality of his crystal plates for looking-glasses and spectacles. For his 'ordinary' glass, which was similar to crystal but cheaper, Mansell said that he used an English variety of soda made from certain marine plants.[7] The plant to which he was referring was kelp or 'sea-oare', which was gathered, burned and sold commercially in both England and Scotland;[8] production was stimulated by this new demand from the glass industry, but the kelp was also used in dyeing cloth, and in the alum industry.[9]

Apart from sand, and ashes or soda, only one other ingredient was consistently added to the glass batch—cullet, or broken glass. This was done (as it still is done today) not only for economy, but chiefly because it reduces the melting point and actively assists in the melting process.[10] Although it might be thought that cullet would need to be purchased only before glassmaking was started in a new location, in fact there was seldom enough waste from scraps and breakages to make up the proper proportion needed for new batches, and nearly all glassmakers had to buy broken glass. As the cullet heaps found on abandoned sites testify, all sorts of broken glass were utilized. Cullet was sold commercially and was often shipped round the coast, and also at times either imported or exported.[11] After Mansell took control of the industry he complained that

[1] S.P. 16/418, no. 90; 16/448, no. 37.

[2] The Book of Rates of 1604 seems to use the term 'saphora' as synonomous with barilla, but saphora usually meant zaffre, or cobalt. See p. 160 and n. 3.

[3] S.P. 12/42, no. 42; 14/112, no. 28; Port Books, E. 190/8/1, London, 1588.

[4] Ibid., E. 190/8/2, London, aliens, 1589.

[5] Merret, unnumbered page preceding Introd.

[6] HMC, *Fourth Report*, House of Lords MSS., p. 103.

[7] 'The True State of the Businesse of Glasse'; and Lansd. MS. 162/97, fol. 67.

[8] *Cal. S.P.D.* x. 131; *R.P.C. Scot.* xii. 771–2.

[9] *Cal. S.P.D.* ix. 377, 475.   [10] Phillips, p. 26.

[11] See many Port Books, from E. 190/5/5, Imports, 1571/2, to E. 190/43/1, Exports, 1640; and coastal books such as E. 190/757/21, Chichester, 1613, and E. 190/7/6, London, coastal, 1585.

cullet was hard to procure and the price had gone up.[1] He himself may have contributed to the scarcity, for since the quality of his window glass made at Newcastle had deteriorated, he started using a higher proportion of cullet than was normal 'to helpe ye badness of ye ashes'. Yet the London glaziers, who controlled the largest supply of cullet, that from the cuttings in their shops, could sell to the French glassmakers at higher prices than Mansell wished to pay, and they frequently shipped their cullet abroad.[2]

Two other ingredients were sometimes added to the batch as decolourizing agents—manganese and cobalt (generally called 'zaffer' in the seventeenth century).[3] Their effect is to provide a different but complementary colour which neutralizes the greenness induced by the presence of iron oxide in the sand. The chemical reaction varies with the alkali employed, however, and while manganese alone is usually successful in decolourizing potash glass, the two used together produce a better effect in soda glass.[4] Manganese, the 'glassmaker's soap', had been used from ancient times;[5] but the earliest written references to zaffer, meaning cobalt, date from the mid sixteenth century.[6] Possibly earlier than that, but certainly by 1600, Venetian glassmakers used both. The Italian workmen at Winchester House said that both in Murano and in Southwark they had used 'two kinds of stone mine called mangese and zafer' to give the glasses clarity,[7] and it is very probable that Verzelini's workmen before them and Mansell's after followed the same practice. The supply of these substances was never a problem: cobalt was imported from time to time from Germany, and manganese came from the Mendip Hills in Somersetshire.[8]

In the making of forest glass decolourizers were seldom used.[9] The makers of green glass made no attempt to disguise the colour of their wares: in fact, they often sought out sands which would produce the rich colour which their customers found attractive. Yet even without the addition of any decolourizers, much of the window glass made in the sixteenth century and even much earlier was almost colourless—though some of it had a decided green tinge. The lack of colour has sometimes been attributed to 'purer materials' or washing of the sand, but such measures would hardly suffice. Turner's chemical analysis of the ashes of every kind of plant material used for glassmaking in the sixteenth century supplies a satisfactory explanation, for he found manganese in the ashes of beech wood, derived in particular from the leaves, which occasionally

[1] S.P. 14/113, nos. 49, 50.   [2] See pp. 89, 129.
[3] Hodkin and Cousen, p. 117. Impure cobalt earth is still called zaffre.
[4] Ibid., p. 133.   [5] Turner, *JSGT* p. 296^t.
[6] Ibid., p. 41^t.   [7] Exch. K.R., Barons' Depositions, E. 133/25/21, *Bowes* v. *Salter*.
[8] Merret, p. 289.
[9] Scoville found no evidence for the use of decolourizers in window-glass making in France.

yielded manganese to the extent of one to eleven per cent of the ash.[1] The smaller amounts were sufficient to decolourize the glass, and the larger amounts could even have tinted the glass flesh-colour or lavender if the metal had been allowed to stand in the pots before working. This extraordinary occurrence of manganese in beech wood, not previously recognized, explains why window-glass makers preferred that wood as fuel (since they used ashes from their own furnaces); and also why, as Isaac Bungar said, they used the 'lop and top' whenever enough was available.[2] It also explains why Mansell had such difficulty making clear glass when he was forced to buy all sorts of ashes mingled together. Mansell was well enough informed to realize that some substance must be added to clarify the glass, and by 1619 he began using 'materialles called Saphur', a thing which he said had not been used before in England for window glass.[3] Zaffre without the addition of some manganese as well would not have been very effective in potash glass, but it is possible that he mentioned only the more unusual substance. He was not correct in claiming to be the first, apart from the crystal-makers, to use it in England: Carré, probably following Flemish usage, made one purchase for his Lorrainers in advance of their arrival,[4] and another purchase was made by the workmen at Knole House, one of whom was an Italian.[5] Nevertheless the practice was unusual in any kind of glassmaking, except crystal, until the Mansell regime. The use of manganese supplanted zaffre, which no doubt Mansell found did not work particularly well, and by the 1660s Merret could say that manganese was 'the most universal material used in glassmaking of every kind'.[6]

Apart from the increased use of decolourizers and the increased proportion of cullet in the batch—measures adopted to offset the poor quality of the ashes—there is no real evidence of changes in the composition of the batch or in the founding process during this period. The possible exception may have been changes in the formula to increase the silica content of the metal for strong dark bottles. There seems to have been no experimentation with the addition of lead oxide. It is clear that the aliens, both Italians and forest-glass makers, brought with them improved techniques in founding, for their glass metal is generally superior to that made in England during the Middle Ages.[7] After their arrival, however, there is no indication of continued improvements in the formulae or the process; rather, their glass varied in quality according to the kind of the supplies available to them in the locations where they chose to settle.

[1] Turner, *JSGT*, p. 289[t].   [2] S.P. 14/162, no. 231 A.

[3] S.P. 14/113, no. 29.   [4] Lansd. MS. 59, no. 76, enclosure.

[5] Lennard, p. 128.   [6] Merret, p. 282.

[7] Crossley discusses the improvements in founding techniques, based on the amount of waste and scum found on sites worked before and after the coming of the aliens. Crossley, *EcHR* p. 432.

VII

OWNERSHIP, MARKETING, AND CAPITALIZATION

THE high economic and social status of continental glassmakers in the early sixteenth century reflected the fact that they combined the roles of owner, manager, and craftsman. Both the *gentilhommes verriers* and their Italian counterparts owned their own furnaces, and apparently had either enough land to provide them with fuel or sufficient capital to purchase it without recourse to outside sources of finance. Glassmaking was a small-scale family business, passed on from father to son; effective monopolies based sometimes on exclusive privileges from royal grants, as in Lorraine and Normandy, sometimes on a tightly guarded monopoly of skill, as in Murano, protected the status and prosperity of the glass-making families.[1] At that time problems of distribution and marketing did not arise: but when overproduction in Lorraine, the disruption of trade, and religious persecutions prompted migration of large numbers of glassmakers to England, the migrants faced new problems. They needed, if possible, to bring sufficient capital with them to finance new furnaces and fuel supplies until profits began to accumulate; and in addition they would want either to secure the same sort of legal monopolies which many of them had enjoyed on the continent, or to preserve their monopoly of skill. Jean Carré,[2] an alien himself, clearly perceived this, and his successful relationships with the glassmakers he brought to England resulted from his attempt to maintain as much as possible of the status and prosperity they had enjoyed on the continent.

Carré's 'fellowship', or company, which was organized to finance both window-glass making in the Weald and crystal-making in London, was formed largely from imported capital—though this was not drawn exclusively from the glassmakers themselves. Carré himself held a half interest,[3] and Peter Appel, his Flemish son-in-law who was a cloth merchant, also invested in the company.[4] Peter Briet, another merchant who came from the Low Countries at about the same time as Carré,[5] contributed capital and aided in management and marketing, as we have seen. The fourth member of the company who is known by name, Jean Chevalier, chaste-

---

[1] See Chap. I, *passim*.
[2] See Chap. II, pp. 17f.
[3] Lansd. MS. 59, no. 76, enclosure.
[4] Lansd. MS. 22, no. 7.
[5] Ibid.; *Returns of Aliens*, pt. iii, p. 360.

lain of the castle of Fontenoy in Lorraine,[1] seems never to have come to England. He was, however, related to the glassmaking family of the de Hennezells[2]—he may even have been its head.[3] Thus, while part of the capital was drawn from merchants, none of these were native Englishmen and they all had close ties with practising glassmakers. The company took total responsibility for capital expenditure, operating costs, and marketing for two of the three original glasshouses; but the two members of the Hennezell family who operated the third glasshouse contributed half the capital spent on it and were thereby half-owners of their furnace, entitled to half its profits.[4] The glassmakers who operated the other furnaces, the Venetians in London and the Norman de Bongars, were not part-owners, but were paid extremely high salaries in keeping with their earning capacity on the continent.[5] In addition they were all protected from competition by the royal grant from the Queen. The unwanted intrusion into the company of Anthony Becku as a condition of the grant for window-glass making, however, marks the entrance of the entrepreneur. As an outsider, his attempts at dictation were fiercely resented by both Normans and Lorrainers, and as has been related,[6] they managed to thwart his plans for training Englishmen who might then provide dangerous competition.

After Carré's death and the demise of his company, Jacob Verzelini was the most successful of the men Carré had brought from the continent, and he died far richer than he arrived.[7] Verzelini succeeded, partly because he had accumulated enough capital to assume sole ownership of the Crutched Friars furnace in London, and partly because he was able to secure a royal grant which protected his market from both foreign and domestic competition. In addition he sold most of his glass retail, pocketing the middleman's profit, which the glass-sellers had made when Venetian wares were imported. He had no need either for the capital or for the services of middlemen and entrepreneurs.

Two other families who had been brought from the continent and financed by Carré's company—the Bungars and the Vinions[8]—also preserved their independence, and it is hardly a coincidence that they remained leaders in their respective branches of the trade until 1618. Their prosperity, however, was hardly comparable to Verzelini's. In Bungar's case the price of rebellion against Becku's domination, and the result of

---

[1] Lansd. MS. 59, no. 76, enclosure.

[2] Kenyon, p. 125, quoting M. G. Varlot, who did extensive genealogical research on the family of Hennezell.

[3] Since *chevalier* was the title and rank held by the de Hennezell family, it was possibly not his true surname, which may have been omitted in the English translation of the contract (Lansd. MS. 59, no. 76. enclosure.)

[4] Ibid.

[5] See below, pp. 185–6, 188.

[6] See Chap. II, pp. 23–5.

[7] See Chap. II, p. 31.

[8] See above, Chaps. II, III, IV, *passim*.

the eventual demise of the patent for window glass, was the growth in competition from newly arrived immigrants and from imported glass. The drinking-glass makers, who had never been protected, faced the same sort of competition. Like most refugees, the newly arrived immigrants who came in increasing numbers in the 1570s and 1580s brought only a few belongings and very little capital. Though some could afford to build their own furnaces, which seldom cost more than twelve pounds,[1] they needed long-term credit for their fuel, which was by far the most expensive item in their costs apart from the skilled labour, which they could provide. They turned most frequently to the gentry on whose land they wished to settle, and entered into contracts which often amounted to partnerships. Since the woods within easy reach were likely to be exhausted quickly, and the furnaces needed to be rebuilt frequently because of internal damage,[2] the glassmakers made short-term agreements, frequently for as little as three years,[3] and thus preserved their freedom of movement. In general the glassmakers themselves took the initiative in moving on and negotiating new arrangements. On the whole the role of the gentry was passive, though most of them were delighted to arrange for the sale of wood when glassmakers appeared. Occasionally an enterprising steward, eager to profit from handling the marketing, urged his master to seek a bargain with them;[4] and in a few instances, notably that of the Bishop of Lichfield and the Bagots of Blithefield, the owner himself may have actively sought their presence.[5]

The contracts varied to some extent according to the circumstances of the glassmakers involved. At Knole House there were two teams of glassmakers, operating independently, and each master workman 'undertook one halfe the charge of the furnace'.[6] They arranged for deliveries of wood and sand on credit, to be paid for in finished glass, with accounts kept by the steward who went every day to the glasshouse. Other expenses and the salaries of the unskilled workmen who tended the fires were presumably paid by the glassmakers in cash; but they undertook no responsibility for marketing. When they first began operating a 'Mr. Smyth', presumably a merchant and very possibly John Smith, an important importer of glass in the 1560s, handled the marketing and seems to have supplied some of the credit,[7] but later the steward arranged for the sale of all the glass, not just for the portion received in return for wood. In the same year (1585) Ambrose Hensey arrived at the Bagot estates with no capital at all with which to begin operations. Richard Bagot not only paid for his furnace

---

[1] See below, p. 181.   [2] See Chap. VI.
[3] Folger, Bagot MS. L. a. 445; PRO Star Chamber Proc. 8 Jac. I, 179/7.
[4] Lennard, pp. 127–9; Midd. MS. 5/165/139, 1st. doc.
[5] For the Bishop of Lichfield, see Chap. II, p. 36; The Bagots had a long tradition of glass-making on their estates and seemed anxious to continue it.
[6] Lennard, p. 127.   [7] Ibid., pp. 128–9.

and glasshouse but supplied free rent, a cash advance of £40 for supplies, and credit for the purchase of fuel.[1] Hensey was to repay him for the loan and the fuel 'in money or in glasse' (valued at 18s. the case) within a year, giving Bagot each week half the glass produced or its value. In this case it seems clear that Hensey, who supplied all the labour (his own, and the wages of the others), and Bagot, who supplied nearly everything else, were in practice operating as equal partners and dividing the glass between them. No mention of marketing was made in the contract; but probably demand in the area at that time was sufficient for the glass to be sold to local glaziers at the furnace door. In about 1607 another team of glass-makers who were clearly in better circumstances entered into very different arrangements with Richard Bagot's son, Walter. Since they apologized for not being able to 'speak so playne as wee wold', the glassmakers were probably newly arrived immigrants who had brought some small amount of capital with them. They insisted that they would 'build the glass house and fornes of [their] owne chargise'[2] and so 'leave it when we go', paying Bagot for the stone and brick. Instead of asking for credit they offered to 'paye your worship every fortnyghte moneye and make levell with your worshipe everye monthe when we worke', and furthermore they offered to give a bond for £40 for the faithful performance of their contract. Again nothing was said about marketing, but in this case it was clearly not Bagot's responsibility.

In all of these arrangements, except for the brief involvement of John Smith at Knole House, the role of the merchant and of mercantile capital is noticeably absent, a circumstance unusual enough at the time to call for some comment. In many industries merchants supplied both credit and marketing facilities without which the craftsmen could not pursue their trade. Verzelini, as we have seen, had no need of either, and for some time other glassmakers were equally fortunate, especially if the gentry were willing to supply credit. The makers of green drinking glasses and other common articles found a ready sale to travelling chapmen who sought out the glassmakers.[3] As the supply of such articles increased, some chapmen came to specialize in selling only glassware, and 'glassmen of good behaviour' were numerous enough to be noted in the statutes regulating vagabonds and given special licence to travel.[4] They served a useful func-tion and throughout the period continued to provide marketing facilities for most of the green-glass men,[5] but they were far below the glassmakers

[1] Contract between Ambrose Hensey and Richard Bagot, 5 June 1585, printed in full in Horridge, p. 27.   [2] Folger, Bagot MS. L. a. 445, Hensey and Gellatt to Bagot.

[3] Winchester, Dioc. R.O. Consistory Court Book, no. 62, 21M65, fol. 45.

[4] *Statutes of the Realm*, 39 Eliz. cap. 4 and 1 Jac. I, cap. 7. The first statute permitted 'glass-men of good behaviour' to travel the country on licence from three Justices of the Peace, but the second withdrew the privilege.

[5] In 1636 the Glass-sellers Company was protesting about the activities of the travelling 'glassmen'. Howard, pp. 20–3.

in the economic scale and certainly could not aspire to finance them. The London glass-sellers were not yet organized as a separate guild, though they belonged to other London companies. While they sold some forest glass, their capital was employed in importing glass specialities not yet made in England.[1] As for window glass, the London Glaziers Company, though a long-established guild, ranked almost at the bottom of the list of the London companies in wealth.[2] In the country there were very few glaziers and they were also poor. Some could not even afford to glaze their own windows,[3] and few could buy more than three or four cases of glass at a time for their orders.[4] In the early years, therefore, since glaziers did not have the capital to import glass the trade was in the hands of merchants who belonged to other companies. Thomas Walker, a Leather-seller, for example, imported half the Norman glass brought into London in 1567,[5] and John Smith, described simply as 'merchant', imported nearly all that came from Burgundy.[6] Except for Smith, who purchased an interest in the bead and bugle factory at Rye in 1580[7] and probably helped finance the Knole house glasshouse for a time, none of these merchants was in any way connected with financing the production of glass in England.

As the number of glasshouses in England increased, the organization of the industry became more complex and middlemen began to appear. With the help of the gentry most of the green-glass makers and a few of the window-glass makers preserved their independence until 1615, but others, particularly in the Midlands and in the Weald, fell under the domination of men who were essentially merchants. Isaac Bungar was one such man who came to control the enterprises of many of his fellow glass-makers.[8] The dealings of another, Nicholas Gellatt, throw light on the strained financial situation of some glassmakers, which at last gave merchants their opportunity. When Jacob Hensey abruptly ceased glass-making at Bagot's Park in 1615 and went into Mansell's employ at Wollaton,[9] he left behind a debt of £300 to Bagot for fuel which had already been cut and a debt to Gellatt, who was described as a merchant of Leicester, for £240 which represented a cash advance for supplies and running expenses.[10] In a letter to Coke complaining of his losses, Gellatt

---

[1] Port Books, *passim*. See also Chap. X.   [2] C. Ashdown, p. 24.

[3] *Household and Farm Inventories in Oxfordshire*, ed. M. A. Havinden (Oxfordshire Record Society, Publication no. 44), (London, H.M.S.O. 1965), pp. 282, 287, 296.

[4] Lichfield J.R.O., will of John Watkys, glazier, 5 May 1588.

[5] Port Books, E. 190/4/2, London, 1567/8.

[6] Ibid. The abbreviation 'mer.' applied to Mr. Smith may, however, stand not for 'merchant' but for 'mercer'.

[7] See above, p. 32.

[8] See Chaps. II, III, IV, *passim*, but especially pp. 55-7, 72-3.

[9] Folger, Bagot MS. L. a. 144, Bagot to Willoughby, Aug. 1615.

[10] Ibid.; Gellatt to Coke, 5 Aug. 1615, quoted in Horridge, p. 31.

claimed that he 'owned' the glasshouse, though to Bagot he implied that
he and Bagot were in partnership.[1] In effect Gellatt did own the glasshouse, for he marketed all the glass, and from the proceeds he, not
Hensey, was obliged to pay Bagot for the wood. In any case Hensey was
hardly independent, nor was he prosperous. Had work continued in
Bagot's Park he would no doubt have received some recompense for his
labour, but it would most certainly have been small in comparison with
the profits his forebears had realized. The fact that he accepted Mansell's
offer of a weekly wage so readily indicates that he was more than willing
to escape the burden of debt and the uncertain hope of profits. He was not
alone. Gellatt claimed that he had a string of glasshouses besides the one
at Bagot's Park, for he had given 'greate creditt to manie poore men
[glassmakers] in manie cuntries [counties]'.[2] He had three apprentices
who helped him to manage the enterprises and market the glass. All
would be undone, he claimed, by the proclamation forbidding the use of
wood; but it is significant that it was not the glassmakers whom he
financed, but Gellatt himself and Bagot who complained about losses
when the wood-burning glasshouses were shut down.

Though nothing definite is known about Gellatt's background it is
possible that like Bungar he had risen from the ranks of practising glassmakers. Several Gellatts from a prominent glassmaking family in Burgundy are known to have made glass in London and the Weald, and one
had worked earlier in Bagot's Park.[3] Nicholas may have belonged to this
same family, and have accumulated enough capital to engage in the more
profitable role of merchant by financing his less fortunate fellow craftsmen and marketing their wares. Certainly Bungar's career had followed
this pattern. The Isaac Bungar of 1620, 'Freeman and Glazier of the City
of London', accused by his fellow members of the company of once
having had a corner on the London window-glass market and of aspiring
to another, was a man of far different interests from the Isaac Bungar of
1590, the part-owner of one small furnace.[4] One can no longer imagine
him, skilled as a craftsman though he must have been, standing at the
furnace door blowing crown glass, as his kinsmen the de Bongars of
Normandy continued to do for over a hundred years.[5] Like Gellatt he
had come to control other glasshouses through supplying them with fuel
and credit and marketing their glass. Moreover by 1605 some members

<hr/>

[1] Folger, Bagot MS. L. a. 508, Gillot to Bagot, 17 June 1616. When writing to Mansell,
Bagot referred to the glasshouse as his own (Horridge, p. 3), yet Hensey would have claimed
to have been independent.

[2] Horridge, p. 31, Gellatt to Coke, 5 Aug. 1615.

[3] Wisborough Green P.R.; Folger, Bagot MS. L. a. 445, 446; VCH Surrey, ii. 298–9;
List of Foreign Protestants and Aliens . . ., p. 99. The name is found spelled in various ways,
e.g., Gillot, Gelat, Gilot.

[4] See above, p. 55.   [5] Scoville, p. 84.

of the Glaziers Company, such as Lionell Bennett and John Dines,[1] had become prosperous enough to replace the Goldsmiths and Leather-sellers as wholesale dealers in window glass. When Isaac became a dealer, it behoved him to join the company, too. Separation between combined ownership and marketing on the one hand, and craftsmanship on the other, had arisen within the glass industry.

In the same period, the tendency toward separation of capital and labour was accentuated by the policy of the Crown. With the granting of monopoly rights to persons other than glassmakers, the arrangements for financing the industry necessarily changed. Bowes, the soldier and diplomat who received the first such grant (1592), was in no position to supply capital, for the patent was granted specifically as a source of revenue to alleviate his impoverished condition. He was unable to exploit his privilege until he sub-let his rights to the City men, Robson, Turner, and Lane,[2] none of whom had any previous connection with the glass industry. Turner, who supplied the largest share of the capital for the crystal works at Blackfriars,[3] was a speculator who soon turned from active participation in glassmaking to the alum industry, another royal monopoly, with greater hopes of quick profits. Robson, a member of the Salters Company, was presumably a merchant. Robson exemplifies, un-like Bungar, the entrepreneur with no technical experience in glassmaking. Both could be unscrupulous in their pursuit of profit, but Bungar, even after he abandoned actual glass-blowing, represented the conservative medieval tradition of glassmaking. Since he and his like had never been subject to a guild or to government regulation in France or in England, he was an ardent individualist who preferred fiercely to oppose royal interference rather than to change his methods and techniques. He resorted to an economy of scarcity and artificial restriction of the market in order to preserve his position; and with the pride of his ancestors he fought the Mansell monopoly with every means at his disposal. Unlike Bungar, William Robson, nicknamed 'Roaring Robson',[4] went into glass-making with energy unrestrained by preconceptions or long traditions. A more modern type of industrialist, he took a purely pragmatic attitude towards the problems of glassmaking. He accepted new methods of glass-making easily, since all methods were relatively new to him. He sought royal privileges if they were to his advantage, resisted them if it suited his purposes, and showed himself willing to admit defeat quickly and come to terms with a former enemy, such as Mansell, if favourable agreements could be made.

Robson also exemplifies the entrepreneur who with very little capital of his own could 'project' a manufacturing enterprise, raise the necessary

---

[1] See above, pp. 55, 89–90.
[2] See above, pp. 41–3.
[3] See above, p. 42.
[4] Clavell MS. B2/3, Baggeley to Clavell.

funds, supply a technical manager and get the business under way. Though he started in glassmaking by managing the Blackfriars glasshouse, the Irish venture was his own. After buying the patent rights for glassmaking in Ireland he persuaded Sir John Levingston, one of the Grooms of His Majesty's Chamber, and Humphrey and John Holloway, both merchants and the latter a Controller of the Customs, to invest in his scheme. His kinsman John Hawys, who was like Robson a member of the Salters Company, had had enough experience in glassmaking at Blackfriars to manage the new Irish glasshouse, and the five men became partners. The five-part indenture drawn up between them,[1] however, indicated that they did not make equal investments. There were to be six shares, but Robson as holder of the patent rights was to receive his without payment. Hawys also paid nothing for his share, which he received in return for his management, or if he preferred he could collect a salary of 100 marks per annum. Humphrey Holloway held one share, John Holloway two shares and Levingston one share, for which they were to contribute £200 per share. Eventually the Holloways paid in their entire £600, but they claimed that Levingston did not. Robson asserted that he paid in £200 for Sir John according to a private understanding between them, so it seems obvious that Robson made Levingston a present of his share in order to have a friend at Court. A second indenture stipulated that if any further expenses were contracted above the £800 capital specified in the original agreement, they were to be borne in equal parts, the Holloways contributing one half, and Robson, for himself and Levingston, the other. Thus the Holloways were the chief financial backers, supplying three-quarters of the original capital and liable for half of further indebtedness, but they were to receive only half the profit, which, judging from the equation of Hawys's share with 100 marks (£66. 12s. 8d.), was expected to amount to £400 yearly.

The suit between Robson and the Holloways when the glasshouse was shut down indicated that the Holloways had not had £600 in ready assets. They were able to supply £100 in cash, which with Robson's £200 was sufficient to dispatch Hawys to Ireland. At the same time they gave Robson their penal bond for £200, and later were forced to borrow £200 jointly with Robson in order to pay the bond. The last £300 was paid in some time later; and the full capitalization of £800 was indeed expended. After the works were in production Humphrey Holloway went to Ireland to assist Hawys and drew several bills of exchange in amounts from £45 to £60 upon John Holloway and Robson for further expenses, but Robson claimed that these bills did not represent capital investment[2] and could

---

[1] Exch. K.R., Bills and Answers, E. 112/100/1122, *Holloway and Holloway* v. *Robson*. The enterprise was discussed in Chap. III.

[2] Whether or not the bills of exchange represented capital investment or running expenses was the principal point at issue in the lawsuit cited in the preceding note.

have been paid from the sale of finished glass then arriving in London in quantity. At the most conservative estimate, however, the full £800 was invested in the Irish factory. There is no indication of precisely how this was spent or of the size of the establishment, except that it is clear that there was only one furnace, and that this was wood-burning. Most of the capital was probably used not so much for land and buildings as for advance purchase of a year's supply of fuel, and for dead wages to the workmen while the furnace was being built and the pots and supplies prepared: one may compare Jacob Hensey's known debt of £540 at Bagot's Park for a year's fuel and other supplies.

The financial arrangements for Robson's venture help to throw light on the nature of the company, composed of Sir Edward Zouch, Thelwell, Mefflyn, and Percival, which secured in 1611 the patent for the coal process. There is little direct evidence about the financial arrangements, although Mansell said later that £5,000 was spent at a loss before he joined the firm.[1] This figure seems high, but may be somewhere near the true one, for it represented capital expenditure and running expenses on not one but two furnaces, not only during the experimental period but for the years from 1612 to 1615 when the furnaces operated at a loss. Costs were higher in the London area and considerably more capital was needed to experiment with the new process, build the expensive brick tunnels, and pay workmen during unproductive periods. During the same years Sir William Clavell lost over £2,000 trying to make alum with his own coal at Kimmeridge in Purbeck.[2] Undoubtedly in the case of Zouch's company the capital came not from merchants but from the two courtiers involved—Sir Edward Zouch himself and Bevis Thelwell. Zouch, a courtier and cousin of Lord Zouch, the Privy Councillor, was a man of considerable wealth who at his death owned land worth £1,500 per annum and a personal estate valued at £15,000 'at the least'.[3] Thelwell, a Page of the Bedchamber and Clerk of the Great Wardrobe, was also engaged in lending large sums of money to members of the aristocracy.[4] They were thus in a position to supply the necessary capital as well as to expedite the grant through the favour in which they both stood at Court. On the other hand Mefflyn, the King's Glazier, who took little part in the enterprise (he died soon after its inception) was not a man of means,[5] but he was familiar with the London market for window glass. Thomas

[1] S.P. 16/282, no. 99, 'Costes, charges difficulties and losses sustayned by Sir Robert Mansell in the busines of glasse'.

[2] Clavell MS. B1/1, Acquittance for Sir William Clavell, 15 Jac. I. Clavell owed the Crown £3,650 lent for the alum works. See also Mansel, p. 16; Price, p. 88.

[3] Chancery, C. 108/226.

[4] Cal. S.P.D., 1603-10, pp. 42, 349, 474; 1611-18, pp. 209, 123.

[5] At least, Baggeley, his successor, was little better off than most glaziers (Clavell MS. B 2/3, Baggeley to Clavell) and there is no indication that Mefflyn was more prosperous.

Percival seems also to have been in modest circumstances; since the invention of the coal process was attributed to him by the other patentees, he had undoubtedly supervised the experimentation,[1] and probably received his share, as did Hawys in the Robson company, in return for his services.

Judging by the experience of Robson's firm, it is probable that though a sum of about £5,000 may have been spent without yielding any return during the period from 1611 to 1615, such a sum would not all have been paid in immediately upon formation of the company, and much of it may have represented borrowed money. Nevertheless if this sum was actually spent in industrial production and not in graft or waste, it indicates that the amount of capital necessary to bring the coal process from tentative experiments to profitable production was beyond the means of most of the forest-glass makers. So far as is known, Isaac Bungar was the only one of them who could command or borrow capital of that proportion, and he was at the time investing in further woodlands.

As was shown in an earlier chapter, Zouch's company was still in debt in 1615, and the 'weariness' of the partners with further demands for money without a return prompted an enlargement of the company in January of that year by the addition of five new members, including Sir Robert Mansell. The shares were reorganized and a nine-part agreement was signed. Although no particulars are available, it is possible to reconstruct from Mansell's statements some estimate of the total capitalization. In the 1630s he stated that £30,000 was invested before the works 'could be broughte to any state of substance or could be perfected with Cole'. 'This was proved,' he asserted 'in the Parliament of 19 Jacobi and the particulars thereof delivered to Sir Edward Coke.'[2] Later in the same statement Mansell said that 'If he had then failed in perfecting the making of glasse with Newcastle cole . . . he would have beene inforced to have sitten downe with the loss of 36,000 li.'[3] In addition we know that when Mansell took over the sole direction of the monopoly late in 1615, he agreed to pay each of the nine patentees, including himself, the sum of £200 annually for his share. It seems likely then that the sum of £36,000 represented the total paper capitalization, which was divided into nine equal shares of £4,000 each, on each of which Mansell paid the sum of £200 per annum, amounting to interest at 5 per cent. The sum of £30,000, which is mentioned by Mansell twice as the amount invested,[4] may have represented the actual amount spent, so that the company began with at least £6,000 of what would today be called 'watered stock'.

Even though the nine shares were nominally equal, on the basis of the

---

[1] See Chap. III, p. 65.
[2] S.P. 16/282, no. 99, Mansell's 'Costes, charges, difficulties'.
[3] Ibid.   [4] Ibid.; S.P. 16/467, no. 66, 'State of my Workes for windowe glasse'.

Robson agreement one cannot assume that each of the nine patentees actually supplied an equal amount of capital. Of the original patentees Sir Edward Zouch was in the best position to contribute more capital and probably did so. Apart from Mansell the new share-holders consisted of two wealthy members of the aristocracy (the Earl of Montgomery and Sir Thomas Howard), a rich young merchant (Thomas Hayes), and a country squire (Sir Thomas Tracy). While the aristocrats were prominent at Court and were certainly recruited for their influence in maintaining the monopoly against opposition, it is likely that they contributed considerable capital as well. All of the five, in fact, had been investing in new and speculative enterprises.[1] Hayes and his father, a prominent Merchant Adventurer, had recently been exporting large amounts of cloth to the continent, but they ceased to do so after the adoption of Alderman Cockayne's project, so that young Hayes had fluid capital to spare.[2] Some of the share-holders, however, seem to have given bonds in lieu of cash: as late as 1624 all the capital had not yet been paid in.[3] As a result Mansell probably contributed more than his share to the stock of capital, for James Howell spoke of the 'great sums' which his employer 'melted in the glass business'.[4] In addition Mansell frequently borrowed on his own credit, although as he admitted his creditors were willing to lend him 'great somes of money vpon their special confidence in the validity of his Majesties letters patent, the only assurance they have for their indemnity'.[5] Although the shares may not have represented equal investments, they were nevertheless negotiable. In 1621 Sir William Herbert said that he owned one of the shares in the glass company as a result of a bad debt,[6] and in 1623 three others were in the hands of persons not in the original company—Sir Richard Smith, Sir Edward Leech, and the Lady Vere, who had inherited hers from Sir Thomas Tracy, her brother.[7] If Mansell is to be believed, he paid the share-holders their full annual payments until 1623,[8] but thereafter he seems to have paid only in proportion to actual investment. In this connection it is interesting that 'Doctor Percivall', an original share-holder and the technical man in the company, was among those complaining in 1623 that he stood to lose from the issue of a new patent to Mansell alone—a further indication that he, like Hawys in the Irish venture, had contributed no capital.

Considering the fact that the new company controlled by Mansell was obliged to set up enough coal-burning glass furnaces to supply the entire country with glass of all kinds, and that the two furnaces of that type

---

[1] For further biographical details and their business dealings with each other prior to becoming partners in the glass patent, see above, p. 78.

[2] A. Friis, pp. 93, 96, 472. Before 1615 Hayes and Co. usually exported over 1,000 cloths yearly.

[3] S.P. 16/521, no. 148.   [4] Howell, p. 103.   [5] S.P. 16/521, no. 148.

[6] *Commons Debates, 1621*, iv. 354.   [7] *A.P.C.* xxxviii. 464.   [8] S.P. 16/521, no. 148.

then in production were still debt-ridden, the projected total capitalization was hardly inflated. A full understanding of how the money was spent and whether or not the amount of the expenditure was justified must await more detailed investigation of costs of production with the coal process. It can be said here, however, that the abortive attempts to relocate the furnaces near coal-fields certainly involved heavy losses, and that there is no evidence of mismanagement or of unnecessary waste and graft, except for the annuities which did not represent return on actual investment. Contemporaneously the holders of the royal monopoly in alum were squandering large amounts of capital not only in Purbeck but in Yorkshire with far less eventual success.[1] A comparison between the management of the two monopolies speaks well for Mansell's honesty and for his ability in employing his limited amount of capital to the best advantage. He never had enough capital to own the industry outright, however, and in order to supply England with glass he was forced to resort to sub-leasing the privilege of using the coal process.

Even in the glasshouses which Mansell's firm controlled directly there were few innovations in management and marketing, and many glass-makers experienced little change in either their economic status or their relationship to outside capital when Mansell's company took over control. Certainly this was true in the London crystal-glass houses, where English capital had provided resident management and marketing for the Italian workmen since the turn of the century. In other furnaces, which Mansell technically owned, in fact he simply supplied the same sort of credit and marketing facilities that merchants and landowners had previously supplied, except that the workmen were generally, though not always, paid a salary. The enterprise at Wollaton on the Willoughby estates provides the clearest example. The glasshouse (the building and two furnaces) was built by Mansell's workmen, but apparently at Willoughby's expense, and the quality of the glass was tested before the formal contract between Mansell and Willoughby was signed. By its terms Mansell[2] leased the land, the glasshouse, and other buildings, and agreed to buy supplies of coal and other materials at specified rates. Willoughby, in spite of the urgings of Fosbrooke, his coal factor, wanted no further financial involvement, 'being', as he wrote, 'little acquainted either with the men or their occasions'.[3] Pauncefoote, Mansell's 'undertaker' for this project, served in two capacities, from which he profited in different ways. First, he came at intervals to settle accounts[4] and to make cash advances to each of the two chief workmen; he paid the broad-glass maker (Jacob Hensey) a

---

[1] Price, pp. 88–96; Upton, *passim*; see also above, p. 170, n. 1.

[2] Midd. MS. 5/165/140, Contract between Mansell and Willoughby.

[3] Folger, Bagot MS. L. a. 962, Willoughby to Bagot, 8 Oct. 1615. Willoughby's refusal to finance the works is discussed further on p. 85. See also Midd. MSS. 5/165/139, 141.

[4] Midd. MS. 5/165/133.

straight salary and the vessel-glass maker the cash equivalent of a third of the glass made.[1] For working capital he received from Mansell a flat rate of 15s. per case for the broad glass, 2s. a dozen for the vessel glass, and the difference between this price and the actual costs of operation was his profit for management. Secondly, he handled all the marketing of the glass, for which he received 1s. a case. So far as the workmen were concerned, he fulfilled the same function as had the merchant Nicholas Gellatt when Hensey was working at Bagot's Park. Willoughby's role was also little different from Walter Bagot's, for though technically he was in no sense an owner, in fact the sums owed to him for coal and sand were allowed to accumulate for months without interest,[2] so that he was actually supplying Pauncefoote with nearly as much credit as Bagot had supplied to Gellatt. Mansell sold the glass for 22s. 6d. the case; but in addition to paying Pauncefoote his commission, he was responsible for all the costs of transportation and of storage in Hull and London, along with other overheads (including the Crown rent and payments to the other patentees).

That arrangements of this nature were customary throughout the Mansell regime is suggested by correspondence during 1633–4 between Wentworth and his steward Robert Marris concerning the new glasshouse on the estates at Wentworth-Woodhouse.[3] Like Willoughby, Wentworth refused his steward's advice that he should finance the enterprise, and would not even pay for building the glasshouse, since he was concerned that 'if either the commodity failed or Sir Robert die I lose my money, the profit I looke for being principally in the uttering of my Coles'.[4] In this case Mansell seems not to have supplied the services of an agent, and Bristow, the glassmaker, acted as his own 'undertaker'. He asked the customary 15s. the case to cover his expenses and profit, but it was immaterial to him whether it was Mansell or Wentworth who financed his venture, so long as he obtained the credit, cash advances, and marketing facilities which he needed. Marris undertook the marketing for a time with Wentworth's reluctant consent, but Mansell supplied the cash and credit, which he had apparently already been doing for Bristow in another location.

Though there is no direct evidence, it is likely that the same sort of arrangements prevailed at Newcastle, too. One of the chief workmen, a Hensey or a Tysack, no doubt acted as foreman and manager of production, since it is known that the undertakers, Hobson and Robson, resided in London[5] and performed the usual functions of checking accounts,

---

[1] Midd. MS. 5/165/140, 141.2.   [2] Midd. MS. 5/165/135, 136.
[3] Straff. MS. 20/30 Marris to Wentworth, 12 Apr. 1631; 21/69, Wentworth to Marris, 19 May 1631.
[4] Ibid.
[5] Various petitions of the glaziers, discussed above on pp. 88–90, 110, make this clear.

making payments, and arranging for shipment of the glass during their visits to Newcastle. The workmen were largely free of the close super-vision which would have caused resentment, and most of them were no doubt as well off as they had been earlier. Certainly few of them fought against the Mansell regime after the Newcastle works were established and none appeared to testify against the monopoly in the Parliamentary investigation.

The window-glass makers who found it galling to give up nominal ownership, and who had enough capital of their own or could find proper backing could avail themselves of Mansell's leasing system. The yearly rent to Mansell presented no particular problem, for the fee was relatively low (£60 per annum in one instance)[1] and the lessees were allowed to sell their glass at the furnace door at the same price per case (22s. 6d.)[2] that Mansell charged in London after paying transportation costs. Even those who set up such semi-independent establishments, how-ever, usually fell back eventually into dependence upon merchants. Paul Tysack is a notable example. Though he was one of the more prosperous and was able to hold leases in his own name for land and a coal-burning glasshouse near Stourbridge by 1618,[3] his descendants did not profit greatly. When a fire destroyed his glasshouse in 1658 after his death, his son and son-in-law could not afford to rebuild it and were forced to work for a daily wage in Somerset for Robert Foley, an ironmaster who was also dealing in glass.[4] Since this occurred long after the Mansell patent had been cancelled, it is clear that economic factors rather than the patent of monopoly kept his descendants in economic subjection to merchants. Although the younger Paul Tysack eventually rebuilt the furnace on the same land that his father had leased, he was still dependent upon the Foleys for marketing and credit.[5]

The green-glass makers seem to have fared no better. Abraham Bigo could not finance his furnace without help in 1617, and after making leasing arrangements with Mansell he went into partnership with Sir William Clavell,[6] the landowner. The terms of their contract imply equal shares in ownership, for they were to bear equally the cost of the new glasshouse (which Bigo could thereafter use without payment of rent), Mansell's fee, and the charges of 'all tooles and materiales necessary about the glasshouse'. Since the lengthy contract was specific about all other financial details, it is notable that nothing at all was said about the price of Clavell's coal or about wages for the glassmakers, except that Bigo was to receive 'such rates as other men doe vsually worke in other glasshouses', and that he was to be responsible for hiring other workmen. It would

[1] Guttery, pp. 7–8.   [2] Ibid; and 'The True State of the Businesse of Glasse'.
[3] Guttery, p. 6.   [4] Ibid., pp. 9–10.
[5] Ibid., p. 9.   [6] Clavell MS. B2/1, Clavell–Bigo contract, 17 Nov. 1617.

seem logical to assume, therefore, that Clavell supplied the coal and Bigo the skilled labour and that these were considered to be roughly equivalent in value. Clavell in addition handled all the marketing, allowing free use of his quay in Kimmeridge Bay. Under this arrangement Bigo became indebted to Clavell, and later on the debt grew larger when Clavell forced Bigo into a new contract[1] by which Bigo in theory became sole owner, obliged to pay Clavell rent and assume all costs of production, including payment for the coal and all of Mansell's fee. In practice, however, Bigo paid Clavell in finished glass. Though the glass sold readily in Dorchester,[2] at fairs,[3] and in London, Bigo's share of the returns was so small that when he left for Ireland he managed to take enough capital to begin glassmaking again only by leaving Mansell's rent unpaid for several years and by leaving Clavell with insufficient glass to cover this and other financial obligations. Clavell, however, had clearly profited greatly while the works were operating, not only from the sale of his coal but by acting as merchant for all the finished glass, as his clamour when the furnace was shut down indicates.

The other chief drinking-glass factory for green drinking glasses— the one at Ratcliffe—was also originally owned by merchants, all of whom were shopkeepers, though they belonged to various London companies. The amount of capital which they invested and the details of their agreement with the glassmakers were never made clear in the quarrel which ended in their 'giving over' the works, but their yearly fee to Mansell (£300, three times that of Bigo's) is known.[4] Nor is it clear to whom Mansell re-let the works when they 'gave over' as a result of the sale of Clavell's glass in the London area, but it was probably another merchant.

The glass-sellers prospered under the Mansell regime, as their support of his patent and their ability to pay Charles I a large sum for their charter attested.[5] They seem not to have invested directly in the production of glass, however, until their charter was regranted in the Restoration period.[6] Like the glaziers, they were retailers of glass, and it was clearly neither retailers nor skilled glassmakers who dominated the industry in this period, but rather wholesale merchants who controlled the supply by furnishing the necessary capital and credit, as did Mansell's company.

The opposition to Mansell's monopoly in 1621–4 came largely from

[1] For the circumstances surrounding this contract and the documentation, see above, pp. 101, 104.

[2] Exch. K.R., Depositions by Commission, E. 143/James I/East. 22, *Mansell* v. *Clavell*, Deposition of Robert Short, Skinner of Dorchester.

[3] Harl. MS. 6715, fol. 48. Robert Jones of Barnstaple testified that he came to Woodbury Fair to buy Purbeck glasses.

[4] Exch. K.R., Barons' Depositions, E. 133/84/64, Depositions of Roger Culliford and John Jenkins.

[5] See above, p. 130.

[6] Thorpe, pp. 154–6.

other men who had been controlling the supply in this way, and who were struggling to maintain their position. Bungar, with Dines and Bennet, had been in control of the London market for window glass, and through the Vinions he had interests in the production of vessel glass as well. Clavell's interest in the production of and wholesale trade in green drinking glasses was similar to Bungar's in window glass; while John Worrall, though he claimed to have been trained in glassmaking at Blackfriars,[1] was like Robson a 'City' man and member of a London company. Those who knew him described him as 'broker'[2] or dealer. Together Bungar, Dines, Clavell, and Worrall supplied most of the capital for the Scottish glasshouses which provided the only serious competition to Mansell. There is no need to recount again the long struggle between this group and Mansell, and the efforts of the former to overthrow the patent by any means available, but it is worth pointing out that it was Bungar and his friends and not the glassmakers themselves who led and financed the attack on the patent, for they stood to gain most heavily by its overthrow. Though they were supported by a few glassmakers, on the whole the struggle was between two factions who were essentially merchants. Apart from the merchants, Mansell's partners included members of the aristocracy, the gentry, and the City of London; and while there were no peers among Bungar's allies, the gentry and the City were represented. Most glassmakers were indifferent as to which group financed them and sold their wares. A clear distinction between capital and labour had come about in the glass industry, and as compared with their proud forebears, the *gentilhommes verriers* of the continent, glassmakers of the mid seventeenth century made a precarious living in relatively humble circumstances. It would seem that the greatest change in their position had occurred before the changeover to the use of coal as fuel and arose from purely economic factors rather than from the imposition of a monopoly.

[1] S.P. 14/162, no. 64, petition of John Worrall.
[2] S.P. 16/521, no. 147, statement of the Glaziers Company.

VIII

COSTS OF PRODUCTION

THE information is not as complete as one would like concerning the costs of production in different branches of the industry at different periods of time and with different fuels. The most complete and reliable cost accounting[1] was made by Mansell's agent for two separate furnaces housed under one roof, which were built in 1615, one to make window glass, the other, green drinking glasses. The cost accounting shows that not only were the two under separate local management, but they used both coal and ashes at different rates. The term 'forest glass' is used by most writers to cover both types of glassmaking[2] and it has usually been assumed that there was little difference in the founding process and that the two were often carried on in the same furnace. This may have been the case (it was certainly so in the Middle Ages), but since Carré also, built separate furnaces for green and window glass, it seems likely that the aliens brought the tradition of separate furnaces, and of some differences in the batch and in the founding process, with them. When reading the following discussion of costs, the possible variations in the three branches of the industry—window, green, and crystal glass—must be kept in mind.

I. LAND, BUILDINGS, AND FURNACES

Capital investment in land and buildings was not a major factor in financing any glasshouse, but it was of least importance for the migrant forest-glass makers. Many of them paid no rent at all, for in the partnership arrangements which they negotiated with the gentry, the land and sometimes the buildings were often supplied free in anticipation of profits. Such seems to have been the case at Knole House, on the Bagot estates, and in the first arrangements between Bigo and Clavell in Purbeck.[3] When land was leased, the rental varied obviously with the amount of land and the value of the buildings. Albert Hensey paid only £3 per annum in 1607 for rent of his glasshouse,[4] while in the same year Liscourt paid £10 as tenant-at-will for land and a glasshouse near Newent in

---

[1] Midd. MS. 5/165/140, printed in full in the Appendix.
[2] In this work the term is used in the same way.
[3] Lennard, p. 128; Horridge, p. 27 (Bagot–Hensey contract, 5 June 1585); Folger, Bagot MS. L. a. 445; Clavell MS. B 2/1.   [4] Star Chamber Proc., Jac I, 179/7.

Gloucestershire.[1] Larger and more expensive furnaces and buildings sent the rentals up after the coal furnace was developed. In a new arrangement with Clavell in about 1620 Bigo agreed to pay £16 per annum for the facilities he had formerly been using free.[2] Mansell paid Willoughby £26. 13s. 4d. for land and buildings at Wollaton,[3] but this sum included not only land and the 'great barn' housing two furnaces, but a dwelling house and several other buildings formerly used for malting. On the Wentworth estates Mansell expected to pay £8 or £10 rent for land and the glasshouse, and another £6 annually for a dwelling-house for the glassmaker.[4]

A few glassmakers rented sufficient land to supply at least part of their fuel supplies. Jean Carré's lease of Fernfold near Alfold, Surrey, for a rental of £35 per annum included not only a 'fair dwelling' and two glasshouses but also the extensive wooded tract known as Fernfold Wood.[5] Similarly, when Bigo left Purbeck for Ireland he assumed all the feudal rents and obligations for the 'Castle, town and part of the plowland of Clonoghill with all the woods there, to be spent and employed on the premises' at a yearly rent of '24 li sterling at Michaelmas and our Lady Day equally with a fat hog at All Saints, two capons at Christmas and two hens at Shrovetide, his best beast for a herriot and 12 li sterling for a fine of alienation'.[6] Certainly he was in a position to supply his own fuel (wood) for the duration of his short stay. The right of a leaseholder to mine coal on leased land was less clear legally, unless specifically granted.[7] It is possible, however, that Paul Tysack's lease of property known as Colemans near Stourbridge in 1618 for £30 per annum may have stipulated the right to dig both coal and the valuable Stourbridge clay which lay beneath the surface.[8]

In London leases of land and suitable buildings were naturally more expensive. Although there is no record of what Verzelini paid for the Crutched Friars property or for his extensive woodlands in Kent,[9] some indication of London property rentals come from the Bowes venture. Bowes, acting for his assignees, Turner and Robson, first leased a large part of the former Blackfriars monastery for £66. 13s. 4d. per annum and then later added another lease for two rooms adjoining, formerly used for the Pipe Office, at a rental of £14. 6s. 8d.,[10] a total of £81. In addition to the 'greate vault . . . at the southwest end of the garden used and

---

[1] Glos. R.O. D4 21/13, Rental of the Wintour estates, 1607.

[2] Exch. K.R., Depositions by Commission, E. 143/James I/East. 22, *Mansell* v. *Clavell*, Deposition of John Jenkins.

[3] Midd. MS. 5/165/131.1.   [4] Straff. MS. 20/30.   [5] Add. MS. 5701, fol. 150.

[6] Westropp, p. 31. The terms of the lease are printed in full.

[7] For this right see Nef, *British Coal Industry*, i. 309–14.

[8] Guttery, p. 8, assumes that this was the case.   [9] GMR, Misc. MS. 20/2/12.

[10] Folger, Loseley MS. 349/63. The entire Blackfriars property owned by Sir George More and Sir Robert More was sold in 1609 for £1,300 to four London merchants with the leases to Bowes guaranteed for their duration. The agreement describes the property in detail.

employed for a glasshouse' the leased property included a 'great house' surrounded by 'a great garden . . . water courses and fountains' which Robson used as a residence. It is likely that the quarters in the complex of buildings known as Winchester House leased first by Salter and later taken over by Zouch and Mansell were at least as spacious,[1] though perhaps not as grand. Since Mansell used part of the Winchester House property as a storehouse for glass brought from Newcastle,[2] he probably rented (in addition to the buildings used for glassmaking) the 'large piece of ground inclosed with a Brick wall between the Pallace [Winchester House proper] and the River of Thames called St. Mary Overyes Wharfe'.[3] In that case the wharfage fee due to the Bishop cost him £20 per annum in addition to the rent of the buildings. At one time Mansell said that 'the rentes of his howses' cost him £400 altogether,[4] and since he had glasshouses at several locations in the London area, this is not unlikely. The Newcastle rents, if they were included, were probably a small part of the total. While there is no indication of Mansell's costs in Newcastle, in 1645 a Mr. Harris leased from the Mayor and Burgesses of Newcastle a parcel of ground on Tyneside 150 yards in length, 90 yards in breadth at one end and 40 at the other, and half the dock for a yearly rent of £10, but this did not include the 'toll of the two glasshouses' already built on the property, which he also leased for an unspecified fee.[5]

While the rental of land usually included the use of buildings to be used as dwellings and storehouses, occasionally these were rented in addition.[6] Nearly always, however, except when existing monastic buildings could be converted successfully, a new 'glasshouse' as well as the furnace proper had to be built. Though they sometimes asked for some abatement of their rent as compensation,[7] the glassmakers usually preferred to build the 'great barn' and furnace at their own charge, which was not great in the case of the wood-burning glasshouses. In Ireland, for example, a glasshouse 40 feet square and 36 feet high, framed and shingled, cost £8 to

---

[1] Winchester House, a London residence and palace for the Bishops of Winchester, was built in the twelfth century on a manor of fifty-eight acres, most of which had been built on and leased by the seventeenth century. Though the bishops still used the sprawling mansion occasionally, the Liberty of the Clink Token Book in 1614 lists fifteen tenants, one of whom was 'John Leech, Clerke of the Glasshouse'. There is no indication of the amount of space rented or the rental fee. See London County Council, Bankside: the Parishes of St. Saviour and Christchurch, Southwark, (Survey of London, ed. C. R. Ashbee et al., vol. xxii), (London, The London County Council, 1950), p. 47.   [2] S.P. 14/113, no. 51.

[3] Winchester, Dioc. R.O., MS. 155, 646 1-2/2. Parliamentary Survey of 1647, a description of the general layout of the buildings and notation of a few fees, including the wharfage fee.   [4] S.P. 16/282, no. 99.

[5] Newcastle-upon-Tyne, Council Minute Books, pp. 54-5. Later when the leases were renewed Harris and his partner were required not 'to cast rubbish from their glasshouse forward toward the river but backward'—an early concern for control of river pollution.

[6] Midd. MS. 5/165/137. Pauncefoote wished to rent two houses already built for £2 per annum, and a third for £5.

[7] Folger, Bagot MS. L. a. 445; Strafford MS. 20/30.

construct, while the furnace itself cost only £4.[1] The total cost was comparable to the estimated cost of a furnace and glasshouse in Staffordshire of twenty marks (£13. 6s. 8d.),[2] and was probably usual. The coal furnaces, especially the larger ones, were considerably more expensive to build, partly at least because of the bricked-in wind tunnels beneath the hearth. Abraham Bigo's coal furnace not counting the glasshouse which housed it, cost an estimated £30 to build, plus an additional amount for the cost of white bricks.[3] Wentworth's steward said that the glasshouse just finished at Wentworth-Woodhouse in 1631 cost exactly £37. 8s. 4d.[4] This last was intended for window glass; Bigo's for drinking glasses. Since both were coal-burning, we can assume that between £35 and £40 was usual for a glasshouse containing a single coal-burning furnace during Mansell's time, as opposed to about £12 for a wood-burning one. Later the size and cost increased, for though the original cost of Paul Tysack's glasshouse in Stourbridge is not known,[5] after it was destroyed by fire in 1658 his son estimated that it would cost £200 to replace it; though the young man's father-in-law claimed that it was actually replaced for £90.[6] By 1658 brick buildings may have been coming into use, even in the country, in an attempt to prevent such disastrous fires, and they were probably already in use in Mansell's day in urban areas. Mansell's attorney claimed that the total cost of the glasshouse at Ratcliffe was £300[7] including the furnace itself, and such a large sum suggests brick construction.

Mansell said that all told his buildings, in addition to his rents, cost him £5,000, and of this amount £2,000 was spent on buildings in Newcastle.[8] He said that 'the particulers thereof [were] delivered to Sir Edward Coke' at the time of the Parliamentary investigation, and the figures may well be true. At Newcastle he built not only the 3 large glasshouses and other necessary buildings, including storehouses for glass and for materials, and probably dwellings for the workmen, but also 2 of the 6 quays on the Tyne for shipping the glass. 'Forty sayle of shipps',[9] he said, were constantly employed in bringing the glass to London. It is evident that

---

[1] Westropp, p. 30. There is an interesting architect's drawing for a glasshouse dated 30 July 1615 in the Wollaton papers (Midd. MS. 5/165/130), which is also 40 feet square, probably the usual size for forest-glass houses; but since it was made before the arrival of the glassmakers and shows only one furnace it was probably not used when the furnaces were built later in the summer. The plan shows a 'master's lodging' 25 feet square, with two floors, and two smaller 'cabynets' about 8 feet by 10, presumably for storage of supplies.

[2] Folger, Bagot MS. L. a. 445, Hensey and Gellatt to Bagot.

[3] Clavell MS. B 2/1.   [4] Straff. MS. 20/30.

[5] Guttery (p. 7) assumes that the cost of Tysack's coal furnace was the same as that of the wood-burning furnace at Ballynegery, but in view of the design changes this is unwarranted.

[6] Guttery, p. 7, n. 2, and p. 10.

[7] Exch. K.R., Depositions by Commission, E. 134/Jac I/East. 22. *Mansell* v. *Clavell*.

[8] S.P. 16/282, no. 99.

[9] S.P. 14/164/231 B. Mansell said that no ship carried more than 50 cases on a single voyage. The ships from Newcastle carried coal for the London glass furnaces in the same cargo.

capital expenditure in land and buildings increased enormously after the change to the use of coal as fuel.

II. TRANSPORTATION

For most glasshouses in England transportation was not a serious problem, as we have seen, for they customarily sold their glass at the furnace door. There were of course exceptions. The request of one pair of glassmakers to keep 'two or three nags' in the park on the Bagot estates[1] suggests that they may have been keeping their own pack horses for transporting the glass. In the Weald where there was a concentration of furnaces the separate trade of glass carrier grew up,[2] and the services of these carriers could be hired by merchant and glassmaker alike, as desired.

Even if glass carriers were available, land transportation by pack horse or cart was costly, sometimes twenty times as expensive as sea carriage.[3] Some of the early glassmakers settled near ports such as Rye and when their furnaces were closed down because of the shortage of wood, they tried to move to sites near navigable rivers whenever possible. The right combination of cheap fuel and suitable supplies of sand and clay was not always available on a river, however; and in the Weald in particular, where many glassmakers stayed, there were few navigable streams. The Wey seems not to have been navigable before 1653,[4] but it was possible, though slow and tortuous, to manœuvre barges on the Arun[5] below Wisborough Green to the small 'outports' of Arundel and Littlehampton. Some land transportation was still necessary from the furnaces in the vicinity of Kirdford, North Chapel, and Wisborough Green, but the water route lessened the cost for the rest of the way. When Isaac Bungar began to gain control of the London market in window glass he assumed responsibility for delivering the glass to London and it was this route that he seems to have employed.[6] He charged 2s. a case more for glass delivered at Broken Wharf in London than for that sold at the furnace door,[7] so presumably this was the cost of transportation by the water route.

---

[1] Folger, Bagot MS., L. a. 445.

[2] Kenyon, pp. 111–12.

[3] T. S. Willan, *The English Coasting Trade, 1600–1750* (New York, Kelley Reprint, 1967), p. xiv. Transportation by river cost more than by sea, but less than by land. See Willan, *River Navigation in England, 1600-1750* (New York, Kelley Reprint, 1965), chap. vii.

[4] Willan's map of navigable rivers shows the Wey navigable from Guildford, but his authority is dated 1653 (Willan, pp. vi, 147). That is about when it became navigable, according to P. A. L. Vine (*London's Lost Route to the Sea* (London, David and Charles, 1965), p. 22).

[5] Vine, p. 11.

[6] Guildhall MS. 5758, no. 5; Port Books E. 190/756/21, Chichester and outports.

[7] *A.P.C.* xxxiv. 409, 3 Apr. 1616.

Cheap water transportation was equally important to Mansell, for like Bungar he attempted to supply the London market with window glass made at some distance from London, and he naturally sought sites on coal-fields near the sea or navigable rivers. Since he in part blamed high transportation costs for the shutting down of the glasshouse near Nottingham on Sir Percival Willoughby's estates it is worth detailing the exact costs, which fortunately are known. Willoughby's steward Fosbrooke, eager to see glassmaking undertaken, made an estimate before work was begun that was optimistically low—18s. for the transportation of a ton of window glass (10 cases).[1] A later document with more specific figures[2] shows that to carry a ton of glass by land from Wollaton to 'Nottingham Bridges', a distance of 2 miles, cost 4s., from thence by water to Hull it cost 7s. 6d., and from Hull to London only 8s. Certain fees in addition, 'wharfage and howseroome' at Hull, the King's custom, fees to the factor, and charge for the cockett[3] added another 3s. 1d. per ton, so that the total cost of transportation to London is given as £1. 2s. 7d. Fosbrooke had put one item in the first account, of 6d. per ton for storage and wharfage at Nottingham Bridges, which was omitted, no doubt mistakenly, in the second. These facilities were important: for the coal dealers sometimes complained that 'though the Trente be almost continuallie banke full and bootes might go downe at pleasure . . . not one boote styrreth or one boote moveth'.[4] If 6d. more is added, the total cost of shipment from the furnace at Wollaton to the wharf in London was about 23s. the ton. In spite of the slow journey down the Trent, the cost was comparable to the cost of shipment from Bungar's furnaces near Wisborough Green (20s. a ton). Nevertheless Mansell needed cheaper transportation in order to cut costs further and Newcastle offered advantages in this respect. Mansell's furnaces there were located close enough to the Tyne[5] for glass to be loaded directly onto ships from his storehouse, eliminating the expensive land- and river-carriage as well as the fees incurred in transferring loads from ship to ship. There are no direct figures, but it is likely that the cost of shipping the glass to London was cut by half.

III. LABOUR AND WORKING CONDITIONS

Skilled labour was one of the most expensive as well as the most necessary of the prerequisites for glassmaking, but its cost is one of the most difficult of the industry's costs to ascertain with precision. Skilled glassmakers, whether they were independent or under contract, usually worked

[1] Midd. MS. 5/165/139.2.   [2] Midd. MS. 5/165/139.4.
[3] A cockett was a warrant for the shipment of goods.
[4] R. S. Smith, 'Huntington Beaumont', *Renaissance and Modern Studies*, i (1957), 146.
[5] Brand, ii. 43–6.

in teams of two or three, and their recompense was generally calculated in relation to their total output of glass. Several references to the 'glass-makers third'[1] imply that the wages of skilled labour amounted to roughly a third of the value of the glass made, and sometimes the team took a third of the glass in lieu of cash. For drinking-glass making three men constituted the normal team, called a 'chair'.[2] For crown-glass making there were only two in a team. For glass made by the Lorraine or cylinder method, it has usually been assumed, on the basis of Carré's contract[3] with the Hennezells, that three men were needed in a team, for the contract seems to imply the employment of six skilled glassmakers working in teams of three at each of two 'ovens'. At Bagot's Park and at Wollaton, however, (where in each case one of the Henseys, anglicized descendants of the Hennezells, was working), the evidence is reasonably clear that teams of two made 'broad' glass.[4] Perhaps improvements in technique had permitted a reduction in the size of the team from three to two (though it is also possible that they were actually making crown, not cylinder glass).[5] Whether the team was composed of two or three glass-makers, differences between the members in status and in pay are not always clear. Since there were no craft guilds to enforce regulations, and close ties of kinship prevailed between masters and younger men being trained, arrangements as to apprenticeship or journeyman status seem to have been most informal. Sometimes it would appear that the wages of the 'principal workman' included the labour of an apprentice as well,[6] at other times two workmen received separate wages of unequal amount,[7] and in still other arrangements two or three master workmen seem to have received equal pay or to have operated as equal partners.[8]

The earliest specific information on both wages and the rate of output comes from Carré, who negotiated separate contracts with the men from Lorraine and with the Normans. The Hennezells from Lorraine, who were part-owners of their furnace, stipulated that they were to receive 'two hundreth crowns [£50] every yere . . . for recompense of our third of the glass' and in addition half the profits of the enterprise when all expenses had been paid.[9] Each team was to produce 30 bundles per day,

---

[1] Lansd. MS. 59, no. 76, enclosure; Midd. MS. 5/165/140.

[2] The term derives from the chief glassmaker's use of a chair with flat wooden arms on which the pontil, an iron rod fixed to the vessel, was twirled.

[3] Lansd. MS. 59, no. 76, enclosure.

[4] Folger, Bagot MS. L. a. 446; Midd. MSS. 5/165/139.1 and 140.

[5] The term 'broad' seems to have been used for either kind at that time (see above, p. 5, n. 3), and contacts and intermarriage in England between glassmaking families of different traditions would account for the Henseys acquiring the crown-glass technique.

[6] This seems to have been the case for the furnace at Ballynegery, Ireland, since the weekly expenses include the salary of only one glassmaker. See Westropp, p. 25.

[7] Midd. MS. 5/165/140.

[8] Lennard, p. 129; Folger, Bagot MS. L. a. 446; Lansd. MS. 59, no. 76, enclosure.

[9] Ibid.

the equivalent of 1½ cases. The wording of the contract is slightly ambiguous and might be taken to mean that each team was to receive only £50 yearly, but it is much more likely that each man was to receive that sum, making a total of £150 for the team. Since the contract said that their wages represented a third of the value of the glass, which was probably worth about £1 a case at the furnace door,[1] the Hennezells must have estimated that they would make about 450 cases in a year. At the stated rate of 1½ cases a day, however, they would have had to work six days a week for fifty weeks a year in order to produce 450 cases, a highly unlikely working pattern which would not have allowed sufficient time for furnace repairs. In Ireland at the furnace of 'Davy the glassmaker' the working year consisted of only 'twenty-four or . . . (blurred) weeks, if the furnace fire keep in so long'.[2] This must not be taken to mean that half a year of work was followed by half a year of resting, but rather that there were three or four periods during the year when the fires were allowed to die down so that repairs could be made and new pots and batches prepared.[3] The periods for resting and repairs seem to have varied in length, but in some cases, such as Davy's, half the normal working year was lost. Moreover, information from every other glasshouse where rates of production are mentioned indicates that the making of 3 cases a day, or 18 a week, was expected when the men were blowing glass.[4] It would seem, then, that the Hennezells, who negotiated their contract on a yearly rather than a daily or weekly basis (as was more usual) inserted the reference to 1½ cases per day as an indication of their average daily production over a period of a year with allowance for non-productive periods for repairs, and not as an indication of their actual rate when working. Carré, who was familiar with the working patterns of glassmakers, would have understood this.

The Norman glassmakers who worked contemporaneously for Carré's firm were employed on a different basis. According to Becku, Carré's associate in the glassmaking patent, the 'principall workeman' (Peter Bungar) received the very high wage of 18s. per day and was bound to produce 3 cases of glass daily.[5] Becku complained, however, that he did not hold to that rate, for in a period of about five months he had made

---

[1] Cylinder glass then sold in London for 35s. a case (see below, Table I, p. 202); but a margin of 15s. for over-land transportation, the services of agents, and the high profits in which the Hennezells shared seems reasonable.

[2] Westropp, pp. 29–30.

[3] The steward at Knole House said that 'the men work . . . only whyles the founder is tempering his metal' (Lennard, p. 128), and in crystal-glass making firing took place four times a year. S.P. 14/162/, no. 231 B. See also the discussion of fuel deliveries below, pp. 194–5.

[4] This was true of Bungar (Lansd. MS. 59, no. 76), of Davy (Westropp, p. 25), of Paul Tysack (Guttery, p. 8), of Jacob Hensey (Midd. MSS. 5/165/139.1 and 140), and of Bristow (Straff. MS. 20/30); in fact the two latter sometimes made 19 to 20 cases in a week.

[5] Lansd. MS. 59, no. 76.

only 200 cases, a little over half the amount that Becku expected had Bungar worked steadily for six days a week. It is clear that Bungar lost almost as many working weeks in a year as did Davy in Ireland, but Becku, a newcomer to the industry who had had no share in negotiating either contract, did not understand the reason for the unproductive periods. If Becku's assertion of Bungar's actual production in five months is correct and if this average was usual for him throughout the year, then in a year he would have made slightly more glass than the Hennezells (about 480 cases as compared with 450). His wages were far higher, however, even though he was almost certainly paid only for the days when he was actually working, as were other glassmakers on a daily or weekly salary,[1] in spite of Becku's imputation to the contrary.[2] At 18s. a day or £5. 8s. a week for the twenty-five weeks that he probably worked in a year his annual salary would have amounted to £135, more than twice as much as the £50 that each of the Hennezells received. It must be remembered, however, that the yearly remuneration for the team, not the individual, was in rough proportion to the value of the glass made. The three Hennezells, apparently equal in status, worked as a team whereas Bungar needed only one helper, his brother,[3] who may have been an apprentice or at most a journeyman. Though the younger Bungar's wages are not given, he undoubtedly received far less than Peter. He may have been paid as little as £1 a week, and if so, his yearly wages for working twenty-five weeks, plus Peter's wages (£135), would have been £160, again a third of the value of the glass.[4] The method of computing wages on the basis of output per team thus helps explain the discrepancy in the rate of pay for individuals and also the pressure to reduce the size of the team from three to two.

Though they sometimes described themselves as 'poor men', the rates of pay for all skilled glassmakers certainly indicate that they were poor only in comparison with rich merchants or the gentry on whose estates they settled.[5] They were far above the ranks of the average craftsmen,

---

[1] This is specifically stated in Bristow's case (Straff. MS. 20/30), and implied in the weekly cost accounting for Davy's furnace (Westropp, p. 25) and for Jacob Hensey's at Wollaton (Midd. MS. 5/165/140).

[2] Although Becku said that Bungar was bound to make 3 cases of glass daily 'which is . . . not accomplished and yet payd for' (Lansd. MS. 59, no. 76), it must be remembered that Becku had had no share in negotiating the contract or paying the workmen. See above pp. 21–5.

[3] See above, p. 22.

[4] £480 calculated at 20s. per case at the furnace door, the same as for glass made by the Lorrainers (see above, p. 185 and n. 1). Judging by contemporary London prices (see below, Table 1, p. 202) I think this estimate may be slightly high for crown glass, but it suffices to demonstrate the relationship between wages and value of the glass, a relationship which was only approximate.

[5] According to Hammersley (*Business History*, p. 13) a solid country gentleman had an income of over £300 as compared with Bungar's income of about £135 or a little more.

and when they owned their furnaces, they were employers themselves. Bungar's wage of over £5 a week when working enables one to understand his wrath when Becku attempted to force the training of Englishmen in so lucrative a craft, for once the monopoly of skill preserved by the glassmaking families was broken, wages might very well decline. Actually they did decline, even though few Englishmen were trained, largely it would seem because of the rapid influx of alien glassmakers from the continent in the 1570s and 1580s and the fall of the price of glass on the London market.[1] The value of the 'glassmaker's third' was rapidly reduced, since by 1596 a member of the Bungar family was forced to sell glass delivered in London at 14s. a case. In 1621 in Ireland Davy was paid 3s. the case for making glass and since he normally made 3 cases a day or 18 a week,[2] the same as Bungar in 1568, his wages of 54s. weekly were exactly half those paid to Bungar. Even such a drastic reduction in salary left him better off than the glassmakers hired by Mansell. The Wollaton accounts[3] show that Jacob Hensey, the master workman at the window-glass furnace, received only 30s. a week, and his assistant was paid 20s. They too normally made 18 cases a week, though Mansell's agent said that sometimes they made 20. In either case they no longer received the equivalent of a third of the glass, for it was then valued at 15s. at the furnace door and they received only 50s. between them instead of the 90s. to 100s. theoretically due to them. The number of weeks worked in the year had been increased, however, for instead of 25 to 30 which seems to have been usual in 1568, 35 to 40 was considered more usual,[4] and about 700 cases a year may have been made altogether. Whether the technique in furnace building and repair had been improved to prevent such long delays or whether the men had deliberately shortened their resting periods cannot be clearly determined, but desire to increase their yearly income no doubt provided the motivation.

All these examples pertain only to window-glass makers, but the makers of green drinking glasses also traditionally received a third of the glass or its value. There is no indication of the rate of production or of the value of the glass during the early period; but at Wollaton the drinking-glass makers were faring better than the makers of window glass. The item in the accounts[5] for their pay reads simply 'the workemens third— £5', but since a team of 3 was normal it would be reasonable to suppose

<hr />

[1] See Tables 1–3, and discussion of prices, pp. 201–4.   [2] Westropp, p. 26.

[3] Midd. MS. 5/165/140.

[4] Guttery, p. 7. Fosbrooke also estimated that 800 cases might be made in a year at the rate of 16 to 18 cases weekly, which implies 45 to 50 weeks' work in a year (Midd. MS. 5/165/139.1), but Hensey was not making more than about 600 cases a year, though he said that he could make 1,000 cases if Mansell built a larger furnace (probably a 'double' one) and lent him more money (ibid., 5/165/133). Presumably he would then have employed a second team.

[5] Midd. MS. 5/165/140, printed in Appendix A.

that of this amount the chief workman received 40s. weekly and each of two assistants 30s. That 40s. was Mansell's usual weekly wage for a master drinking-glass maker is corroborated by his offer of that sum to Paul Vinion in 1618.[1] At Wollaton, however, the tradition was followed of giving the skilled workmen as a team not a set wage, but the cash equivalent of a third of the value of the glass (the total value in this case being £15 exactly). Since the drinking glasses were worth 2s. the dozen at the furnace door, they must have normally turned out 150 dozen a week. In view of the tenacity of the tradition, it is very likely that when Abraham Bigo began making drinking glasses in Purbeck he was paid in the same way under his first contract with Clavell, which specified only that he be paid at the same rate as 'other men doe usually work'.[2]

The highly skilled Italian glassmakers employed in London earned considerably more than green-glass makers. Their rate of production must have been lower (at least when they fashioned intricate shapes) but their glass was much more valuable and their remuneration no doubt bore some relationship to the value of their product—even though most of these glassmakers were paid a straight weekly salary. Maria del Aqua, one of Mansell's employees, said that he 'came over to England at Sir Robert Mansells charges, upon the salary of 38s. a weeke certaine besides his extraordinaries which came sometimes to 20s. and sometimes to 40s. over and above his wages'.[3] How these 'extraordinaries' were calculated is not specified, but they were probably based on the number of difficult commissioned orders which he completed. Much later the Venetian Ambassador tried to persuade Gaspero Brunoro, a well-known glassmaker trained at the famous Three Crowns Works in Murano, to return to his native land, but was unable to do so because the man had made a contract with Mansell for seven years 'enticed by earning 20 ducats a week'.[4] Since the silver ducat of Italy was worth between 3s. 6d. and 4s. at the time,[5] Brunoro must have received between 70s. and 80s. a week, or about what Maria del Aqua earned at his peak. By the Ambassador's own testimony, Brunoro could make any of the specialities of Venice—the finest crystal glass, coloured glass, and large mirrors—so that the disparity between his and his fellow craftsmen's wages on the one hand, and those of the green-glass makers on the other is readily understandable.

If the Venetians are left out of consideration as a special case, it is clear that by 1615 the wages of window-glass makers had declined by at least half; although those of the makers of green drinking glasses held their level somewhat better so that there was a decided differential in the

[1] S.P. 14/105, no. 18.
[2] Clavell MS. B 2/1, Contract between Clavell and Bigo, 1619.
[3] S.P. 14/112, no. 28, 1st document.
[4] Cal. S.P. Ven. 1636-39, p. 391.   [5] OED, 'Ducat'.

two rates of pay. All wages, partly as a result of the traditional method of remuneration, bore at least some relationship to the price level of the wares. The fact that Jacob Hensey was willing to accept Mansell's terms of 30*s*. a week without protest indicates that he can hardly have been earning more on his own account before the monopoly took effect; thus the decline in the wages of window-glass makers cannot be blamed on the royal patent. Rather it was the greater availability of skilled labour, resulting from continued immigration, the natural increase in population of the glassmaking families, and the training of some Englishmen (in spite of strenuous efforts to prevent this) that was responsible for the reduction in wages. The green-glass makers may have been less numerous and more prosperous, for Vinion at least refused Mansell's offer of 40*s*. a week for several years, and instead offered to pay him the high fee of 20*s*. a week for the privilege of continuing as an independent workman.[1] The fact that most of the green-glass makers worked as independent subsidiaries rather than accept Mansell's salaries perhaps indicates that he was attempting to use his monopoly to force wages down in that sphere of glassmaking.

When glassmakers were independent there were few wage disputes or other labour troubles. Occasionally we hear of quarrels between close kin,[2] but most of the time, as the steward at Knole reported, 'the men agree very well, God be praysed'[3] even when they were of different nationality. The determination of Mansell and his subordinates to force wages down in crystal-making, however, led to serious labour difficulties. For some crystal-glass makers there was always the option of returning to the continent or crossing the border to Scotland. It is interesting in this respect that Lady Mansell was a more severe taskmaster than her husband. The Broad Street works suffered most from continual defections, and in spite of his high wages, Maria del Aqua was one of those who broke his contract in order to go to Scotland.[4] Pickayes, the agent who lured him away, shed some light on his dissatisfaction by asserting that Lady Mansell 'would have him [Maria] to make more glasses in a weeke than he was wont to make before, and his wages to be no more than before'.[5] Somewhat later several English-born glassmakers commented further on the reasons for discontent at Broad Street. They charged that 'the Lady Mansell of late received fforraigne glassmakers and compelled some of your petitioners to serve them, which said strangers by abatement of their wages and some other discontents offered them by the Lady Mansell . . . departed the kingdome.'[6] While jealousies between the English

---

[1] S.P. 14/105, no. 19. See also above, p. 94.   [2] Horridge, p. 29.
[3] Lennard, p. 129.   [4] S.P. 14/112, no. 28, statement of John Maria del Aqua.
[5] Ibid., statement of Agmondesham Pickayes.
[6] S.P. 14/148, no. 52, 'petition of James Lambart, John Williams, and William Tudman to the Privie councill', July 1623.

glassmakers and the Italians no doubt contributed to the difficulties, the chief source of trouble was undoubtedly the required rate of production and the terms of pay. Somewhat later this same group of English glassmakers complained that 'Lady Mansell will neither give them work nor discharge them of her service',[1] but since they had been employed at Broad Street making crystal and there was an extreme shortage of workmen skilled enough for this task, it is likely that their unemployment was a temporary result of their refusal to work at the wages and the rate of production offered. Without continental connections they could not flee the country in search of higher pay.

The expenses of constant recruiting on the continent for skilled glassmakers must be added to their wages in assessing the labour costs of the industry. There is no way of estimating the amounts spent in this fashion, though we know from Howell's extended stay on the continent at Mansell's expense,[2] and the frequent mention by men such as Maria del Aqua that they had come at Mansell's request and expense, that the cost of such recruiting cannot have been insignificant. It is not surprising then, that Mansell complained of the Scottish glassworks not only because of the competition they provided in the sale of glass but because of their enticement of men from his works; and that he eventually found it cheaper to buy out the Hay patent rather than face the need for constant recruitment.

The glassmakers were not the only wage-earners in the industry. Of the other people employed in making glass, the founder was the most highly skilled. At Davy's furnace in Ireland the founder received 7s. weekly, with the promise of a rise to 8s. if his work proved especially good.[3] At Wollaton the founder for the drinking-glass furnace also received 7s. a week, although the broad-glass founder was paid 10s.[4] At about the same time carpenters, masons, and plumbers received an average wage of 1s. a day[5] (6s. weekly), so the founders' wages were only slightly above those of skilled workers in the building trades. The 'tezeurs' or fire-tenders received less, 5s. a week at Wollaton, or about the same as agricultural workers received.[6] There were at least two tezeurs for each furnace and in Ireland there seem to have been four.[7] The pot-maker was nearly as highly skilled as the founder and as essential; but it is difficult to estimate his usual wage. The only indication, which comes from the Wollaton accounts, give the sum of 6s. 8d. weekly—but this included the cost of 'poot clay' as

---

[1] S.P. 14/118, no. 53. At the time of this dispute Sir Robert was in England and not at sea, but Lady Mansell took an active part in management of the business at all times, as in fact did Abraham Bigo's wife, who kept his accounts. See Exch. K.R., Barons' Depositions, E. 133/84/64.

[2] See above, p. 81.   [3] Westropp, p. 25.

[4] Midd. MS. 5/165/140.   [5] Rogers, v. 664–5.

[6] Ibid.

[7] Westropp, p. 25. Westropp transcribes the MS. as '1 Tezeurs or men to tend the fire—18s.' but I think it likely that the first number is '4'.

well as of the making of the pots, and in addition it seems as though the
two furnaces may have shared the services of a single man and that the
expense of his work was divided between the two (the same figure is
given for each furnace). This is the more likely since the case-maker at
Wollaton, who was certainly less skilled, received 8s. a week, a sum
which did not include the lumber, while the packer of the window glass
was paid 5s. There is no mention of case-making and packing at the green-
glass furnace, but the full-time clerk who kept the accounts received
7s. 6d. a week, slightly more than the founder.[1]

IV. FUEL: WOOD AND COAL

Fuel was another major item of expense in operating a glasshouse. The
cost of fuel showed the widest variation; and since the price of each type
of fuel varied according to source, the difference in cost between the two
fuels was not as great as is sometimes imagined. That the cost of wood
was rising in general throughout the Elizabethan period has often been
demonstrated,[2] but more detailed information is needed in order to
estimate the actual cost for glassmakers. One of the earliest indications
comes from the accounts of the glasshouse at Knole House in Kent,
which show that in 1585 a cord of wood cost 3s. 4d.[3] Deliveries of at
least 30 and frequently of 60 cords were made regularly to the glasshouse,
but since the steward said the furnace did not operate continuously, it is
difficult to be certain of the average rate of consumption per week. However, the purchase of 452 cords in a period of about 25 weeks (27 July to
18 January 1584–5), an average of 18 cords a week, suggests that over
900 cords, perhaps closer to 1,000, were used in a year at a total cost of
from £150 to £166. That the price at Knole was not unrepresentative is
indicated by the fact that in 1596 a cord of wood cut from the Bacon
estates was sold for exactly the same amount (3s. 4d.).[4] In about 1585
wood was substantially cheaper in Staffordshire, however, for the glassmakers who settled on the Bagot estates in that year paid only 2s. 4d. a
cord.[5] Assuming that the rate of consumption was the same at Bagot's
Park as at Knole House, the total yearly cost of the fuel in the former
location was only £112—certainly a sufficient saving to induce some
glassmakers to move away from the south. But scarcity of wood and
rising prices followed them, for about twenty years later Walter Bagot
raised the price of wood for a new team of glassmakers to 4s. 2d. a cord,[6]
almost doubling the cost of fuel. Since this second team stated during
their bargaining with Bagot that at the agreed rate of 4s. 2d. they would

[1] Midd. MS. 5/165/140.   [2] Nef, British Coal Industry, i. 221–2.
[3] Lennard, p. 126.   [4] Univ. of Chicago, Bacon MS., 'Wood sold Anno 1596'.
[5] Horridge, p. 27, quoting in full the agreement between Ambrose Hensey and Richard
Bagot, 5 June 1585.
[6] Folger, Bagot MS. L. a. 445.

consume wood to the value of £200 yearly,[1] the number of cords they expected to burn (960) agrees to a remarkable extent with the estimate from Knole House, and can be taken to be the usual level of consumption. By 1615, when the glass furnace at Bagot's Park was closed down by the proclamation forbidding the use of wood, both Bagot and Gellatt (the merchant who had been marketing the glass) claimed that wood already cut, which represented a year's supply, was worth £300.[2] There is no reference to the price of wood by the cord. By this time Jacob Hensey had replaced the earlier glassmakers at Bagot's Park, under a new contract; if the statements of Bagot and Gellatt were true, Jacob was paying almost half again as much for wood as his immediate predecessors, and fuel costs had almost tripled since 1585. Though there is no indication that Jacob Hensey tried to lower costs by experimenting with the use of coal as fuel, there is no doubt that he left Bagot's Park abruptly and willingly to enter Mansell's employ,[3] largely because he was seriously in debt. When trying to recover damages for his unused fuel, Bagot claimed that he had no other purchaser for it:[4] since it was already cut and cleft into small pieces for the glasshouse, this may have been true. There is ample evidence, however, of the sale of wood from the Bagot estates for conversion into charcoal for the iron furnaces and forges in the area,[5] so that it was clearly demand from both the glass and the iron industry, as in the Weald, that had forced up prices.

There were still areas of England, however, where glassmakers could obtain wood at moderate rates. This was probably true for Abraham Liscourt near Newent in Gloucestershire;[6] and the glassmakers who migrated to north Wales, to Devon, and to Yorkshire were certainly motivated by lower fuel costs. Ireland was even more desirable. The estimate of weekly expenses for the glasshouse at Ballynegery, County Waterford, as late as 1621 gives the cost of wood as only 12d. per cord.[7] This clearly refers only to the cost of 'cutting, cropping and cleaving small' wood belonging to the owner of the glasshouse, and is hardly comparable to the selling price of wood in England; but since the owner did not think it worthwhile to estimate any further charge for the fuel in his cost accounting, it may be assumed that he made no extra charge, because he had no other market for his wood.

In London the cost of wood throughout the period for the crystal-glass

[1] Folger, Bagot MS. L. a. 445.

[2] Horridge, pp. 31–2, quoting in full Gellatt to Coke, 5 Aug. 1615; Bagot to Mansell, 1616. In 1617 Bagot asserted that the wood was worth £400. See Folger, Bagot MS. L. a. 147, Bagot to Mansell.

[3] See above, p. 84.   [4] Folger, Bagot MS. L. a. 147.

[5] Folger, Bagot MSS. L. a. 305, 328, 974.

[6] Notes kindly lent by G. Hammersley indicate that wood at Newent in 1607–14 was plentiful and cheap.

[7] Westropp, p. 30.

furnaces was naturally higher than in the country, because of transportation costs and competing demand from other users. Verzelini bought by the billet[1] rather than the cord, and at the time that fire destroyed his first glasshouse, he is said to have had stored there 400,000 billets of wood.[2] Thus the glass-sellers' complaint, a year later, that he consumed annually about 500,000 billets in his furnace,[3] was probably not an exaggeration— the amount of wood in store was normally close to a year's supply. Thorold Rogers has shown that billets of wood sold for 12s. per thousand in London in 1574[4] (the year of the fire), so it is probable that during his first years of operation Verzelini spent annually about £300 on fuel. This was twice the amount that the glassmakers at Knole House paid for fuel in 1585, but the high value of the crystal glass made it possible to absorb higher fuel costs and still operate at a profit. Even so, Verzelini's purchase of extensive woodlands, in order to avoid some of the increase in price and protect his supply, shows that he was concerned about the price of fuel.[5] The English patentees who supplanted him in crystal production were more severely affected, for the price of 1,000 billets of wood rose in London to 13s. 4d. in 1580, then to 14s. 8d. or 16s. in 1594, and 18s. 8d. in 1608.[6] This steady increase, though not as great as that at Bagot's Park (perhaps because supplies of wood were drawn from a larger area) was large enough to cause serious concern. Assuming that the annual rate of consumption in the crystal furnaces remained the same, it must have cost Robson at least £466 per annum for fuel for the Blackfriars glasshouse in 1608, as opposed to £300 for Verzelini in 1575. Estimated in another way, by the load instead of the billet, if Robson had burned 900 loads, as did the furnace at Knole House, his costs would have run from £450 to £540 a year—for wood by the load sold for from 10s. to 12s. in London in 1602.[7] All other costs in crystal-making at the time remained relatively constant; but the rise in fuel costs forced Robson to charge higher prices than did Verzelini or the importers of Venetian crystal, and to crush cheaper competition by enforcing his monopoly.

It was in London, where the first successful experiments with the use of coal began, that pressure seems to have been greatest for the change to the new fuel. In general coal was cheaper than wood, though its price

---

[1] A billet was a bundle of firewood which in Essex in 1502 was legally 'in length . . . iii foote and a half of assise and in gretnes in ye middle xv inches', (*OED*).

[2] Holinshed, iv. 329.

[3] During the Parliamentary investigation of 1621 counsel instructed by Lady Mansell said that two to three thousand *loads* of wood, rather than billets, were used in the crystal factory (presumably Robson's) prior to the granting of Mansell's patent for coal. *Commons Debates, 1621*, iii. 255; iv. 354.

[4] Rogers, iii. 276.

[5] Since Verzelini's sons considered the sale of wood their principal source of income, coppicing was probably practised.

[6] Rogers, iii. 277; iv. 363, 366.   [7] Nef, *British Coal Industry*, i. 221–2.

varied widely. The price of good Scottish coal rose in London from 14*s.*
a ton in 1615, to 16*s.* then 20*s.* and finally 24*s.* a ton in 1620 (according
to Mansell—who blamed much of the rise on a deliberate attempt of the
Scottish colliers to take advantage of his dependence on the supply).[1]
Good quality coal from the Wollaton mines cost 5*s.* 6*d.* a ton,[2] though
a few miles away at Awsworth another grade of coal—'the softer sort that
doe not sparkle'—could be bought at the pithead for 2*s.* 6*d.* a ton.[3] At
Newcastle-upon-Tyne the price varied from as little as 2*s.* a ton to about
10*s.*, depending upon the grade,[4] though transportation increased that
price when the coal reached London. The change to the use of coal as
fuel did not necessarily involve a reduction in costs; any reduction was
dependent upon the quality of coal used and the location of the glasshouses
in regard to the mines.

Before any detailed comparison of the costs of the two types of fuel
can be made, the amount of coal burned in glass furnaces must be estimated. The most specific evidence on the rate of consumption concerns
the two coal-burning furnaces operated by Mansell's firm at Wollaton,
one producing broad glass and the other green drinking glasses. Before
work began, Fosbrooke, Willoughby's factor, collected information on
the cost of making window glass for his master, who owned the land and
mines. He estimated that in a year 800 cases of window glass (80 tons)
could be made from coal costing £125.[5] At the agreed rate of 5*s.* 6*d.* per
ton, this would amount to about 450 tons of coal, or between 5½ and 6
tons of coal per ton of glass. Since he expected glass to be made at the
rate of 16 to 18 cases per week, he must have anticipated a 45 to 50
week working year, and a weekly consumption of coal of between 9 and
10 tons. After work had continued for several years Pauncefoote, Mansell's
agent, who managed the works and paid the bills, drew up a weekly
estimate of costs[6] which for broad glass indicates a larger amount of 11
tons of coal per week with which 20 cases of glass 'might welbe made'.
On the other hand the only surviving accounts of money due to Willoughby for coal, clay, and sand over a period of sixteen weeks[7] show a very
low average of 7 tons of coal per week. Careful examination of these

[1] S.P. 14/162, no. 231 B; 14/113, no. 49. See also National Library of Scotland, Denmilne
MS. 148/77/13; and p. 105, above.

[2] Midd. MS. 5/165/131, contract between Mansell and Willoughby; Ibid., 5/165/140,
account of weekly expenditure. Both sources state clearly 5*s.* 6*d.* per *ton*, though Fosbrooke
said the price was 5*s.* 6*d.* per rook (ibid., 5/165/139.1). Nef, who apparently used only the
printed summary of the latter (H.M.C. *Middleton MSS.*, pp. 500-1), assumes that the rook was
slightly more than a ton, so his estimate of the amount of coal burned at Wollaton in glassmaking is rather higher than mine. See Nef, *British Coal Industry*, i. 219, n. 6; ii. App. C.

[3] Midd. MS. 5/165/137.   [4] Nef, *British Coal Industry*, ii. App. E.

[5] Midd. MS. 5/165/139.1 Fosbrooke said that 'one case is a horse load' and '10 horse load
or ten case is a ton'.

[6] Midd. MS. 5/165/140.   [7] Ibid., 5/165/135 and 136.

accounts, however, reveals that in periods when the furnace was obviously working, 11 tons a week, Pauncefoote's estimate, were actually delivered. In other weeks less than 3 tons, and sometimes none at all, was delivered: but the deliveries of sand and clay increased, an indication that, while the melting-furnace was not operating, pots were being prepared and new batches of frit mixed. Allowing for a 40 week working year with 11 tons of coal delivered each week, and the delivery of an average of less than a ton in each remaining week, the total is 450 tons, which confirms the original estimate by Fosbrooke. We may assume then that about 450 tons of coal were needed yearly in a broad-glass furnace operated by a single team.

In advance of production Fosbrooke said that 'broad glass spendeth bothe more coales and asse (ash), quantitie for quantitie, then drinking glasse dothe';[1] and Pauncefoote estimated the weekly consumption of coal for the drinking-glass furnace as 10 tons instead of 11.[2] These figures would seem to be contradicted by Merret's testimony, for he said that the workmen told him that the green-glass furnaces required the hottest fire of any kind of glassmaking.[3] At first glance the actual deliveries of coal at Wollaton would appear to corroborate Merret's evidence, for when the furnace seems to have been working a very high average of $12\frac{1}{2}$ tons of coal a week was consumed. On the other hand it seems that the interruptions in working were more frequent and of longer duration than in the case of the broad-glass furnace, and that the coal delivered during these periods was less, averaging only $\frac{1}{2}$ a ton per week: so it is possible to reconcile a higher level of coal consumption during the melting process with a lower annual average consumption—and it was with the latter that Fosbrooke and Pauncefoote were chiefly concerned. It would seem reasonable to assume, then, that the drinking glass furnace consumed on average from 400 to 425 tons of coal a year, costing (at Wollaton) from £110 to £117.

It is immediately obvious that the cost of coal at Wollaton was dramatically lower than the cost of wood at Bagot's Park in the preceding year (a saving, however, which was offset, as we shall see, by the necessity of purchasing ashes). It is difficult to compare the cost of coal with that of wood in London; but if we take 450 tons of coal as the usual annual rate of consumption, there would be a considerable saving when Scottish coal (at the lowest price of 14s.) was burned, for the total cost of fuel would then have been about £300, a saving of at least £150 per annum over the estimated cost of wood for Robson's furnace. Indeed, fuel costs had been reduced to about what Verzelini had paid. When Scottish coal in London rose to the prohibitive price of 20s. a ton, however, it became even more expensive than wood; but the change to the use of Newcastle coal

[1] Midd. MS. 5/165/139.1.   [2] Ibid., 5/165/140.   [3] Merret, p. 245.

in London (which Lady Mansell bravely adopted)[1] brought the annual cost down to about £225. It should be noted that when Zouch's firm during its first years of operation (1611–15) made window glass instead of crystal with coal their fuel costs (about £300) would have been the same that Hensey was paying for wood in Bagot's Park: they had made no saving at all by changing to the supposedly cheaper fuel.

V. MATERIALS AND TOTAL OVER-ALL COSTS

The cost of sand and of clay for the pots was never high, nor was it a particularly important item in the over-all cost of glassmaking; but securing materials of proper quality was sometimes troublesome.[2] At Wollaton the cost of the clay was included with that of the labour for 'pounding and making' the pots, and no specific figures are available. As for the sand, Merret said with reference to the London works, 'it costs but little except for the bringing by water'.[3] At Wollaton, where a local sand was used, one load costing a shilling was delivered each week to each of the furnaces, and from that amount glass was made in each valued at £15.[4] There is no indication that the price of either clay or sand varied to any great degree during the period, except when Mansell was forced to import clay for a short time.[5]

When soda was used for crystal-making, barilla was imported. This was expensive. The Book of Rates listed barilla at 10s. per hundredweight in 1604;[6] but glassmakers at the Scottish firm operated by Ord said that they paid £1 a hundredweight for Spanish barilla,[7] and Mansell said that he paid the same in 1615, while later he paid as much as 30s., or £30 the ton.[8] Since listings in the Book of Rates were for customs purposes only and are often far below the actual value, the statements of Ord and Mansell are probably correct. All the crystal-makers used barilla in large quantities; they were its sole users at that time, so the amounts of barilla imported reflect the level of production of crystal. Mansell imported far more than his predecessors: in 1621, for example, he imported 1,371 hundredweight, and in 1631 880 hundredweight, worth at least £1,371 and £880 respectively[9] (though valued at only half that for customs purposes). Except for the skilled labour of the Venetians, this was certainly the most expensive item needed for operating the crystal-works—far more costly than fuel.

For forest-glass making, ashes in their natural state were used. When wood was burned as a fuel, the ashes were taken from the furnaces: they

---

[1] S.P. 14/162, no. 231 B. See also above, p. 105.   [2] See above, p. 88.
[3] Merret, p. 261.   [4] Midd. MS. 5/165/140.   [5] See above, p. 88.
[6] Exch. K.R., Customs, E. 122/173/3, 'New Book of Rates, 1604'. The entry reads 'Barila or Saphora to make Glasse the barrel of 200 wgt—20s.'
[7] S.P. 14/112, no. 28.   [8] 'The True State of the Business of Glasse'.
[9] Port Books, E. 190/24/4 and 34/2, London imports, 1621, 1630.

cost nothing at all and the supply normally seems to have been ample.[1]
But when coal was burned, the ashes were not suitable and the purchase
of ashes became a sizable item in the cost of production. The most remarkable disclosure from the Wollaton accounts is the difference between
the two furnaces in the rate of consumption of ashes. The window-glass
makers used 20 loads of ashes a week, as opposed to 7 used by the green
drinking-glass makers,[2] though each group used only a single load of
sand. Such a great difference must reflect a difference between the formulae of the two batches, involving different proportions of silica to
alkali. Ashes for either furnace (from fern and bracken cut in the nearby
forests) cost 6s. a load, and for the window-glass furnace this amounted
to £6 a week as opposed to £3. 6d. a week for coal; or 42 per cent of the
total cost, as opposed to 21 per cent for fuel, and 17½ per cent for the
wages of the glassmakers. For the green-glass furnaces the percentages of
the cost of ashes (£2. 2s. a week, or 17 per cent) and for the wages of
glassmakers (41 per cent) are almost exactly reversed, while the percentages for fuel (22 per cent) and for all other expenses (20 per cent) remain about the same.[3] It is easy to see that in window-glass making, even
when coal at moderate price from nearby pits was burned, the necessity
of buying ashes more than offset the saving in fuel costs, and became by
far the largest single item in the cost of production. This fact adds more
weight to the supposition that window-glass makers such as Paul Tysack
and Isaac Bungar had no real incentive to experiment with the use of coal
as fuel, for the chances of reducing their over-all costs were slight.[4]
But if, as has been suggested earlier, the first experiments were carried
out by an English inventor unfamiliar with the trade, employing technical advisers from the crystal-works who were already accustomed to
heavy expense for soda (hence not concerned about the necessity of purchasing ashes at high cost for window-glass making when coal was
burned), the experiments are more comprehensible. So, too, is the early
transfer to crystal-making from window-glass making at Winchester
House,[5] and Bungar's claim that he could undersell glass from the coal-
burning furnaces[6] before Mansell reduced fuel costs still further by moving to Newcastle from Nottingham. Mansell later claimed that the price
of ashes went up from the 6s. a bushel which he paid during the early
years (as the Wollaton accounts show), to 9s. and then 11s. a bushel, and

---

[1] See above, p. 158.

[2] Midd. MS. 5/165/140. Except where otherwise noted, all of the figures cited in the remainder of this chapter are from this document, printed in Appendix A.

[3] The percentages are based on the cost of production, not the value of the glass.

[4] See above, pp. 62–5, 86. Though Bungar certainly experimented with the use of coal as
fuel at some date, Mansell said that this only occurred after the success of the coal process had
been demonstrated and the monopoly granted. See S.P. 14/162, no. 231 B. It seems likely
that the same was true of Paul Tysack.

[5] See above, p. 67.   [6] S.P. 14/162, no. 231 A, Bungar's statement.

that this explained the rise in price of window glass late in his career.[1]
Certainly there was competition for the supply at that time from the saltpetre men which may well have inflated the price.[2]

The Wollaton accounts show another interesting difference between
the two furnaces, in the costs of repair. The same amount is listed for
both for repair of the tools used—the blow-pipes, shears, wooden moulds,
and other implements (which were small in original cost but, like the
furnaces, were constantly damaged by the molten glass). For repair of the
furnaces themselves, however, the cost for the window-glass furnace was
only half that for the green-glass furnace; and the figures for the latter
made a distinction between repairs to the furnace itself—no doubt meaning the crown—and to the sieges, whereas the sieges are not mentioned
in the figures for the window-glass furnace. There is little doubt that a
higher furnace heat was used for green-glass, as Merret said, than for any
other kind of glass, and that the higher furnace heat necessitated more
frequent and more extensive repairs. It is notable that the cost of repairing
the coal-burning green-glass furnace at Wollaton (exclusive of the mend-
ing of tools) amounted in a year to more than the original cost of a wood-
burning furnace plus the glasshouse itself (£17. 10s. as opposed to £12).
The necessity for the long delays for repairs is obvious, as is also the un-
importance of the investment in furnaces and tools during the years
when small furnaces were usual. Replacement and frequent rebuilding
made both more of an operating expense than a capital investment.

The differences between the costs for the two furnaces also indicate
that when coal was burned and ashes bought, it cost more to make window
glass per week (£14. 8s. 6d.) than green glass (£12. 7s. 2d.), though the
amounts produced were assumed to be equal in value (£15). When wood
was burned the reverse was true, for the ashes were free, and window-
glass making consumed less fuel. The profit to the producer when coal
was burned was therefore greater in green glass, and this explains why
more of the green-glass makers than the window-glass makers remained
semi-independent as Mansell's lessees, instead of accepting salaries.
(John Squire, for example, remained at Wollaton on a salary for less than
a year before becoming Mansell's lessee.)[3] As Mansell's agent pointed out,
the selling price of window glass at the furnace door in 1615 (15s. the case)
allowed for almost no profit when expenses were paid; for if 20 cases
were made a week, the profit was only 11s. 6d., while if 18 were made,
there was a loss of 18s. 6d. But Mansell felt that he could not allow his
agents more than 15s. a case at the furnace door and still sell the glass in
London at 22s. 6d. the case (the price the wood-burners had charged),[4]
since he paid more than 2s. a case for transportation to London and in

---

[1] 'The True State of the Business of Glasse'.   [2] See above, pp. 158–9.
[3] Midd. MS. 5/165/131 and 133.   [4] See below, p.202.

addition had to pay the cost of storage in London, the fees of his agents who handled the sale, the high Crown revenue, and the annuities to the patentees. Bungar, however, using wood as fuel, had produced window glass for about 12s. the case at the furnace door in 1596,[1] and even in 1616 when the cost of wood was much higher he offered to sell Mansell window glass at 16s. the case at the furnace door or 18s. delivered to London.[2] It is understandable that Mansell accepted the offer on a temporary basis, until the more profitable Newcastle works were in operation.[3]

It is obvious, then, that the change to the use of coal as fuel did not bring about an immediate reduction in the cost of producing window glass, and probably reduced only slightly the cost of producing green drinking glasses; but in the field of crystal-making the saving was immediate and substantial, since soda costs remained the same for some time whereas the fuel cost less.

[1] Muniments of the Glaziers Co., Guildhall MS. 5758, no. 5. Bungar's price was 14s. the case delivered to London, but transportation to London cost him 2s. a case.

[2] A.P.C. xxxiv. 469–70. See also pp. 85–6, above.

[3] See above, p. 88.

IX

PRICES, PRODUCTION, AND THE MARKET: WINDOW AND VESSEL GLASS

THE cost of production was by no means the only factor which determined the selling price of glass. Artificial conditions of monopoly at home, prohibition on importation from abroad, and the ratio between supply and demand were also important—especially the latter, for the demand for glass was elastic to a high degree. Low prices could put such 'unnecessary' luxuries as glass windows and tableware within the reach of persons of moderate means and thereby expand the market considerably. On the other hand it is well known that the sixteenth century experienced serious inflation which affected the purchasing power of money and drove up the level of most prices. The sharpest increase came during the middle decades of the century, but thereafter prices continued to rise, though at a somewhat slower rate.[1] During the early years of Elizabeth's reign the price of glass followed the general trend; but it soon became a notable exception.

I. WINDOW GLASS

Although window-glass makers sometimes sold directly to the ultimate consumers (the owners of building projects), it was a more usual and in London an almost universal practice for middlemen to buy from producers in large consignments and resell to glaziers, who then installed the glass for the ultimate consumers. Wholesale prices by the case bear a more direct relationship to costs and level of production in the industry than do retail prices by the foot charged by the glaziers, for the glaziers' charges customarily included the cost of materials other than glass—especially lead—as well as their own remuneration. The number of feet in the case varied: crown glass made in Normandy or in England was packed into cases of 24 tables, or crowns, averaging 30 inches in diameter (5 square feet per crown), giving a total of 120 square feet (though variations in the size of the crowns from 4½ to 6 square feet altered the number of feet in the case).[2] The roughly rectangular cylinder glass made in

---

[1] E. H. Phelps Brown and S. V. Hopkins, 'Wage-rates and Prices, Evidence for Population Pressure in the sixteenth Century', *Economica*, n.s. xxiv (1957), Table 4, p. 306.

[2] Lansd. MS. 21, no. 68; MS. 22 no. 6; Guildhall MS. 5758 no. 5.

Lorraine or Burgundy was sold by the bunch or bundle, called the 'wisp' in Scotland and northern England, which contained 3 sheets tied together with straw, each sheet being a little under or a little over 3 square feet. Lorrainers in England continued the practice, and glaziers bought by the bundle during the reign of Elizabeth, but for wholesale purposes twenty bundles were packed into cases, or 'cradles',[1] which varied in total from 160 to 200 square feet. After about 1600 there are no further references to any measure but the case in the wholesale trade. Since the kind of glass was seldom specified (the term 'broad' could refer to any kind of window glass), and since men of different traditions had been working together, it is thereafter difficult to tell from references to cases of glass which type of glass was meant or how many feet there were to the case until Mansell took over control of the industry. Under his administration the size of the cylinder glass sheets was increased to about 4 square feet. They were packed in bundles of 3 as usual, but there were only 15 bundles to the case giving a total of 180 square feet,[2] the standard amount required by his contracts.

The variation in the size of the sheets or crowns was generally deliberate, not accidental, and therefore the number of feet to the case or bundle was usually specified in all agreements or complaints. This makes it possible to construct a table of window-glass prices with reasonable accuracy (Table 1). Except as otherwise explained, the prices given in the table are wholesale prices paid by glaziers to middlemen and refer largely to the London area. The two prices indicated by asterisks are not strictly comparable to the others. The first, that for crown glass in 1596, is not the price paid by the glaziers but the price paid to the producer (Isaac Bungar) by a middleman for crown glass delivered to London; and the second, that for cylinder glass in 1585, is also the price paid to the producer, this time at the furnace door in Staffordshire. The figures in parenthesis are estimates of the probable price paid by the glaziers, allowing for profit to the merchant in London, and in Staffordshire for transportation to a market town, in order to make them comparable. Using the figures in parenthesis one can then construct a graph[3] of the price level which gives a clearer picture of the relationship between date and price. The prices of crown and cylinder glass are shown separately until after 1620, when one price prevailed in London for all window glass, which was probably all of the cylinder type. It is immediately obvious that the wholesale price of glass rose from the 1540s to the 1570s in accordance with the general rise in prices, but that the increase in the price of Lorraine glass was less than in that of the Norman type. Both increases were followed by a sharp decline, a moderate recovery, and then a general levelling-off under monopoly conditions.

[1] Lansd. MS. 21, no. 68; MS. 59, no. 76. [2] S.P. 14/120, no. 71; R.P.C. Scot. xxi. 439.
[3] See p. 204.

TABLE I

Wholesale Prices of Window Glass in London

Reference	Person	Date	Price per case	No. of ft. in case	Price per ft.
CROWN GLASS					
Lansd. MS. 21, no. 68	King's Glazier	Time of Henry VIII	15s.–16s.	140	1·3d.–1·4d.
Lansd. MS. 59, no. 76	Carré	1568	32s.	120	3·2d.
Lansd. MS. 21, no. 68	King's Glazier	1574	31s.	110	3·4d.
Lansd. MS. 22, no. 8	Briet and Appel	1576	32s.	120	3·2d.
Guildhall MS. 5758, no. 5	*Bungar–Lawrence	1596	*14s. (16s.–18s.)	110	1·5d (1·7d.–2·0d.)
BROAD OR CYLINDER GLASS					
Lansd. MS. 21, no. 68	King's Glazier	Time of Henry VIII	10s.	160	1·3d.
Lansd. MS. 59, no. 76	Carré	1568	35s.	200	2·1d.
Lansd. MS. 21, no. 68	King's Glazier	1574	35s.	200	2·1d.
Lansd. MS. 22, no. 6	Briet and Appel	1576	35s.	200	2·1d.
Horridge, p. 27	*Hensey in Bagot's Park	1585	*18s. (20s.–22s.)	140–160?	1·3d.–1·5d. (1·5d.–1·9d)
EITHER CROWN OR BROAD, PROBABLY ALL BROAD					
S.P.14/120, no. 71	Wealden glass sold in London	1600–15	22s. 6d.	136	2d.
Midd. MS. 5/165/139	Mansell	1615–17	22s. 6d.	180	1·5d.
Exch. K.R., E. 122/99/103	Robson (Ireland)	1616	21s.	180?	1·4d.
S.P. 14/120, no. 89	Wealden (Bungar)	1617–18	25s.–26s.	136	2·2d.–2·3d.
S.P. 14/120, no. 71	Scottish firm	1620	20s.	180	1·35d.
S.P. 14/164, 231 B	Mansell	1621–35	22s 6d.	180	1·5d.
S.P. 16/378, no. 58	Mansell	1636–40	24s. 6d.	180	1·6d.

Note: A question mark indicates that the number of feet to the case is not entirely certain.

TABLE 2

Retail Price of Window Glass Installed in London, the lower Thames area, or Royal Buildings

Reference	Date	Price per foot (d.)	Place or Person
Lansd. MS. 21, no. 63, 2nd doc.	Time of Henry VIII	5	Coxe, Royal Glazier
Rogers, iv. 473	1541–50	5	Lower Thames
Rogers, iv. 473	1551–60	7½	Lower Thames
Lambeth Churchw. Accounts,ᵃ p. 70	1562	7½	Lambeth
Rogers, iv. 473	1571–80	6½	Lower Thames
Rogers, v. 499	1587	7	Lower Thames
Clavell MS. B2/3	1590–1621	6	Baggeley, Royal Glazier
Rogers, v. 499	1604	6	Oxford
Rogers, v. 499	1605	4½	Eton
Surr. Arch. Coll. xix,ᵇ 183–4	1617	5	Wandsworth Churchwardens Accounts
Clavell MS. B2/3	1621	5	Baggeley, Royal Glazier

ᵃ *Lambeth Churchwardens' Accounts, 1504–1646, and Vestry Book, 1610*, ed. C. Drew (London, for the Surrey Record Society, 1940).
ᵇ 'Wandsworth Churchwardens' Accounts from 1603 to 1620, *Surrey Arch. Col.* xix (1906), 145–94.

TABLE 3

Retail Price of Window Glass Installed in the North, Chiefly Co. Durham

Reference	Date	Price per foot (d.)	Place
Exch. K.R., E. 134/19	1577	8	Keldolme Abbey, Yorks.
Durham Parish Books,ᵃ p. 33	1592	8	Pittington, Co. Durham
Ibid., p. 274	1598	6½	Houghton-le-Spring, Co. Durham
Ibid., p. 140	1604	6½	St. Oswald's, Durham city
Ibid., p. 73	1617	6½	Pittington
Ibid., p. 292	1617	7	Houghton-le-Spring
Ibid., p. 296	1625	5	Houghton-le-Spring
Ibid., p. 181	1626	5	St. Oswald's

ᵃ *Churchwardens' Accounts of Pittington and Other Parishes in the Diocese of Durham from 1580 to 1700* (Publications of the Surtees Society, vol. lxxxiv, 1888).

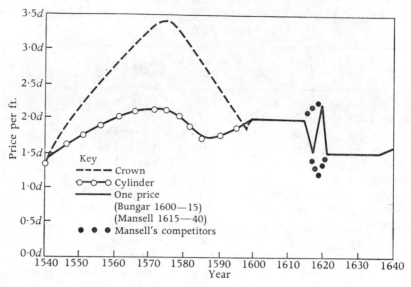

Movement in Prices of Window Glass

In comparison with wholesale prices it is worth looking at the retail prices charged by the glaziers (Tables 2 and 3). Though they follow the same general pattern, that is, a rise in price from the time of Henry VIII to the 1570s and 1580s (which was maintained for a longer time in the north), followed by a gradual decline until the level of the price in the 1540s was reached again, there are two points to note. The rise in retail price follows more closely the rise in the wholesale price of Lorraine than that in the price of Norman glass; and secondly, the discrepancy in price between London and the north, which might be expected owing to the latter's distance from sources of supply, disappears after 1620, when Mansell's furnaces at Newcastle supplied most of the market.

Before discussing the price of window glass in relationship to the monopoly and to the costs of production, it is necessary to explore the situation of supply and demand.

The history of the architecture of the period indicates that large expanses of glass were becoming fashionable for those who could afford them. After the Wars of the Roses the long years of internal peace made a defensible home less of a necessity. The windows of the early Tudor days were generally small, sometimes with only one light or at most two or three. As the century went on, the lights increased in number and the bay window became more popular. While bays had been common near the dais in the great hall of country houses from early times, the size and height of the bays increased until they became two storeys in height or even the full height of the building. They were used also in pairs symmetrically on either side of the entrance, until finally the whole facade of the house might seem to be made of glass.[1] The most famous example of this sort of house was Hardwick Hall, the residence built by Bess of Hardwick[2] who married four rich husbands, including the Earl of Shrewsbury. The contemporary rhyme, 'Hardwick Hall, more glass than wall',[3] indicates the amazement of the common folk at the extravagant use of glass.[4] Wilton House, remodelled early in the reign of Charles I by the Earl of Montgomery, is another example. All windows were then stationary and in the early Tudor period most were composed of small quarrels, diamond-shaped pieces leaded into large frames. Later on, architects such as Robert Smythson, who designed both Middleton Hall and Wollaton for members of the Willoughby family, used panes much the same size as conventional panes today, mullioned with cross bars of wood or stone. Crown glass cut to better advantage into quarrels, but the rectangular broad glass was more easily cut into panes.

Some indication of the amount of glass used in building new houses is found in building accounts. In the reign of Henry VIII, while the King's palaces and the mansions of the greater nobility contained considerable amounts of glass, the houses of the gentry were certainly not entirely glazed. The accounts of the building of Redgrave Hall, belonging to the Bacon family and completed in 1546, show that a total of £147. 12s. was paid for the entire house, but payments to the glazier amounted to only £4. 4s. 2d.[5] The plumbers on the other hand were paid £6. 14s. 6d. and the carpenters £23. 10s. 8d. The small individual payments to the glazier imply that he was paid by the foot, and since 5d. a foot was usual at that time, we can assume that only about 200 feet of glass were installed. When William More built Loseley House between 1561 and 1569, however, he spent a total of £1,666. 19s. 7d. on the entire house, and of that £29. 11s. 2d. was for glazing.[6] Prices had risen considerably, but also far more glass was used. The Loseley accounts show that the glass was bought by the case and the glazier paid by the day for installation. Eleven cases were bought at 29s. each[7] and since this was the approximate cost of Norman glass, we may assume 120 feet or thereabouts to the case, bringing the total to over 1,300 feet. Most persons who built new houses or glazed windows in old ones paid glaziers by the foot which proved more expensive. Robert Smythson itemized the glazing costs for Middleton

---

[1] J. A. Gotch, *Early Renaissance Architecture in England* (London, Batsford, 1901), pp. 109–10.
[2] *DNB*, 'Elizabeth Talbot, Countess of Shrewsbury'.
[3] Ashdown, p. 12.   [4] See illustration, Plate IVf.
[5] Univ. of Chicago, Bacon MS., 'The charges of building Redgrave Hall', pp. 160, 191.
[6] 'Extracts from the Private Account Book of William More of Loseley in Surrey . . .', ed. J. Evans, *Archaeologia* xxxvi (1855), 303, 306, 309, 310.
[7] Ibid., p. 309.

Hall built about 1587 and the total bill came to £50. 9s. 5d. for 1,700¾ feet at 7d. the foot.[1] In 1627 the Earl of Winton paid a little over £55 for glass in his new house in Aberdeenshire,[2] probably for about the same footage. The owners of all these residences were decidedly well-to-do: but the few who were richer still wanted even more glass. Glazing the royal residence at Nonsuch cost £348,[3] and the Earl of Northumberland had plans drawn up in 1615 for a new house at Petworth which called for large expanses of glass. There were to have been twin towers each with 26 windows containing a total of 1,092 feet of glass, and in the rest of the house 216 windows 10 feet high, making an estimated grand total of 9,732 feet of glass at 6d. a foot, costing £245. 12s. Apparently the total cost of the house was too high, even for so rich an earl, for it was never built and he contented himself with an extension to the existing house at Petworth, including 1,410 feet of additional glazing.[4] It would be futile to try to count the number of large manor houses constructed, but there was undoubtedly a building boom in Elizabethan and early Stuart times, as both contemporary and modern commentators on social change have noted. Francis Bacon remarked that 'there has never been the like number of fair and stately houses as have been built and set up from the ground since her Majesties reign; insomuch that there have been reckoned in one shire that is not great to the number of three and thirty, which have been all new built within that time.'[5]

In spite of the amount of glass which went into new buildings, not all the rooms in large manor houses were glazed, and what glazing there was was often allowed to fall into bad repair. An interesting example comes from a detailed inventory made in 1608 of Thornage Hall in Norfolk[6] which belonged to Sir Nicholas Bacon (though he resided normally at Redgrave). The steward listed the number of glazed windows in each of the 33 rooms or auxiliary buildings and the state of their repair. Rooms for general use, such as the parlours and the hall, had been completely glazed, but there were 30 quarrels broken in the hall and the windows in the long gallery were 'much broken'. The chambers had been completely or partially glazed roughly in order of their importance; and there were a few glass windows in such rooms as the maids' chamber and the kitchen and buttery, though they were all 'much decayed' and broken. Only the windows in the chapel were intact. Since both panes and quarrels are mentioned, one gets the impression that the glazing had

---

[1] Midd. MS. 5/165/129.   [2] HMC Second Report, p. 19.
[3] J. Dent, The Quest for Nonsuch (London, Hutchinson, 1962), p. 47.
[4] G. Batho, 'Notes and Documents on Petworth House, 1574–1632', Sussex Arch. Col. xcvi (1958), 114–19.
[5] Francis Bacon, The Crown and the Aristocracy, quoted in L. Stone, Social Change and Revolution in England (London, Longman, 1965), pp. 131–3.
[6] Univ. of Chicago, Bacon MS., Inventory of Thornage Hall, 3 Oct. 1608.

been done piecemeal over a long period and then allowed to fall into
disrepair.

One might think that the inventory of Thornage was atypical if there
were not ample evidence, from the accounts of churchwardens and of the
stewards of great houses, that necessary repairs were almost as large a
part of a glazier's business as setting new glass. The household accounts
of the Earl of Northumberland record frequent repairs at Petworth,
Syon House, and Boswell House.[1] At St. Oswald's, Durham, it was necessary to reset 11 feet of old glass and repair 5 dozen holes in 1626 and the
very next year to re-lead 8 more feet and repair 7 dozen holes.[2] In 1574
Lancelot Yonge, the Queen's Glazier, spent his entire time journeying
from place to place 'repairinge and maynteyning of the glasse and glasse-
works of the Queenes Majesties mancon howses'.[3] Records of debts owed
to glaziers at the time of their death tell the same story. John Watkys of
St. Ives, Huntingdon, for example, was owed 53s. 4d. out of a total of
109s. 8d. for repairing the chancel windows at St. Ives church after 'the
lead was blowen up with the wynd'.[4] In order to avoid such repairs the
churchwardens at Wandsworth, Surrey, in 1610 ordered 'duble wickers
for all the wyndowes' and wire and nails to fasten them on in an effort to
protect the glass; but in spite of their precaution, in 1619 they had to replace 'divers windows in ye church blowne downe by the great wind'.[5]
The poor quality of much of the window glass, especially the fact that it
was blown too thin, accounts for some of the necessity for repairs. The
glaziers were not anxious to have the defects remedied,[6] because it made
them more business: but the purchasers frequently complained, since the
continuous need for expensive repairs, added to the original cost, made
glass windows more of a financial liability than a permanent improvement.

Largely because of the expense involved, glass windows continued to
be considered a luxury until the last decade of the sixteenth century. They
were listed separately in inventories, which indicates that they were regarded as movable property and not as a permanent part of a house. Many
great lords who had more than one house had their windows taken down
when they were not in residence, to be stored away from exposure to the
weather, or took the windows with them when they moved from one
house to another.[7] As late as 1590 an alderman of Doncaster bequeathed

[1] BM, Alnwich MS., Ser. U. I., 1–3, Household accounts of Henry Percy, ninth Earl of
Northumberland, on microfilm, *passim*.

[2] *Churchwardens' Accounts of Pittington* . . ., pp. 180–1.

[3] Lansd. MS. 21, no. 68. In that year repairs were made at Hatfield, Somerset Place, White-
hall, St. James, Richmond, Hampton Court, Windsor Castle, Reading, and Woodstock.

[4] Lichfield J.R.O., Inventory of John Watkys, 1588.

[5] Wandsworth Churchwardens' Accounts', p. 194; see also R.P.C. *Scot.*, 2nd ser. ii. 352–3.

[6] So it was claimed in 1619. See above, p. 100.

[7] Ashdown, p. 13.

his dwelling house to his wife, but left the windows to his son.[1] In 1599, however, a judgement by Sir Edward Coke in the Court of Common Pleas established a principle that prevented this practice, by declaring that glass fixed to a window frame with nails was deemed to be an essential part of the house and must remain with it.

Coke's judgement reflects the fact that glass had become less of a luxury: as it became cheaper and more plentiful, glass windows were no longer bought only by the upper classes and the Church. From Leicestershire inventories Hoskins concluded that while very wealthy merchants might own glass windows, few craftsman, even those who were relatively prosperous, had any in the 1560s, though by the 1580s and 1590s the situation had changed.[2] Oxfordshire inventories confirm his findings. There are almost no glass windows in the houses of craftsmen before the 1580s; but at their deaths during that decade the inventories of a saddler, a haberdasher of Banbury, and a blacksmith of Oxford show that their houses had some glass in 3–4 of their 6–9 rooms (though the house of a glazier of Banbury had none at all).[3] All of the persons having glass windows were townsmen, however (with the exception of one yeoman, Thomas Taylor of Witney, whose large house of 25 rooms with 17 glass windows together with his sizable income from the wool trade placed him on the level of many of the gentry).[4] The ordinary yeomen, and most of the craftsmen, still had no glass at all. It is difficult to tell whether the trend for persons of moderate prosperity to install glass continued at the same rate or accelerated during the seventeenth century, for once windows were legally considered part of the house, they disappeared from the inventories.[5]

Important cathedrals and chapels were already largely glazed with coloured pictorial windows. Since these were associated with Roman Catholicism, they were no longer popular with most Anglicans, particularly those of Puritan persuasion. However, they were not replaced on a large scale. Harrison's *Description of England*, published in 1577, says of churches in Essex:

As for our churches themselves . . . all images, shrines, tabernacles, rood-lofts, and monuments of idolatry are removed, taken down and defaced, only the stories in glass windows excepted, which, for want of sufficient store of new stuff, and by reason of extreme charge that should grow by the alteration of the same into white panes throughout the realm, are not altogether abolished

---

[1] *Notes and Queries*, 4th ser. iv (1869), 111.

[2] W. G. Hoskins, *Provincial England: Essays in Social and Economic History* (London, Macmillan, 1963), p. 107.

[3] *Household and Farm Inventories*, pp. 144, 267–8, 245–6.

[4] Ibid., p. 282.

[5] *Jacobean Household Inventories*, ed. F. G. Emmison (*Publications of the Bedfordshire Historical Records Society*, vol. xx, 1938), *passim*.

in most places at once, but little by little suffered to decay, that white glass may be provided and set up in their rooms.[1]

It would seem that both the scarcity and expense of window glass prevented large orders from churches before the 1580s; but later, as the supply increased and the price went down, not only were replacements made in larger structures, but small parish churches which had never been glazed had white glass installed as and when the churchwardens could afford it. There was still some demand for coloured window glass, but it was very limited. The north and west windows of Laud's chapel were reglazed in 1636 at the rate of 18*d*. the foot for new leading and 6*s*. the foot for new glass,[2] twelve times the rate for ordinary glass. Since Archbishop Parker had paid only 10*s*. for two 'pictures in glass' in 1575,[3] the cost of pictorial windows had undoubtedly gone up, rather than down. A few of the gentry bought armorial windows of coloured or stained glass, which also increased in price. Sir William More, for example paid 10*s*. for the window at Loseley bearing his arms,[4] but Lord William Howard paid 20*s*. for a similar window in 1621.[5] Howard, a Roman Catholic, also bought a number of sacred pictorial windows, (including one for 40*s*. in 1625).[6] However, the demand for coloured window glass was never large enough to prompt glassmakers to make it in England: it was probably all imported.[7]

It seems that the demand for window glass in England climbed sharply in the 1580s and 1590s, and then continued to increase steadily but less spectacularly. The reduced price of glass helped to stimulate demand by tempting the rich to use glass more extravagantly, and enabling people of moderate means to afford it; but it might have been expected that increased demand would in turn have led to an increase in price. The reasons why that did not happen must have been related to supply.

Apparently no window glass was being made in England at the time of the arrival of the aliens in 1567.[8] The records of importation into London show that only a little over 200 cases (or rather its equivalent in continental measures)[9] was imported by English merchants in 1567–8; if this is doubled to allow for importation by aliens in London, and doubled

---

[1] W. Harrison, *Elizabethan England*, ed. L. Withington (London, Walter Scott, 1876), p. 77. The original title was *Description of England*.

[2] S.P. 16/35, no. 56, 4 June 1636.

[3] 'Copy of the Inventory of Archbishop Parker's Goods', *Archaeologia* xxx (1844), 28.

[4] 'Extracts from the Private Account Book of William More', p. 310. The window may still be seen.

[5] *Selections from the Household Books of Lord William Howard of Naworth Castle*, ed. G. Ornsby (Publications of the Surtees Society, vol. lxviii, 1877) hereafter cited as *Household Books of Lord William Howard*, p. 195.

[6] Ibid., p. 234.

[7] Mansell made no mention of making coloured window glass.

[8] See above, pp. 11–12, 19.   [9] See Table 4.

TABLE 4

Window Glass Shipped In or Out of the Port of London

Reference and Date[a]	Amount	Origin or Destination	Value[b] £	s.	d.
IMPORTS					
4/2, English, 1567/8	110 cases	Normandy	110.	0.	0.
	25 chests[c]	Burgundy	50.	0.	0.
	22 wey[c]	Rhineland	55.	0.	0.
5/5, Aliens, 1571/2	138 cases	Normandy	138.	0.	0.
	30 wey	Rhineland	75.	0.	0.
7/8 and 8/1, English, 1587/8	None	—	—		
11/1, Aliens, 1600	3 cases	Normandy	3.	0.	0.
14/5, Aliens, 1609	None	—	—		
18/6, English, 1615	26 cases	Normandy	26.	0.	0.
24/4, English, 1621	225 cases	Scotland	224.	0.	0.
	20 cases	Normandy	20.	0.	0.
31/3, English, 1626	34 cases	Normandy	34.	0.	0.
34/2, English, 1630	70 bunches	Rhineland	3.	10.	0.
38/5, English, 1635	2 cases	Normandy	2.	0.	0.
43/5, English, 1640	None	—	—		
44/3, Aliens, 1640	None	—	—		
EXPORTS					
38/7, English, 1634	Misc. amounts, about 40 cases	New England	40.	0.	0.
43/1, English, 1640	Misc. amounts, about 12 cases	New England, Ireland	12.	0.	0.

[a] Since every reference is to the Port Books, Series E. 190, that portion of the reference is omitted. Until 1600 one book usually covers a year from Michaelmas to Michaelmas and the date is indicated thus, 1567/8, though in a few years there are two books covering the same period, e.g. 1587/8. After 1600 entries run from Christmas to Christmas and only one year is given as though the book began on 1 January, e.g. 1600. Books were kept separately for English and alien merchants, as indicated. The series is extremely incomplete and many of the books are defaced or defective. Though an attempt was made to select those in the best condition, the figures given must nevertheless be used with caution.

[b] When valuations were found in the Port Books, they were used in the table, even if they seemed incorrect (as in the entry for 1621). Otherwise valuations were taken from the Book of Rates of 1558 (Patent Rolls, C. 66/920, mm. 12^d–22^d) extracts from which are printed in the Appendix, p. 259. Valuations of window glass for customs purposes did not change throughout the period and were generally lower than the actual wholesale value of the glass.

[c] The chest was roughly equivalent to 2 cases; the wey to 2½.

again to include importation at the outports, this gives a very generous estimate of the amount of glass imported to supply the English market— a maximum of 900 cases (equivalent to the annual output of 2 furnaces).[1] Carré established two furnaces with the intention of supplying the entire market himself, but in 1571–2 about the same amount of glass was still coming from the continent. By 1590 a contemporary said that there were 14 or 15 glasshouses in England.[2] This number included the crystal furnace and furnaces making green drinking glasses, and there is no way to tell how many made window glass: from the predominance in the records of glassmakers of men from the Lorrainer families which had a tradition of making window glass, however, we may assume that at least half, and probably over half, of the 15 glasshouses made window glass. If there were 7 furnaces producing window glass at the rate of 450 cases a year (the rate achieved by the first Lorrainers in England), something over 3,000 cases were being made in 1590. If there were 8 furnaces and if the rate of production had been stepped up to 600 cases yearly, then over 4,000 cases were produced. By that time no window glass was being imported, and none was imported from then on, except when Mansell faced shortages from his furnaces or competition from Scotland, or to supply small amounts of coloured glass. Independent glassmakers said that early in 1614 there were 8 furnaces making only window glass[3] (though this number seems not to have included the coal-burning furnace at Lambeth, where production was limited because it was working at a loss). It is obvious that the number of furnaces had not increased significantly in the quarter century since 1590, though if 600–700 cases were being made regularly in each furnace, as seems likely, total production would have gone up to a possible maximum of 5,000–6,000. The proclamation of 1615 prohibiting the use of wood, and Mansell's difficulties in relocating his coal-burning furnaces, temporarily reduced the number of furnaces, resulting in importation from Ireland, Scotland, and Normandy, in spite of Mansell's strenuous efforts to prevent it. By 1624, however, he said that he had established 9 furnaces for window glass 'in remote places of the kingdom', and then later a tenth at Woolwich to supply London when the shortage of shipping from Newcastle was restricting the supply.[4] The number of furnaces suggests that the change to the use of coal had not increased production: but there is reason to think that the three furnaces at Newcastle were larger than the usual wood-burning furnaces. Occasionally during the wood-burning period more than one team of glassmakers may have been employed at a furnace working what were called 'double furnaces'[5]—though there is only one instance of a definite

---

[1] See pp. 184–7, for the output per furnace.
[2] Lansd. MS. 59, no. 75.
[3] *Proc. and Debates*, ii. 72.
[4] S.P. 14/162, no. 231 B.
[5] Midd. MS. 5/165/133; Westropp, p. 29.

example from documentary evidence.[1] Mansell, however, said that he employed 60 men at Newcastle,[2] and that the three furnaces there would supply the kingdom as well as the eight wood-burning furnaces had done.[3] Since in glassmaking there were 2 or 3 men in a team, and the labour staff was composed roughly half of glassmakers and half of less skilled labour,[4] it is likely that Mansell had 8 or 9 teams in his large new glasshouses. By 1624 he was actually shipping 3,000–4,000 cases to London alone from Newcastle,[5] and supplying east and south coast ports with perhaps 2,000 more. Not all of Mansell's six window-glass furnaces outside New-castle can be located,[6] but it seems likely that they were each manned by one team;[7] probably in total they produced less than the three in Newcastle, which continued to supply London and most of England. It is doubtful if production towards the end of the Mansell regime reached as high as 10,000 cases a year, or 1,000 tons.[8] Mansell never mentioned any particular expansion in this sphere of the industry, and though glass-houses appeared in new locations, they were set up by his lessees, some of whom continued to move about much as they had done when they burned wood.[9]

It is the interaction of costs, prices, level of production, and demand that explains certain developments within the industry. The rise in the price of window glass from the last years of Henry VIII's reign to the mid-1560s clearly reflected the price of continental glass, for though some glass may have been made in England early in that time, most glass was imported. Since glass was more plentiful in Lorraine[10] than in Normandy, the general inflation did not force up the price as high in Lorraine, and this differential was reflected in English prices both before and after 1567. The attempt of the first immigrants to maintain continental prices through royal monopolies kept the price high throughout the early 1570s, as Table 1 indicates; but once the Council wisely refused to issue a new and more complete monopoly in 1576,[11] the way was open for a flood of new immigrants. Most of them were Lorrainers, and when their numbers increased and the amount of glass on the market rose to a figure three to four times the amount in the 1560s, the price fell drastically. As the glaziers remarked in 1541, 'the plentie or scarcytie in the market al-

---

[1] Lennard, p. 127. Both the sources cited in the preceding note mention the possibility of double furnaces, but it is clear that only one team was then working at each.

[2] S.P. 16/476, no. 66.   [3] S.P. 14/105, no. 58, c. 1618.

[4] Midd. MS. 5/165/140.   [5] S.P. 14/162, no. 231 B.

[6] There were two near Stourbridge, one near Chester, and one or two near Scarborough (Proc. and Debates, ii. 361).

[7] Guttery, p. 7; Straff. MS. 20/30.

[8] Ten cases equalled a ton in 1615. Midd. MS. 5/165/139, no. 1.

[9] For example, Francis Bristow, who after working in other locations appeared on the Wentworth estates in 1631. Straff. MS. 20/30.

[10] See above, p. 23.   [11] See above, p. 27.

ways maketh the pryce thereof'.[1] At the same time wood was becoming dearer in the Weald (where most of the immigrants had settled) raising their costs of production: in their migrations to the west and the midlands, the glassmakers sought not only cheaper fuel but markets which had not previously been well supplied. As the tables show, the price soon came down in the country as well; though the easy availability of glass and cheaper prices was expanding the market considerably. Meanwhile the London market, supplied by the glassmakers who stayed in the Weald, was still glutted, as Bungar discovered in his dealings with a merchant; he saw the necessity for limiting the supply from the Weald in order to uphold prices at a level somewhat above that to which they had fallen in the 1590s.[2]

The over-supply was clearly a determining factor in the fall of prices; faced with this situation, the industry in order to survive must have been forced either to reduce the cost of production or profits or both. The way in which this occurred has already been explored in the discussion of the lowered economic status of independent glassmakers by the turn of the century[3] and the drastic fall in wages for the men who were on a salary.[4] Continental glassmakers had been able to achieve the status of members of the minor nobility through very large profits which placed them socially and economically far above other craftsmen. The first immigrants brought some capital which they had accumulated as a result of high continental prices, and even during their first years in England some were able to pay cash for their fuel and stayed ahead in their payments to the landlord,[5] whereas by 1615 the lower prices in England had wiped out their profits (except for the equivalent of a wage far lower than they were accustomed to think their due), and many were in serious debt.[6] The fall in wages is a far more convincing explanation for lowered costs than any possible saving in fuel from more efficient furnaces or founding techniques introduced by the aliens,[7] since the saving could not have been great in window-glass making and was certainly offset by the doubling and sometimes tripling of the cost of wood. Even after prices became stabilized at about the turn of the century, through Bungar's control of the London market and the gradual expansion of demand which upheld prices in the country, few glassmakers improved their lot. Instead they fell under the domination of merchants who could find a sale for their product, whereas previously merchants had failed to control production because their services were unnecessary.

[1] Ashdown, p. 11, quoting a petition of the glaziers.
[2] See above, pp. 55–7, and Table I.   [3] See above, p. 167.
[4] See above, p. 187.   [5] Lennard, p. 128.   [6] See above, p. 166.
[7] Crossley, EcHR, pp. 421–33, suggested this saving as an explanation, but his evidence for a reduction in costs comes from archaeological remains on sites of glasshouses making vessel, not window, glass.

DEG—H

The most surprising thing about the price level is the long period from about 1600 to 1635 when the price of window glass remained steady at 22s. 6d. One might suppose that the change from the use of wood to coal as fuel would have made possible a lowering of prices, or that Mansell's complete internal monopoly with heavy debts and overhead payments might have caused a price rise, yet neither happened. The constant price, which both preceded and followed the brief period of 1615–21 when importation was prohibited, was certainly below that of continental glass, (since almost no continental glass was imported, even when importation was allowed), but it was not below the price of glass made in Ireland (with wood)[1] or in Scotland. The necessity of purchasing ashes as material for the batch offset the saving in fuel, once coal was burned; for, as we have seen, Mansell's cost of production with coal at Wollaton (14s. 8d. a case)[2] was higher than Bungar's price per case delivered to London in 1596,[3] and only slightly less than Bungar's price at the furnace door in 1616.[4] There is no doubt than Mansell could be undersold by glass made in Ireland, even as late as 1633,[5] for wood was available there very cheaply. The Scottish competition, however, seems to have been a short-lived effort to drive him out of the market and break his monopoly in England;[6] and when that failed the Scottish firm ceased to produce window glass, though it continued to compete in the field of drinking glasses. Once Mansell began using the cheaper grades of Newcastle coal he had indeed reduced his costs below those of most wood-burning furnaces in England, but he was still paying off debts owed by the company for losses during the experimental period. It is notable that under conditions of complete internal monopoly and with heavy debts and overheads to the Crown he did not raise the price. For a time during the difficult years from 1615 to 1621 he did indeed try, but the clamours of his customers soon forced him to return to the previous price. Surely demand was a factor, for the glaziers who bought his glass would not have minded paying him higher prices if they could have passed on the increase to their customers and still have received as many orders. The ultimate consumer, then—the ordinary householder and churchwarden, as well as the nobility in the Council who called Mansell to account and threatened loss of his privilege unless he reduced his prices—helped maintain the constant price. Since he controlled all internal production either through outright ownership or discretion in granting leases, he could adjust the supply to the demand to prevent a fall in price, as the occasional complaints of scarcity indicate, yet keep the market sufficiently supplied to satisfy the glaziers. The careful cost accounting which he required of his agents, and

---

[1] See Table I, and also pp. 86–7.   [2] Midd. MS. 5/165/139.
[3] Guildhall MS. 5758, no. 5.   [4] A.P.C. xxxiv. 470.
[5] Straff. MS. 13/165.   [6] See above, Chap. IV.

his sensitivity to market conditions, show that he indeed had the brains of a businessman. The only permanent price increase during his long administration of the monopoly was imposed in 1637 to meet the financial necessities of Charles I. That his prices were not inordinately high is best proved by the fact that after the monopoly was swept away, prices of window glass did not fall, and during the Restoration period they rose slightly.[1]

II. DRINKING GLASSES AND OTHER TABLEWARE

The price level and rate of production of table glass are less easy to determine than those of window glass, since drinking glasses, the most common product, varied so widely in size and quality. Brief notations in inventories are hard to identify with excavated fragments or with price lists, which may have been easy for a contemporary to understand but are less so today.

In 1624[2] and again in 1635[3] Mansell issued schedules of his prices in statements defending his patent and his policies for the benefit of members of Parliament and the Privy Council respectively. Since as he said they could be easily checked with any glass-seller, there is no reason to doubt their accuracy—and both lists give prices for 1621 which correspond. The second statement also adds prices on imported Venetian glasses, both current and before 1615 when Mansell assumed control of the monopoly. From these two documents a table of prices for crystal and ordinary 'white' glass has been constructed (Table 5). None of the prices in this schedule refer to green glasses of any shape, for later in the statement of 1635 Mansell said that he had sub-leased the making of all green glasswares; whereas he said that the prices listed referred only to glass made in his own furnaces. He did say, however, that although materials for green glass had gone up in price in the preceding years, the price of the green glass had remained the same 'for many years since [it was] set down by the Agreement of all the Glass-Sellers and Glasse-makers'.[4] The 'ordinary' glasses in the schedule must have been 'white' glass made from native soda (kelp), in contrast to his domestic crystal, which was made from the far more expensive imported barrilla.[5] The mortar glasses were made from the cheaper metal, the looking-glass plates from true crystal. Though there is no mention of the prices of plates, bowls, cruets, or other household items, such tableware was certainly made of crystal in England by Salter's men, and probably by Mansell as well,

---

[1] *Churchwardens' Accounts of Pittington*, p. 352. Glazing by the foot went up to 6*d*., as opposed to 5*d*., by 1683.

[2] S.P. 14/162/231 B.

[3] 'The True State of the Businesse of Glasse', undated, but from internal evidence clearly written in 1635.

[4] Ibid.   [5] See above, p. 196.

TABLE 5

Price of Drinking Glasses per Dozen

Kind of Glass	Before 1615	1621	1624	1635
Large ordinary glasses (for beer)	—	6s.– 7s. 4d.	4s. 6d.	4s.
Small ordinary glasses (for wine)	—	4s.	2s. 6d.	2s. 6d.
Mortar glasses	—	2s. 6d.	1s. 3d.	1s. 4d.
Crystal beer glasses (imported from Venice)	20s.–24s.	—	—	10s.–11s.
Crystal wine glasses (imported from Venice)	18s.	—	—	7s.–8s.
Crystal beer (domestic)	—	18s.	15s.	9s.
Crystal wine (domestic)	—	16s.	12s.	5s. 6d.– 7s.
Smallest crystal glasses	—	12s.	10s.	—
Looking-glass plates	—	11s.	8s.–10s.	—

for he was hardly one to neglect a profitable branch of the trade. He seems to have listed only his best sellers in attempting to prove his point that prices had been substantially reduced.

Mansell's lists leave us without any information about the prices of Verzelini's crystal, of imported glassware from Flanders, France, and Germany, or of the green glasswares made in England both before and after the change to the use of coal as fuel. Though household accounts and inventories seldom specify styles, size, or origin, they provide some clues which supplement the table and in some instances corroborate Mansell's prices. The earliest of these show remarkably few glasses valued at very low prices. In an inventory of Loseley House taken in 1556 coloured beer glasses predominate, and most were valued at 2d. apiece, including a 'lyttle blewe bereglasse'; however, a 'lyttle bereglasse of whyte and grene' was listed at 6d., and two with covers at 8d. and 1s. each. Three 'glasses lyke chalisys' probably meant for wine were valued at 4s. each— but the description indicates the novelty of drinking wine from glass rather than from plate or pewter. Though Loseley was near the furnaces of the Peytoes and Strudwicks (English glassmakers who had been making vessels for decades),[2] it seems likely that all of these glasses were of foreign origin.

In contrast the household accounts of the Earl of Northumberland for the period 1585 to 1603[3] list many purchases of glasses, usually bought

[1] 'Account Book of William More', pp. 292–3.   [2] See above, p. 11.
[3] Alnwick MSS., Ser. U. I., 1–3.

by the dozen or simply listed as 'glasses bot' for amounts up to £10. The price varied from 8s. a dozen, to 16s. a dozen (paid both in 1585 and in 1598), though the usual price seems to have been 11s. to 13s. a dozen—too low, according to Mansell's price list, for imported Venetian crystal, which was in any case then forbidden except on special licence. The large numbers bought and the variety of prices suggest rather that the glasses were different styles and shapes bought from Verzelini or from Robson. The highest price paid on the Earl's behalf, 16s. the dozen, corresponds with Mansell's price for crystal wine glasses at the beginning of his regime, and suggests that at first Mansell maintained Robson's prices for crystal, just as he maintained Bungar's price for window glass.

Lord William Howard of Naworth kept a less fashionable household than the Earl of Northumberland and lived a long way from London, but his accounts (which coincide with a large part of the Mansell regime) indicate large purchases of glassware,[1] and on the whole substantiate Mansell's claim to have reduced prices. For example, one purchase of crystal glasses 'for wine and beer' at an average price of 9s. the dozen is slightly above Mansell's schedule, but transportation to the north easily explains the difference. Most of his glasses, however, were the ordinary kind at from 2s. 6d. to 5s. the dozen.

It is almost impossible to document any trend in the price of green drinking glasses, for the entries in the account books of great households make no distinction between green glass and the ordinary white glasses which Mansell made. It is certain that green drinking glasses made at Wollaton with coal in 1616 were valued by Mansell's agent at 2s. the dozen at the furnace door;[2] allowing for the profits of the chapmen or the merchants, they would probably have sold elsewhere for 3d. or 4d. apiece. The Howards' steward frequently bought glasses 'at the gates', and a purchase of two glasses for 6d. in 1612 before Mansell began making ordinary white glass probably refers to green glasses, which had no doubt been bought by a chapman from a forest-glass maker at 2s. the dozen. Efforts to determine the price between 1566, when coloured beer glasses were valued at 2d., and 1612, when drinking glasses of some sort were 3d., are thwarted by the fact that the few instances in inventories which can be found lump several objects together, such as an item which reads simply 'potts and glasses—4s.'[3] One cannot say with any certainty that the price went down, as did the price of window glass.

Demand for glass tableware was affected by fashion as much as by price. Little is known from the fragments that remain of the styles produced by the English glassmakers before the coming of the aliens, but it seems clear that such drinking cups as they made were simple and of a rather poor

[1] *Household Books of Lord William Howard, passim.* [2] Midd. MS. 5/165/139.
[3] *Household and Farm Inventories,* p. 272.

quality.[1] Apothecaries' wares seem instead to have been their staple product. The Huguenots, particularly the Flemings such as Vinion and the Du Houx, introduced a vastly superior technique both in the quality of the green-glass vessels and in their shapes and decoration.[2] Tall beer or ale glasses seem to have predominated, judging from fragments found on excavated sites.[3] A contemporary described a beer glass as 'six or eight inches in height and being of one equal bigness from the bottom to the top',[4] in other words a straight-sided beaker which seems to have been a typically English shape, although continental fashions for footed, flute-shaped glasses, sometimes incurved and sometimes everted at the top, are even more common. All shapes were often decorated with mould-blown ribs, sometimes wrythen, and trails or prunts of glass were also applied.[5] The colour varied from pale green to a dark and blue-toned olive-green, and at its best the metal was hard and stable. The attractiveness of this glass, and its easy availability after the aliens spread throughout England, certainly contributed to the growing popularity of drinking glasses. Use of the coal process did not change the quality or styles of the forest glass, except for the appearance at two sites of unusual black glass objects and fragments,[6] which resulted from colouration of the glass by coal smoke either deliberately or accidentally. Many other products besides beer glasses were made by the forest-glass makers, including a few short-stemmed wine glasses.

Stemmed ware in crystal was the chief product of Verzelini's furnace, and fortunately a number of specimens survive intact.[7] The styles follow the Venetian fashions, as might be expected, except that coloured glass applied as decoration seems not to have pleased the English taste. Instead clear goblets were generally engraved to order. Acceptable quality, a price undoubtedly below that of crystal imported from Venice (since transportation and breakage hazards were avoided), and a larger supply quickly popularized them. Robson (who supplanted Verzelini), Salter, and Mansell all employed highly skilled Venetians who could reproduce Venetian styles or 'bespoken fashions' as desired, and in addition Mansell claimed to have introduced the making of beer glasses in crystal, similar in shape to the forest-glass beer glasses. As for his usual styles for wine

[1] Kenyon, pp. 32, 105.

[2] Ibid.; J. S. Daniels, *The Woodchester Glasshouse* (Gloucester, Bellows, 1950); and other sources. Fragments may be seen in the Guildford Museum, Winchester City Museum, Gloucester City Museum, the London Guildhall, and elsewhere.

[3] One of the best analyses of fragments found on a forest-glass site is that by R. J. Charleston, Keeper of Ceramics, Victoria and Albert Museum, in the article by Crossley and Aberg, *Post-Med. Arch.* vi. 128–57. His drawings are especially helpful.

[4] H. Platt, *Jewell House of Art and Nature* (London, P. Short, 1594), p. 76.

[5] See Plate II.

[6] See above, pp. 150–1. A black glass bowl from Denton is now in the Pilkington Museum; fragments from Kimmeridge are in the possession of the author.

[7] See above, p. 3, n. 4, and Plate III.

glasses, they are on the whole simpler than those characteristic of Venice at the time. Hollow inverted baluster stems, known as 'cigar' stems today[1] seem to have been the most common; but stems impressed with lion masks, fluting, and other decoration were made, and sometimes convoluted ears and wings were added.

During the early part of the period drinking glasses of any sort were most unusual, even in households of the upper classes. William More, who owned eight beer glasses in addition to three wine glasses had more than most of the gentry. When Lord Buckhurst entertained a cardinal and a bishop in 1568 he remarked: 'Such glasse vessels as I had, I offered them which they thought too base.'[2] The use of glass drinking vessels did not show the same remarkable growth during the 1580s and 1590s as did window glass. In 1613, for example, Sir Robert Drury of Drury Lane, London had four 'cabinet glasses', which were probably cased bottles used as decanters,[3] but only four wine and three beer glasses,[4] fewer than William More. One wonders how he managed to serve guests, but a contemporary enlightens us: 'Neither used they to sit drink upon the table, for which no room is left, but the cuppes and glasses are served in upon a sidetable, drinke being offered to none till they call for it'.[5] In addition, goblets of plate were far more common than crystal ones. Drury may have been a bit old-fashioned, for, as we have seen, the Earl of Northumberland bought several dozen drinking glasses besides glass plates and twenty-four fine 'Venice glass' dishes.[6] On the whole, however, the greatest increase in the use of drinking glasses seems to have come in the 1620s and 1630s. By that time inventories no longer specify the number of drinking glasses, but lump them together at one valuation.

The trend was the same for ordinary folk. Oxfordshire inventories of the 1570s and 1580s show remarkably few drinking glasses, although it is common to find an hour-glass, a looking-glass, a urinal or a few small glass bottles. The craftsmen who were mentioned earlier as possessing some glass windows in the 1580s had no drinking glasses at all. Even Thomas Taylor, the well-to-do yeoman who lived in a large well-glazed house, had only one drinking glass.[7] It is significant that at his death in 1583, a shopkeeper of Henley-on-Thames had twelve urinals and four 'glassys with rose water' but no drinking glasses of any sort among his stock of household goods—which was chiefly earthen pots and bottles,

[1] See Plate III (c). For fuller discussion, see Thorpe, pp. 131, 168–70.
[2] *Shakespeare's England* (Oxford, Clarendon Press, 1916), ii. 120.
[3] For a discussion of cased bottles see below, p. 227.
[4] Univ. of Chicago, Bacon MS., Inventory of the household stuff of Sir Robert Drury in his house in Drury Lane, 19 May 1613.
[5] *Morvson's Itinerary* (1617), quoted in S. M. E. Ruggles-Brise, *Sealed Bottles* (London, Country Life, 1949), p. 29.
[6] Alnwick MSS. Ser. U. I., 2, accounts of Francis Lucas and George Dutton.
[7] *Household and Farm Inventories*, p. 154.

TABLE 6
Drinking Glasses Shipped In or Out of London

Reference and Date[a]	CRYSTAL[b] Amount	Value £ s. d.	Amount	ORDINARY Origin[c] or Destination	Value[d] £ s. d.
IMPORTS					
4/2 Eng., 1567/8	43 doz.	14. 0. 0	None	—	—
5/5 Aliens, 1571/2	50 doz.	10. 0. 0	2,942 doz.	France, Germany	93. 13. 4
7/8 and 8/1 Eng. 1587/8	None	—	None	—	—
8/4 Eng. 1589 (½ yr.)	None	—	70 doz.	?	2. 6. 8
11/1 Aliens, 1600	8 doz.	1. 12. 0	717 Rhenish wines & vials	Amsterdam	35. 17. 10
18/6 Eng., 1615	None	—	700 Rhenish wines	Amsterdam	2. 18. 4
24/4 Eng., 1621	280 doz.	94. 0. 0	1,000 doz.	Holland	50. 0. 0
			1,800 glasses	France	7. 10. 0
			4,500 glasses	Scotland	18. 15. 0
			300 glass bowls	Caen	5. 0. 0
31/3 Eng., 1626	890 doz.	267. 0. 0	142,500 glasses	Scotland	593. 15. 0
			35,400 glasses	France, chiefly	147. 10. 0
			3,207 doz.	France	160. 7. 0
			250 doz.	Flanders	12. 10. 0
32/2 Aliens, 1627	None	—	250 doz.	France	12. 10. 0
34/2 Eng., 1630	430 doz.	129. 0. 0	48,400 glasses	France	201. 13. 4
			223 doz.	Amsterdam	11. 3. 0
			1 doz. glass dishes	Amsterdam	3. 15. 0
43/5 Eng., 1640	None	—	800 glasses	Scotland	3. 6. 8
44/3 Aliens, 1640	None	—	None	—	—
EXPORTS					
38/7 Eng., 1634	None	—	210 doz. green	Canary Islands	10. 10. 0
			63 doz. coarse	Guinea, Barbary	3. 3. 0
			24 cwt 'English green cups'	Ireland	?
			Misc. amounts	Ireland	?
43/1 Eng., 1640	23 doz. (Venetian)	6. 18. 0	150 doz. green	Ireland	1. 10. 0
	38 doz. (Eng. fine)	7. 12. 0	1,601 doz. coarse	Ireland & ?	180. 1. 0

buttons and so on;[1] though he did have one drinking glass in the hall, among his personal possessions. In 1581 a pewterer of London[2] left plate and silver goblets worth £20, but only three objects of glass—an hourglass, one crystal drinking glass valued at 8s., and a 'longe glass candlestick' which was given a place of honour in the parlour along with a pair of virginals. Ale-house keepers and tavern-owners were better customers than individual householders, however, and quickly took up the fashion for drinking glasses. In taverns, as Sir John Falstaff remarked to Dame Quickly, 'Glasses, glasses is the only drinking,' but it was still enough of a novelty to call for comment until almost the end of our period.

Importation of drinking glasses did not follow the same pattern as importation of window glass; in crystal, in fact, the pattern is almost reversed, as the tables show.[3] Fifty dozen or less came in before Verzelini set up his furnace at the Crutched Friars, and thereafter none at all until Bowes had difficulty in starting production in a new furnace about the turn of the century. The prohibition in Verzelini's monopoly of importation from Venice explains these figures, but his prosperity certainly indicates that he was supplying the market with far more glasses than had ever been imported. During Mansell's time importation on a commercial scale was resumed in Venetian crystal, in spite of his own production and the fact that his glasses were cheaper. Instead of decreasing, as time went on the numbers imported increased to an all-time high in 1634. Though the price of imported as well as of domestic-made crystal had fallen, imported wares were still far more expensive; one can only assume that for the luxury trade Mansell's glasses could not compete successfully. There is every indication that the quality of the metal itself in England remained high,[4] and it was rather the constant defection of Italian workmen who

---

[1] *Household and Farm Inventories*, p. 146, Inventory of Thomas Barrett.
[2] S.P. 13/C Eliz., no. 9, 11 Mar. 1581, Inventory of Thomas Elliott.
[3] See Tables 4, 6.
[4] See above, pp. 125–6 and below, p. 249. Fragments in the Guildhall, London, are difficult to distinguish from possibly imported glass.

---

[a] See above, p. 210, Table 4, note *a*.

[b] All the crystal came from Venice, except for 60 doz. which came from the Levant in 1621; all the crystal was exported to Ireland.

[c] The port of origin is no certain indication of the origin of the glasses, especially for Dutch ports. Some glasses are described as 'Rhenish', some as 'Flemish', and some may have been Dutch.

[d] Since the Book of Rates of 1582 lists French drinking glasses at 8d. per dozen (see Appendix, p. 260) this figure was used for ordinary glasses until 1621. In that year declared values for French, Dutch, and Scottish glasses (given in the Port Books) were uniformly 1d. per glass, whether imported by the dozen of by the hundred. Thereafter that figure was used, although the Book of Rates of 1642 (see Appendix, p. 261) made a distinction in value between Flemish on the one hand and French and Scottish on the other. The declared valuations seem to be about half that of the wholesale value of the glasses. The glass dishes imported from Amsterdam in 1630 (declared value given) must have been unusually fine.

could produce the more intricate styles that made imported wares more attractive. In green drinking glasses and *façon de Venise* from Flanders and France (not clearly differentiated in the Port Books) importation was freely allowed before 1615. More of these glasses were being imported than of crystal made in Venice before the coming of the alien glassmakers. Thereafter the amount dropped, but importation did not cease as with window glass; and unlike window glass also, these foreign glasses reappear in substantial numbers during the Mansell administration. At that time most came from the Scottish glasshouse owned by English capital, however; and although drinking glasses were still coming in from France and Flanders in 1630, by 1634 they finally disappear from the Port Books. Instead small amounts of 'English drinking glasses' were being exported.[1] We can say rather precisely then that it was only after 1630 that English-made glass supplied the market entirely. This confirms the impression from household accounts and inventories that drinking glasses did not become common in most middle-class households until that time.

It is difficult to assess the rate of production of vessel glass. The number of furnaces for crystal is known for the first part of the period, for there was only Verzelini's furnace at the Crutched Friars, but the number of teams or chairs working there is uncertain. At least three seems likely.[2] Verzelini's successors were Robson's Blackfriars furnace, the furnace operated first by Salter and then by Zouch at Winchester House, and Mansell's at Broad Street. Robson probably had two chairs, since he was operating under a monopoly similar to Verzelini's and attempting to supply the same market, though with less success. In a law suit it was said that his men made 10,500 drinking glasses (875 dozen) in about seven weeks, in other words about 125 dozen weekly.[3] At Wollaton one chair of green-drinking glassmakers turned out 150 dozen weekly,[4] but their products were probably not stemmed and perhaps could be made much more quickly. At Wollaton the men seem to have worked only about thirty weeks in the year and on this basis they made 4,500 dozen yearly while Robson's men made only 3,750 dozen. Since Mansell said that at one time fourteen men deserted from Broad Street he must have employed five or six chairs at peak production but at other times he had almost no workmen at all.

His 'ordinary' white glass seems to have been made elsewhere than Broad Street, possibly at the Minories glasshouse operated by Bevis Thelwell,[5] one of his original partners. The output of these glasses was certainly larger than that of crystal. By 1635 when he was supplying the

---

[1] See Table 6.   [2] Cf. Thorpe, p. 100.
[3] Exch. K. R., E. 122/569b, Bills and Answers, *Bowes* vs. *Turner, Robson and Lane*, Bill of complaint.
[4] Midd. MS. 5/165/139.   [5] See above, pp. 79–80.

country well with ordinary glass Mansell said that his reduction in price of 2*s*. the dozen saved the country yearly the sum of £1800,[1] which implies that he was selling 18,000 dozen yearly. At the rate of production at Wollaton, this would imply four chairs at work.

As for green glass, it is difficult to count the number of furnaces in operation at any one time, for both before and after the change to the use of coal as fuel the forest-glass makers frequently moved site. Since 1 of the 15 glasshouses operating in 1590 made crystal, and 7 or 8 made window glass, 6 or 7 must have made vessel glass. Their output, however, was seldom restricted to drinking glasses alone before 1615. Excavated fragments show that a large part of the output of these furnaces consisted of bottles, urinals, apothecaries' wares, linen-smoothers, and other household items;[2] and the glass listed in household inventories confirms the impression that drinking glasses formed only a part, and probably the lesser part, of the products made. After 1615 Mansell attempted to impose standardization on the industry and to concentrate the production of drinking glasses in furnaces that made nothing else, as at Wollaton[3] and at Kimmeridge in Purbeck[4] (the drinking-glass furnace at Ratcliffe, however, also made vials for hour-glasses,[5] and possibly fulfilled orders for apothecaries and chemists). His furnaces for vessel as well as for window glass were considerably larger than earlier ones. Though only one chair worked at Wollaton, Bigo built his furnace at Kimmeridge to accommodate four pots,[6] and the Ratcliffe furnace was at least as large.[7] The making of bottles soon became a separate branch of the industry.[8] Efficiency in the use of coal and in management and marketing, seem to have been his motives for imposing the use of larger furnaces with specialized production. Late in his regime, the evidence that the supply of drinking glasses was adequate for the English market with a surplus for export,[9] indicates that 50 per cent more furnaces and chairs than in the wood-burning era were in operation by 1640.

A relationship between the price level and supply and demand cannot be established for drinking glasses, since the information is so imprecise. There is no evidence that the price varied in any dramatic way before 1615, however; as did the price of window glass. The continued importation from abroad (though reduced after the influx of aliens), shows that there was no over-supply to force down prices and profits. Moreover, the share of the glassmakers in the profits of production—the

---

[1] S. P. 16/282, no. 99.

[2] R. J. Charleston's analysis of the fragments at Hutton-le-Hole and Rosedale, in Crossley and Aberg, *Post-Med. Arch*. vi. 128–57.

[3] Every mention of the furnace in the Midd. MSS. confirms this.

[4] Clavell MS. B 2/1, Bigo–Clavell contract.

[5] See above, p. 101.   [6] Clavell MS. B 2/1, Bigo–Clavell contract.

[7] See above, p. 181.   [8] See below, p. 228.   [9] See above, p. 220.

'glassmakers third'—was not reduced and wages remained higher than for window glass, as did profits for the producer. Though improved techniques in annealing and founding introduced by the aliens in the 1570s may have reduced their fuel consumption compared with that of English glassmakers in the preceding century,[1] there is no indication that this had any effect on the price of vessel glass in the years before 1615. During the Mansell regime there was no reduction in the price of green glass; but his claim that the prices of both domestic crystal and white drinking glasses had been reduced is substantiated. This reduction was certainly not the result of pressure from over-supply, since continental glassware was being imported long after the price was reduced, and in any case Mansell controlled production and would not have permitted a glut. Rather the lower price was a result of the reduction in costs, applicable only to crystal and white glass,[2] achieved by burning coal as fuel. It is notable that Mansell though in possession of a monopoly, passed on the saving to the consumer. He was not forced to do so by competition from abroad; in fact, it was probably his lower prices that forced the reduction in the price of Venetian crystal sold in England. He was undoubtedly sensitive to market conditions and aware that more glass could be sold at cheaper rates than at his previous prices, and since he could still make a profit at the lower rate, it was to his advantage to increase production. As he wrote to Wentworth late in life,[3] Mansell thought and acted not as Vice-Admiral of England but as an industrialist.

[1] Crossley, *EcHR*, pp. 421–33.   [2] See above, p. 199.
[3] Straff. MS. 18/65, Mansell to Wentworth, 21 June 1638.

X

SPECIALIZED GLASSWARE: BOTTLES, HOUR-GLASSES, MIRRORS, AND SCIENTIFIC WARES

THE expansion in the glass industry and its effect on the total economy of England cannot be properly understood by a concentration on window-glass and drinking-glass making alone. Though these were the largest and most specialized branches of the glass industry at this period, glassmakers producing green drinking glasses also made many other kinds of containers and household objects, and crystal was blown not only into vessels but into sheets for looking-glasses and spectacles. Of all the various 'specialities' made of glass, only one type—glass beads, bugles, and buttons—seem never to have been important in the English industry in this period or made for any length of time,[1] in spite of the fact that considerable quantities were imported.[2] Nearly all the beads bought in England came from Venice, and it was undoubtedly the difficulty of keeping Venetian workmen that deterred English entrepreneurs from attempting to enter this branch of the trade—together with the fact that the level of production of coloured glass in England for other uses whether for windows or for decoration on drinking glasses, was never large. Other specialities which were imported from the continent during the early part of the period under study were later made in England, however (chiefly during the Mansell administration of the monopoly); one extremely important introduction was a new sort of bottle.

I. THE BOTTLE TRADE

Some types of glass bottle were made in ancient times. The practical Romans blew bottles in square moulds for easy shipment in cases. During the Middle Ages cylindrical and 'steeple-shaped' bottles were made in various sizes as apothecaries' wares, and also for holding perfumes, sweet waters, and household remedies.[3] The forest-glass makers made bottles in England along with cups, beakers, and urinals long before the coming of the Huguenots; and the aliens made them throughout the reign of Elizabeth. The quality of the metal was improved by the aliens, who made

---

[1] See above, pp. 32–3.　　　　[2] Port Books, *passim*.　　　　[3] Thorpe, pp. 85, 119.

DEG—I

bottles in a variety of shapes: square, hexagonal, and cylindrical.[1] Sometimes ribbed and decorated styles were blown, as the market and the whim of the glassmaker demanded.

It is impossible to judge the proportion of a furnace's output in the later sixteenth century that was devoted to bottles, as opposed to drinking cups and ale glasses, urinals, and ewers; but from the inventories it seems that drinking glasses probably amounted for less than half of the output of a furnace. Containers of all types made of glass were relatively scarce and fragile as compared with those of the Restoration period. Evidence from Elizabethan household accounts, inventories, records of importation, and archaeological excavations all point to the same conclusion—that the commonest bottles, pots, and jugs were made of earthenware or stoneware.[2] Stone bottles were made in England and imported from the continent, chiefly France, in far larger quantities than glass bottles.[3] The common use of leather 'jacks' is familiar to students of Shakespeare; and for babies wooden 'sucking bottles' were imported from Germany.[4] English-made pewter bottles (which were sized by volume before 1618) were extremely common,[5] as were bottles of tin, which churchwardens especially seemed to favour 'to carry wyne in'. It is difficult to compare the prices of different types of bottle, for there is seldom any indication of size;[6] but it is worth noting that tin bottles were probably about as expensive as glass ones. The parish of Hartland in Devon, for example, apparently replaced a glass bottle worth 18d. with a tin bottle, probably about the same size, costing 16d.[7] Usually it was not so much expense as fragility that limited the use of glass bottles. Whenever glass bottles or ewers are found in inventories, they appear in the 'wyfs closet' or in the parlour, whereas stone bottles were 'left in the buttery',[8] the pantry, or the brewhouse.

Glass bottles at this time were usually small (two to three inches in height), often square or hexagonal, thin-blown, and made of green glass with mould-blown ribbing or wrythen designs, or occasionally of *cristallo*.[9] Plain ones were often used for medicines, whereas the more ornamental were commonly filled with 'sweet water'[10] or perfume. Larger

[1] Some of the shapes are illustrated in Plate IV. See also Honey, p. 13.

[2] It is my own conclusion, corroborated by W. S. Thorpe, late Curator of the Victoria and Albert Museum, that unless the word 'glass' is included, references to bottles meant stone bottles.   [3] Port Books, *passim*. See especially E. 190/14/5; 24/4; 31/3.

[4] Port Books, E. 190/43/2 and others.

[5] There are numerous references to pewter bottles in inventories of the period.

[6] For the Tudor period I found only one reference, to a 'pynt glasse bottell'. *Household and Farm Inventories*, p. 161, inventory of 1583.

[7] HMC, *Fifth Report*, 573, Churchwardens' accounts of the parish of Hartland.

[8] Univ. of Chicago, Bacon MS., Sir Robert Drury's inventory, 1613.

[9] Fragments of many such bottles, and a few still intact, are in the Guildhall Museum, the Guildford Museum, the Winchester City Museum, and elsewhere. See Plate IV.

[10] *Household Books of Lord William Howard*, p. 343; Port Books, E. 190/8/1.

ones were frequently protected by casings of wicker and leather,[1] and seem to have been used chiefly as decanters for serving wine in large households or for use in the sacristies of parish churches. About the turn of the century such use clearly became more common, and fairly large, square bottles, still thin-blown of green glass, appear in greater number.[2] Hampers and 'cellars' (apparently wooden boxes with compartments) protected them from breakage. An entry in an inventory of 'a very fine cellar for wyne with eight glasses'[3] is typical. Large households usually bought wine by the hogshead and stored it in wooden casks; but two entries in Lord Howard's accounts of the purchase of 19 quarts of sack 'to fill the cellars of glasses'[4] would indicate that occasionally such cellars were used for storage by the wealthy. The common folk could hardly afford such luxuries, and there is nothing to connect glass containers with either beer or ale. Occasional references, such as 'three pounds of cork for the brewer'[5] and a curious entry in the Northumberland accounts which reads simply 'bottle ale, £5',[6] indicate that these beverages were sometimes bottled, but undoubtedly in stone.

In addition to the perfume and medicine bottles, and the cellar bottles, some other glass flasks and vials, of varying sizes, were made to hold other liquids. The Mores of Loseley owned a 'great bottell glasse' worth 6d., a coloured bottle of glass worth 2s., and a 'great glasse ewere to keepe oyle in'.[7] Except for the small bottles of sweet water, bottles were not customarily sold filled with any sort of merchandise. Entries from account books such as 'payde for a pint of inke and a bottell then'[8] and 'a quarter of a pint of oyle for the coachman and a bottle'[9] imply simultaneous but separate purchases. Unbroken bottles were too expensive to be thrown away and demand for new bottles was clearly small, met largely by glasshouses in England. During the Tudor period, in comparison with the sizable imports of drinking glasses, very few glass bottles of

---

[1] After 1557 the Book of Rates distinguished between 'uncovered' glass bottles, those 'covered with wicker', and those 'with [de]vices covered with leather'. Patent Rolls, C. 66/926, mm. 12d–22d, Book of Rates, 1558; T. S. William (ed.), *A Tudor Book of Rates* (Manchester, Univ. of Manchester Press, 1962).

[2] Numerous fragments have been found in excavations. See I. Noel-Hume, 'A Century of London Glass Bottles, 1580–1680', *Connoisseur Yearbook* (1956), pp. 98–103; J. P. Hudson, 'Seventeenth Century Glass Excavated at Jamestown', *Florida Anthropologist* xvii, no. 2 (1964), pp. 95–103.

[3] J. C. Halliwell, *Ancient Inventories of Furniture, Pictures, Tapestry, Plate...* (London, Privately Printed, 1854), p. 217.

[4] *Household Books of Lord William Howard*, p. 217.

[5] Ibid., p. 43.

[6] Alnwick MSS., U.I., 3, Account of G. Greene, Steward, 8 Mar. 1603—28 Mar. 1604. The entry is puzzling, and it is not certain whether bottled ale or bottles for ale is meant. The entry occurs between one for 'divers wines' costing £49. 17s. 5d., and for wine bottles costing 4s. 4d.

[7] 'Account Book of William More', pp. 292–3.

[8] *Household Books of Lord William Howard*, p. 44.

[9] *Lambeth Churchwardens' accounts*, p. 217.

any kind came into the country.[1] However, the number of imported glass bottles was noticeably greater during the reign of James I. By that time importation by 'shocks' consisting of 5 dozen in a case[2] (instead of 2 or 3 dozen in a chest or basket) would seem to indicate the packaging of a bottle more uniform in size and shape than was common earlier. Since these bottles came largely from the Low Countries, they were probably of the square type, with a capacity of about three-fifths of a quart, often referred to as 'Dutch gin bottles'.[3] Far fewer bottles of glass than of earthenware were imported, however; and the number sold, whether imported or made at home, was never large enough to sustain bottle-making as a separate branch of the glass trade. The green-glass makers, and perhaps also the crystal-makers, made them as a lesser part of their production of other kinds of vessel glass.

During the early part of the Mansell regime it is impossible to point to any startling change in the bottle trade. Thin-blown square, hexagonal, or sometimes round bottles in green and clear glass continued to be made in his subsidiary furnaces. By the middle of the century, however, a new sort of bottle appeared: a thick, strong, dark bottle produced by a separate branch of the industry. The main evidence as to how this type of bottle originated comes from an incident early in the Restoration period. On 1 September 1661 John Colnett, a descendant of a Flemish family of glassmakers,[4] received letters patent from Charles II for the sole making of glass bottles in standard sizes—'Gallons, Pottles, Quarts, Pintes and half Pintes'—on the pretext that he 'first invented, made and attained to ye perfection of making glass bottles'.[5] Since he claimed that 'during the late rebellious tymes' others had appropriated his invention and made bottles below the lawful sizes, his were to be set with a distinctive seal to indicate full measure, and all bottles without a seal were to be broken. Early the next year a bill was introduced in Parliament for the confirmation of Colnett's privilege;[6] but shortly afterwards two petitions asked that the patent should be cancelled.[7] The four bottle-makers who signed the second petition—John Vinion, Robert Ward, Edward Percival, and William Sadler—claimed that Sir Kenelm Digby, not Colnett, was the true 'first inventor' of the new bottles, and that he had employed them and Colnett to make the bottles; but that Digby had later

---

[1] See Table 7.

[2] Port Books, E. 190/4/5, London, Aliens, 1608–9. 170 dozen glass bottles were imported, mostly in shocks of 5 dozen.   [3] See Hudson, p. 98.

[4] R. Chambon, L'Histoire de la verrerie en Belgique du IIième siècle à nos jours (Brussels, Le Librairie Encyclopédique, 1955), pp. 93–95.

[5] House of Lords MS., 'An act to confirm the invention and manufacture of glass bottles . . ., 10 April 1662. The act recites the terms of Colnett's patent.

[6] Ibid.

[7] House of Lords MSS., Petitions from Vinion and Ward, and from Vinion, Ward, Percival, and Sadler, 1662.

Plate I

An early fifteenth-century glasshouse in the forest-glass tradition. From Sir John Mandeville's *Travels*, BM Add. MS. 24189, fol. 16.

Plate II

a   b

c

a. Unstable urinal, *c.* 1500, from a pit in St. Swithin's Lane. Ht. 9 in. b. Ale glass (reconstructed) of blue-green metal with incurved rim and mould-blown pattern, excavated at Cheapside. Ht. 7⅛ in. c. Beaker with chequered spiral-trail decoration (see Tait, *JGS* ix (1976), 94–8). Ht. 3¾ in. d. Green-glass goblet (reconstructed) from the Gracechurch St. excavation (see Oswald and Phillips, *Connoisseur,* Nov. 1949, pp. 30–1). Ht. *c.* 5 in.

d

e. Green drinking glasses with mould-blown, wrythen and trailed decorations. Conjectural replicas by James Powell & Sons from fragments from the Woodchester glasshouse.

Plate III

a   b   c

a. A Verzelini glass, engraved for the marriage of John and Jone Dier, and dated 1581. Ht. 8¼ in.
b. The Barbara Potters glass, dated 1602, probably made at the Blackfriars glasshouse (see p. 46).
Ht. 8³⁄₁₆ in.   c. A 'cigar-stem' wine glass, a common type made by Mansell. From the Gracechurch
St. excavation (see Oswald and Phillips, *Connoisseur,* Nov. 1949, pp. 31–3). Ht. 5³⁄₅ in.

d. Laddered-stem wine
glass, excavated at the Bank
Station. English-made,
probably between 1600
and 1630. Ht. 6⅛ in.
e. Nonsuch wine glass
with a simple knopf and
baluster stem. From a
cesspit at Nonsuch
Palace filled in *c.* 1650.
Possibly made by Mansell
and supplied by him to
the royal Household.

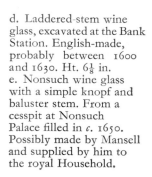

d   e

Plate IV

a

b

c

d

e. Wine bottle in dark-green bottle glass, with long neck and seal on an onion-shaped body. English, *c.* 1655.

a. Bottle of light apple-green, a modification of the 'steeple-shaped' apothecaries' bottle. Ht. 4⅜ in.
b. Green-glass bottle with wrythen ribbing. Ht. 4⅜ in.   c. Hexagonal bottle from the Woodchester glasshouse. Ht. 5⅛ in.   d. Square bottle excavated at Waltham Abbey. (See Charleston, *Post-Med. Arch.* iii (1969), 88–9.) Ht. 5¼ in.

f. Hardwick Hall, built (1591–7) by Elizabeth, Dowager Countess of Shrewsbury.

abandoned his interest and that the trade 'had been of Publique use at several glasse houses in England' for many years. The matter was referred to the Attorney-General, who submitted a report on 2 April 1662, confirming the facts asserted by the glassmakers and stating that 'Colnett offers nothing material in opposition'.[1] The report killed both the bill and Colnett's patent.

The significance of the dispute lies in the fact that all parties concerned, themselves bottle-makers, agreed that there had indeed been a new 'invention'; that Digby was the true inventor; and that the date was 'neer thirty years since', or about 1632–3. The nature of the 'invention' is clear from an examination of bottles dating from the 1650s which represent a clear break with the earlier tradition in bottle-making. Instead of being thin-blown, light in weight, pale in colour, and frequently square at the base, they are heavy, strong, and globular in shape with a high 'kick' in the bottom and a long tapering neck ending in a collar for tying down corks. The colour was always very dark, varying from dark olive to brown or black. Most of these bottles were impressed with a seal (a blob of glass, on which initials or other devices were imprinted); but this usually bore the mark of the owner rather than, as Colnett wished, that of the maker.[2] Whereas the fragile type of bottle made earlier is the ancestor of the modern decanter, this new strong dark type is the ancestor of the modern beer or wine bottle, and in Merret's day bottles of this type were commonly used for storage both of wine and of beer.[3] Pepys proudly related going to the Mitre Tavern to see wine put in his new crested bottles.[4] The new type of bottle seems to have been made by a formula developed after the invention of the coal process in glassmaking. The wind tunnels in the new furnaces produced a higher internal furnace heat, and if the covers were omitted from the pots, increasing the temperature within them still further, a batch with a higher silica content and less potash and lime could be melted. Though the metal was darkened by the coal fumes, this was not considered a disadvantage; in fact, it came to be regarded as a sign of glass of a superior strength. Scoville comments on the fact that the French preferred the dark 'English' bottles and began to copy them soon after 1700 in coal-burning furnaces using open pots.[5]

The striking difference between the two types of bottle has long been noticed; but it has usually been assumed that the new sort first appeared during the 1650s, largely because the earliest date found on a sealed bottle is 1657.[6] Most seals did not bear dates, however, and there is no

---

[1] Ibid., Report of the Attorney-General, 1662.

[2] For an illustration see Plate IV. There are many such bottles in museums and in private collections.

[3] Merret, p. 226.   [4] Quoted in Ruggles-Brise, p. 26.   [5] Scoville, pp. 11–12.

[6] A bottle marked R. M. P. 1657, probably from the King's Head Tavern, now in the Northampton Museum.

reason to doubt the statement of the bottle-makers that the time of the discovery was about 1633, and that Sir Kenelm Digby was the true inventor. Digby was a well-known courtier and dilettante who was interested in science and later became one of the founders of the Royal Society.[1] Such persons customarily made their own apparatus from glass vessels for distilling and other experiments by lamp-working, or had it specially blown at a glasshouse. From 1633 to 1636 Digby was resident at Gresham College, so that the alleged date of the invention was precisely the time when he was most likely to have been in contact with glassmakers. Though he was acquainted with Mansell (from serving with him on commissions regarding the Navy), they were not particularly friendly;[2] but he was on excellent terms with Mansell's former manager at the Broad Street glassworks, James Howell, whose injured hand Digby cured with his famous sympathetic powder.[3] This friendship would have provided him with easy access to technical information about the coal process and also, perhaps, with an introduction to the men long-experienced in the trade who later became his employees—a Colnett, a Vinion, and a Percival. With the help of one or more of them Digby, who prided himself on scientific inventions, could easily have worked out the new formula. Presumably when he hired the glassmakers to begin work in a new furnace making only bottles, he must have paid Mansell, who owned the monopoly in glassmaking, a fee. However, after Digby's imprisonment as a Royalist and Roman Catholic in 1642,[4] and the ending of Mansell's patent in the same year, the trade was undoubtedly 'of publique use'. Thereafter bottle-makers increased in numbers.

There is a possibility that Digby's furnace may have been at Newnham-on-Severn, for there, near the site of an early coal-fired glass furnace, many seals (described as 'rough buttons') and a considerable amount of black-glass slag have been found.[5] Local tradition ascribes the furnace to Mansell in the reign of Charles I. In 1673 there was a newly-built bottle-works at Newnham;[6] and soon Gloucester, Bristol, and Newcastle, too, became prominent in the trade. In all the bottle-works standardization by size, which had previously been rare, became common (as indicated in Colnett's claim). Once specialization in separate factories began, the trade increased enormously. 'I would have the bottles all pints,' a would-be

[1] DNB, 'Sir Kenelm Digby'. R. T. Peterson, Sir Kenelm Digby, The Ornament of England (London, Jonathan Cape, 1956).
[2] Cal. S.P.D. 1631–3, pp. 90, 142, 313, 326, 328. They disagreed on naval matters; but both disliked Buckingham.
[3] B. J. Dobbs, 'Studies in the Natural Philosophy of Sir Kenelm Digby', Ambix, xviii (Mar. 1971), 6–7.
[4] Peterson, p. 163. Digby was imprisoned in Winchester House, and on this basis Peterson ascribes the invention of bottles to 1642; but in view of other evidence this seems unlikely.
[5] M. K. Wood, Newnham-on-Severn, a Retrospect (Gloucester, Albert Smith, 1962).
[6] Glos. R.O. BRA 267. Indenture, 15 Feb. 1672/3.

TABLE 7
Glass Bottles Shipped In or Out of London[a]

Reference and Date[b]	Amount	Value £ s. d.			Origin or Destination
IMPORTS					
4/2 Eng., 1567/8	None	—			—
5/5 Aliens, 1571/2	29 doz. covered w. wicker	29.	0.	0	Rouen
	40 doz. small @ 4s. doz.	8.	0.	0	Flushing
	18 doz. flasks	?			Emden
	36 doz. 'water glasses'[c]	7.	4.	0	Lübeck, Emden, and Flushing
7/8 and 8/1 Eng., 1587/8	34 doz. small, for 'sweet' water	6.	16.	0	Hamburg
	4 doz. covered @ 20s. doz.	4.	0.	0	Dieppe
	3 cases	1.	16.	0	Elbing
8/2 Aliens, 1589 (½ yr.)	15 doz. uncovered	1.	2.	6	Amsterdam
8/4 Eng., 1589 (½ yr.)	23 cases @ 12s. a case	13.	6.	0	?
11/1 Aliens, 1600	30 doz. small @ 8s. doz.	12.	0.	0	Venice
15/5 Aliens, 1609	170 doz. uncovered	12.	15.	0	Amsterdam, Dansk, and Dormst
18/6 Eng., 1615	40 small cases	?			
	200 doz. small with devices	8.	18.	4	?
24/4 Eng., 1621	58⅓ doz.	4.	7.	6	Caen
31/3 Eng., 1626	72 doz. @ 18d. a doz.	5.	8.	0	Amsterdam
	22 sellers with glass bottles	?			Flanders
34/2 Eng., 1630	None	—			—
38/5 Eng., 1634	None	—			—
43/5 Eng., 1640	None	—			—
44/3 Aliens, 1640	None	—			—
EXPORTS					
38/8 Eng., 1634	3 doz. covered with leather	4.	10.	0	Hamburg
	100 doz. 'English' bottles	7.	10.	0	Canary Islands
	12 gross green glass bottles	10.	16.	0	?
43/1 Eng., 1640	260 doz. 'English' bottles	19.	10.	0	Canary Islands, Rotterdam, and ? Robordence
	21 doz. covered with leather	31.	10.	0	Rotterdam and ?

[a] Since earthern bottles, both covered and uncovered, were imported more frequently and in larger numbers than those of glass, entries of 'bottles' without a qualifying phrase have been omitted from the Table, although some may well have been glass. Valuations were frequently given in the Port Books; when they were not, those in the Book of Rates for 1558 (Patent Rolls, C. 66/920, mm. 12d–22d) were used for reign of Elizabeth, those in the Book of Rates of 1604 (Exch. K.R., Customs, E. 122/173/3, 2 Jac. I) thereafter.

[b] See above, p. 210, Table 4, note a.

[c] The meaning of 'water glasses' is uncertain, but containers for 'sweet' or 'strong' waters were probably meant.

purchaser wrote in 1654, 'and of glasse, which you may buy of any glass-man.'[1] It would seem that the new bottles were popular not just for their greater strength, but because they were cheaper. As opposed to 6d. or 8d. apiece (the usual price for bottles, apparently of similar size, for use in churches), bottles sealed with the owner's crest cost only 5s. a dozen in 1671, and plain bottles 3s. 6d. a dozen.[2] Since prices of window glass and other glassware were higher in the Restoration period than during the Mansell regime, Digby's bottles probably sold for no higher a price, even allowing for his fee to Mansell.

The notable increase in the production of bottles during the reign of Charles I applied also to the old type of thin-blown bottle which was either covered with straw or leather, or packed in compartmentalized cases for shipping. As the table of importation shows (Table 7), it was unnecessary to import any of these bottles after 1626; moreoever, by 1634 small quantities of the cased bottles, along with 'English bottles' (the usual term for the dark strong sort), were being exported. Trade in the dark bottles soon far exceeded that in the cased bottles, however; and the new bottles entirely supplanted those of stone. Taverns bought them by the dozen, and planters in Virginia ordered large quantities bearing the impression of their seals.[3] Shipments of bottles became increasingly large as the century progressed (in 1684, 3,000 dozen were shipped along the coast from Newcastle alone)[4] and the production of bottles rivalled that of window glass in size and importance. Much of this expansion occurred after Mansell's regime was ended, and Mansell himself cannot be given credit for the development of this new branch of the industry; but the foundations seem to have been laid during his regime, and would not have been possible without the use of the coal process.

II. HOUR-GLASSES

Hour-glasses were made from small vials, especially blown for that purpose by filling them with sand and then joining the narrow necks over a flame, a process known today as lamp-working. The process required no great skill, but was apparently not practised in England in Tudor times. In 1563 hour-glasses were listed among 'necessary imports' from the Low Countries.[5] Large numbers were imported from the continent,[6] worth considerably more in total than the bottles imported during the same

---

[1] HMC *Second Report*, Field MSS., p. 394.   [2] Ruggles-Brise, p. 27.

[3] Noel-Hume has excavated hundreds of fragments on Virginian sites, and has identified many of the initials on the seals with known owners of large houses on the James River or in Williamsburg. See I. Noel-Hume, *Here Lies Virginia* (New York, Knopf, 1963), *passim*.

[4] T. S. Willan, *The English Coasting Trade, 1600–1750* (New York, Kelley reprint, 1967), pp. 99, 116.

[5] H. Hall, *A History of the Custom-Revenue in England* (London, E. Stock, 1892), i. 238.

[6] See Table 8, p. 234.

periods. The Book of Rates of 1558 values ordinary hour-glasses which came chiefly from Germany at 20d. a dozen wholesale, those of *cristallo* from Venice at 20s. the dozen, and those 'of Flanders making the fyne sorte' at 6s. 8d. the dozen.[1] The coarse type, being within the means of ordinary folk, was naturally the most popular; importation of this kind of hour-glass increased substantially after the early years of Elizabeth's reign, to reach a peak in about 1590 before it began slowly to decline. The hour-glasses were ordered, chiefly from Hamburg and Stade, by haberdashers, skinners, and other shop-keepers, to be sold with other common household wares. They appear in nearly every inventory[2] (even in those of persons who owned no other glassware), and they were purchased by churchwardens 'for the preacher'—that is, to time his sermons.[3] They were valued at from 2d.[4] to 18d.[5] apiece (though Archbishop Parker seems to have possessed an hour-glass worth 20s.,[6] which must presumably have been of the finest crystal, beautifully embellished). Since clocks cost as much as £6[7] (restricting their use to the upper classes and to a few parish churches), hour-glasses were a comparatively cheap method of time-keeping. Moreover, the price of those in the middle price range seems to have dropped during the second decade of the seventeenth century: the churchwardens of a parish in Surrey bought an hour-glass for 10d. in 1610, but replaced it for 6d. in 1619.[8]

It was precisely during this decade that hour-glasses seem first to have been made in England. In 1637 five hour-glass makers said that they had pursued their trade for several years before the granting of Mansell's patent in 1615, and that they then bought 'hower glas vialles redye prepaired for there use at the prizes of 7s. the gross and 7s. 6d. at the dearest'.[9] They implied that these vials were made in England, and their cheap price indicates that they came from the green-glass furnaces. When Mansell leased the making of green glass to subsidiaries, and restricted their sales to certain areas, an hour-glass maker soon petitioned the Glass Commissioners for permission to buy at any of Mansell's glasshouses instead of at the furnace in London, where the price was high and glass suitable for working was scarce.[10] Though the request was granted for a time, Mansell sought to reimpose his restrictions: neither he nor his lessees were much interested in hour-glass vials. Nevertheless the vials continued to be made in sufficient numbers to supply the increasing number of hour-glass makers and English-made vials slowly took over the supply of the

[1] Patent Rolls, C. 66/920 mm. 12ᵈ–22ᵈ, Book of Rates, 1558.
[2] See especially *Household and Farm Inventories, passim.*
[3] HMC, *Hartland MSS.*, v. 573.
[4] 'Account Book of William More', p. 292.   [5] *Hartland MSS.*, v. 573.
[6] 'Copy of the Inventory of Archbishop Parker's goods', *Archaeologia*, xxx (1844), 28.
[7] Wandsworth churchwardens' accounts, p. 145.   [8] Ibid.
[9] S.P. 14/113, no. 20 Mar. 1620.   [10] S.P. 16/373, no. 82, Dec. 1637.

English market. In 1634 only three cases of hour-glasses (probably 15 to 18 dozen) were imported, while at the same time 61½ dozen were exported to Ireland.[1]

In 1637 five hour-glass makers complained that the price of vials had

TABLE 8

Hour-glasses Shipped In or Out of London[a]

| Reference and Date[b] | FINE | | | COARSE | | |
	Amount	Origin or Destination	Value £ s. d.	Amount	Origin or Destination	Value £ s. d.
IMPORTS						
4/2 Eng., 1567/8	1 doz. 4 doz.	Venice Flanders	1. 0. 0 1. 6. 8	22 doz. 18 doz.	Antwerp	1. 22. 8 1. 10. 0
7/8 and 8/1 Eng., 1587/8	4 doz.	Flanders	1. 6. 8	1,150½ doz.	Hamburg, Stade, and Emden	95. 15. 10
8/4 Eng., 1589 (½ yr.)	12 doz. cased		4. 0. 0	401 doz.	?	34. 5. 0
24/4 Eng., 1621	None		—	687 doz.	Hamburg, Amsterdam	56. 10. 0
34/2 Eng., 1626	192 doz.	Venice	517. 2. 0	420 doz.		35. 0. 0
34/2 Eng., 1630	18 doz.	Flanders	3. 12. 0	180 doz.	Hamburg, Middleburg	15. 0. 0
38/5 Eng., 1634	None		—	18 doz.	Hamburg	1. 10. 0
43/5 Eng., 1640	None		—	None		—
EXPORTS						
38/7 Eng., 1634	None		—	61½ doz.		5. 2. 6
43/1 Eng., 1640	None		—	30 doz.	Ireland, ? Robordence	2. 10. 0

[a]All valuations are from the Book of Rates of 1558, since they remained unchanged for hour-glasses throughout the period. See Appendix, p. 260. Figures from the Port Books for several years which yielded slight or negative results were omitted from the table.

[b] See above, p. 210, Table 4, note *a*.

risen from 7s. to 9s. a gross[2] an increase that is not surprising in view of Mansell's recent new indenture obliging him to pay the Crown a high rent for his monopoly. (Indirectly they admitted that the price had remained unchanged for twenty years under monopoly conditions.) The hour-glass

[1] Port Books, E. 190/38/5; 38/7. The case seems to have varied as a measure; but it usually consisted of 5 or 6 dozen, not a gross.

[2] S.P. 16/373, no. 82.

makers' chief complaint, however, was not of the price rise or even of the quality (which they said was poor), but of a serious scarcity which they attributed to the fact that vials were being 'delivered to insufficient workemen such as never served [apprenticeship] for the said arte'. The petitioners were members of the newly formed Company of Glass-Sellers, which was trying at that time to enforce its privileges against the wishes of the Aldermen of London,[1] and their petition was clearly motivated by a desire to have the sale of vials limited to members of the Company and their apprentices.[2] The Council decided that their complaints of high prices and poor quality were 'merely clamourous', and Mansell's agent negotiated a new agreement which assured them of a constant supply at an agreed price.[3]

III. LOOKING-GLASSES

Until Mansell's control of the glass monopoly, traffic in looking-glasses showed many similarities to that in hour-glasses, except that the trade was more lucrative and a much higher degree of skill was required in the finishing trades. Throughout most of the Middle Ages small metallic mirrors of steel or silver were the only ones in use, and they were still imported and sold in England until 1640—though apparently never made here. Early in the fourteenth century small convex mirrors were made in Nuremberg by introducing a mixture of tin, antimony, and resin into a hot globe of molten glass and then cutting the cooled globe into lenses,[4] which produced a small but well-defined image. Again there is no firm evidence for production of this sort of mirror in England during the Tudor–Stuart period; but the large number of 'pennyware' and 'halfpenny ware' looking-glasses imported from Germany indicates their steady popularity.[5] Their valuation for excise purposes at 8s. and 4s. per gross of twelve dozen (far lower than that of the steel mirrors)[6] meant that from a commercial point of view they accounted for a relatively insignificant part of the total trade in glassware. In about 1500 a new process of silvering cold, flat plates of glass, by applying thin sheets of tin foil with mercury as the cementing medium, was developed, possibly in Flanders.[7] It was quickly adopted by Venetian looking-glass makers who used plates

---

[1] See above, pp. 130f.

[2] G. Unwin (*Industrial Organization in the Sixteenth and Seventeenth Centuries* (Oxford, Clarendon Press, 1904) p. 130) has shown that other Stuart corporations of small masters sought to secure monopolies by enforcing membership of their guilds.

[3] S.P. 16/373, no. 82, 2nd doc., Order in Council.

[4] The account of this process and of the silvering process developed later in Flanders and Venice is taken from B. Schweig, 'Mirrors', *Antiquity* xv (1941), 257–88.

[5] See Table 9, pp. 238–9.

[6] Patent Rolls C. 66/920, mm. 12d–12d, Book of Rates, 1558. Looking-glasses 'of steale' were valued at 6s. 8d. the dozen (small), 13s. 4d. the dozen (large), and the valuation held until 1657 when there was a slight reduction.   [7] Schweig, p. 259.

of Italian *cristallo*, called 'sites', which were ground and polished before silvering, producing the finest and largest mirrors in Europe. Though the Venetians guild of looking-glass makers sought to maintain their monopoly of the trade, by 1570 workmen in both Antwerp and Rouen were producing similar looking-glasses, very probably from exported Venetian 'sites'.[1] By that year also sizes had been standardized: they were numbered from 1 to 8, the smallest (no. 1) being $3\frac{1}{2} \times 2\frac{1}{2}$ inches, the largest 8×10 inches, and the most popular, middle size (no. 6) $7 \times 5\frac{1}{2}$ inches.[2] For customs purposes the 'middle sort' were valued at 20s. the dozen; those under no. 6 at 10s. the dozen; and those of size 7 and upwards at 40s. the dozen.[3] These valuations represent wholesale prices for looking-glasses imported without frames or cases. When they were framed, sometimes in silver, and embellished in other ways the valuation on a single small Venetian mirror might be as high as £2. 10s.[4]

Though small in size by modern standards these mirrors were a highly prized luxury at the time. Goldsmiths imported them from Antwerp, Rouen, and Venice itself in increasing amounts during the reign of Elizabeth. The quantity imported (as indicated in Table 9) does not seem particularly impressive; but the total valuation of these imported looking-glasses in 1587–8 was higher than that of any other imported glass product (with the possible exception of beads,[5] another Venetian speciality). By that time the closing of the Scheldt to shipping (following the fall of Antwerp to Spanish troops) had forced many of those engaged in the finishing trades to move from Antwerp to Amsterdam and Flushing; but as with hour-glass makers, the first looking-glass makers do not seem to have come to England until the reign of James I. Neither Verzelini, Robson, or Salter made plates from *cristallo*, and there is no firm evidence that they were made by Zouch's men before Mansell took control of the monopoly. Mansell's statement that he introduced such manufacture into England may well be true.[6] In 1615 looking-glasses were still being imported, but a Flemish looking-glass maker was training English apprentices in the parish of St. Saviour's, Southwark, near the Winchester House works. From that time on the finishing trades were firmly established in England.

Mansell estimated that the cost of finishing looking-glasses amounted

[1] The Port Books, which distinguish between the value of Venetian and Flemish for all other kinds of glass, make no distinction for mirrors.

[2] Young, p.18. The sizes are from the charter of 1635, but the numbering system appears in the Port Books as early as 1570.

[3] Port Books, E. 122/173/3, Book of Rates, 2 Jac I. Though not listed in the Book of Rates of 1558, the same distinction by size and value appears in the Port Books of 1571–2 (E. 190/5/5).

[4] Port Books, E. 190/32/1, London, 1627.

[5] Port Books, E. 190/7/8 and 8/1. See also Appendix B.

[6] S.P. 16/521, no. 148.

to $2\frac{1}{2}$ times the cost of the unground plates—which was about 11*s*. a dozen in 1615, reduced to 8–10*s*. later.[1] Probably 4 or 5 times as many men were employed in the finishing processes as in blowing the plates, for the Glass-Sellers listed among their members 'Grinders, Foylers, Pollishers, Finishers, and Casers' as separate persons,[2] and the work though less skilled was slow. In 1624 Mansell estimated that if all the glassmakers engaged in blowing plates and all those in the finishing processes together with 'their severall families' were counted, the number would come to no less than 500 persons supported by the industry.[3] From time to time Mansell recruited new finishers from the continent, though most of his finishing staff were English-born, and he defended their interests against the attempt of the Bingleys to secure a monopoly in finishing the plates.[4] Unlike the hour-glass makers, who complained of Mansell's supply of glass periodically, the looking-glass makers supported him consistently whenever his patent was in jeopardy.

Partly because of the value of looking-glasses and the prospect of great profits from them, Mansell gave high priority to their manufacture in the allocation of his time, energy, and resources. Moreover, since this manufacture provided employment and made expensive imports of looking-glasses unnecessary, he listed the bringing of the production of looking-glasses 'to a state of perfection' as one of the three principal benefits of his regime to the commonwealth (the other two being the saving of wood and the general reduction in prices).[5] His claim to success in producing glass plates of high quality is supported by the testimony of the Venetian Ambassador[6] and by the standard of the scientific equipment that was made from the plates.[7] However, he encountered many difficulties in keeping the level of production high enough to satisfy the men in the finishing trades. When importation, except with his permission, was cut off by the Proclamation of 1615, he began production of the plates with high hopes, but in 1619 his workmen were making so few that he was forced to authorize the importation of 600 dozen.[8] In the same year he sent Howell to the continent to recruit more skilled glassmakers from Murano and to arrange for the importation of large amounts of barilla.[9] According to both the Venetian Ambassador and the looking-glass makers, he was succeeding well in meeting the demand for looking-glass plates by 1621. In June of that year, however, complaints against his monopoly in Parliament led to the relaxation of the restrictions on importation.[10] As a result, more finished mirrors were imported from Venice during the remainder of the year than in any other year during the

---

[1] S.P. 14/162, no. 231 B.

[2] S.P. 16/475, no. 57, Petition of the Glass-sellers of London.

[3] S.P. 15/162, no. 231 B. [4] See above, pp. 101–2. [5] S.P. 16/521, no. 148.

[6] See above, p. 82. [7] See below, pp. 245–7. [8] *A.P.C.* xxxvii, 220–1.

[9] See above, p. 81. [10] See above, pp. 116–18.

TABLE 9
Looking-glasses Shipped In or Out of London[a]

Reference and Date[b]	CRYSTAL Amount	Destination	Value £ s. d.	COARSE Amount	Destination	Value £ s. d.
IMPORTS						
4/2 Eng., 1567/8	87 doz. and 1 chest		91. 0. 0	48 gross		12. 12. 0
	3 coffers		4. 0. 0			
7/8 & 8/1 Eng., 1587/8	35 doz. large		70. 0. 0	46½ gross		13. 3. 0
	146 doz. small		146. 0. 0			
	12 doz. medium		13. 0. 0			
11/1 Aliens, 1600	5 doz. large		10. 0. 0	None		—
	25 doz. small		25. 0. 0			
14/5 Aliens, 1609	5 doz. no. 6		5. 0. 0	None		—
	19 doz. under no. 6		9. 10. 0			
	20 small		16. 8			
18/6 Eng., 1615	2		14. 0. 0	None		
	5 doz. large		10. 0. 0			
	2 doz. small		2. 0. 0			
24/4 Eng., 1621	50 doz. large		100. 0. 0	25 gross		7. 14. 0
	416 doz. small		208. 0. 0			
31/3 Eng., 1626	10 doz. large		20. 0. 0	80½ gross		23. 6. 0
	3 doz. no. 6		3. 0. 0			
	1		4. 0. 0			
	88 + doz. sites (unfinished plates)		105. 10. 0			
	1 chest and 2 coffers of sites		162. 10. 0			
34/2 Eng., 1630	8 doz. large		16. 0. 0	82 gross		30. 14. 0
	2		3. 0. 0			
38/5 Eng., 1634	12 doz. large		24. 0. 0	None		
	½ doz. medium		10. 0. 0			
	23 doz. small		11. 10. 0			

43/5 Eng., 1640	None		27 gross	—		5. 14. 0
44/3 Aliens, 1640	None		9 gross	—		1. 18. 0

EXPORTS

38/7 Eng., 1634	1 doz. small	Dunkirk	18 doz.		10. 0
	12½ doz. no. 6	Lisbon, Madeira Islands		Guinea	12. 10. 0 12. 0
	15 doz. size uncertain^c	Portugal			13. 0. 0
43/1 Eng., 1640	35 doz. small	?Robordence, Guinea, Barbary	5½ gross 20 dozen^d	?Sapho Dublin	17. 10. 0 1. 2. 0 6. 0. 0
	11½ doz. no. 6	Robordence, Barbary St. Lucia, Malta, East India			11. 10. 0
	2 very large	Calais			3. 0. 0
	1 very large	Bilboa			7. 0. 0
	4 very large^e	Elsinore			?6. 0. 0

^a Except when valuations were given in the Port Eooks, they were computed from the Book of Rates of 1604 (Exch. K.R., Customs, E. 122/173/3). Before 1615 the origin of the crystal glasses was usually given as Middleburg, occasionally as Stade, Emden, or Venice; but since the glasses were described as 'Venice' and included in cargoes of Mediterranean goods such as Spanish silks and Italian velvets, they had presumably been reshipped from Venice. After 1615 the crystal ones came directly from Venice. The coarse looking-glasses came from Antwerp in 1567, after 1585 from Hamburg, Emden, Stade, and Lubeck. Amounts and values of pennyware and halfpennyware looking-glasses have been put together.

^b See above, p. 210, Table 4, note a.

^c This entry is ambiguous. It appears to read 'xv dozen obware [halfpennyware] looking glasses costing xiii li', but normally halfpennyware glasses were bought by the gross and were worth only 4s per gross. Since valuations were seldom given except for unusual items of moderate or high value, I have assumed that the valuation rather than the descriptive words is correct and that the glasses were of crystal of a special size not numbered in the usual way.

^d Since the valuation (6s. a dozen) is clear, these glasses (and possibly those exported to Guinea in 1634 listed above) would appear to be of a new sort, perhaps intermediate between the pennyware and the small crystal.

^e This entry is extremely difficult to interpret. It could mean 4 looking-glasses, or 40, written iiii^d rather than xl; and the valuation of 30s. could be for each (as I have assumed in the chart) or for the total.

period of this study.[1] Though the large number of mirrors imported late in 1621 might seem to be a reflection on the quality of Mansell's plates, it is more likely to be related to the struggle between the merchants, who wanted to increase their overseas trade by destroying the monopoly, and the glass-sellers, who were co-operating with Mansell and were perhaps financing the men in the finishing trades, who later became members of the Glass-Sellers Company. Certainly English-made mirrors could compete successfully with those made in Venice or elsewhere on the continent, for from 1624 to 1635 there was no prohibition of importation and yet the number of imported mirrors remained relatively low. In some years, however, Mansell had great difficulty in supplying enough plates, sometimes because of the continuing problem of defection of workmen, sometimes because of a shortage of the essential barilla, and at such times the 'sites' reappear in the imports. It was only after the Venetian Council prohibited the export of any unfinished plates that Mansell's production was finally secure. Nevertheless, by 1634 small numbers of finished looking-glasses were being exported to Dunkirk, Lisbon, and the Madeira Islands, and the number increased somewhat in 1640.[2] In 1657 the new Book of Rates omitted looking-glasses entirely[3] indicating that by then importation was uncommon.

'Sites', as opposed to finished mirrors, were not included in earlier Books of Rates. When an item was not found in the Books, merchants were required to declare its value: the declared value of the Venetian 'sites' in 1634 was 25s. a dozen,[4] an extremely high price compared with Mansell's (which he said was 11s. the dozen in the period 1615–21, and from 8s. to 10s. thereafter).[5] It is hard to account for the difference in price; and even harder to reconcile it with Mansell's statement that the English manufacture was not secure until the Venetian supply was cut off. Perhaps Mansell's low price was possible only if labour costs were kept low—which would explain why his men were constantly defecting to the continent.

There are plentiful references to looking-glasses in the inventories of the time. One is listed for almost every household, varying in type from the small half-penny variety to the most expensive, valued at several pounds. There must have been a sizable market for them; but the level of demand and supply is not known in detail. Certainly a large amount of the crystal produced in England in Mansell's time went into the production of looking-glasses. The successful development of this manufacture in England—which had no parallel in France until the foundation of the

[1] See Table 9, pp. 238–9 A. All the looking-glasses imported in 1621 arrived in London after June.   [2] Port Books, E. 190/38/7, Exports, 1634; E. 190/43/1, Exports, 1640.
[3] Hall, ii. 249–73.   [4] Port Books, E. 190/38/5, Imports, 1634.
[5] S.P. 14/162, no. 231 B.

Royal Plate Glass Company in 1665,[1] can surely be attributed largely to Mansell's efforts; though his accomplishments have been overshadowed by the fact that the French, once they began the manufacture, soon developed a method of casting plates which was far superior to the technique of blowing them.

IV. SPECTACLES

Spectacle lenses were cut and ground from the same flat sheets of *cristallo* that were used for looking-glasses, so Mansell's 'exceeding great charge in perfecting the worke'[2] of making the plates affected both products. Moreover, the development of the finishing trade of spectacle-making was similar to that of looking-glass making, except that in the case of the spectacle-makers recruitment from the continent seems not to have been necessary, and the craft was organized into a separate guild much earlier. The charter of the Spectacle-Makers was secured from Charles I in 1629;[3] unlike the hour-glass makers and the looking-glass makers they were never associated in any way with the Glass-Sellers Company.

Though the use of spectacles as an aid to reading seems to date from the end of the thirteenth century,[4] it was not until after the invention of printing that demand reached any proportions. During the sixteenth century their use increased noticeably, and spectacle-makers were practising their craft in several of the chief cities of northern Europe, especially in Germany and the Low Countries. It is possible that spectacles were made in London, too, at this time, for the date when the craft was introduced into England is uncertain. The pattern of importation, however, which parallels that of hour-glasses and looking-glasses for the Elizabethan period, suggests rather that most if not all were imported from abroad—chiefly from Stade, Hamburg, and Rouen. As indicated in Table 10, the numbers imported increased during the early part of the reign of Elizabeth. However, these imports fell off sharply by 1621, and they disappeared from the records after 1630, the year following the incorporation of the guild. By 1634 modest numbers of spectacles (about equal in number, however, to those imported in 1621) were being exported.[5] What is more significant, they were going chiefly to Germany, France, and the Low Countries, as well as to Ireland and Portugal.

Such exportation to areas that had formerly been the chief source of supply suggests that English spectacles were more plentiful and also of better quality by 1634 than those of continental manufacture. The English spectacles were made of Mansell's crystal plates, blown especially thick

---

[1] Scoville, p. 27.   [2] S.P. 16/282, no. 99, 'Costes, charges, difficulties'.
[3] Ashdown, p. 39.
[4] S. Bradbury, *The Evolution of the Microscope* (Oxford, Pergamon Press, 1967), p. 4.
[5] Port Books, E. 190/38/7, Exports, 1634.

TABLE 10

Spectacles Shipped In or Out of London

Reference and Date[a]	Amounts	Value[b] £ s. d.	Origin or Destination
IMPORTS			
4/2 Eng., 1567/8	40 gross	20. 0. 0	Flushing, Antwerp
7/8 and 8/1 Eng., 1587/8	75½ gross	37. 10. 11	Hamburg, Rouen, and Stade
14/5 Aliens, 1609	39½ gross	19. 15. 0	Stade
24/4 Eng., 1621	16 gross	8. 0. 0	Hamburg
31/3 Eng., 1626	4 gross	2. 0. 0	Amsterdam
34/2 Eng., 1630	2 gross	1. 0. 0	Middleburg
43/5 Eng., 1640	None	—	—
EXPORTS			
38/7 Eng., 1634	13 gross	6. 10. 0	Hamburg, Dunkirk
43/1 Eng., 1640	21¾ gross	10. 17. 6	Canary Islands, Amsterdam, Dieppe, Portugal, and Robordence

[a] See above, p. 210, Table 4, note *a*.

[b] The valuations for customs purposes remained stationary at 10*s.* per gross throughout the period. See Appendix, pp. 260–1.

to take the grinding of either looking-glass makers or spectacle-makers, and no such plates seem to have been made in northern Europe. (They were occasionally imported from Venice, but at a much higher price than Mansell charged.) Lenses could also be ground from clear forest glass; this was probably done in Europe, and in England before Mansell's time. There are even examples of the occasional use of green glass. Lord Norris wrote to a friend in London in 1607 asking him to send a particular book and 'a green crystal glass to do good offices between the small print and my eyes'.[1] In that instance, some sort of magnifying glass rather than mounted spectacles seems to have been intended; but as late as 1633 Lord William Howard ordered 'one payre of green spectacles' and 'one payre

[1] S.P. 15/39, no. 28, Lord Norris to Carleton, Nov. 1607.

of multiplying spectacles' at the same time.[1] After Mansell began making good quality crystal plates, however, his plates seem to have been used almost exclusively, and the quality of the lenses improved. The spectacle-makers supported Mansell's monopoly when it was under attack[2] and never complained of the price he charged, the quality of his plates, or the adequacy of the supply.

It is not possible to estimate the amount of glass that went into spectacle-making, or the output (measured in gross); but it can be seen from inventories that demand increased and the price was lowered as the supply in England became more plentiful. The accounts of Lord William Howard supply an excellent example. He was an avid reader with a large library and also an amateur scientist who owned an astrolabe, and made various archaeological discoveries.[3] The accounts show that he bought his first pair of spectacles in 1620 for 18d. and had them mended later the same year.[4] Thereafter, however, he bought within 13 years the amazing number of 27 pairs (at the very least)—on 3 occasions buying 4 pairs at once. Among this impressive array were some with horn rims, and one pair with silver frames, valued at 3s. 8d.;[5] but by 1624 the usual price paid by Howard was 9d. a pair. Lord William could hardly have been so careless as to break or mislay so many spectacles;[6] there is a simple explanation for the purchases. There were no opticians at the time to prescribe or grind lenses to order, though there was some knowledge of optics. Merret said that convex spectacles were used for the aged and concave for the purblind;[7] and lenses were numbered when ground, the number generally indicating the radius of the tool. In London a prospective buyer could try out several pairs, but this was not possible for a man such as Lord William who seldom left his northern castle. Instead he ordered numerous pairs in an attempt to help his eyesight as it grew worse from constant reading. Though he was richer and more studious than the average Englishman, his purchases reflect the growing demand for spectacles by those who could afford them.

V. SCIENTIFIC EQUIPMENT

The volume of production is not the only indication of the importance of an industry for a nation. Social and other intangible benefits may accrue which have little to do with the number of persons employed. During the seventeenth century the development of science, especially

---

[1] *Household Books of Lord William Howard*, p. 293.

[2] *Commons Debates, 1621*, iii. 256.

[3] *Household Books of Lord William Howard*, p. 257. The Introduction gives an account of his life and interests.

[4] Ibid., pp. 144, 147. [5] Ibid., p. 257.

[6] The accounts distinguish between purchases made for various members of the family and the spectacles were all for Lord William. [7] Merrett p. 3.

in England, is one of the most significant factors in cultural and intellectual history. The attention to accurate scientific observation and measurement which was then a chief characteristic of science depended upon new instruments. Out of the six most important of these, four—the microscope, the telescope, the barometer, and the air pump—were fashioned partly of glass. Any relationship between the production and use of such instruments and between glassmakers and scientists is of great interest.

Both the microscope and the telescope are obviously connected with the production of lenses; in fact, the invention of both is attributed to Dutch spectacle-makers at about the turn of the century. There is some doubt, however, as to the actual inventor in each case.[1] Lenses of good quality were essential if these instruments were to be made. Hans Lippershey, one of three spectacle-makers of Middleburg in the Netherlands (the others being Hans Janssen and his son Zacharias) whose names are most often associated with the invention, in constructing his telescope used lenses ground from natural rock crystal, because of the poor quality of the available glass lenses, which he said were often greenish in colour and marred by air bubbles. It would seem that the Dutch spectacle-makers were grinding their lenses from forest glass, not from *cristallo* from Venice. Better lenses were undoubtedly available to Galileo. In May 1609 he heard in Venice from friends in the Netherlands about the new invention, and made his own telescope from glass lenses (no doubt made in Murano); he then spent a considerable time in improving it and putting it to use in astronomical observations.

Galileo's fame was such that his telescope, usually called a 'perspective glass', was soon widely used by astronomers and the invention was often attributed to him.[2] In England one of the first purchases of a telescope was made not by a scientist but by a sea-captain, a Captain Bruz of London. By February 1610 (less than a year after Galileo first heard of the invention) Bruz had already received one telescope, ordered through a friend named William Trumbull residing in Brussels, and he had placed an order for more, since the first was not satisfactory.[3] Trumbull ordered these 'perspective glasses' in Antwerp, not in Brussels, and soon received three with glass lenses at 10s. each and one with a lens of rock crystal at 20s. He returned the rock crystal one as too expensive, but sent the others on to Bruz in London asking him for 40s. for the three. Captain Bruz thought the price was too high, for he said that they were not much better than the one he already had, which had only cost 4s.; yet he offered to buy one for 10s., or to pay 20s. for the three.[4] The particular interest of this incident is two-fold: first, the Dutch lenses were obviously not of a

[1] Bradbury, pp. 5, 21.   [2] Merret, p. 3.
[3] HMC, *Downshire MSS.*, ii. 228, 239.   [4] Ibid., 229, 239.

very high quality, and secondly, an English sea-captain had perceived the practical uses for telescopes at sea, almost as soon as the invention appeared, and was intent upon securing a satisfactory one.

The precise date of the first English-made 'perspective glasses' is not known, but it is clear that production began during the Mansell regime, undoubtedly using lenses made from his crystal plates. In 1634 the Port Books show that 3 dozen 'perspective glasses' were exported to Hamburg,[1] and there is no record of importation in that or the preceding years. Since we know that there was some demand for telescopes from sea-captains, and also that spectacle-makers were flourishing in London in the 1620s, it is very likely that there were by that time some English-made telescopes. Mansell stressed his great interest in the production of fine quality plates. Though he makes no particular mention of 'perspective glasses' (none of his private correspondence, which might have revealed an interest, survives), when one remembers that he was trained as a sea-captain, held the title of Vice-Admiral of the Navy throughout his life, and saw frequent service on commissions relating to the Navy throughout his career as glass monopolist, one cannot but wonder whether his great interest in improving the quality of the plates for lenses was stimulated at least in part by an interest in the production of telescopes for the Navy. Mansell was also by his first marriage a brother-in-law of Sir Francis Bacon, author of the *Advancement of Learning*; and another Bacon, Captain Francis, probably a kinsman of Sir Francis, was his supervisor at the Broad Street furnace.[2] Since the telescope was the most 'practical' of all the new scientific inventions of the period, it was fitting that its development was furthered by good quality lenses made in a furnace owned and supervised by seamen, at least one of whom was related to the great exponent of the practical application of new knowledge.

A simple magnifying lens, as distinct from the compound microscope, was used both before and after the discovery of the true microscope as an aid to the naked eye in close scientific observation. Prior to his great discovery of the circulation of the blood (first expounded in his lectures in about 1616) William Harvey had observed 'with the aid of a magnifying glass' a pulsating heart in such seemingly bloodless insects as wasps, hornets, and flies.[3] Shortly afterwards one of the first true microscopes, which was made by the Janssens of Middleburg for the Archduke Albert of Austria, came for a time during 1619 into the possession of Cornelius Drebbel, an Englishman.[4] Soon Drebbel journeyed to Middleburg for the express purpose of purchasing one of his own so that he could copy it in England. Thereafter he made a number of such instruments which

[1] Port Books, E. 190/38/7. [2] See above, pp. 81–2.
[3] *The Works of William Harvey*, trans. R. Willis (London, The Sydenham Society, 1847), p. 29.
[4] Bradbury, p. 21.

circulated widely in Europe.[1] We can be relatively certain that he used lenses made of crystal plates from Mansell's furnaces. Remembering the statement of the Venetian Ambassador that the plates were not 'sensibly inferior' to those made in Murano, and were sometimes even better,[2] the popularity of Drebbel's instruments on the continent no doubt resulted from the superiority of his lenses as well as from his own skill in manufacture. Since the microscope had little practical use except in scientific investigation, and even scientists regarded it as nothing more than a curious toy until after the work of Boyle and van Leeuwenhock, it did not attract as much interest as did the telescope, and probably few were made. English scientists were among the first to appreciate its uses, however, and a book entitled *Theatre of Insects* published in 1634 extolled the uses of 'lenticular glasses of crystal' as a means of opening up a large 'field of Philosophy' hitherto unknown.[3] The micrometer, an instrument applied to both telescopes and microscopes for measuring small angles, was invented in England before 1639 by William Gascoigne, a young gentleman of Yorkshire, although it was little known before it was exhibited at a meeting of the Royal Society in July 1667.[4]

Together, the influence of Bacon's philosophy (with its stress on the practicality of new knowledge), the patent system (which offered tangible rewards to inventors), and the spirit of discovery in all areas of life produced a host of new inventions and minor improvements in others.[5] As might be expected, many of these proved to be insignificant; but they provide evidence on the connections between industrialists and scientists, not least in the glass industry. Rolvenson, the projector who tried to invent new furnaces for glass and other metals, describes an invention useful for night-time work at furnaces of a 'newly-devised luminary of glasse, or glasses filled with water and candle placed to give light through it, which giveth a very great light a great distance off, with small charge; and may be converted to excellent use, being placed in high places, in crossways and streets of citties and townes.'[6] The association of Sir Kenelm Digby, who achieved considerable fame in his own day as a scientist, with the use of a new formula for making glass, and, consequently, with developments in the bottle-trade, has already been noted.[7] The most important connection, however, between scientists or inventors on the one hand, and glassmakers on the other, resulted from the dependence

---

[1] Bradbury, pp. 21–2.   [2] *Cal. S.P. Ven.* xvi. 212.

[3] M. Nicholson, 'The Microscope and English Imagination', *Smith College Studies in Modern Languages*, xvi (1934–5), 8.

[4] *Encyclopaedia Britannica*, 11th ed. 'Micrometer'.

[5] W. E. Knowles Middleton, *The Invention of Meteorological Instruments* (Baltimore, Johns Hopkins Univ. Press, 1969), chaps. i, ii; A. Wolf, *History of Science, Technology and Philosophy in the Sixteenth and Seventeenth Centuries* (London, Allen & Unwin, 1935), *passim*.

[6] Rolvenson, p. C. 2b.   [7] See above, pp. 229–30.

of the experimenter upon equipment made of glass. Whereas lenses, as we have seen, were important, the innumerable flasks, vials, retort heads, stills, tubing, and other glass equipment were indispensable. Easy access to blowers skilled enough to fashion such equipment to order could be the crucial factor in determining whether or not experiments could be carried out, as an example from the early history of the barometer makes clear. In the autumn of 1645 Father Mersenne of Paris, who served as a sort of international exchange agent for new scientific discoveries, tried to repeat one of Torricelli's experiments with air pressure in connection with the principle of the barometer. Mersenne was not able to do so in spite of explicit directions, because he could not obtain adequate glass tubes in Paris. Instead he wrote about it to another scientist, Pierre Petit, and since Petit was at Rouen where there was a good glass-works he was able to perform the experiment successfully with a larger tube.[1] In England, the work of Robert Boyle, Hooke, and other members of the Royal Society was certainly expedited by their nearness to glasshouses staffed with competent workmen: this experiment was repeated there before 1648.[2] So necessary was the association between scientists and glassmakers that Boyle's off-hand remark about 'the last time I visited a glass-house' to see 'an eminently skillful workman whom I had purposely engaged to make some vessels for me'[3] would hardly seem worthy of comment, did it not prompt the reflection that fifty years earlier he might not have found such a workman so close at hand.

It is true that simple apothecaries' wares, such as beakers, flasks, and simple tubing, had been made continuously at Chiddingfold throughout the Middle Ages, and were later made elsewhere in England. The making of complicated retorts, however, demanded a much higher skill. A petition against Mansell's monopoly in 1621 makes clear that 'chimicall glasses, as retorte heades and bodies, boulte heades and other like used for extractions distillacion and other Chimicall and Physical uses' had been imported from Germany before the granting of the monopoly, and that the German ones were both cheaper and better than those sold by Mansell.[4] As shown in Table 11, the Port Books record frequent imports of vials, flasks, and 'water glasses';[5] and since some such vessels were being made in England, the imported ones were presumably of better quality. Stilling glasses were imported in substantial numbers (300 in 1587–8)[6] at a price that varied from 16d. each to £8 a dozen, and small 'glass pipes' (probably glass tubing) came in in 1574 and 1612.[7] No doubt

---

[1] Middleton, p. 18.   [2] Ibid., p. 24.

[3] Robert Boyle, *Works*, ed. T. Birch (London, 1772), i. 339.

[4] Harl. MS. 6847, fol. 271, printed in *Commons Debates, 1621*, vii. 544.

[5] Port Books, E. 190/5/5, Imports, 1571/2. The meaning of 'water glasses' is unclear, but they were certainly not drinking glasses.

[6] Ibid., E. 190/7/8 and 8/1.   [7] Ibid., 11/1, 63/3, 18/3.

the petitioners were right in their assertions that Mansell's chemical glass was inferior and dear in his early years; but after 1624 no more stills were imported. He had introduced another specialized skill, and had begun the training of men who could eventually satisfy even Robert Boyle.

Once the specialized production of scientific equipment was established, the quality of the glass proved as satisfactory to the scientists as the dex-

TABLE II

Scientific Equipment Made of Glass Shipped In or Out of London

Reference and Date[a]	Kind and Amount	Origin or Destination	Value[b] £ s. d.
IMPORTS			
7/8 & 8/1	100 stills @ 15d. each	Dort	5. 0. 0
Eng., 1587/8	200 stilling glasses @ 16d. each	Emden	13. 6. 0
11/1 Aliens, 1600	480 stilling glasses	Amsterdam	?
18/3 Aliens, 1613	40 lb. glass pipes (?tubing)	Venice	5. 0. 0
EXPORTS			
83/7 Eng., 1634	3 doz. perspective glasses	Hamburg	?
	3,700 lanthorne (lantern) lenses	Hamburg	?
43/1 Eng., 1640	Apothecaries' wares[c]	Dublin	?
	19 cases glass vials	Dublin	?
	4 doz. urinals	?	?
	4 doz. lanthornes	Dublin	?
	6 doz. 'cuppinglasses'[d]	Canary Islands	?

[a] See above, p. 210, Table 4, note a.

[b] All valuations given are those declared by the merchants. Although this was required when merchandize was not listed in the Book of Rates, merchants frequently declared the value of an entire consignment of miscellaneous items, and although these are named, the value of each cannot be determined.

[c] Since apothecaries' drugs were listed separately, this item must pertain to equipment.

[d] Though this term is obscure, it seems to refer to glass vessels used for blood-letting and other medicinal purposes, not to cups for drinking.

terity of the blowers. Thomas Sprat, the historian of the Royal Society, comments as follows: 'Toward the exactness of all manner of Optick glasses, the English have got an advantage of late years, by the Art of making glass finer and more serviceable for Microscopes and Telescopes, than that of Venice.'[1] Samuel Hartlib wrote to Boyle in 1659 that the French naturalist Bressieux had written to ask him for 'some peice of

[1] Thomas Sprat, *A History of the Royal Society of London* (London, 1667), p. 250.

glass, good and fine'. Hartlib suggested to Boyle that 'if some peice of good glass could be sent to him to work upon (seeing he complaineth of the difficulty of getting good stuff, and that at Venice they degenerate very much in that art) it would, I believe oblige him to permit us some-times to look on his workmanship, which he is very shy to do.'[1] If English glass was bartered in exchange for the sharing of the results of experiments by continental scientists, the industry had indeed come a long way from the time when Carré talked with the glassmaker in Chid-dingfold who could make only the simplest articles of forest glass. Since Sprat uses the phrase 'of late years', some of the improvement in English crystal glass probably occurred during the period of the Interregnum; for want of further evidence we cannot date its superiority over continental glass exactly. Nevertheless, in the face of Mansell's recurring and in-sistent statements as to the amount of time and money he had put into the improvement of the quality of crystal, especially of that used for looking-glasses and lenses, we can hardly deny him a fair share of the credit.

The Royal Society furthered the connection between scientists and glassmakers. The Society's early proceedings show that numerous experi-ments were made on the properties of glass, particularly on the curious behaviour of little glass globules known as 'Prince Rupert's tears'.[2] It was the Royal Society, also, which encouraged Christopher Merret to translate and write a commentary on Neri's *Art of Glass*, which has been so often quoted in the present study. He dedicated the work to 'the Honourable and true Promoter of all solid Learning, Robert Boyle, Esquire' and added: 'You [Boyle] have shewed the world not onely your great progress into singular knowledge but have also taught it the true use of that most beneficial Art [glassmaking]'.[3] Boyle was certainly a most appropriate choice for the dedication, for he had already taken a serious interest in the chemistry of glass and its physical properties. In his 'Essay on the porousness of solid bodies' he remarked that 'glass itself is not all of one sort, as men unacquainted with chymistry are wont to presume', and then went on to distinguish between glass of lead, glass of antimony, soda glass, and ordinary green glass.[4] He seems to have understood no more of the chemistry of glass than a contemporary glassmaker would have done; yet in the drawing together of scientist and industrialist[5] in

---

[1] Boyle, vi. 135. It is important to note that this incident occurred before the invention of lead crystal in England.

[2] Merret appended the paper read before the Royal Society on 'Prince Rupert's tears' to his commentary on the *Art of Glass*.

[3] Merret, Dedication.

[4] Boyle, iv. 787.

[5] There are other references in Boyle's works to his frequent consultations with practising glassmakers about the physical properties of glass, information which he incorporated into his scientific treatises. See especially, ibid., i. 455.

mutual concern for the improvement of a product in common use may be seen the beginning of an alliance which was to have far-reaching effects. Since the Royal Society was not founded until 1660, this awareness of a community of interest, which can be recognized in the tentative exchange of information between members of the Royal Society and industrial glassmakers might seem to date exclusively from the period of the Restoration. However, it is well known that the informal meetings in Gresham College which preceded the formation of the Society by several decades were of much the same character as the later, formal meetings, and both Boyle and Merret imply that their interest in glass was of long standing. It does not seem unwarranted, then, to say that in the period of our study, glassmaking took its first tentative steps toward its close connection with science, and began, in a sense other than an economic one, to assume its modern role.

XI

CONCLUSION

IT hardly needs to be said that the eighty years from 1560 to 1640 saw a variety of changes in the English glass industry. The most obvious was the growth in scale from 2 small furnaces in the Weald making simple apothecaries' wares and household glass of poor quality, to a sizable industry of probably 25–30 glasshouses, some much larger than those of 1560, supplying all of a greatly expanded English market and beginning to export some glass to Europe and the colonies. It is difficult to estimate the total value of English-made glass in 1640, for so little is known of the price and level of production of some of the wares made; yet since more than 9,000 cases of window glass, selling at 24s. 6d. a case, seem to have been produced, window glass alone would have been worth over £11,000 and the value of the other kinds of glasswares would at least have doubled that figure.

The influx of alien glassmakers, whose numbers and skill infused new life into English glassmaking, was unquestionably the greatest single factor contributing to growth in the industry. In this connection the policy of the Crown in encouraging such immigration deserves some credit. Though the granting of numerous royal monopolies for all kinds of projects has been criticized, no general condemnation of all the glass patents is warranted. The policy of the Elizabethan Government during the early part of the Queen's reign, in granting special concessions to the first aliens on the basis of the introduction of a new industry, was on the whole a sound one. Admittedly the Crown took little initiative in recruiting glassmakers and they might have come without royal protection, but they were certainly encouraged to choose a haven in England and to remain there permanently through the issue of the letters patent. No harm came to the English consumer as a result of this policy; in fact, the country soon benefited from a much larger supply of glass in the three principal branches of the trade—tableware both of crystal and of green glass, and window glass. As the number of aliens increased, the price of window glass fell, and sales accordingly increased; while at the same time the easy availability of other kinds of glassware increased sales in other sectors of the industry. With reference to window glass, the Privy Council in 1576 wisely refused to grant a monopoly patent with a prohibition on importation that would have held prices at the former level. Late in Elizabeth's reign, however, the new policy of rewarding favourites and pensioners with monopoly rights in order to relieve the Exchequer of expense can justifiably be blamed for saddling a part of the industry with high overheads, a burden which, unfortunately, was carried over into the early Stuart period.

The invention of the coal process was a factor in the development of glassmaking second in importance only to the influx of aliens, for it insured the continued growth of the industry by setting it on a sound economic basis. The assumption, however, that the scarcity and high cost of wood for fuel forced glassmakers to make the change, and the imputation that this occurred in the forest-glass industry before the granting of the Zouch patent of 1611, need to be revised. Examination of the evidence presented in the Parliament of 1621 leads to the conclusion that it was one of the partners in Zouch's firm, Thomas Percival, who was the first person to burn coal successfully in glassmaking. The amount of capital that was invested in his experiments supports this attribution: few window-glass makers (to whom the invention has sometimes been ascribed) had the necessary capital. Moreover, they lacked sufficient motivation to experiment (except in a small way), for window-glass makers well knew that the need to purchase wood or fern ashes in sufficient quantity for their batches might offset the saving in fuel. This was particularly true in country districts where wood was still reasonably priced (as it was in parts of Gloucestershire), or when glassmakers controlled sufficient woodlands to supply their minimum needs (as did Bungar in the Weald). It was no accident, then, that the experiments took place in the London area, with the experience of men trained in crystal-making as a guide, for it was only in crystal-making that the saving from burning coal was immediate and substantial. The first users of the new process might not have made window glass at all, had not the monopolies in crystal-making granted to Bowes and Salter, which Robson controlled, prevented them from making crystal, whereas Bungar's restriction of production in the Weald had left the London window-glass market in short supply. When the new patentees found that window glass could not be made at a profit in London using coal, they were forced to challenge Robson by making crystal in spite of his exclusive privileges, in an effort to make a profit from their invention. Yet though the unfortunate royal policy of grants to favourites was responsible for the early losses incurred by the patentees for the coal process, the wiser policy of making grants for new inventions was a positive stimulus to experimentation and change. The ease with which monopoly privileges for new inventions could be secured, and the hope of eventually making large sums of money, encouraged Zouch and his partners to invest substantial amounts in experimentation and to push the experiments to a successful conclusion. Examination of the technical problems involved in the new process has shown that Percival indeed made sufficient changes in furnace structure to warrant calling his process an invention: the royal patent which followed was certainly justified.

To point out that the invention of the coal process was made by out-siders hiring technical help, and not by established glassmakers pressed by high fuel costs, is not to deny the importance of the shortage and rising cost of wood for fuel. The prospect of using coal would not have been so attractive to the group financing the invention had it not been for the high cost of wood, which was forcing up the prices of crystal drinking glasses in London and would soon have done the same in other branches of the industry. There is plentiful evidence that in the years between 1585 and 1615 the cost of wood bought by glassmakers at Bagot's Park in Staffordshire had almost trebled, but the effect had been not to raise prices but to depress the earnings of glassmakers, because market conditions would not permit the volume of glass then being made to be sold at prices much above those of 1585. The rising price of wood at Bagot's Park also indicates that the glassmakers themselves contributed to the high cost of wood when they stayed in one location for long. Since the necessity to be near markets or cheap transportation for their products somewhat limited their search for fresh woodlands, if consumption of wood in glasshouses had continued unchecked during the seventeenth century, there is little doubt that the price of glass would have risen and many buyers would have been priced out of the market. At best, produc-tion would have remained stationary, as it was to do in France during the next century, and as it already had done in the Weald before 1615 through the artificial restriction of production by Bungar and Hensey. Since many of the conservative descendants of the alien glassmakers were reluctant to abandon the wood-burning tradition, (as the long battle between Bungar and Mansell indicated) and since they knew—as they frequently asserted—that the saving from the use of coal was (at this time) slight in their branch of the trade, it is hardly credible that they would have adopted the new fuel had not the royal grant forced them to do so. When the coal process became more efficient and cheaper grades of coal were burned, there was a genuine saving in total costs, and eventually the entire industry profited from enforced use of the new invention.

There is no reason to doubt that when they issued the first coal patent and its successors up to the year 1623 James I and his advisers thought that they were acting in the best interests of the nation. Until the patent of 1635, which was obviously granted to help relieve the financial diffi-culties of Charles I, there is no evidence of graft or bribery in connection with the glass patents granted for the coal process, or of any substantial monetary advantage to the Exchequer from the rents. Whether or not the shortage of fuel and timber was really serious enough to warrant granting a complete monopoly of all glassmaking (not just the right to use the new process), responsible statesmen thought that it was. Relief of the pressure on woodlands by forcing even a relatively small industry to use a more plentiful type of fuel was deemed desirable, even if this caused temporary hardship to some individuals. Moreover the thoroughness with which the Privy Council investigated the adequacy of the supply, the price, and the quality of the glass indicated that they had not given free rein to a group of courtiers to exploit the English consumer. It is true, however, that politics and favouritism had some influence both on the granting of the patents and on the attacks made upon them by various Parliaments. If the previous, unwise policy of granting unwarranted glass monopolies to Bowes and other courtiers had not been perpetuated, some of Mansell's early troubles and the rise in the price of glass in the period before 1620 might have been avoided: he needed a high margin of profit in order to pay off the previous patentees. In addition he had to pay interest on watered stock which resulted from the somewhat loose methods of raising capital then employed. Until he was relieved of both kinds of unproductive overheads in 1623, they were a genuine cause of loss. So, too, were his efforts to relocate the industry near coalfields, since technical reasons which no glassmaker then understood and the high cost of ashes which more than offset the saving on coal brought about failure in several locations. Indeed it is remarkable that Mansell showed as much grasp as he did of the technical problems and of the necessity both for careful cost accounting and for a reduction in fuel costs by means of larger and more efficient furnaces.

Because of these losses and the persistent and ingenious opposition of Isaac Bungar, who wanted to return to the use of wood, there was every justification for prolonging the monopoly in 1623. By that time Mansell had demonstrated that the coal process was bringing economic benefits to the nation. The price of window glass had fallen, for even though Mansell had retained the customary price by the case, the increase in the number of feet to the case meant a reduction in the price by the foot. After 1621 there was never any question that the supply was adequate—which had not been the case in the years just preceding the granting of the monopoly of 1615. In crystal glass, also, prices had come down, and though the price of green drinking glasses remained stable, the market was supplied with more English-made drinking glasses than before. It was only after 1623 that Mansell's company was able to recoup its losses and expand production further. There was no justification, however, for the extension of the monopoly in 1635, which led to a rise in prices as a result of the high rent paid to the Crown.

Mansell's administration of the glass monopoly is not above criticism, especially the local restrictions which he placed on the marketing of green drinking glasses and his labour policy in regard to the Venetian workmen. Nevertheless the standardization and centralized control which he imposed resulted in a more efficient and modern organization of the industry. Moreover the separation between capital and labour and the declining status of the glassmakers which resulted in lower wages had already begun before he took control of the monopoly. The proud *gentilhomme verrier*, who owned his own establishment and considered himself the social equal of the gentry and the minor nobility, had almost disappeared in England. Isaac Bungar was the last true representative of the medieval tradition of owner-craftsman: and he was almost alone in refusing to become Mansell's salaried employee. Capitalists and merchants had come to own and control the furnaces, and they included not just Mansell's firm but other men, independent of him, such as Sir William Clavell. Though government policy in granting monopolies had speeded up the process, the change had begun much earlier as a result of economic factors (such as the oversupply of window glass and rising cost of wood) which cut into the independent glassmaker's profits. In spite of his opposition to the Mansell monopoly, Bungar himself had become both merchant and capitalist before the patent of 1615. The wages then paid to glassmakers still placed their income far above the average for skilled workmen: £60–£80 a year in straight salary was extraordinarily high pay in the seventeenth century, and for those who became managers, this sum could be doubled. Moreover the wages seem to have been as high as the industry could bear. Entering the production of glass was hardly the easiest route to quick wealth, as Clavell discovered, and as both Sir Percival Willoughby and Thomas Wentworth realized. Even Mansell made no large fortune. There was no heavy accumulation of capital in the industry during this period (though the amount of capital necessary to begin operations had increased, and the scale of the enterprises tended to be larger).

One of the chief benefits to the nation from the Mansell administration was his production of various kinds of glassware not made in England before his time. The making of crystal plates for looking-glasses and spectacles created employment not only for an additional number of glassmakers, but for a substantial number of men engaged in subsidiary finishing crafts. Towards the end of his career Mansell claimed that 4,000 persons were supported by the glass industry. The number was probably not exaggerated if the families of all persons connected with glassmaking are taken into account—those of the glassmakers themselves; of casemakers, clerks, and unskilled labour; of ship-masters and sailors who transported the glass; of craftsmen in the finishing processes; of glaziers, merchants, and wholesalers who specialized in selling glass; and of Mansell's staff of managers and factors. The production of strong, dark bottles as a separate branch of the industry, though small during his life-time, eventually became extremely important economically: during the Restoration period it was one of the largest branches of glassmaking. However, the importance of the glass industry in the total economy of England before 1640 should not be over-stressed, for compared with iron-making it was still a relatively small industry and the rate of its growth after the 1580s was hardly comparable to that in later periods. Nevertheless royal protection of the 'infant industry' during its most difficult years in order to accomplish the successful change to the use of coal as fuel pro-vided the necessary conditions of cheap fuel, improved technology, and a climate of opinion congenial to experimentation that allowed the industry to make great strides thereafter.

In another respect glassmaking underwent a significant change. In 1560 most of the glass sold was considered a luxury for the well-to-do; yet in 1640 glass for the luxury trade, especially fine drinking glasses in true *cristallo*, was the kind least able to compete with imported products. Though many of these luxuries were made, the emphasis in production was directed rather at supplying windows (for houses of medium size as well as for the mansions of the wealthy), standardized bottles (for com-mercial storage of beverages), and thousands of dozens of ordinary drinking glasses (for taverns and for middle-class buyers). Practicality and greater consumption seem to have been the guiding principles. Even the one exception, Mansell's emphasis on improving the quality of crystal plates, a luxury item, may have been motivated in part by their use in making lenses for telescopes used by seamen; certainly it was English scientists who believed that their work in extending knowledge of the universe would result in practical improvements who profited most from his efforts. The trend towards ordinary usage continued to grow. In 1620 James Howell had remarked about the 'dainty pellucid' goblets emerging from the glass pots, but a century later Samuel Johnson, equally impressed with the transformation of sand and ashes into glass, marvelled rather that in the shapeless mass of molten glass 'rugged with excrescences and clouded with impurities . . . lay concealed so many conveniences of the world'.[1] By 1640 the pattern had been laid, and the transformation of glassmaking from a medieval to a modern industry was well under way.

[1] Quoted in L. M. Angus-Butterworth, *The Manufacturing of Glass* (London, Pitman, 1948), p. 220.

APPENDIX A

COSTS OF PRODUCTION BASED ON YEARLY COSTS AT TWO GLASS FURNACES ON THE ESTATES OF SIR PERCIVAL WILLOUGHBY AT WOLLATON IN NOTTINGHAMSHIRE, ABOUT 1617[1]

Mr. Pauncefoote the glasse makinge and provisions
A note of the particular charges of both the fornaces at Wollaton weeckly and first for that for broadglasse.

	£	s.	d.
Imprimis eleven ton of coles at 5s. 6d. per ton	3.	0.	6.
Item twenty loades of ashes at vis. per load	6.	0.	0.
Item sand one load	0.	1.	0.
Item case timber	0.	4.	0.
Item a packer of glasse	0.	5.	0.
Item case maker	0.	8.	0.
Item to the smyth for tooles mending	0.	5.	0.
Item poot clay pounding and making	0.	6.	8.
Item mending the fornace	0.	3.	4.
Item two teasers 5s. a peece	0.	10.	0.
Item the founder	0.	10.	0.
Item a blower and gatherer	1.	0.	0.
Item the master workeman	1.	10.	0.
Item rent	0.	5.	0.
	14.	08.	06.

The weeckly charge of the greene glasse fornace

	£	s.	d.
Imprimis ten ton of coles at 5s. 6d. per ton	2.	15.	0.
Item ashes 7 load at vis. per load	2.	2.	0.
Item sand	0.	1.	0.
Item poot clay pounding and makeing	0.	6.	8.
Item fornace mending	0.	5.	0.
Item seeges mending	0.	2.	0.
Item tooles mending	0.	5.	0.
Item rent	0.	5.	0.
Item two teasers	0.	10.	0.
Item a founder	0.	7.	0.
Item clerckes wages	0.	7.	6.
Item the workemans third (makeing 15 li. per weeck)	5.	0.	0.
	12.	07.	2.

[1] Midd. MS. 5/165/140, reprinted by the kind permission of the owner, Lord Middleton, and of the custodians, the Council of the University of Nottingham.

DEG—K

£   s.   d.

The weeckly charge of both fornaces at the rentes aforesaid come
  to . . . .   26. 15. 8.
for which charge may welbe made 20 case of broad glasse and
  15 li. of drinkeing glasses which come to . . . .   30. 0. 0.
soe the gaine is weeckly (above the charges) besides the expense
  of provisions all rated at deare rates . . . .   03. 4. 4.
Then the greene glasse must be delivered Sir Robert at 2s. the
  dozen towards his rent for which (yf the workemen worke at
  the same rates they now doe) wilbe lost every weeck   . . .   1. 14. 0.
soe the cleere weeckly gaine wilbe but . . . .   1. 10. 4.

And yf it please Sir Percival to take the workes and workemen into his owne
hands (which I presume they wilbe well content withall) and which he may
best doe by reason most of all the provisions are his owne, we wille take of
all the glasse both broad and greene, the broad at 15s. per case and the greene
at 2s. per dozen. And (haveing cleered the old reckonings) beginne a new, and
pay him 10 li. every weeck and cleere with him for all once every quarter for
the time to come.

And yf this course be not acceptable, nor the weeckly charge can be drawne
into this proporcion, for my parte (I soe well understand my owne business)
that I will not adventure any longer undertaking.

APPENDIX B

SELECTIONS FROM THE BOOKS OF RATES

Explanatory Note: The term Book of Rates is a conventional term used to refer to official lists of merchandize commonly imported or exported with valuations for the use of the customs officials in computing the *ad valorem* duties. An attempt was made when the valuations were reviewed and changed in 1558 to assign official values which were roughly equivalent to the actual wholesale price of the merchandize,[1] though some goods, including many glass items, were undervalued. The valuations were never changed during the reign of Elizabeth, though several new editions of the Book of Rates of 1558 were issued with some additional items listed. Many items were revalued when the Book of 1604 was issued, though few valuations for glass were changed, and no new Book of Rates appeared thereafter until 1635. When articles imported were not listed, merchants were required to declare their value. The extracts to follow include all the items in the Books of 1558 and 1604 comprised wholly or partly of glass, with a few additional items for comparison. They must not be taken as reliable indications of actual value, although they do indicate the kind of articles most commonly imported with a rough approximation of comparative value. They were used to compute the value of glass in Tables 4 and 6–11 found in the text,[2] except when declared valuations given in the Port Books varied from those in the appropriate Book of Rates.

THE BOOK OF RATES OF PHILIP AND MARY, 1558 PATENT ROLLS, C. 66/920, mm. 12ᵈ–22ᵈ

Cristal beads the thousand	xl*s.*
Bottels of glasse uncovered the dozen	xviij*d.*
Bottels of glasse the dozen covered	xx*s.*
Bottels of glasse with vices covered with lether the doz	xxx*s.*
Drinking glasses of Venys making the dozen	iiii*s.*
Glass broken the barrel	iiii*s.* iiij*d.*
Glasse white—Normandy glas the case	xx*s.*
Glasse colored the case	xl*s.*
Glasse white—Burgon glass the cheste	xl*s.*
Glass colored—Burgon glass the cheste	l*s.*
Glasse the way or wake cont' lx bunches	lx*s.*
Looking glasses of christall small the dozen	xx*s.*

---

[1] Willan (ed.), *A Tudor Book of Rates*, introduction, p. xxxii. Willan reviews the history of the Elizabethan Books of Rates.

[2] The Tables are on pp. 210, 220, 231, 234, 238–9, 242, and 248 respectively.

Looking glasses of christall large the dozen . . . . xl*s.*
Ower glasses the dozen . . . . xx*d.*
Ower glasses of Venis making the dozen . . . . xxs.
Ower glasses of Flanders makeing of the fyne sorte the dozen . . . vi*s.* viii*d.*
Spectacles the gross . . . . x*s.*
   Glass items added to the above list when the Book of Rates was reissued
   in 1582.[1]
Balme glasses the groce . . . . iij*s.* iij*d.*
Drinking glasses of the french making the dozen . . . . . . viij*d.*
Glasses to look in, peny ware the groce . . . . viij*s.*
Glasses called halfpeny ware the groce . . . . iiij*s.*

THE BOOK OF RATES UNDER THE GREAT SEAL.
EXCH. K.R., CUSTOMS ACCOUNTS, E. 122/173/3, 2 JAC. I
(1604)

The Rates for the Subsidy of Poundage Inwards

Barilia or Saphora to make glasse the barrell of ij^cwaight . . . . xx*s.*

Bottles {
of earth covered wth wicker the dozen . . . . xx*d.*
of glass covered wth wicker the dozen . . . . . . vi*s.* viii*d.*
of glass w^t vices covered in lether the dozen . . . . . xxx*s.*
of glass uncovered the dozen . . . . xviii*d.*
of wood for sucking bottles ye groce of xii dozen . . . v*s.*
}

Braceletes or   { of glasse the small groce of xii bundles or dickers . . xij*d.*
  Necklaces   { Red the smale groce of xii bundles or dickers . . . xij*d.*

Bugles {
great the pounde . . . . ij*s.*
smale or seede bugles the pounde . . . . . . iiij*s.* iiij*d.*
lace the pounde. . . . . iiij*s.*
}

Glasse for Windows {
Burgundie white the cheste . . . . xl*s.*
Burgundie colloured the cheste . . . . l*s.*
Normandy white the case. . . . . xx*s.*
Normandy colloured the case . . . . .xl*s.*
Renish the waigh or webb of lx bunches . . . . . l*s.*
}

Glasse for burning glasses the dozen . . . . xij*d.*

Glasses vor Looking glasses {
half penny ware the groce of xii doz . . . . iiij*s.*
pennyware the groce of xii dozen . . . . . viij*s.*
of steele smale the dozen . . . . . vi*s.* viii*d.*
of steele large the dozen . . . . . . xiii*s.* iiij*d.*
of Christall smale the dozen under no. 6 . . . . x*s.*
of Christal midle sorte the dozen of no. 6 . . xx*s.*
of Christall large the dozen of no. 7, 8 & upwards. xl*s.*
}

Glasses vor hower glasses {
of flaunders makeing course the groce of xii dozen xx*s.*
of flaunders makeing fyne the dozen . . . vi*s.* viii*d.*
of Venis makeing the dozen . . . . xx*s.*
}

---

[1] Printed in full in Willan (ed.), *A Tudor Book of Rates.* The entries below are found on pp. 6,
23, 29.

Glasses vor
- Balme glasses the groce of xii dozen . . . . . iii*s*. iiij*d*.
- [1]vialls the C of v^{xx} . . . . viii*s*. iiij*d*.
- waterglasses the dozen . . . . iiij*s*.

Saffora to make glasse the C waight . . . . x*s*.

Spectacle without cases the groce of xii dozen . . . . x*s*.

The Rates of Merchandize . . . London, R. Badger for Lawrence Blaikloch, 1642.[2]
Rates Inward:

	£	*s*.	*d*.
Venice drinking glasses the dozen . . .	0.	12.	0.
Flanders drinking glasses the hundred glasses	0.	16.	8.
Scotch and French drinking glasses the hundred containing 5 score	0.	10.	0.
course drinking glasses the dozen . . .	0.	2.	0.

Drinking glasses {

Rates Outward:

Glass broken the barrell	0.	3.	4.
Glasses { to drink in fine English the dozen	0.	4.	0.
to drink in, course English the dozen	0.	0.	8.

---

[1] This entry means 'the hundred of five score'. Sometimes the 'hundred' contained 120.

[2] These extracts were not used in computing valuations for drinking glasses in Table 6 (p. 220) but they are of interest in giving some indication of the relative value of various kinds of imported glasses in 1642 and also for their evidence that by that date the exportation of English glasses was sufficiently large to warrant their inclusion in the Book of Rates.

BIBLIOGRAPHY

MANUSCRIPT SOURCES

Bodleian Library, Oxford University
    North MS. a. 2, fol. 145, 'Notes touching Sir Edward Zouche his sute for making
       of glass with seacoles'.
British Museum, Manuscript Room
    Additional MSS.
    Alnwich MSS., Series U. I., Household Accounts of Henry Percy, ninth Earl of
       Northumberland, on microfilm.
    Harleian MSS.
    Lansdowne MSS.
Chatsworth House
    Hardwick MSS.
East Sussex Record Office, Lewes
    Rye MSS.
Folger Shakespeare Library, Washington
    Bagot MSS.
    Loseley MSS.
Gloucester City Library
    Bishop's Transcripts of Parish Registers
Gloucester County Record Office
    Court Records
    Manorial Rental Records
Greater London Record Office
    Parish Registers
    Records of the Archdeaconry of Surrey
    St. Saviour, Token Books of the Liberty of the Clink
Guildford Muniment Room
    Loseley MSS.
    Miscellaneous MSS.
    Sadler Deeds
Guildhall Library, London Guildhall
    Muniments of the Company of Glass-Sellers
    Muniments of the Company of Glaziers
    Muniments of the Company of Spectacle-Makers
    Parish Registers
Hampshire Diocesan Record Office, Winchester
    Consistory Court Books
    Diocesan Surveys
House of Lords Library, Victoria Tower
    House of Lords MSS.
Lichfield Joint Record Office
    Wills
Longleat House
    Marquess of Bath MSS.
    Whitelock Collections

Loseley House, Guildford
  Loseley MSS.
National Library of Scotland, Edinburgh
  Denmilne MSS.
Public Record Office, London
  Prerogative Court of Canterbury
  Wills and Probates of Wills
  Records of the Chancery, Enrolments
    Close Rolls
    Patent Rolls
  Records of the Chancery, Judicial Proceedings
    Chancery Proceedings
    Decree Rolls
    Master's Exhibits
  Records of the Exchequer, King's Remembrancer
    Customs Accounts
    Judicial Proceedings (equity side)
      Barons' Depositions
      Bills and Answers
      Decrees and Orders
      Depositions by Commission
    Port Books
  Star Chamber Proceedings
  State Papers, Domestic Series
Sheffield Central Library
  Strafford MSS.
Smedmore House, Kimmeridge, Dorset
  Clavell MSS.
Society of Genealogists, London
  Transcripts of Parish Registers
University of Chicago Library
  Bacon MSS.
University of Nottingham Library
  Middleton MSS.
West Sussex Record Office, Chichester
  Chichester Consistory Court Diary, vol. C.
Worcestershire Record Office, Worcester
  Palfrey Collections
  Parish Registers
Parish Registers in the Custody of Various Incumbents.

OFFICIAL PUBLICATIONS

Great Britain, Board of Trade. *Working Party Reports: Handblown Domestic Glassware.*
  London, H.M.S.O., 1947.
Great Britain, HMC. *Reports.* London, H.M.S.O., 1870–.
Great Britain, Parliament. *Journals of the House of Commons.* London, 1803–.
Great Britain, Parliament. *Journals of the House of Lords.* London, n.d.
Great Britain, Parliament. *Statutes of the Realm.* London, Eyre, 1811–28.
Great Britain, PRO. *Calendar of the Patent Rolls.* London, H.M.S.O., 1926.

Great Britain, PRO. *Calendar of State Papers and Manuscripts Relating to English Affairs, Existing in the Archives and Collections of Venice* . . ., vols. vii–xxv (for 1558–1642). London, H.M.S.O., 1890–1924.

Great Britain, PRO. *Calendar of State Papers, Domestic Series*. Elizabeth–Charles I. London, Longman, Bowman, Green, Longman, 1856–80.

Great Britain, PRO. *Calendar of State Papers, Colonial Series*, vols. i–vi (for 1574–1660). London, Longman, 1860–84.

Great Britain, Privy Council. *Acts of the Privy Council of England*. 39 vols., London, H.M.S.O., 1890–1938.

Private Parliamentary Journals and Semi-Official Publications

Calendar of Sussex Marriage Licenses, ed. E. H. W. Dunkin, pt. iii. (Suss. R.S. Publications, vol. ix), Lewes, 1909.

Commons Debates, 1621, ed. W. Notestein, F. H. Relf, and H. Simpson. 7 vols., New Haven, Yale Univ. Press, 1935.

D'Ewes, Sir Simonds. *Journal of the Votes, Speeches, and Debates both of the House of Lords and House of Commons* . . . London, 1693.

'Lay Subsidy Assessments for the County of Surrey in the year 1593 or 1594', *Surr. A. Col.* xix (1960), 39–101.

Letters of Denization and Acts of Naturalization in England, 1509–1603, ed. W. Page. (Publications of the Huguenot Society of London, vol. viii), Lymington, The Huguenot Society of London, vol. viii), Lymington, The Huguenot Society, 1893.

List of Foreign Protestants and Aliens, Resident in England, 1618–1688, ed. W. D. Cooper. (Publications of the Camden Society, O.S. vol. lxxxii), 1862.

Newcastle-upon-Tyne. *Extracts from the Newcastle-upon-Tyne Council Minute Books, 1639–1656*. Newcastle-upon Tyne, Northumberland Press, 1920.

[Nicholas, Edward.] *Proceedings and Debates of the House of Commons in 1620 and 1621, Collected by a Member of that House* . . ., ed. T. Tyhwhitt. Oxford, 1766.

The Port Books of Boston, 1610–40, ed. R. W. K. Hinton. (Lincoln Record Society Publications, vol. i), 1956.

The Port Books of Rye, ed. R. F. Dell. (Suss. R.S. Publications, vol. lxiv), 1965–6.

Rates of the Customs House. London, 1590.

The Rates of Merchandize . . . London, R. Badger for Lawrence Blaikloch, 1642.

Records of the Virginia Company, ed. S. M. Kingsbury. 3 vols., Washington, Govt. Printing Office, 1906–35.

Register of the Privy Council of Scotland, ed. J. H. Burton and D. Masson, vols. viii–xiii. Edinburgh, H. M. General Register House, 1887–96.

Registre des Baptismes, Marriages et Morts . . . *de L'Eglise Wallone de Southampton* (Publications of the Huguenot Society of London, vol. iv), Lymington, The Huguenot Society, 1890.

Returns of Aliens Dwelling in the City and Suburbs of London from the Reign of Henry VIII to that of James I, ed. R. E. G. Kirk and E. F. Kirk. (Publications of the Huguenot Society of London, vol. x in 4 parts.) Aberdeen, Univ. of Aberdeen Press, 1900–08.

Transcripts of Sussex Wills, pt. iii, ed. W. H. Godfrey. (Suss. R.S. Publications, vol. xliii), 1938.

A Tudor Book of Rates, ed. T. S. Willan. Manchester, Univ. of Manchester Press, 1962.

PRINTED CONTEMPORARY SOURCES

AGRICOLA, GEORGIUS. *De Re Metallica*, trans. and ed. H. C. Hoover and L. H. Hoover. New York, Dover Publications, 1950.

BIRUNGUCCIO, V. *La Pirotechnia*, trans. and ed. C. S. Smith and M. T. Gnudi. New York, American Institute of Mining and Metallurgical Engineers, 1942.

BOYLE, ROBERT. *Works*, ed. T. Birch. 6 vols., London, 1772.

Churchwardens' Accounts of Pittington and Other Parishes in the Diocese of Durham from 1580–1700. (Publications of the Surtees Society, vol. lxxxiv), 1888.

COKER, JOHN. *Survey of Dorsetshire*. London, J. Wilcox, 1732.

'Copy of the Inventory of Archbishop Parker's Goods at the Time of his Death', contributed by W. Sands, *Archaeologia* xxx (1844), 1–30.

DUDLEY, DUD. *Metallum Martis*. 1665 edn.

'Extracts from the Churchwardens' Accounts of the Parish of Wing in the County of Buckinghamshire; submitted by F. Ouvry', *Archaeologia*, xxxvi (1855), 221–41.

'Extracts from the Private Account Book of William More of Loseley in Surrey, in the Time of Queen Mary and Queen Elizabeth', ed. J. Evans, *Archaeologia*, xxxvi (1855), 284–92.

GLAUBER, JOHANN. *A Description of New Philosophical Furnaces, or a New Art of Distilling . . .*, set forth in English by J. F., D. M. London, T. Williams, 1651.

HALLIWELL, J. C. *Ancient Inventories of Furniture, Pictures, Tapestry, Plate . . .* London, Privately printed, 1854.

HARRISON, WILLIAM. *Elizabethan England*, ed. L. Withington. London, Walter Scott, 1876.

HARVEY, WILLIAM. *The Works of William Harvey*, trans. R. Willis. London, The Sydenham Society, 1847.

HAUDICQUER DE BLANCOURT, F. *The Art of Glass*. London, 1699.

HOLINSHED, R., *The Chronicles of England . . .* 6 vols., London, J. Johnson etc., 1807.

Household and Farm Inventories in Oxfordshire, 1550–1590, ed. M. A. Havinden. (Oxford-shire Record Society, Publication no. 44.) London, H.M.S.O., 1965.

HOWELL, JAMES. *Epistolae Ho-Elianae . . .* London, 1737.

Jacobean Household Inventories, ed. F. G. Emmison. (Publications of the Bedfordshire Historical Records Society, vol. xx.) 1938.

KNOWLER, W. *The Earl of Strafford's Letters and Dispatches.* 2 vols., London, W. Bowyer, 1739.

Lambeth Churchwardens' Accounts, 1504–1646, and Vestry Book, 1610, ed. C. Drew. London, for the Surrey Record Society, 1940.

MERRET, CHRISTOPHER. See Neri, Antonio.

NERI, ANTONIO. *The Art of Glass . . .*, trans. with some observations by Christopher Merret. London, 1662.

PERCY, HENRY, ninth Earl of Northumberland. *Advice to His Son, 1609*, ed. G. B. Harrison. London, Benn, 1930.

PLATT, HUGH. *Jewell House of Art and Nature*. London, P. Short, 1594.

ROLVENSON, JOHN. *Treatise of Metallica*. London, T. Thorpe, 1613.

Selections from the Household Books of Lord William Howard of Naworth Castle, ed. G. Ornsby, (Publications of the Surtees Society, vol. lxviii), 1877.

SPRAT, THOMAS. *A History of the Royal Society of London*. London, 1667.

STURTEVANT, SIMON. *Metallica*. London, George Eld, 1612.

Surrey Wills. *Surrey Record Society Publications*, no. iii, pt. 1, London, 1915.

THEOPHILUS. *On Divers Arts: The Treatise of Theophilus*, trans. J. Hawthorne and C. S. Smith. Chicago, Univ. of Chicago Press, 1963.

'The True State of the Businesse of Glasse of All Kindes', n. p., n. d., BM pamphlet 669, f. 4 (7).

Tudor Economic Documents, ed. R. H. Tawney and E. Power. 2 vols., London, Long-mans, 1924.

'Wandsworth Churchwardens' Accounts from 1603 to 1620', *Surr. A. Col.* xix (1906), 145–94.

Wills and Inventories from the Registry at Durham. (Surtees Society Publications vol. cxcii.) 1929.

SECONDARY WORKS

ABDURAZAKOV, A. A. 'Medieval Glass from the Tashkent Oasis', *J.G.S.* xi (1969), 32.

ABERG, F. A. and CROSSLEY, D. W.: see under Crossley.

ALBION, R. G. *Forests and Sea-Power.* Cambridge, Mass., Harvard Univ. Press, 1926.

ANDREWS, CHARLES M. *The Colonial Period of American History.* 4 vols., New Haven, Yale Univ. Press, 1934–8.

ANDREWS, J. H. 'Two Problems in the Interpretation of the Port Books', *EcHR* 2nd ser. ix (1956–7), 119–22.

ANGUS-BUTTERWORTH, L. M. *The Manufacture of Glass*, London, Pitman, 1948.

ANON.—'The earliest Recorded Glassmaker in England', *Glass Technology*, vol. 1 no. 4, August 1940, p. 137.

ASHDOWN, C. H. *History of the Worshipful Company of Glaziers of the City of London.* London, Black, 1919.

ASHTON, T. S. *Iron and Steel in the Industrial Revolution.* Manchester, Univ. of Manchester Press, 1924.

Baddeley, W. St. Clair. 'A Glasshouse at Nailsworth', *Bristol and Gloucestershire Archaeological Society Transactions*, xlii (1920), 89–95.

BARRELET, J. *Le Verrerie en France de l'époque gallo-romaine á nos jours.* Paris, Larousse, 1954.

BATHO, G. 'Notes and Documents on Petworth House, 1574–1632', *Suss. A. Col.* xcvi (1958), 108–34.

BECK, G. M. A. 'Omniabene Lutheri: A Surrey Glassmaker', *Surr. A. Col.* lii (1952), 90.

BINDOFF, S. T. *Tudor England.* Pelican, 1950.

BOURNE, HENRY. *History of Newcastle.* Newcastle-upon-Tyne, J. White, 1736.

BRADBURY, S. *The Evolution of the Microscope.* Oxford, Pergamon Press, 1967.

BRAND, JOHN. *History and Antiquities of the Town and County of the Town of Newcastle-upon-Tyne.* 2 vols., London, B. White, 1789.

BRETT-JAMES, N. G. *The Growth of Stuart London.* London, Allen and Unwin, 1935.

BRIDGEWATER, N. P. 'Glasshouse Farm, St. Weonards: A Small Glassworking Site', *Transactions of the Woolhope Naturalists' Field Club*, xxxvii (1963), 300–15.

BUCKLEY, FRANCIS. 'Early Glasshouses of Bristol', *JSGT* ix (1925), 36–60.

—— 'Glasshouses of Dudley and Worcester', *JSGT*, xi (1927), 287–93.

—— *A History of Old English Glass.* London, E. Benn, 1925.

—— *Old London Glasshouses, Southwark.* Sheffield, for the Society of Glass Technology, 1930.

BUCKLEY, WILFRED. *Diamond Engraved Glasses of the Sixteenth Century, with Particular Reference to Five Attributed to Giacomo Verzelini.* London, Benn, 1929.

Chambon, R. 'The Evolution of the Processes used for Hand-fashioning of Window Glass from the Tenth Century to the Present', *Advances in Glass Technology*, pt. ii. New York, Plenum Press, 1963, 165–78.

—— *L'Histoire de la verrerie en Belgique du IIième siècle á nos jours.* Brussels, Le Librairie Encyclopédique, 1955.

CHARLESTON, R. J. 'Ancient Glass-making Methods'. Typescript, Circle of Glass Collectors, no. 24, Mar. 1961.

—— 'The Glass', in Huggins, E. J., 'Excavations at Sewardston Street, Waltham Abbey, Essex', 1966', *Post-Med. Arch.* iii (1969) 88–9.

—— 'Medieval and Later Glass', in Cunliffe, B., *Winchester Excavations, 1949–60*. Winchester, City of Winchester Museum and Libraries Committee, 1964, i. 145–51.

CLARK, E. G. 'Glassmaking in Lorraine', *JSGT* xv (1931), 107–19.

CLARK, G. T. *Some Account of Sir Robert Mansell, Kt.* Dowlais, privately printed, 1883.

CLEPHAM, J. 'The Manufacture of Glass in England and the Rise of the Art on the Tyne', *Archaeologia Æliena*, n.s., viii (1879), 109–24.

CROSSLEY, D. W. 'Glassmaking in Bagot's Park, Staffordshire, in the Sixteenth Century', *Post-Med. Arch.* i (1967), 44–83.

—— 'The Performance of the Glass Industry in Sixteenth Century England', *EcHR* 2nd ser. xxv (1972), 421–33.

CROSSLEY, D. W. and ABERG, F. A. 'Sixteenth-Century Glass-Making in Yorkshire: Excavations at Furnaces at Hutton and Rosedale, North Riding, 1968–71', *Post-Med. Arch.* vi (1972), 107–59.

CUNNINGHAM, W. *Alien Immigrants in England*. Social England Series. London, Swan, Sonnenshein, 1897.

DANIELS, J. S. *The Woodchester Glasshouse*. Gloucester, Bellows, 1950.

DAVIES, S. S. 'The Early History of the Patent Specification', *LQR* l (1966), 86–189; 260–74.

DENT, J. *The Quest for Nonsuch*. London, Hutchinson, 1962.

DeVOS, CHARLES. 'Les Colnet, maitres verriers en Brabant wallon', *Brabantica*, viii (1966), 155–66.

DIDEROT, D. and D'ALEMBERT, J. *Encyclopédie ou dictionnaire raisonné des sciences, des artes and des métiers*. 1st ed., Geneva, 1751–65.

—— *Receuil de planches sur les sciences, les arts liberaux les arts mechaniques avec leur explication*. 10 vols., Paris, Chez Briasson, 1762–71.

DIETZ, F. C. 'The Receipts and Issues of the Exchequer during the Reigns of James I and Charles I', *Smith College Studies in History*, xiii, no. 4, (July 1928).

DILLON, EDWARD. *Glass*. London, Methuen, 1907.

DOBBS, B. J. 'Studies in the Natural Philosophy of Sir Kenelm Digby', *Ambix*, xviii (Mar. 1971), 1–25.

FISHER, F. J. 'London's Export Trade in the Early Seventeenth Century', *EcHR*, 2nd ser. vol. iii, no 2 (1950), 151–61.

FRIIS, ASTRID. *Alderman Cockayne's Project and the Cloth Trade; The Commercial Policy of England in its Main Aspects, 1603–25*. London, Oxford Univ. Press, 1927.

GARDINER, S. R. *History of England from the Accession of James I to the Outbreak of the Civil War, 1603–1642*. 10 vols., London, Longmans, Green, 1894–96.

GERSPACH, E. *L'Art de la verrerie*. Paris, A. Quantin, 1887.

GODFREY, E. S. 'The Development of English Glassmaking, 1560–1640'. Unpublished Ph.D. thesis, Univ. of Chicago, 1957.

GOLDSMITH, J. N. and HULME, E. W. 'History of the Grated Hearth, the Chimney and the Air Furnace', *Transactions of the Newcomen Society*, xxiii (1942–3), 1–12.

GOTCH, J. A. *Early Renaissance Architecture in England*. London, Batsford, 1901.

GRAS, N. S. B. *The Early English Customs System*. Cambridge, Mass., Harvard Univ. Press, 1918.

GRAZEBROOK, H. S. *Collections for a Genealogy of the Noble Families of Henzey, Tyttery and Tysack*. Stourbridge, J. T. Ford, 1877.

GROSS, C. *The Gild Merchant*. 2 vols. Oxford, The Clarendon Press, 1890.

GUNTHER, R. 'Raugaskegel auf alten Glashütten', *Glastechnische Berichte*, xxiv (1961), 559–62, Bgira Translation no. 493 entitled 'Old Glasswork Cones'.

GUNTHER, R. T. *Early Science at Oxford*, vol. i. Oxford, The Clarendon Press, 1923.

GUTTERY, D. B. *From Broad Glass to Cut Crystal*. London, Hill, 1956.

HALAHAN, B. C. 'The Frome Copse Glass-house, Chiddingfold', *Surr. A. Col.* xxiv (1921), 24–31.

HALL, BERTHA. 'The Trade of Newcastle and the Northeast Coast'. Unpublished M.A. thesis, Univ. of London, 1933.

HALL, HUBERT. *A History of the Custom-Revenue in England*. 2 vols., London, E. Stock, 1892.

HALLEN, A. W. 'Glassmaking in Sussex, Newcastle and Scotland', *Scottish Antiquary; or Northern Notes and Queries*, vii (1893), 145–56.

HAMMERSLEY, G. 'The Crown Woods and their Exploitation in the Sixteenth and Seventeenth Centuries', *Bulletin of the Institute of Historical Research*, xxv (1972), 136–59.

—— 'A History of the Iron Industry in the Forest of Dean Region, 1562–1660'. Unpublished Ph.D. thesis, Univ. of London, 1972.

—— 'Technique or Economy? The Rise and Decline of the Early English Copper Industry', *Business History*, xv (1973), 1–27.

HAMPSON, C. P. 'The History of Glassmaking in Lancashire', *Lancashire and Cheshire Antiquarian Society Transactions*, xlviii (1932), 65–75.

HARDEN, D. B. 'Domestic Window Glass: Roman, Saxon and Medieval', *Studies in Building History*, ed. E. M. Jope. London, Odhams Press, 1961.

HARRINGTON, J. C. *Glassmaking at Jamestown*. Richmond, Dietz Press, 1953.

HARRISON, F. H. *An Introduction to the History of Medicine*. 2nd edn., rev., Philadelphia, Saunders, 1917.

HARTSHORNE, A. *Old English Glasses*. London, E. Arnold, 1897.

HATCH, C. E. 'Glassmaking in Virginia, 1607–1625', *William and Mary College Quarterly Magazine*, 2nd ser. xxi (1941), 119–38; 227–38.

HENNEZEL D'ORNOIS, J. M. F. de. *Gentilhommes verriers de la Haute-Picardie*. Nogent-le-Ratvov, Charles-Fontaine, 1933.

A History of Technology, ed. Charles Singer *et al.* Oxford, the Clarendon Press, 1957.

HODKIN, F. W. and COUSEN, A. *A Textbook of Glass Technology*. London, Constable, 1929.

HONEY, W. B. *English Glass*. London, Collins, 1946.

HORRIDGE, W. 'Documents Relating to the Lorraine Glassmakers in North Staffordshire with some Notes Thereon', *Glass Notes*, xv (1955), 26–33.

HOSKINS, W. G. *Provincial England: Essays in Social and Economic History*. London, Macmillan, 1963.

HOUDOY, J. *Verreries à la façon de Venise*. Paris, A. Aubry, 1873.

HOWARD, A. L. *The Worshipful Company of Glass-Sellers of London*. London, for the Company, 1940.

HUDSON, J. P. 'Seventeenth Century Glass Excavated at Jamestown', *Florida Anthropologist*, xvii, no. 2 (1964), 95–103

HUGHES, E. *Studies in Administration and Finance, 1553–1825*. Manchester, Univ. of Manchester Press, 1934.

HULME, E. W. 'English Glass-Making in the Sixteenth and Seventeenth Centuries', *Antiquary*, xxx (July-Dec. 1894), 259–63.

—— 'History of the Patent System under the Prerogative, and at Common Law', *LQR*, xii (1896), 141–54; xvi (1900), 44–56.

—— 'Sir Kenelm Digby and the Green Glass Manufacture', *Notes and Queries*, 8th ser. viii (1895), 67.

Jenkins, Rhys. *Links in the History of Engineering and Technology from Tudor Times*. Cambridge, Cambridge Univ. Press, for the Newcomen Society, 1936.

—— 'The Reverberatory Furnace with Coal Fuel, 1612–1712', *Transactions of the New-comen Society*, xiv (1933–4), 67–80.

Kenyon, G. H. *The Glass Industry of the Weald*. Leicester, Univ. of Leicester Press, 1967.

—— 'Petworth Town and Trades, 1610–1760', *Suss. Arch. Col.* xcvi (1958), 35–107.

KNOWLES, J. A. 'Medieval Glazing Accounts', *Journal of the British Society of Master Glass Painters*, ii (1927–8), 116–25; 179–92; iii (1928–9) 1–29.

—— 'The Source of the Coloured Glass used in Medieval Stained Glass Windows', *Glass*, Mar.–June, 1926.

LAFOND, J. 'Was Crown Glass Discovered in Normandy in 1330?', *JGS*, xi (1969), 37–8.

LENNARD, T. BARRETT, 'Glass-making at Knole, Kent', *Ant.* xli (1905), 127–9.

LE VAILLANT DE LA FIEFFE, O. *Les Verreries de la Normandie*. Rouen, 1873.

LONDON COUNTY COUNCIL. *Bankside: The Parishes of St. Saviour and Christchurch, Southwark. Survey of London*, ed. C. R. Ashbee *et al.*, vol. xxii. London, The London County Council, 1950.

McNULTY, R. H. 'Common Beverage Bottles; Their Production, Use and Form in Seventeenth and Eighteenth Century Netherlands', *JGS*, xiii (1971), 91–119; xiv (1972), 141–8.

MANSEL, J. C. *Kimmeridge and Smedmore*. Dorchester, Friary Press, n.d.

MANSELL, W. W. *An Historical and Genealogical Account of the Ancient Family of Maunsell (Mansell, Mansel)*. London, Buck and Straker, 1850.

MARSON, P. *Glass and Glass Manufacture*. London, Pitman, 1918.

MIDDLETON, W. E. KNOWLES, *The Invention of Metereological Instruments*. Balti-more, Johns Hopkins Univ. Press, 1969.

MILLARD, A. M. 'The Import Trade of London, 1600–40'. Unpublished Ph.D. Thesis, Univ. of London, 1956.

NEALE, J. E. *The Elizabethan House of Commons*. New Haven, Yale Univ. Press, 1950.

NEF, J. U. 'A Comparison of Industrial Growth in France and England from 1540 to 1640', *Journal of Political Economy*, xliv (1936), 389–403.

—— 'The Progress of Technology and the Growth of Large Scale Industry in Great Britain, 1540–1640', *EcHR*, v (1934), 3–24.

—— *The Rise of the British Coal Industry*. 2 vols., London, Routledge, 1932.

NICHOLSON, M. 'The Microscope and English Imagination', *Smith College Studies in Modern Languages*, xvi (1934–5), no. 4.

NOEL-HUME, I. 'A Century of London Glass Bottles, 1580–1680', *Connoisseur Year-book*, 1956, pp. 98–103.

—— *Here Lies Virginia*. New York, Knopf, 1963.

—— 'Tudor and Early Stuart Glasses Found in London', *Connoisseur*, Aug. 1962, —— pp. 269–73.

Notes and Queries, 1st ser. x (1854); 4th ser. iv (1869).

OPPENHEIM, M. 'The Royal Navy under James I', *EHR*, vii, pt. 2 (1892), 471–96.

OSWALD, A. and PHILLIPS, H. 'A Restoration Hoard from Gracechurch St., London', *Connoisseur*, Sept. 1949, 32–6.

PAPE, T. 'The Excavations at Blore Park', *Connoisseur*, xcii (1933), 172–7.

—— 'Medieval (and later) Glassworkers in North Staffordshire', *Transactions of the North Staffordshire Field Club*, lxviii (1933–4), 74–121.

PETERSSON, R. T. *Sir Kenelm Digby, the Ornament of England, 1603–65*. London, Jonathan Cape, 1956.

PHELPS BROWN, E. H. and HOPKINS, S. V. 'Wage-rates and Prices, Evidence for Population Pressure in the Sixteenth Century', *Economica*, n.s. xxiv (1957), 289–306.

PHILLIPS, C. J. *Glass: The Miracle Maker*. New York, Pitman, 1941.

PILBIN, P. 'The Influence of Local Geography on the Glass Industry of Tyneside,' *Journal of the Tyneside Geographical Society*, n.s., vol. i, no. 1 (Oct. 1936), 31–45.

POWELL, H. J. *Glassmaking in England*. Cambridge, Cambridge Univ. Press, 1923.

PRICE, W. H. *The English Patents of Monopoly*. Boston, Houghton Mifflin, 1906.

RIDGWAY, M. H. and LEACH, G. B. 'Further Notes on the Glasshouse Site at Kingswood, Delamere, Cheshire', *Journal of the Chester Archaeological Society*, n.s. xxvii (1943), pt. 1, 133–40.

ROGERS, J. E. T. *A History of Agriculture and Prices in England*. 7 vols., Oxford, the Clarendon Press, 1866–1902.

ROLLASON, A. A. 'Early Glassmakers at Eccleshall,' *Transactions of the North Staffordshire Field Club*, liv (Annual Report, 1919–20), 33–5.

RUGGLES-BRISE, S. M. E. *Sealed Bottles*. London, Country Life, 1949.

SALZMAN, L. F. *Building in England down to 1540; A Documentary History*. Oxford, the Clarendon Press, 1952.

—— *English Industries of the Middle Ages*. Oxford, the Clarendon Press, 1923.

SAYRE, E. V. 'The Intentional Use of Antimony and Manganese in Ancient Glasses', *Advances in Glass Technology*, pt. 2, New York, Plenum Press, 1963, pp. 263–82.

SCHWEIG, B. 'Mirrors', *Antiquity*, xv (1941), 257–68.

SCOULOUDI, I. 'Alien Immigration into and Alien Communities in London, 1558–1680', *Proceedings of the Huguenot Society of London*, xvi (1937–41), 27–49.

SCOVILLE, W. C. *Capitalism and French Glassmaking, 1640–1789*. (*University of California Publications in Economics*, vol. xv.), Berkeley, Univ. of Calif. Press, 1950.

Shakespeare's England; An Account of the Life and Manners of His Age. 2 vols., Oxford, the Clarendon Press, 1916.

SMITH, R. S. 'Glass-making at Wollaton in the Early Seventeenth Century', *Transactions of the Thoroton Society of Nottingham*, lxvi (1962), 24–34.

—— 'Huntington Beaumont', *Rennaissance and Modern Studies*, i (1957), 115–53.

STATHAM, E. P. *History of the Family of Maunsell (Mansell, Mansel)*. 2 vols. in 3, London, privately printed, 1917–20.

STONE, L. *The Crisis of the Aristocracy, 1558–1641*. Oxford, the Clarendon Press, 1965.

—— *Social Change and Revolution in England*. London, Longmans, 1965.

STRAKER, ERNEST. *Wealden Iron*. London, G. Bell, 1931.

TAIT, HUGH, 'Glass with Chequered Spiral-Trail Decoration', *JGS* ix (1967) 94–112.

TAWNEY, R. H. *Business and Politics under James I*. Cambridge, Cambridge Univ. Press, 1958.

THORPE, W. A. *English Glass*, 2nd edn., London, A. & C. Black, 1949.

TURNER, W. E. S. 'Studies in Ancient Glasses and Glassmaking Processes', *JSGT* xl (1956), 39^t–52^t; 162^t–86^t; 277^t–300^t.

TURNER, W. E. S. 'Tercentenary of Neri-Merret's *Art of Glass*', *Glass Technology*, iii (1962), 181–213.

UNWIN, G. *Industrial Organization in the Sixteenth and Seventeenth Centuries*. Oxford, the Clarendon Press, 1904.

UPTON, A. F. *Sir Arthur Ingram, c. 1565–1642*. Oxford, Oxford Univ. Press, 1961.

The Victoria County History of the Counties of England. London, A. Constable and Oxford Univ. Press, 1901–.

Viking Glass Company. *From American Sands and Artists' Hands*. New Martinsville, W. Va., The Viking Company, 1950.

VINE, P. A. L. *London's Lost Route to the Sea*. London, David and Charles, 1965.

WAKEFIELD, R. *The Old Glasshouses of Stourbridge and Dudley*. Stourbridge, The Stour Press, 1934.

WESTROPP, M. S. D. *Irish Glass*. London, Herbert Jenkins, 1921.

WILLAN, T. S. *The English Coasting Trade, 1600–1750*. New York, Kelley Reprint, 1967.

—— *River Navigation in England, 1600–1750*. New York, Kelley Reprint, 1965.

WILLIAMS, N. J. 'Elizabethan Port Books', *EHR*, lxvi (1951) 387–95.

WILLSON, DAVID H. *Privy Councillors in the House of Commons, 1604–1629*. Minneapolis, Univ. of Minnesota Press, 1940.

WILSON, C. *England's Apprenticeship, 1603–1763*. New York, St. Martin's Press, 1965.

WILSON, D. M. and HURST, D. G. 'Medieval Britain in 1960. Herefordshire: St. Weonards, Glasshouse Farm', *Medieval Archaeology*, v (1961), 37–9.

WINBOLT, S. E. *Wealden Glass: The Surrey–Sussex Glass Industry, 1261–1615*. Hove, Combridges, 1933.

WOLF, A. *History of Science, Technology and Philosophy in the Sixteenth and Seventeenth Centuries*. London, Allen and Unwin, 1935.

WOOD, E. S. 'A Medieval Glasshouse at Blunden's Wood, Hambleton, Surrey', *Surr. Arch. Col.* lxii (1965), 54–79.

WOOD, M. K. *Newnham-on-Severn, a Retrospect*. Gloucester, Albert Smith, 1962.

YOUNG, SIDNEY. *History of the Worshipful Company of Glass-Sellers of London*. London, Barker, 1913.

INDEX